CRIME, CRIMINAL JUSTICE AND RELIGION

Crime, Criminal Justice and Religion: A Critical Appraisal seeks to bridge a gap in the examination of crime and criminal justice by taking both a historical and a contemporary lens to explore the influence of religion. Offering unique perspectives that consider the impact on modern-day policy and practice, the book scrutinises a range of issues such as abortion, hate crime and desistance as well as reflecting upon the influence religion can have on criminal justice professions.

The book acts to renew the importance of, and recognise, the influence and impact religion has in terms of how we view and ultimately address crime and deliver criminal justice. One of the first books to cover the area of crime, criminal justice and religion, the book is divided into three parts, with part 1 – "Contextualising Crime, Criminal Justice and Religion" – providing an introduction to crime, criminal justice and religion, and reflections on the role religion has had, and continues to have, in how crime is understood and how we respond to it. Part 2 – "Appraisal of Institutions and Professional Practice" –considers the issue of religion through institutions and professions of criminal justice, such as the police and legal profession, while part 3 – "Appraisal of Contemporary Issues" – explores a range of crime and criminal justice issues in on which religion has had an impact, such as the death penalty and terrorism.

Crime, Criminal Justice and Religion will be of primary interest to academics, researchers and students in criminology, law, sociology, psychology, social policy and related Humanities, Arts and Social Sciences disciplines. It will also be of interest to theologians, both as scholars and practitioners. The book is a body of work that will appeal at an international level and will also be a key resource for a range of practitioners across the globe working on issues concerning crime and criminal justice.

Philip Birch is Associate Professor of Criminology in the Faculty of Arts & Social Sciences at the University of Technology Sydney, Australia. During his academic career he has taught in the British, US and Australian university systems. Prior to entering academia, Philip worked as a criminologist in the field, holding posts in the UK prison service as well as in the crime and disorder field, which involved managing a specialist crime unit. Philip has published over 100 books, book chapters, peer-reviewed articles and government reports in his main areas of research – offender management and rehabilitation; police, prisons and probation practices; gender-inclusive violence, with a particular focus on domestic and family violence, and sex work. In 2019, Philip was invited to present his research at the United Nations. He has secured over $860K in research funding and support grants to date, which has addressed a variety of themes within his areas of expertise. Philip also holds an honorary research fellowship in the School of Psychology, University of Central Lancashire, UK, as well as a Professorial Associate at Ashworth Research Centre, Ashworth High Secure Hospital, National Health Services, UK. Philip is a visiting professor (Police Science) in the Faculty of Life Sciences at the University of South Wales, UK, and a fellow of the Higher Education Academy. Philip was the co-founder and inaugural editor-in-chief of the *Journal of Criminological Research, Policy and Practice* (*JCRPP*, 2014–2017) and *Abuse: An International Impact Journal* (2020–Present). He was also editor-in-chief of *Salus: An International Journal for Law Enforcement and Public Safety* (2018–2021) and sits on the editorial board of the *Journal of Aggression, Conflict and Peace Research*.

Conor Murray is a Lecturer in Criminology and Criminal Justice at Ulster University, where he is also the Global Engagement Lead and Postgraduate Tutor within the School of Applied Social and Policy Sciences. He sits on the Executive Board of NIACRO, an NGO dedicated to reducing crime and its impact on people and communities in Northern Ireland. As an early career researcher, he is focused on disseminating the findings of his doctoral research, which included a nine-month ethnographic study in Hydebank Wood (Young Offenders Centre) College. His findings will be published in a research monograph in 2023. While writing the book Conor has also been exploring research interests in disciplines of young adulthood, gender, sexuality, policing, religion, and sport-based interventions. He has secured over £150,000 in research funding and support grants and has published book chapters, peer reviewed articles and reports.

Andrew McInnes is an adjunct associate professor with Charles Sturt University, working in the Australian Graduate School of Policing and Security. Until July 2020, he was a senior lecturer at the Charles Sturt University campus in Port Macquarie, NSW, Australia, where he was a course manager and lecturer in criminal justice, leadership and policing subjects, both on campus and online. He has previously led in the development of a start-up academic institution on behalf of the Abu Dhabi government in the United Arab Emirates, including in the design, accreditation and delivery of new academic programmes in policing, security and crime scene investigation. Dr McInnes served as a police officer in the Royal Ulster Constabulary and Police Service of Northern Ireland for almost 31 years. On retirement in 2013, he held the rank of superintendent and was the deputy head of Training and Development in the Northern Ireland Police College. He served in a wide range of operational and headquarter roles including district commander, criminal justice development, counterterrorism operations and training delivery and evaluation.

ROUTLEDGE STUDIES IN CRIME AND SOCIETY

Motherhood, Respectability and Baby-Farming in Victorian and Edwardian London
Joshua G. Stuart-Bennett

The Intersections of Family Violence and Sexual Offending
Gemma Hamilton and Patrick Tidmarsh

Children, Care and Crime
Trauma and Transformation
Alison Gerard, Andrew McGrath, Emma Colvin and Annette Gainsford

Technology and Domestic and Family Violence
Victimisation, Perpetration and Responses
Bridget Harris and Delanie Woodlock

Crime, Criminal Justice and Religion
A Critical Appraisal
Philip Birch, Conor Murray and Andrew McInnes

Demystifying Modern Slavery
Rose Broad and David Gadd

For more information about this series, please visit: www.routledge.com/Routledge-Studies-in-Crime-and-Society/book-series/RSCS

CRIME, CRIMINAL JUSTICE AND RELIGION

A Critical Appraisal

Edited by Philip Birch, Conor Murray and Andrew McInnes

Routledge
Taylor & Francis Group
LONDON AND NEW YORK

Cover image: gettyimages.co.uk / Fred de Noyelle / Godong

First published 2023
by Routledge
4 Park Square, Milton Park, Abingdon, Oxon OX14 4RN

and by Routledge
605 Third Avenue, New York, NY 10158

Routledge is an imprint of the Taylor & Francis Group, an informa business

British Library Cataloguing-in-Publication Data
A catalogue record for this book is available from the British Library

ISBN: 978-1-032-23288-1 (hbk)
ISBN: 978-1-032-23289-8 (pbk)
ISBN: 978-1-003-27659-3 (ebk)

DOI: 10.4324/9781003276593

Typeset in Bembo
by Newgen Publishing UK

CONTENTS

FIGURES

TABLES

CONTRIBUTORS

Shamila Ahmed, PhD, is based at the University of Westminster and specialises in the "war on terror", terrorism, policing, radicalisation and state crime. In 2021, she was invited to the United Nations Congress on Crime Prevention and Criminal Justice as an expert on radicalisation and terrorism. Her multidisciplinary perspective and expertise, which includes the disciplines of law, criminology, international relations, political science and psychology, have led to various publications which seek to understand the impact of structures, institutions and discourses on individuals' perceptions, beliefs, values and experiences.

Alex Beaumont is currently a lecturer in Criminology and Sociology at University of Law (Manchester campus, UK). His research interests lie within the field of criminal justice, desistance, psychoanalytic theory and religion, as well as the emerging field of digital desistance. Alex is in the last stages of his PhD through the University of Plymouth (UK), where he has spent five years as a doctoral teaching assistant.

Philip Birch, B.Soc.Sci.(Hons); P.G. Cert. (HEP); P.G. Cert. (SSRM); P.G. Dip. (Soc.Sci.); MSc.; PhD, is Associate Professor of Criminology in the Faculty of Arts & Social Sciences at the University of Technology Sydney, Australia. During his academic career he has taught in the British, US and Australian university systems. Prior to entering academia, Philip worked as a criminologist in the field, holding posts in the UK prison service as well as in the crime and disorder field, which involved managing a specialist crime unit. Philip has published books, book chapters, peer-reviewed articles and government reports in his main areas of research – offender management and rehabilitation; police, prisons and probation practices; gender-inclusive violence, with a particular focus on domestic and family violence; and sex work.

Fiona Bloomer is a senior lecturer in the School of Applied Social and Policy Sciences, at Ulster University, UK. Her research centres on abortion policy, with a focus on its intersection with stigma, faith and activism. She has written extensively on this subject, including as co-author of the book *Reimagining Global Abortion Politics* (2018).

Myra Blyth is based at Regent's Park College, University of Oxford. From 2004 to 2020 Myra combined her roles of teaching and research as a fellow and tutor at Regent's Park College, University of Oxford. Since completing her doctoral thesis: "Towards a Restorative Hermeneutic: Churches Responding to Crime and Wrongdoing" (2012). Myra has explored the question of the place – if any – for forgiveness in restorative justice. She guest-edited a special edition of the *Oxford Journal of Law and Religion* on this question and recently co-authored a book entitled *Restorative Justice and Forgiveness* (2022). Other recent publications include a chapter on "restorative justice and human trafficking" (2022).

Emma Campbell is co-convenor of a leading activist group, Alliance for Choice, which campaigns for free, safe, local access to abortion in Northern Ireland. Over the last decade, Emma played a leading role in advocating for legal change. This included advising on national and international interventions such as membership of the ad hoc advisory panel working with Stella Creasy MP, whose efforts in the UK Parliament resulted in the decriminalisation of abortion in Northern Ireland.

Jodi Death is an Associate Professor and member of the QUT Centre for Justice. Jodi's primary research interest is in child sexual abuse in institutional care. This includes identifying and responding to the voices and needs of survivors and developing an understanding of historic paedophile networks. Jodi has completed research for the Australian Royal Commission into Institutional Responses to Child Sexual Abuse, considering young peoples' perspectives of safety in out-of-home care.

Ioan Durnescu is Professor at the University of Bucharest, Faculty of Sociology and Social Work. He teaches and conducts research in the areas of probation, prison and deradicalisation. His special interest is comparative probation and re-entry. He is one of the editors of *Probation in Europe* (WOLF) and the *Understanding Penal Practice* (Routledge). Ioan Durnescu is also co-editor of the *European Journal of Probation*, published by the University of Bucharest, and co-chair of the RAN Rehabilitation Working Group.

Miranda Forsyth is Professor at the Australian National University (ANU) with over 20 years of research and practical experience in the operation of justice systems in Melanesia. She has a PhD in law from the ANU that examined the relationship between customary justice and the state criminal justice system in Vanuatu. She has led a multi-year research project on sorcery accusation-related violence in Papua New Guinea since 2013.

Isabelle R. Gunning (she, her) – Professor of Law, Southwestern Law School. Isabelle is a member of a small, Christian-derived independent religious teaching called New Thought. She is licensed as a practitioner/spiritual counsellor by her home church, the Agape International Spiritual Center.

Michael Hallett is Professor of Criminology and Criminal Justice at the University of North Florida. His work has appeared in numerous books and journals including *Punishment & Society*, *Justice Quarterly*, *The Prison Journal*, and others. Dr Hallett led a three-year study on-site at America's largest maximum-security prison, Angola (aka Louisiana State Penitentiary) exploring the religious lives of long-term inmates. His most recent book stemming from this research is titled *The Restorative Prison*, with colleagues from Baylor University's Institute for Studies of Religion.

Garth den Heyer is a professor with Arizona State University and senior research fellow with the US National Police Foundation. He is also a contributing faculty member at Walden University and an associate with the Scottish Institute of Policing Research. He served with the New Zealand Police for 38 years, retiring as an Inspector. His main research interests are policing, counterterrorism and homeland security; militarisation; service delivery effectiveness; strategic thinking; organisational reform; and transnational gangs.

William Hoverd is a senior lecturer in Defence and Security Studies at Massey University, New Zealand. He is a sociologist of religion who works in the multidisciplinary area of security studies with specific focus on New Zealand. He has most recently published in the areas of the Christchurch Call, terrorism, cybersecurity, Covid-19, New Zealand religious diversity and New Zealand national security.

Jonathan Kearney is a commissioner with the Northern Ireland Human Rights Commission. Prior to that, he was an assistant professor in an academy in the United Arab Emirates, drawing upon a 32-year background in operational policing. He has worked with European academics, examining European Union policy and practice in crisis-management operations, and his research activities have taken him to the United Nations in New York, and the Balkan states of Bosnia and Herzegovina, Kosovo and the Republic of North Macedonia.

Gary Manders is a criminologist and senior lecturer in Applied Social Studies at the University of Bedfordshire, United Kingdom. Formerly, a probation officer and senior practitioner in Youth Justice, he has over 12 years of experience in the criminal justice system within England.

Maureen Mansfield is a community organiser, advocate and campaigner for feminist abolition and anti-carceral approaches to violence. Mo has extensive experience working in the voluntary sector with organisations critical of state violence such as

INQUEST, Women In Prison, and Women at WISH. Mo organises with Abolitionist Futures, a collective focused on political education, creating abolitionist resources, writing, network building and public events building a movement towards work without prisons, detention and punishment.

Kim McGuire holds a PhD in History (Lancaster University), and master's degrees in Law (UCLan) and in Social History (Lancaster University). Her main research interests, on which she has published extensively, include interpersonal conflicts in various political, social and economic contexts. Whilst interested in conflict constructions, including "hate crime", (linguistically, legally, emotionally, factually), ultimately her concern is how these are perpetuated, and also how they can be mediated, regulated and resolved. She teaches criminal law, criminology and mediation.

Andrew McInnes, BA (Hons), MEd, PhD, PGCE (FE), FCMI, is an adjunct associate professor with Charles Sturt University, working in the Australian Graduate School of Policing and Security. Until July 2020, he was a senior lecturer at the Charles Sturt University campus in Port Macquarie, NSW, Australia, where he was a course manager and lecturer in criminal justice, leadership and policing subjects, both on campus and online. He has previously led in the development of a start-up academic institution on behalf of the Abu Dhabi government in the United Arab Emirates, including in the design, accreditation and delivery of new academic programmes in policing, security and crime scene investigation.

Kathleen McPhillip's is an Australian sociologist of religion and gender in the School of Humanities, Creative Industries and Social Sciences at the University of Newcastle, Australia. Kathleen's work examines the difficult issue of child sexual abuse in religious organisations in Australia. As a sociologist of religion, gender and mental health, Kathleen has been investigating the impacts of child sexual abuse on survivors as well as the responses from institutions. Kathleen is a member of the Centre for the History of Violence and the Society Health and Disability Research Group at the University of Newcastle, Australia.

Conor Murray, BSc (Hons), MSSc, PhD, PgCHEP, FHEA, is a Lecturer in Criminology and Criminal Justice at Ulster University, where he is also the Global Engagement Lead and Postgraduate Tutor within the School of Applied Social and Policy Sciences. He sits on the Executive Board of NIACRO, an NGO dedicated to reducing crime and its impact on people and communities in Northern Ireland. As an early career researcher, he is focused on disseminating the findings of his doctoral research, which included a nine-month ethnographic study in Hydebank Wood (Young Offenders Centre) College. His findings will be published in a research monograph in 2023. While writing the book Conor has also been exploring research interests in disciplines of young adulthood, gender, sexuality, policing, religion, and sport-based interventions. He has secured over £150,000 in research funding and support grants and has published book chapters, peer reviewed articles and reports.

Gabriel Oancea is head of the Bucharest Probation Service and associate lecturer at the University of Bucharest, Faculty of Sociology and Social Work. He teaches effective methods used in offenders' supervision and rehabilitation, and aspects related to the specific of social work in criminal justice. He is involved in studies regarding the effectiveness of preventive measures and the transfer of prisoners and probationers within EU.

Brian Payne, BSc (Hons), MSSc, PhD, SFHEA, is a senior lecturer in Criminology and Criminal Justice and the subject lead for Criminology and Criminal Justice at Ulster University, Northern Ireland. His primary research interests lie in the areas of restorative justice, policing and transnational organised crime. Brian has conducted extensive research with community restorative justice projects in Belfast and evaluated the work of police and justice agencies and associated stakeholders in England and Northern and Southern Ireland. He has previously worked on a major research council project entitled "North-South Irish Responses to Transnational Organised Crime" and has been principal investigator on several large research projects totalling over £400K in funding, including a review of the public value of forensic services in Northern Ireland, an evaluation of the extent and practice of illegal money lending in Northern Ireland, and an exploration of the relations between young people and the police in the south-west of England. Brian is a visiting fellow (Criminology) of the University of Gloucestershire and sits on the editorial board of the *Irish Probation Journal.*

Russell G. Pearce (he, him) – Professor of Law, Edward & Marilyn Bellet Chair in Legal Ethics, Morality & Religion, Fordham University School of Law. Russ "views his Judaism as the foundation for his life and his work, including his commitment to liberatory and redemptive practices within Jewish and American law". He co-authored, with Laynie Soloman, (2022), "'Nothing about Us without Us': Toward a Liberatory Heterodox Halakha," *Touro Law Review, 37*(4), p. 1776.

Michael Quinlan is the National Head of School for Law & Business at the University of Notre Dame Australia. Prior to joining the university in 2013, Professor Quinlan had a distinguished career of more than 23 years at the commercial law firm Allens. Professor Quinlan is also vice president of the St Thomas More Society, a board member of Freedom For Faith and the Legal Profession Admissions Board as well as a member of the advisory board of the Catholic Archdiocese of Sydney's Anti-Slavery Taskforce. Professor Quinlan's research interests centre on the relationship between the law, morality and religion.

Kelly Richards is an Associate Professor and member of the QUT Centre for Justice. Kelly has an extensive research track record in the areas of restorative and innovative justice practices, Aboriginal and Torres Strait Islander justice-related matters, and sexual offending. From 2008 to 2012, Kelly was a visiting fellow in the Centre for Restorative Justice at the Australian National University. In 2010, she was named ACT Government Office for Women Audrey Fagan Churchill Fellow, and in 2020 she received a Fulbright Senior Scholar Award.

Michael Salter studied Law at Southampton University, 1975–1978, and completed his PhD on "Law, Sport and Public Disorder" in 1988 from the University of Sheffield. He has published over 45 articles and five books, was Principal Investigator (PI) for a major EU Research Project on hate crime, and is currently teaching at the Chinese University of Hong Kong including courses on international law, legal communications and Shakespeare's Hamlet.

Ian de Terte is a senior lecturer and clinical psychologist based at the School of Psychology, Massey University, New Zealand. He is a former detective with the New Zealand Police. He currently is a reservist with the New Zealand Defence Force, holds the rank of Major and the specialist role of clinical psychologist. His research focuses on traumatic stress, high-risk occupations, first responders, psychological resilience and coping strategies. He has over 50 publications and has secured over NZ$300,000 in research funding.

Matthew P. West is an assistant professor of Criminology and Criminal Justice in the School of Justice and Public Safety at Southern Illinois University Carbondale. His research draws on psychological, sociological and criminological theories to understand decision-making in legal contexts, such as capital cases. He is also interested in quantitative methods, employing a range of techniques to analyse and simulate data. His work appears in outlets such as the *Journal of Quantitative Criminology* and *Psychology, Public Policy, and Law.*

Tobias Winright (PhD, University of Notre Dame) is Associate Professor of Theological Ethics and Health Care Ethics at Saint Louis University in St. Louis, Missouri (USA). With professional experience in law enforcement as a correctional officer and a reserve police officer, his doctoral dissertation was "The Challenge of Policing: An Analysis in Christian Social Ethics" (2002), and his book *Serve and Protect: Selected Essays on Just Policing* (2020) includes several of many essays on the subject spanning over 25 years. Most recently he edited the *T&T Clark Handbook of Christian Ethics* (2021).

Logan A. Yelderman is an assistant professor of Psychology at Prairie View A&M University. His research lies at the intersection of psychology, law and religion. With an emphasis on legal decision-making research, he studies fundamentalist beliefs, religious priming, parole release decisions, juvenile justice and mock juror decision-making in death penalty and insanity defence cases. His recent publications have appeared in *Psychological Reports*, *Psychology, Public Policy, and Law*, *Psychiatry, Psychology and Law*, *Legal and Criminological Psychology*, and *Mental Health, Religion, and Culture.*

PART 1

Contextualising Crime, Criminal Justice and Religion

1

INTRODUCING CRIME, CRIMINAL JUSTICE AND RELIGION – A CRITICAL APPRAISAL

Philip Birch, Conor Murray and Andrew McInnes

Background to the Volume

Since 9/11, there has been a rapid growth in the use of scientific- and technology-driven methods and techniques in responding to crime by institutions of the criminal justice system. This approach to crime prevention and crime reduction has seen the rise of an abundance of "hard" and "soft" strategies, as identified as early as 2004 by Levi and Wall. Through increased surveillance and control measures, not only has there been a shift in criminal justice policy and practice but also a shift in scholarly and academic discourse concerning crime and criminal justice. Arguably, the dominance of science and technology within this context has led to overlooking other (important) factors that impact on crime and the criminal justice system.

Religion has had a substantial history in regard to seeking to offer an understanding of criminality as well as having an influence on criminal justice institutions. Prior to the Enlightenment period, religion played a significant role in understanding society and addressing a range of social ills. However, with the Age of Enlightenment during the seventeenth and the eighteenth century, a rejection of religion occurred, replaced by reason and scientific method. Nevertheless, the influence of religion within the context of crime and criminal justice has never really diminished; rather, it has, arguably, been merely overlooked. Illustrations for such a position can be offered in various ways; it is well documented how probation as a practice and a criminal justice institution has its origins in religion (Philips, 2010, 4), while Kerley (2018) noted that during the 1960s a growth in the social scientific study of religion occurred, albeit culminating in the controversial work of Hirschi and Stark's (1969) Hellfire Study. In this work, it was concluded that there was no relationship between crime and religion, a position that has been subsequently challenged (Burkett & White, 1974). More contemporaneously, restorative justice has gathered significant support as a response to crime and has a connection

DOI: 10.4324/9781003276593-2

to religion (Hadley, 2001), while the study of the "criminology of religion" has recently been recognised as a subdiscipline, although it is still considered to be in its infancy (Jang, 2013), as reflected in the small amount of literature that exists in this area (see: Hill et al., 2020; Johnson & Vanderbank, 2014; Kerely et al, 2018; Millie, 2020 and Sadique, & Stanislas, 2016).

With such a rich history between the interface of religion and crime, and as noted by Jang (2013), this being an area that is still under-researched, with very little published in the area, the proposed volume seeks to redress this imbalance. While there have been more published peer-reviewed articles than books in the arena of crime and religion (e.g. Chitwood, Weiss & Leukefeld, 2008; Dew et al., 2008; Kelly et al., 2015), most publications fail to move beyond a historical and/or theoretical review, and the spectrum of issues considered is limited. This volume seeks to bridge that gap in the examination of crime and criminal justice by taking both a historical and a contemporary lens to explore religion in the context of crime and criminal justice and offer a unique perspective by considering the impact on modern-day policy and practice, while considering a range of issues such as criminal justice professions, abortion and hate crime. Therefore, this volume will act to set the agenda for the renewed recognition of the importance that religion has in terms of how we view and ultimately address crime and deliver criminal justice. It will be one of the first texts by Routledge to cover the area of crime, criminal justice and religion, and will serve as a major influence and essential point of reference in the field.

Focus of the Volume

The book is composed of 20 chapters, written by authors affiliated with academic institutions, human rights commissions and non-governmental organisations from a broad range of jurisdictions and each providing an original contribution to the literature on crime, criminal justice and religion. While many of the chapters focus primarily on Christianity, there is reflection and consideration of religions outside of this denomination. The book is divided into three parts. The first part, which includes this chapter, is entitled "Contextualising Crime, Criminal Justice and Religion", and seeks to reflect on the relationship between religion, crime and criminal justice, both historically and contemporaneously. Chapter 2 also falls into the first part, in which a reflection on the influence of religion in understanding and defining crime as well as consideration of the response by the criminal justice system is provided. This chapter, by Philip Birch (University of Technology Sydney, Australia), Conor Murray (Ulster University, Northern Ireland), and Andrew McInnes (Charles Sturt University, Australia), cerebrates how over time the importance and significance of religion has shifted, impacting on the social, cultural and civil aspects of society in various ways on a variety of issues, none so much as that of crime and criminality. In this chapter, the authors consider the religion–crime nexus by first acknowledging it is complex; however, they illustrate the connection in a number of ways, including theoretically drawing upon theories such as social control theory and social bond theory, as well as recognising the connection between morality, religion and criminality. This reveals the crime prevention element the religion–crime nexus can foster. Equally, attention is paid to the fact that religion has, arguably, created crime, illustrating the position through social issues such as abortion and homosexuality. The chapter then moves on to reflect on the relationship between religion and the criminal justice system and, while the system has largely been considered secular in most parts of the world, the values and principles that underpin the operations of the criminal justice system align with religious values and principles. The concluding message is religion, crime and criminal justice are intertwined, with religion and the criminal justice system sharing a number of values and principles that govern the role and function of each institution, while playing a role in the prevention of crime.

The second part of this volume comprises Chapters 3–10 and is entitled "Appraisal of Institutions and Professional Practice". This part of the book explores how religion impacts policies and practices of criminal justice institutions around the world. It commences with Chapter 3, where Tobias Winright (St. Louis University, USA) explores the impact of religion on the practice of policing. He argues that, while many members of society have moved away from adherence to institutional religion or subscription to religious beliefs, most people worldwide still identify with, or acknowledge having a background in, religion. Winright suggests that the same is true of those who are police officers. He identifies the numerous ways that religion has informed and impacted the institution and practice of policing as well as individual police officers. Historically, policing has reflected deeply held beliefs about the human condition, crime and justice, and the need for social and political arrangements to safeguard the peace. For individual police officers, their world view, often rooted in religion, impacts their view and practice of policing. For example, religion provides spiritual solace for police officers who experience strife and stress from their work. Also, religion motivates police officers' efforts to serve and protect their fellow citizens and the community in accordance with certain moral values and commitments.

Chapters 4 and 5 build on the points of discussion raised by Winright in Chapter 3 by examining the ways in which contemporary policing intersects with religion. Chapter 4, by Andrew McInnes (Charles Sturt University, Australia), commences this exploration with a discussion on police professionalisation and the policing of religious communities. McInnes argues that policing has become an increasingly complex and challenging profession with many strategic and operational considerations to take into account when developing a service that is community focused, representative, and that has earned the trust and confidence of citizens. He suggests that police organisations across the world have been responding to the wide-ranging needs of a more global society that are becoming much more diverse in a range of ways, including that of religion. The need for police officers to be able to understand the wide range of needs of communities across the religious spectrum is critical to the success of a community-focused policing service. McInnes takes the issue of religion in police training for new recruits as the focus of his examination. In doing so, he explores the theoretical foundations of religious awareness and development training. As a result, McInnes brings together key concepts of police professionalism, community policing, trust and confidence to a discussion on the role of training and development in supporting religious communities. In Chapter 5, Conor Murray, Brian Payne (both Ulster University, Northern Ireland) and Philip Birch (University of Technology Sydney, Australia) suggest that policing in divided societies – societies in which overt and hidden forms of division exist – is a complex issue driven by many facts, with religion being a common catalyst. The authors explore how a fallout of such division is the sectarian bias that typically occurs through police practice. Through the consideration of both Israel and Northern Ireland as case examples, Murray et al. explore the interface of religion and social cohesion in divided societies. In doing so, they consider the structural impediments to effective policing and difficulties faced in maintaining police legitimacy. The authors also highlight the continued importance of police reform in diverse contexts as a means for improving police legitimacy, particularly within divided societies that are historically polarised and lacking social cohesion.

Moving on from policing, in Chapter 6, Michael Hallet (University of North Florida, USA) offers an update regarding the changing role of religion in US correctional programming. Drawing from archival and site-based research, Hallet explores issues regarding "religious establishment" versus "religious liberty" in US corrections. While religious programmes offer powerfully transformative access to social capital for many prisoners, the growing prominence of religious volunteers with programme authority over US prisoners raises both opportunities and concerns. The changing role of religion in US prisons is explored in four key areas: lack of state neutrality towards religion, excessive state entanglement with religious service providers, inadequate solicitation of alternative programming, and a de facto measure of coercion in delivery of services. Hallet concludes with grades in each area and a set of recommendations.

In Chapter 7, Gary Manders (University of Bedfordshire, England) examines the role of religion in Youth Justice, and how the interplay between a young person's agency, beliefs, values and behaviour generates possibilities for change. In doing so, he explores the dynamics of young offenders' world views and the importance of understanding and utilising this concept as a resource for effective practice in Youth Justice. Manders' particular focus is on young people's religious identity and its implications for supporting the initial transition towards abstinence from offending. He discusses the issues for practitioners of developing "religious literacy" and explores strategies for opening up conversations with young people about their belief systems. The notion of the good life as a life worth living is scrutinised as a strengths-based model of rehabilitation through identifying youth offenders' future goals and intended strategies for achieving them. Furthermore, Manders examines the notion of moral exemplars as a catalyst for transformation and explores the importance of faith communities as a resource for practitioners and young people in conflict with the law.

Based on their own first-hand experiences of working in the profession, Ioan Durnescu and Gabriel Oancea (both University of Bucharest, Romania) in Chapter 8 consider the influence of religion on probation. The authors suggest that, although probation's place of birth is disputed, most scholars agree that its ideological roots are in the Christian religion. In its early days, a probation officer was regarded as a man of God, "a man with experience and tact and full of the milk of human kindness" (Jarvis, 1972:8). Consequently, the missionary had to have faith and treat individuals as holders of the "divine spark". Moral characteristics of the probation officer were more important than his skills. However, compassion, acceptance and empathy were often mentioned as important "tools" of craft. Durnescu and Oancea contend that in one way or another, these "tools" are still found in the profession, sometimes under different umbrellas or different names. They argue that, despite its current secular ideology, probation activity is still animated by strong Christian values and beliefs, such as forgiveness, compassion, acceptance and so on. The authors argue that these values have been metamorphosed into different principles and standards of practice but retained their core messages that place the individual and his uniqueness in the centre of attention.

Chapters 9 and 10 both take the legal profession as their focus of examination. Chapter 9, by Michael Quinlan (University of Notre Dame, Australia), explores the fundamental impact religion has had on the development of the Western legal tradition and on the legal profession in the Western world. As the execution of St Thomas More in 1535 evidenced, there have been periods of stress and conflict between the religious convictions of some lawyers and the laws of the state. As religious belief has declined and become more variegated, the relationship between the laws of the state and the religious beliefs of lawyers has been experiencing a new era of friction. Quinlan suggests that this is evidenced through the scrutiny of the religious beliefs of recent appointments to the US Supreme Court and the Canadian Supreme Court's rejection of Trinity Western University's appeal from the denial of its accreditation. He concludes that the legal profession must be open to, and supportive of, membership by lawyers from differing religious backgrounds to maintain public confidence and be representative. In Chapter 10, Isabelle R. Gunning (Southwestern Law School, USA) and Russell G. Pearce (Fordham University, USA) consider the "calling" of lawyers in the criminal justice system. The authors explore the implications for lawyers of the prophet Micah's teaching that they should "do justly," "love mercy" and "walk humbly with your God" (Micah 6:8). Gunning and Pearce suggest that the dominant conception of the lawyer's role requires that lawyers "bleach out" identity as neutral partisans. However, instead, the authors augment the perspective of the Religious Lawyering movement that lawyers should integrate their faith and their work. Drawing from that framework, from the authors' beliefs that all people are created in God's image, and from their own respective Christian and Jewish backgrounds, Barret et al. consider how lawyers from different faith traditions can bring the values of doing justice, loving mercy and walking humbly to their work in the criminal justice system. The authors suggest that these values can enhance and enrich lawyers' ability to fulfil their professional roles and allow them to discern a prophetic and a practical understanding of the interrelated challenges of restorative justice, prison abolition and reparations that have drawn greater public attention as a result of the racial reckoning that followed the murder of George Floyd.

The third and final part of this volume contains Chapters 11–20 and is entitled "Appraisal of Contemporary Issues" with regards to crime, criminal justice and religion. This part of the book critically examines key issues which are at the forefront of global debates around the intersection of religion, crime and criminal justice, including human rights, abortion, mass shootings, terrorism and the death penalty. It begins with Chapter 11, written by Jonathan Kearney (Northern Ireland Human Rights Commission), who examines the relationship between human rights, religion and the criminal justice system. Kearney suggests that human rights are often presented as the manifestation of the "golden rule". On the face of it, such a perspective works well when there is agreement. But circumstances can arise in which the relationship is not one of being enmeshed in a common cause; rather, the experience is of one outlook butting against the other. Kearney examines how religious liberties are approached universally and within the regional experience of the European Convention on Human Rights. Drawing upon recent legislative and criminal justice experiences in the United Kingdom and Australia, Kearney critically analyses the extent to which those experiences represent blockages which then create the need for diversion or the opportunity for repair. He concludes with a description of the delicate interplay between human rights, religion and the criminal justice system where alleged offenders may become victims because of the actual processes employed by the police.

In Chapter 12, Emma Campbell (Ulster University, Northern Ireland), Maureen Mansfield (INQUEST, Northern Ireland), and Fiona Bloomer (Ulster University, Northern Ireland) consider the role religion plays in abortion and the criminal justice system (CJS) in Northern Ireland. The authors suggest that religiosity dominates discourse on abortion law and policy in contexts where it is restricted, illegal and difficult to access. In Western societies restrictions bound by religiosity typically stem from a conservative right-wing Christian ethos, impacting on law making, provision of abortion services and support services. Campbell, Mansfield and Bloomer examine the presence of religiosity in the CJS within the UK through two main themes: the attempts by anti-abortion religious groups to maintain influence on the dominant discourse, access and legislation; and how these have changed over time. Analysis of the discourse of key players, including anti-abortion politicians, and judges, and policy documents, will illustrate the harms and contradictions that can be enacted by infusing legal frameworks with religious morality, rather than looking to fundamental need, harm reduction and minimum human rights standards. Particular attention is paid to the criminalisation of abortion and threats of criminalisation of abortion seekers, abortion providers and activists within an environment of anti-abortion religious groups being apparatus of the state.

The issue of the death penalty is the focus of Chapter 13,in which Longan Yelderman (Prairie View A&M University, USA) and Matthew West (Southern Illinois University, USA) examine the intersection between religion, the death penalty and the United States criminal justice system. The authors suggest that the role of religion in the criminal justice system has evolved over time, but the relevance of religion has become increasingly more contentious. Yelderman and West argue that religion plays an important role in the death penalty, suggesting that the primary criminal justice issue that religious institutions voice their positions on is capital punishment. They go on to explore three avenues in which religion pertains to the death penalty. First, they assess religion as a foundation for the development of the death penalty in law. Second, they assess the religious themes in trials and religious appeals. Third, they assess the religious beliefs of jurors and how these beliefs might be related to their verdicts and sentencing decisions. To conclude, Yelderman and West examine the implications of their current research and propose future directions regarding the role of religion in the death penalty and criminal justice system.

The issue of hate crime becomes the focus of Chapter 14, where Kim McGuire and Michael Salter (both University of Central Lancashire, England) use literary and legal analysis to explore issues relating to Islamic hate crime. While their foci are England and Wales, as illustrative of the concerns raised by religion, crime and control, these are relevant to democracies worldwide. The chapter builds upon McGuire and Salter's (2014) previous work which considered the ability to "abuse, ridicule, threaten, defame, mock and insult the religious beliefs, icons, prophets, practices and esteemed figures of believers" (p. 159). The authors revisit such issues, but the foci are the legal definitions of "religious hate crime", and arguments concerning the potential dangers of effectively reinstating "blasphemy" for one specific religion. Currently, as with all "hate crimes offences", a base offence must be committed, motivated by or demonstrate hostility towards, a protected religion, or indeed, atheism. Equally, intention to incite religious hatred is criminalised. The authors analyse "privileging" one religious belief over others, for example, Islam, and their analysis considers support for, but also the implications for, the operation of "hate crime", prosecution, and practices deemed "religious" in nature, by some, but potentially criminal by others.

Connected to the issue of hate crimes is the issue of terrorism, and Chapters 15 and 16 examine the ways religion and ideology intersect with state policies and responses in regards to dealing with terrorism. In Chapter 15, Shamila Ahmed (University of Westminster, England) and Garth de Heyer (Arizona State University, USA) consider the question: is far-right terrorism another form of religious terrorism? In doing so, the authors contrast how the construction of Islamist terrorism, as a non-secular religiously inspired form of terrorism, has amplified the constructed risk of Islamist terrorism; while the construction of far-right terrorism and extreme nationalism, as secular non-religious ideologies, has contributed to minimising and reducing the threat associated with these ideologies. Ahmed and de Heyer argue that the ideological construction of religious terrorism has contributed to Islamophobia and the introduction of draconian national and international policies within the "war on terror". They argue that this contrasts with the construction of non-religious inspired terrorism and extreme nationalism, as secular ideologies continue not only to mask the threat posed by these ideologies but also to underplay their ability to radicalise individuals. Through exposing how religion obscures the construction, risk and policy responses to terrorism, the chapter demonstrates the equally pervasive ability of religious and non-religious terrorism to gain support for ideologies premised on replacing existing social and political structures. Chapter 16, by William James Hoverd (Massey University, New Zealand), Garth den Heyer (Arizona State University, USA), and Ian de Terte (also from Massey University), considers what can be learnt from New Zealand's state policy responses to the Christchurch Mosque shootings. In doing so, they critically analyse the relationship between religion and domestic terrorism from the New Zealand crime and justice context, with a specific focus upon the state's response to the 2019 Christchurch Mosque shootings where 51 people were killed by a lone white supremacist gunman. After the attack, earlier surveillance of the Muslim community was formally critiqued in a Royal Commission of Inquiry, and this has impacted domestic counterterrorism and policing efforts to credibly engage with religious communities whilst remaining attentive to the threat of faith-based extremism. The authors suggest that the chapter has three goals: 1) explain the tensions inherent in policy engagements around religious communities and counterterrorism; 2) explore how in the New Zealand context, government engagement with religious communities might best occur after the Christchurch Mosque shootings, particularly when it comes to concerns around terrorism; and 3) theorise how this relationship between religion and terrorism may be pertinent for international audiences.

Moving the focus on to an area arguably overlooked in the mainstream consideration of crime and criminal justice, in Chapter 17, Miranda Forsyth (Australian National University, Australia) takes as her focus the United Nations Human Rights Council (2021) decision to pass a historic resolution (the UN resolution) which recognises for the first time the harmful practices related to witchcraft accusations and ritual attacks as a form of human rights abuse. The wording of the resolution was the culmination of years of debate as activists, lawyers and scholars struggled with finding ways to condemn violence and stigmatisation, whilst not impacting traditional and new belief systems involving the supernatural. Forsyth uses the resolution as a springboard to explore the tensions in legislating around the concept of magic in contexts of world view pluralism. She argues that such contexts involve radically different views about the role the supernatural plays in issues of causation in everyday life. Sorcery is commonly attributed as a cause of misfortune across the globe, and exorcism of evil spirits is part of the Catholic canon, and yet, for the most part, legislators are wary of regulating in this space. Forsyth concludes that this reticence presents significant challenges to legal systems seeking to effectively minimise ongoing and devastating harm arising from beliefs in the supernatural.

In Chapter 18, Jodi Death, Kelly Richards (both Queensland University of Technology, Australia) and Kathleen McPhillips (University of Newcastle, Australia) consider clergy-perpetrated child sexual abuse (CPCSA) as organised offending. The authors suggest that CPCSA has been recognised internationally as having devastating impacts on individuals, families and communities. They go on to argue that both research and the results of public inquiries have pointed to the systemic nature of CPCSA in religious organisations. Despite these findings, little research has considered CPCSA and subsequent cover-up as organised. Death et al. argue for the significance of understanding CPCSA as organised offending and the importance of this for policymakers and ongoing management of CPCSA. Utilising social network analysis and dark networks theory, the authors point to the potential internationalisation of clergy offending and the vulnerability of developing nation states where disruption of networks may not have occurred. Relevant considerations include the role of a strong democracy, the importance of independent media representations and changing policy in the care and resourcing of vulnerable children away from large-scale children's homes.

Restorative justice becomes the lens through which Chapter 19 considers crime, criminal justice and religion. Myra Blyth (University of Oxford, England) explores the relationship between religion and restorative justice by arguing that attempts to engage theology and the law in dialogue are limited, and the conviction of practical theologians writing on criminal justice is that public debate on issues of justice is enriched and deepened where lawyers and theologians engage with one another. Blyth suggests that viewing theology and law as dialogue partners can be mutually enriching. Each brings something different and distinctive to the discussion. In 1980, Bishop David Jenkins made this case, arguing that theology can best serve the quest for an answer to how society responds to crime by keeping alive in criminology those awkward questions that are frequently neglected about the struggle to be human. In the spirit of theology and law as dialogue partners, the author argues that the shift in focus from retributive to restorative values which has taken place in both the modern criminal justice debate and in contemporary atonement theology offers rich potential for critical dialogue between atonement theology and restorative justice theory. Both speak of justice as relational and, consequently, of the need for a participatory process; both understand the purpose of punishment as being restorative rather than retributive; and both understand the ultimate goal of justice to be reconciliation. The chapter is both theoretical and practical: in part one, critical questions for theology and law are raised through a mutual critical dialogue between restorative justice and atonement theology, and in part two, original case study data demonstrates very practically how atonement themes and restorative justice principles can successfully combine to help address crime within the prison context.

Finally, in drawing the book to a close, Chapter 20 by Alex Beaumont (University of Plymouth, England) presents initial findings from an in-depth psychosocial study into the impact conversions to Christianity have upon prisoner identity, community reintegration and desistance. Drawing upon the self-narratives of 13 ex-prisoners claiming to having had life-changing conversions, Beaumont argues that framing such experiences through both Badiouian and Zizekian philosophical notions of "Event", may provide insight into what is going on in such processes, and revitalise established notions of "turning points" and identity perspectives. The findings reveal how fidelity to the "event" can be easily retained inside prison, but upon release, ex-prisoners are faced with a double vulnerability that entails navigating both a new spiritual "reality" and a non-offending identity – how one is able to maintain this new outlook in an often-unforgiving system and society is the ultimate test and therefore requires more service provision support.

In conclusion, *Crime, Criminal Justice and Religion: A Critical Appraisal* represents a contemporary discourse around the influence and impact of religion on crime and criminal justice, a discourse that is arguably overlooked in the current crime and criminal justice landscape in favour of a focus on science and technological advances. The issues canvassed over the many chapters in this volume act as a timely reminder that religion has and continues to play an important role in the understanding and delivery of justice. This volume is therefore instrumental in bringing to the forefront and (re)developing, new thinking, analyses, paradigms, policies and practices in the field of crime, criminal justice and religion. By bringing together researchers and experts from multiple jurisdictions, utilising numerous theories and covering a range of issues, it serves as a major expansion on the existing literature in the area, which is sparse and spread across historical epochs. The culmination of these elements will serve to spearhead a revival of interest, research, academic discourse and industry recognition with regards to the impact and influence of religion on crime and criminal justice. As a result, this book becomes an important and useful resource for a range of criminal justice institutions and practitioners seeking to enhance their operational capabilities as well as to shape policy and practice, while from an academic perspective, this book becomes an important and useful resource for anyone studying and researching crime and criminal justice.

References

Burkett, S. R., & White, M. (1974). Hellfire and delinquency: Another look. *Journal for the Scientific Study of Religion, 13*(4), 455–462.

Chitwood, D. D., Weiss, M. L., & Leukefeld, C. G. (2008). A systematic review of recent literature on religiosity and substance use. *Journal of Drug Issues, 38*(3), 653–688. https://doi.org/10.1177/002204260803800302

Dew, R. E., Daniel, S. S., Armstrong, T. D., Goldston, D. B., Triplett, M. F., & Koenig, H. G. (2008). Religion/spirituality and adolescent psychiatric symptoms: A review. *Child Psychiatry and Human Development, 39*(4), 381–398.

Hadley, M. L. (Ed.). (2001). *The spiritual roots of restorative justice*. SUNY Press.

Hill QC, M. H., Doe, N., Helmholz, R. H., & Witte Jr, J. (Eds.). (2020). *Christianity and criminal law*. Routledge.

Hirschi, T., & Stark, R. (1969). Hellfire and delinquency. *Social Problems, 17*(2), 202–213.

Jang, S. J. (2013). *Religion and crime*. Oxford University Press.

Johnson, P., & Vanderbeck, R. M. (2014). *Law, religion and homosexuality*. Routledge.
Kelly, P. E., Polanin, J. R., Jang, S. J., & Johnson, B. R. (2015). Religion, delinquency, and drug use: A meta-analysis. *Criminal Justice Review, 40*(4), 505–523. https://doi.org/10.1177/0734016815605151
Kerley, K. R. (Ed.). (2018). *Religion and crime: Theory, research, and practice*. MDPI.
Levi, M., & David S. Wall, D.S. (2004). Technologies, security, and privacy in the post-9/11 European information society. *Journal of Law and Society, 31*(2), 194–220.
McGuire, K., & Salter, M. (2014). Legal responses to religious hate crime: Identifying critical issues. *King's Law Journal, 25*(2), 159–184.
Millie, A. (Ed.). (2020). *Criminology and public theology: On hope, mercy and restoration*. Policy Press.
Philips, J. (2010). The social construction of probation in England and Wales, and the United States: Implications for the transferability of probation practice. *British Journal of Community Justice, 8*(1), 1–17.
Sadique, K., & Stanislas, P. (Eds.) (2016). *Religion, faith and crime*. Palgrave Macmillan.

2

CRIME AND CRIMINAL JUSTICE – REFLECTING ON THE INFLUENCE OF RELIGION

Philip Birch, Conor Murray and Andrew McInnes

Introduction

This chapter reflects on the influence that religion has on crime and criminal justice. The impact religion has had on society over time has been well documented, both in terms of its positive and negative effects, which at times has engendered compassion, while at other times has engendered discrimination. Beginning with a consideration of the broader influence religion has had on society, this chapter first cerebrates how over time the importance and significance of religion has shifted, impacting on the social, cultural and civil aspects of society in various ways on a variety of issues. The chapter then moves on to consider the role religion has played in shaping society's understanding of what crime and criminality is, along with religion's influence on the policies and practices of the criminal justice system and its agencies. In doing so, the commonly held belief that crime and criminal justice operates within a secular context is questioned. The chapter concludes by reflecting on the role religious influence has on crime and criminal justice, even in an age in which technological and scientific innovations are leading the way in the prevention, disruption and reduction of crime.

Religion and Society

The social history of religion has been well documented (Berger, 1969; Brown, 2007); Fasolt, 2006; Lahti, 2009; McGuire, 2008; Possamai & Tittensor, 2022). Over time, religion – represented in its many forms – has drifted from a dominant, authoritative force that governed society and its functioning, to a more diminutive force in contemporary, increasingly secular, societies (Possamai & Tittensor, 2022). In reference to religion's diluted influence, Possamai and Tittensor (2022: 4) suggest that: "As with other social and cultural aspects of our lives, religion is in a constant

DOI: 10.4324/9781003276593-3

state of flux". They suggest that religion has not disappeared from society; rather, it has adapted and morphed into the contemporary landscape it finds itself in. This is a view shared by Berger (2014), who argues that secularisation has been replaced with pluralism – allowing religion to continue to be a part of the societal landscape. Such claims are supported by a study on the importance of religion in contemporary society by the Pew Research Center (2017). Based on global population predictions up to 2060, the Center suggests that over the next 40 years, religious affiliation and membership will more or less be consistent amongst many religious faiths such as Catholicism, Hinduism and Judaism; however, the same research identifies there will be a decline in those who identify as atheist, agnostic or who are not religiously affiliated (Pew Research Center, 2017).

In reflecting on the influence and impact religion has had on society over time, a consideration of the aspects of social, cultural, and civil life that have been shaped by religion is important. The work of McGuire (2008) provides a useful lens to do this as it explores individual, social and structural ways in which religion influences, informs and shapes society. From an individual perspective, McGuire (2008) examines how religious affiliation can be a characteristic around which an individual can construct their identity, for example, a man's self-identity as a husband, or a woman's self-identity as an elderly member of society (McGuire, 2008). This is also applied at a more macro level, for example, in the way in which religion can shape the identity of a family, as this can be both internal, to each member within the family, and external, to those outside of the family. At a broader level, community can also be defined and redefined by religion, in which a sense of belonging, as well as social cohesion, can be formed (Hervieu-Léger, 2006). Equally, religion can be the antithesis of belonging and social cohesion, as evidenced by those who live in divided communities such as Northern Ireland and Israel (Murray, Payne, & Birch, 2022).

At a more societal and structural level, religion has played a significant role in shaping social issues and problems such as sex work (Birch, 2015; Turcescu & Stan 2005), membership of the LGBTQI+ community (Hall, 2017; Hasbany, 2013; Johnson & Vanderbeck, 2014), abortion (Campbell, Mansfield, & Bloomer, 2022; Hussein, 2022; Clements, 2015), and divorce (Tuttle & Davis, 2015). The role by which religion has contributed to such issues and their debate, has meant religion can act both as a catalyst and inhibitor to social change, as reflected in recent shifts in issues such as climate change (Morrison et al., 2015) and same-sex marriage (Lee & Mutz, 2019). Religion is therefore intrinsically linked to society, affecting individual behaviours, social and cultural standards as well as the value systems in place that inform, guide and regulate society. Even within the contemporary societal landscape in which science and technology dominate, the underlying force of religion has remained a factor that both informs and shapes society. While during recent times, a call for better integration of religion into academic and public dialogue has been evidenced, an illustration of this can be offered by Ebaugh (2002), who noted that religion needs to be brought back into the social sciences due to world events. For scholars in the contemporary criminology landscape, they have long recognised that religion and the criminal justice system are on the "criminological agenda" (O'Connor et al., 2006), in which the connection between religion and social life is no better illustrated than through the lens of crime and the criminal justice system.

Understanding the Religion–Crime Nexus

It has been argued that religion has a positive influence on people's lives, whether that be in the form of psychological and physical well-being (Chen & VanderWeele, 2018) or as a source of comfort and strength during life's challenges, such as mental ill-health (Kearns et al., 2018). The application of this notion to the relationship between crime and religion, however, is a difficult one. Traced back to the work of Durkheim (1897), who stated that religion should lead to a reduction in negative behaviours, including deviant and criminal acts, the religion–crime nexus has been a staple issue in the social sciences discourse. However, many regard Hirschi and Stark's (1969) Hellfire and Delinquency study as a watershed moment in the debate concerning crime and religion, in which it was claimed that religion did not prevent delinquency, a finding that, while surprising at the time, went unchallenged, until a steady stream of research began to emerge evidencing a contradictory position, revealing that religion did provide a mediating factor with regards to its effect on reducing criminality (Adamczyk et al., 2017). As a consequence, the religion–crime nexus was re-examined by Stark (1996), who later refined the argument to suggest that there were a number of contexts in which religion can lead to conformity. This position has been supported by a range of studies that have demonstrated a significant relationship between religion and a reduction in crime (Weaver et al., 2005; Yeung et al., 2009). It can be, and it has been, argued that religion is a protective factor, reducing the likelihood of engagement in criminality (Jang et al., 2008; Johnson et al., 2001; Johnson et al., 2000; Regnerus, 2003), reflecting the role that religion plays in not only understanding what crime is but also in preventing crime.

Theoretically, the association between religion and less crime can be aligned with social bonds and social control postulating. As outlined by Jeng and Rhodes (2012), social bonds and social control mediate factors associated with crime; religion therefore helps reduce deviant and criminal behaviour. This position is further illustrated by the work of Salvatore and Taniguchi (2012), who noted that religion, due to its effects on the social bonds and social controls in people's lives, can effectively reduce deviant and criminal behaviour. Such positing offers support for the application of theoretical frameworks, such as Hirschi's (1969) social bond theory and Laub and Sampson's (2003) social control theory, for understanding the relationship between religion and crime.

Areas in which the religion–crime nexus have been studied within the context of crime and criminality have included youth offending, problematic substance use and violence. For example, Johnson et al. (2008) found those who were religiously affiliated were less likely to engage in drug use, while Salas et al. (2014) evidenced young people were least prone to violence if they were religious. Arguably, the religious-crime nexus is underpinned by morality, in which the moral guidance of religion contributes to a reduction in crime and criminality.

Morality, Religion and Crime

A basic dictionary definition of "crime" reveals a connection between morality and religion. For example, a crime can be defined as "an action or an instance of negligence that is deemed injurious to the public welfare or morals or to the interests of the state and that is legally prohibited; any offence, serious wrongdoing or sin" (Word Reference, n.d.). Such a definition exposes the term "crime" to an understanding that has both a legal and a moral interpretation, with Muncie (2001) claiming that the way we define crime reflects the way we think about society. The understanding society has of crime, and the relationship between morality and religion, however, are deeper than a basic definition of what crime is.

Many religions, including Christianity, Hinduism and Islam, believe that God created the world (Cradle of Humankind, 2022). Associated with the creation of the world is the establishment of moral standards or laws, which provide an inextricable link between morality and religion. Through its moral framework, religion embeds ethical principles into the social world that humans apply to their everyday life. Ethics involves making moral judgements about what is right or wrong, good or bad, in which right and wrong are qualities or moral judgements humans assign to actions and conduct (Beckley and Kennedy, 2020). Ethics can therefore provide answers to complex questions that ultimately guide one's behaviour, no more so than when it comes to engagement in deviant or criminal behaviour. The moral and ethical principles associated with religion positively impact on behaviour, negating anti-social behaviour and criminality, which in turn fosters individual self-control and social/community cohesion (Durrant & Poppelwell, 2017). Crime is prevented through the morality created by religion, as evidenced by Stavrova and Siegers (2014), who reported that those who follow a religion are more likely to engage in charity work, disapprove of lying and are less likely to engage in crime. Nevertheless, this sense of right and wrong has led to punishment if such moral standards of laws are broken (Durrant & Poppelwell, 2017). Religion can inevitably be associated with an increase in crime due to its (moral) framing of particular issues such as abortion, membership of the LGBTQI+ community and sex work, to name but a few. Such social issues have been problematised and demonised over time, with religion playing an influential role in such characterisations, which in turn has contributed to their criminal status (Turcescu & Stan, 2005).

According to the Pew Research Center (2009), opposition to abortion is influenced by one's religious beliefs. In the same research it was also reported that if participants believed abortion was morally wrong, they would be more likely to believe abortion should be illegal (Pew Research Center, 2009). A similar picture emerges when membership of the LGBTQI+ community is considered. While many countries across the globe have legalised same-sex relationships, many have not. As Brookes (1993) noted, membership of the LGBTQI+ community has been classified throughout history as a moral wrong, a mental illness, a criminal act or some combination of all three. Views on being gay have changed over time within the medical and psychological fields, and being gay is more accepted by wider society – as reflected in global changes to the law to permit same-sex marriage. However, for many religions, membership of the LGBTQI+ community is still not accepted (Brookes, 1993; García et al., 2008; Pallotta-Chiarolli et al., 2022). Finally, sex work has been subjugated to the moral standards and moral laws dating back to when records began, in which religion has played an important role. As noted in the work of Bartley (2012) and Birch (2015), documentation throughout history, for example in the medieval times, with reference to sex work in Europe, highlights the role of the church and medical science in how the sex work industry was governed and subsequently perceived by society. Brooks Gordon (2006) documents how the church redefined the sex work industry from a business requiring payment to one of promiscuity. This provides a background to the way sex work is still considered to be an immoral act by some social groups in contemporary society, including that of religious organisations (Archdiocese of Baltimore, 2012; Rus et al., 2012) and is still illegal in many parts of the world.

In sum, while the relationship between religion and crime has been shown to lead to a reduction in crime, in particular within areas such as drug use and violence, the relationship has also contributed to the criminalisation of some behaviours and social practices. Religion instils morality and ethical principles into people's lives, which can have a self-controlling effect, contributing to social/community cohesion. By default, this morality intertwines with religion, and can result in an increase in crime, illustrated by the issues considered above. Consequently, a complex relationship between religion and crime is revealed which inevitably impacts the criminal justice system.

The Role of Religion in the Criminal Justice System

While the criminal justice system is claimed to operate within the parameters of secular values and principles, the relationship between religion and criminal justice, both as an institution and as a practice, can be evidenced in several ways. In large part, the influence of religion on the system can be evidenced with the emergence and growth of restorative justice approaches and practices which draw on religious values and principles (Johnston & Van Mess, 2006), as well as the connection between religion and offender rehabilitation approaches and practices (O'Connor et al., 2006; Ziv, 2017). There is also the example of the involvement of prison chaplains and the delivery of religious services in the prison/correctional service which have been offered for some time to prisoners. There is also the impact religion has on the law, with Gatseliuk et al., (2021) illustrating the influence religion has on the criminal law and process, noting: "Criminal law and process play a significant role in regulating public relations [...] religious norms are the broader

TABLE 2.1 Relationship between religion and the law

Religion	*Law*
Religion is an individual value: the denial of the existence of transcendent reality leads to the loss of the influence of religious ideas on human consciousness and the deprivation of religion of regulatory qualities.	The right is a public value: the right does not lose its normativeness in case of non-recognition of its value by an individual.
The authoritarian nature of religious consciousness: the believer always feels the direction of divine authority.	Autonomous nature of legal consciousness: freedom from external authority.
Religious precepts are aimed at regulating thoughts, designed to help in individual suffering, hope, repentance.	The rules of law govern the external side of behaviour.
The norms of religion cover only the believing part of the country.	The rules of law are national in nature.
Consolidation of rules of conduct in religious sources.	The rules of law are enshrined in law.

regulators of public life" (p.226). Based on the work of Tkaschuk (2017), Vovk (2010), and Tsebenko (2019), Gatseliuk et al. (2021) provide an outline of the relationship between religion and the law, illustrated by Table 2.1 below.

(Gatseliuk et al., 2021: 230)

The relationship between religion and the law is understood by examining the violation of (moral/social) norms, and the maintaining and sustaining of these (moral/social) norms. Both religion and delivery of the law centre on the notion of social control. This relationship of maintaining norms and acting as a mechanism of ensuring conformity (social control), which binds religion and law together, reflects the central task of the criminal justice system. This central task of the criminal justice system is underpinned by a set of general principles that ultimately provides public safety to the community. These general principles that underpin the operations of the criminal justice system are to *punish, deter, rehabilitate and protect* (the community), with a view to preventing, disrupting and reducing crime. Such operations are underpinned by the theoretical frameworks of:

- *Individual deterrence* (also termed specific or special deterrence): to dissuade or deter an offender from committing a crime in the future.
- *General deterrence*: to dissuade or deter members of the broader community from committing a crime in the future.
- *Rehabilitation*: to change the attitudes or behaviour of offenders so they do not commit crime in the future.
- *Incapacitation*: to protect community members from certain offenders who may pose a threat to their welfare and safety.

(Daly & Sarre, 2017: 371)

The operationalisation of these theoretical frameworks, values and principles of the criminal justice system are largely delivered by three arms: Investigative, which includes the police and other law enforcement agencies; Adjudicative, which involves the systems of courts; and finally Correctional, which includes prisons and community corrections/probation/parole (Daly & Sarre, 2017). Scholars have recognised for some time now the role religion has had on these three arms of criminal justice. For example, with the investigative arm of criminal justice, the relationship between religion and law enforcement is one that reflects a strong connection, first, as a means of coping with the role of policing; and second, in addressing crime and disorder. It has been well documented that policing is a stressful occupation and as a result, police officer well-being is regularly compromised (Birch et al., 2017; McCreary et al., 2017; Craven et al., 2021). However, those officers who hold religious beliefs have been shown to cope better than those who do not. For example, research into religious coping by police officers revealed they accommodated stress, a pattern that held across several nations (Gumani et al., 2013; Acquadro et al., 2015; McCarty & Lawrence, 2016). These findings offer an insight into how religion facilitates the practice of law enforcement. As well as religion having an impact on policing in this way, a relationship has also been found with regards to dealing with crime and disorder. This is reflected through a range of issues in which a police officer's religious beliefs and affiliations have prevented them from carrying out their duties. For example, in the case of *Rodriguez v. City of Chicago*, Officer Rodriguez refused to guard an abortion clinic due to his Catholic faith (Grunloh, 2005), while Miles-Johnson (2016, 2019 and 2022) reported that a police officer's religious ideals can negatively impact their service response to a community member whose behaviour and/or lifestyle contravene the officer's religion. The relationship between religion and policing is a complex one. While there is evidence to illustrate how a police officer's religious beliefs and affiliations can adversely affect the practice of policing, the application of religious beliefs and ideals to one's practice, those such as compassion and forgiveness, can have positive effects on the practice of policing and the communities police officers serve, as illustrated by the execution of police discretion (Héliot et al., 2020).

Evidence of the fusion between religion and the delivery of criminal justice can also be found in the other arms of the criminal justice system. The systems of courts in many countries worldwide take pride in the separation of powers doctrine and the independence of government. However, when religion is factored into the independence of courts, the premise justice is blind becomes compromised. While research is still limited in the area of court sentencing and the influence of religion, evidence has been provided to show religion has led in some cases to more harsher sentences (Fern, 2005; Ulmer et al., 2008). This is a troubling finding, particularly for countries which impose the death penalty.

With regards to the final arm of criminal justice, that of correctional, prisons have a rich history of religious affiliations delivering programmes to prisoners (Camp et al., 2006, O'Connor et al., 2006; Skotnicki, 2000). Examples of such can be evidenced through prison fellowship organisations that have a global presence and are in existence in countries such as the USA, Australia and the UK. Prison Fellowship seeks to spread the word of God amongst prisoners and offer programmes in prison as well as support ex-prisoners in the community (Prison Fellowship, n.d.; Prison Fellowship Australia, n.d.; Prison Fellowship UK, n.d.; Prison Fellowship International, n.d.). In conjunction with this, faith-based programmes are also offered in prison settings, and to a broad range of cohorts, many with complex needs such as substance users and at-risk juveniles (Dodson et al., 2011). The involvement of religion in the delivery of criminal justice in this way blurs the line between the state and the church as policymakers and criminal justice executives endorse and support the delivery of such initiatives. Dodson et al. (2011: 368) support this by stating that, "during the 21st century, correctional ideology [has] shifted back toward religious strategies for addressing crime". As a consequence, religion and the delivery of criminal justice have become intrinsically linked, offering clear evidence of the direct role religion and religiously affiliated organisations have in the delivery of criminal justice, and questioning the secular nature of the criminal justice system.

Conclusion

Religion influences society at a state, an institutional and an individual level. Contemporaneously, there has been a shift from theocracies and state-led religion to more secular societies, which has taken place in most countries across the globe, leading to a reduction in the hold religion has on society. However, despite this shift, religion has not disappeared, but moulded to fit within modern societies – both ensuring and facilitating large proportions of citizens still have religious affiliations and religiously held views and beliefs. And while a shift from state-led religion to secularisation is evident in the refinement of institutional policies and practices, in particular within Western societies, the practices of criminal justice agencies, including policing, courts and prisons, can be shown to be inextricably linked to and influenced by religion. At an individual level, religious affiliation, in certain contexts, can result in social bonds being formed, whereby individuals adhere to morals and values that align with the laws of the state and subsequently prevent offending behaviour.

In an era in which there is a plethora of literature evidencing factors associated with offending behaviour and desistance from both a psychological and a structural perspective, along with rapid growth in technological and scientific approaches in the prevention, disruption and reduction of crime, the role of religion and its influence on crime and criminal justice must not be overlooked nor underestimated. The influence of religion on crime and criminal justice is very much present in the twenty-first century.

References

Acquadro Maran, D., Varetto, A., Zedda, M., & Ieraci, V. (2015). Occupational stress, anxiety and coping strategies in police officers. *Occupational Medicine, 65*, 466–473.

Adamczyk, A., Freilich, J. D., & Kim, C. (2017). Religion and crime: A systematic review and assessment of next steps. *Sociology of Religion, 78*(2), 192–232.

Archdiocese of Baltimore. (2012). *Church stand against prostitution puts it debate.* Retrieved from: www.archbalt.org/church-stand-against-prostitution-puts-it-debate/

Bartley, P. (2012). *Prostitution: Prevention and reform in England, 1860–1914.* Routledge.

Beckley, A., & Kennedy, M. (2020). Ethics and police practice. In P. Birch, M. Kennedy, & E. Kruger (Eds.), *Australian policing.* Routledge (pp. 93–109).

Berger, P. (2014). *The many altars of modernity: Towards a paradigm for religion in a pluralist age.* De Gruyter.

Birch, P. (2015). *Why men buy sex: Examining sex worker clients.* Routledge.

Birch, P., Vickers, M. H., Kennedy, M., & Galovic, S. (2017). Wellbeing, occupational justice and police practice: An "affirming environment"? *Police Practice and Research, 18*(1), 26–36.

Berger, P. L. (1969). *The social reality of religion.* Faber.

Brooke, S. L. (1993). The morality of homosexuality. *Journal of Homosexuality, 25*(4), 77–100.

Brooks Gordon, B. (2006). *The price of sex: Prostitution, policy & society.* Willan Publishing.

Brown, P. R. L. (2007). *Religion and society in the age of St. Augustine.* Wipf and Stock Publishers.

Camp, S. D., Klein-Saffran, J., Kwon, O., Daggett, D. M., & Joseph, V. (2006). An exploration into participation in a faith-based prison program. *Criminology & Public Policy, 5*(3), 529–550.

Campbell, E., Mansfield, M., & Bloomer, F. (2022). Religion, abortion and the criminal justice system in Northern Ireland. In P. Birch, C. Murray, & A. McInnes (Eds.), *Crime, criminal justice & religion: A critical appraisal.* Routledge (pp. 150–164).

Chen, Y., & VanderWeele, T. J. (2018). Associations of religious upbringing with subsequent health and well-being from adolescence to young adulthood: An outcome-wide analysis. *American Journal of Epidemiology, 187*(11), 2355–2364.

Clements, B. (2015). *Religion and public opinion in Britain.* Palgrave Macmillan.

Cradle of Humankind (2022). Creation beliefs. Retrieved from: www.maropeng.co.za/content/page/creation-beliefs

Craven, R., Marsh, H., Ryan, R., Dicke, T., Guo, J., Gallagher, P., Van Zanden, B. Kennedy, M., & Birch, P. (2020) A critical social justice issue of our time: Enabling police wellbeing. In P. Birch, M. Kennedy, & E. Kruger (Eds.), *Australian policing: Critical issues in 21st century police practice.* Routledge (pp. 71–92).

Daly, K., & Sarre, R. (2017). Criminal justice: Aims and process. In D. Palmer, D., W. de Lint, & D. Dalton (Eds.), *Crime and justice: A guide to criminology.* Thomson Reuters/Lawbook (pp. 358–376).

Dammer, H. R., & Albanese, J. S. (2013). *Comparative criminal justice systems.* Cengage Learning.

Dodson, K. D., Cabage, L. N., & Klenowski, P. M. (2011). An evidence-based assessment of faith-based programs: Do faith-based programs "work" to reduce recidivism? *Journal of Offender Rehabilitation, 50*(6), 367–383.

Durrant, R., & Poppelwell, Z. (2017). *Religion, punishment, and the law: Evolutionary perspective.* Palgrave Macmillan.

Durkheim, E. (1897). *Suicide: A study in sociology.* Free Press.

Ebaugh, H. R. (2002). Return of the sacred: Reintegrating religion in the social sciences. *Journal for the Scientific Study of Religion, 41*(3), 385–395.

Fasolt, C. (2006). History and religion in the modern age. *History and Theory, 45*(4), 10–26.

García, D. I., Gray-Stanley, J., & Ramirez-Valles, J. (2008). "The priest obviously doesn't know that I'm gay": The religious and spiritual journeys of Latino gay men. *Journal of Homosexuality, 55*(3), 411–436.

Gatseliuk,V., Strelbitska, L., Herasymchuk, O., Pavlyshyn, A., & Khrystiuk,V. (2021). The influence of religion on the norms of criminal law and process: an international-comparative study. *Amazonia Investiga, 10*(42), 226–235.

Grunloh, L. A. (2005). Religious accommodations for police officers: A comparative analysis of religious accommodation law in the United States, Canada, and the United Kingdom. *Indiana International & Comparative Law Review, 16*(1), 183–225.

Gumani, M. A., Fourie, E., & Blanche, M. T. (2013). Critical incidents impact management among South African police service officers. *Journal of Psychology in Africa, 23*, 481–487.

Hall, D. (2017). Religion and homosexuality in the public domain: Polish debates about reparative therapy. *European Societies, 19*(5), 600–622.

Hasbany, R. L. (2013). *Homosexuality and religion*. Routledge.

Héliot, Y. F., Gleibs, I. H., Coyle A., Rousseau, D. M, & Rojon, C. (2020). Religious identity in the workplace: A systematic review, research agenda, and practical implications. *Human Resource Management, 59*: 153–173.

Hervieu-Léger, D. (2006). The role of religion in establishing social cohesion. *Religion in the New Europe*, 45–63.

Hirschi, T. (1969). *Causes of delinquency*. Transaction Publishers

Hirschi, T., & Stark, R. (1969). Hellfire and delinquency. *Social Problems, 17*, 202–213.

Hussein, K. A. (2020). Abortion in the eyes of the Christian Religion/Descriptive Study. *Journal of Natural Remedies, 21*(7), 151–156.

Jang, S. J., Johnson, B. R., & Bader, C. (2008). The cumulative effect of religiosity in crime desistance. *Journal of Drug Issues, 38*(3), 771–798.

Jang, S. J., & Rhodes, J. R. (2012). General strain and non-strain theories: A study of crime in emerging adulthood. *Journal of Criminal Justice, 40*: 176–186.

Johnson, B. R., Jang, S. J., Larson, D. B., & Li, S. D. (2001). Does adolescent religious commitment matter? A re-examination of the effects of religiosity on delinquency. *Journal of Research in Crime and Delinquency, 38*: 22–44.

Johnson, B. R., Larson, D. B., Jang, S. J., & Li, S. D. (2000). The "invisible institution" and black youth crime: The church as an agency of local social control. *Journal of Youth and Adolescence, 29*: 479–498.

Johnson, P., & Vanderbeck, R. M. (2014). *Law, religion and homosexuality*. Routledge.

Johnson, T. J., Sheets, V. L., & Kristeller, J. L. (2008). Identifying mediators of the relationship between religiousness/spirituality and alcohol use. *Journal of Studies on Alcohol and Drugs, 69*, 160–170.

Johnstone, G., & Van Ness, D. (Eds.). (2006). *Handbook of restorative justice*. Willan/Routledge.

Kearns, M., Muldoon, O. T., Msetfi, R. M., & Surgenor, P. W. (2018). Identification reduces stigma of mental ill-health: A community-based study. *American Journal of Community Psychology, 61*(1–2), 229–239.

Lahti, D. C. (2009). The correlated history of social organization, morality, and religion. In E. Voland & W. Schiefenhövel (Eds.), *The biological evolution of religious mind and behavior*. Springer (pp. 67–88).

Laub, J. H., and Sampson, R. J. (2003). *Shared beginnings, divergent lives: Delinquent boys to age 70*. Harvard University Press.

Lee, H.Y., & Mutz, D. C. (2019). Changing attitudes toward same-sex marriage: A three-wave panel study. *Political Behavior, 41*(3), 701–722.

McCarty, W. P., & Lawrence, D. S. (2016). Coping, confidence, and change within the academy: A longitudinal look at police recruits. *Police Practice and Research, 17*, 263–278.

McCreary, D. R., Fong, I., & Groll, D. L. (2017). Measuring policing stress meaningfully: Establishing norms and cut-off values for the Operational and Organizational Police Stress Questionnaires. *Police Practice and Research, 18*(6), 612–623.

McGuire, M. B. (2008). *Religion: The social context.* Waveland Press.

Miles-Johnson, T. (2016). Policing diversity: Examining police resistance to training reforms for transgender people in Australia. *Journal of Homosexuality, 63*(1), 103–136.

Miles-Johnson, T. (2019). Policing diverse people: How occupational attitudes and background characteristics shape police recruits perceptions. *SAGE Open, 9*(3), 1–13.

Miles-Johnson, T. (2022). Religious policing: How religion and level of religiosity shape officer's interaction with minority groups. *SN Social Sciences, 2*(5), 1–21.

Morrison, M., Duncan, R., & Parton, K. (2015). Religion does matter for climate change attitudes and behavior. *PloS one, 10*(8), 1–16.

Murray, C., Payne, B., & Birch, P. (2022). Police legitimacy in divided societies: Exploring the interface of religion and social cohesion. In P. Birch, C. Murray, & A. McInnes (Eds.), *Crime, criminal justice & religion: A critical appraisal.* Routledge (pp. 55–67).

O'Connor, T. P., Duncan, J., & Quillard, F. (2006). Criminology and religion: The shape of an authentic dialogue. *Criminology & Public Policy, 5*(3), 559–570.

Pallotta-Chiarolli, M., Sweid, R., & Sudarto, B. (2022). "You can't be gay and do religion": Understanding Muslim LGBTIQ+ experiences of accessing support services. *Journal of Intercultural Studies, 43*(1), 148–165.

Pew Research Center. (2009). Abortion and morality: Religious and moral influence on the debate. Retrieved from: www.pewresearch.org/religion/2009/10/01/support-for-abortion-slips5/

Pew Research Center. (2017). The changing global religious landscape. Demographic Projections. Retrieved from: www.pewforum.org/2017/04/05/the-changing-global-religious-landscape/

Possamai, A., & Tittensor, D. (2022). *Religion and change in Australia.* Routledge.

Prison Fellowship. (n.d.). What we do. Retrieved from: www.prisonfellowship.org/about/

Prison Fellowship. (n.d.). What we do. Retrieved from: https://pfi.org/what-we-do/

Prison Fellowship Australia. (n.d.). About us. Retrieved from: https://prisonfellowship.org.au/about-us/

Prison Fellowship UK. (n.d.). About. Retrieved from: https://prisonfellowship.org.uk/about/

Regnerus, M. (2003). Linked lives, faith, and behavior: Intergenerational religious influence on adolescent delinquency. *Journal for the Scientific Study of Religion, 42*(2), 189–203.

Rus, F. C., Boie, C., & Ilies, V. (2012). Reactions of the Romanian Orthodox Church to the proposed legislation to legalize prostitution. *Journal for the Study of Religions and Ideologies, 11*(32), 206–226.

Salas-Wright, C. P., Vaughn, M. G., & Maynard, B. R. (2014). Buffering effects of religiosity on crime: Testing the invariance hypothesis across gender and developmental period. *Criminal Justice and Behavior, 41*, 673–90.

Salvatore, C., & Taniguchi, T. (2012). Do social bonds matter for emerging adults? *Deviant Behavior, 33*, 738–756.

Skotnicki, A. (2000). *Religion and the development of the American penal system.* University Press of America.

Smith, M. A. (2010). Religion, divorce, and the missing culture war in America. *Political Science Quarterly, 125*(1), 57–85.

Stark, R. (1996). Religion as context: Hellfire and delinquency one more time. *Sociology of Religion, 57*, 163–173.

Stavrova, O., & Siegers, P. (2014). Religious prosociality and morality across cultures: How social enforcement of religion shapes the effects of personal religiosity on prosocial and moral attitudes and behaviors. *Personality and Social Psychology Bulletin, 40*(3), 315–333.

Terrill, R. (2015). *World criminal justice systems: A comparative survey*. Routledge.

Tkachuk, I. D. (2017). Correlation of religion and law as forms of regulation of social relations. *Journal of Kyiv University of Law, 4*, 47–50. Retrieved from: http://nbuv.gov.ua/UJRN/Chkup_2017_4_12

Tsebenko, S. B. (2019). Legal and religious norms as regulators of social. *Law and Society, 1*, 35–39. Retrieved from: http://pravoisuspilstvo.org.ua/archive/2019/1_2 019/part_1/8.pdf

Turcescu, L., & Stan, L. (2005). Religion, politics and sexuality in Romania. *Europe-Asia Studies, 57*(2), 291–310.

Tuttle, J. D., & Davis, S. N. (2015). Religion, infidelity, and divorce: Re-examining the effect of religious behavior on divorce among long-married couples. *Journal of Divorce & Remarriage, 56*(6), 475–489.

Ulmer, J. T., Bader, C., & Gault, M. (2008). Do moral communities play a role in criminal sentencing? Evidence from Pennsylvania. *The Sociological Quarterly, 49*(4), 737–768.

Weaver, A. J., Flannelly, K. J. & Strock, A. L. (2005). A review of research on the effects of religion on adolescent tobacco use published between 1990 and 2003. *Adolescence, 40*(160), 761–776.

Yeung, J. W., Yuk-Chung Chan, K., & Lee, B. L. K. (2009). Youth religiosity and substance use: A meta-analysis from 1995 to 2007. *Psychological Reports, 105*(1), 255–266.

Vovk, D. (2010). Correlation of law and religion in the Christian legal tradition: The stage of post secularization. *Bulletin of the Academy of Legal Sciences of Ukraine, 4*(63), 58–67. Retrieved from: http://dspace.nlu.edu.ua/handle/123456789/6179

Word Reference. (n.d.). *Crime.* Retrieved from: www.wordreference.com/definition/crime#:~:text=crime%20(kr%C4%ABm)%2C%20n.,crimes%3Aa%20life%20of%20crime.

Ziv, R. (2017). *The future of correctional rehabilitation: Moving beyond the RNR model and good lives model debate*. Routledge.

PART 2

Appraisal of Institutions and Professional Practice

3

RELIGION AND POLICE OFFICERS

Exploring the Impact on Police Practice

Tobias Winright

Introduction

Until the early 1990s, scarcely any scholarship addressed the question of how religion might relate to policing. Indeed, at the time, when I first began my research on the police, religion and the ethics of the use of force, the dearth of literature on the subject was striking. During my previous experience in law enforcement, many fellow officers explicitly invoked religious beliefs and iterated theological words on the job. Or, more implicitly, deeply held views and values grounded and infused, consciously or not, their work. It was not uncommon to hear co-workers employing the language of "good" and "evil," "right" and "wrong," "justice" and "injustice," "innocence" and "guilt," as well as more direct references to "God," to scriptural passages, and, as one captain described policing, to "doing the Lord's work." Even those police officers who were nominally, if at all, religious would occasionally utter such words, reflecting the underlying impact of religion on them, their view of the police, and their practice of policing. Yet only a handful of scholarly articles and book chapters at the time were to be found that examined the intersection between religion and the police (Anonymous, 1963; Forster, 1982; Holdaway, 1983).

This chapter explores some ways that religion can impact police practice. The relationship between religion and the police is considered in three steps. First, the state of the question in the literature is more clearly established. Second, anecdotal reflections by police are considered to highlight common themes and concerns. Third, an academic treatment of the subject by a theologian who is also a police officer is gleaned from for further insight, before concluding with a brief proposal regarding religion, the ethos and end (or *telos*) of the police, and ethics regarding police practice.

DOI: 10.4324/9781003276593-5

Two Ships Passing

Like two ships passing in the night, scholarly literature in the field of religion, or theology, and in the field of police studies, or criminology, rarely and barely engage one another. A quarter century ago, when I first began to do research regarding their intersection, a handful of essays that I found focused mostly on ethics and the use of force, since violence-related questions are a perennial concern of religions that emphasize in various ways beneficence (i.e., doing good to others), nonmaleficence (i.e., not harming others), and peace (i.e., a tranquil order). Because of my religious background as a Christian (Roman Catholic) and given that my employment in law enforcement occurred in the United States, a pluralist society wherein most citizens identify as Christians or religious (Smith, 2021), my initial foray into the extant literature was fueled by problems that I witnessed or experienced which seemed in tension not only with democratic policing principles but also with my religious beliefs and values (Winright, 1995). The use of force, especially deadly force, gave me pause both as a law enforcement officer and as a Christian. After all, as Lisa Sowle Cahill (1994) observes, "The challenge to decide about violence, especially statesupported and institutionally perpetuated violence, has been with Christians from the beginning" (p. ix). Similarly, Stanley Hauerwas (1983) claims that "the question of violence is the central issue for any Christian social ethic" (p. 114). It should not be surprising that for me, as a Christian who had been informed by sermons about Jesus' teachings about peace and formed by rituals such as the passing of the peace during worship on a weekly basis throughout my life, the use of force in policing posed a problem.

Racism, too, was a related issue with which I wrestled and that I witnessed while in law enforcement (Winright, 2020b). Unlike the use of force, racism is never morally justified. Pope John Paul II (1999), in a homily delivered while visiting St. Louis, Missouri, condemned "racism, a plague which [...] [is] one of the most persistent and destructive evils of the nation." Similarly, the U.S. Catholic bishops (1979) have decried racism as "a sin" and "a radical evil." Yet, African Americans are 2.5 times more likely to be arrested than white Americans, and although more white Americans than persons of color are killed by police officers, African American men are 21 times more likely than white men to be killed by police (Davis, 2017, p. xv). The disproportionate rate of arrests and killings of Black males by U.S. police was, and is, at odds with both the principles of liberal democracy (e.g., equality, liberty, and justice) and the values of religious traditions (e.g., the "Golden Rule").

Nevertheless, few scholars in religious studies and theology paid attention to the police. Those who did so focused on the question of police violence—its possible justification and its curtailment—as well as the related problem of police brutality toward African Americans. In the wake of the killings of Michael Brown, Eric Garner, George Floyd, Breonna Taylor, and many more Black persons and other persons of color by U.S. police officers, and the protests that swept the United States, proclaiming "Black Lives Matter" and demanding "abolition" and "defunding" of the police, more religious academics and theologians are beginning to grapple with the question of the police, although the attention of these scholars continues to concentrate on the issue of police violence and racism rather than on the relation between religion and policing (Alexis-Baker, 2021; Jaycox, 2020; McCarthy, 2020).

Sometimes the question of the impact of religion on the police comes from the other direction, that is, from scholars of criminology and policing. Lawrence Sherman (1982) observes, "The most basic question of all criminal justice ethics, of course, is whether and under what conditions one can reconcile doing harm to others with our widespread norms against harm" (p. 38). This pivotal question leads Sherman (1982) to ponder, "Can a pacifist be a police officer [...]? Can a Christian? Can a Rawlsian? What is the ethical defense for saying that killing is wrong and then urging killing in response to killing?" (p. 38). Thus, deeper religious and philosophical questions about the police sometimes are raised by criminologists and scholars of policing, too. Robert Reiner (1992) suggests that an "ultimate question" is whether a society could exist without police, and he adds that this is "an essentially metaphysical issue" rooted in "views of morality, justice, and even deeper matters of ultimate ends, meaning, and the nature of being—the province of religious belief" (pp. 32–33). On the question of truth, John Kleinig (1996) mentions the possibility of religious and theological arguments about the problem of deception and lying by police (pp. 300–301). Likewise, Edwin J. Delattre (2011) briefly considers possible conflicts involving a police officer's conscience, on religious grounds, and orders given by a supervisor or policies of a department, such as protecting an abortion clinic even though the officer's religious convictions may be opposed to abortion (pp. 337–340). Yet, while some scholars in both major spheres of study—religious studies/theology and police studies/criminology—have devoted some consideration to the intersection of religion and the police, what James F. Keenan, S.J. (2016) writes on the subject remains accurate at present, "As I approach this topic, I realize that there is very little material published on it" (p. 273).

That is not to say that criminal justice, broadly speaking, and religion have been ignored altogether. After all, as Andrew Millie (2021b) notes, "for good or ill [...] much Western criminal justice has historically drawn inspiration and justification from interpretations of Christian theology, doctrine and tradition" (p. 4). Even were the so-called secularization thesis accurate regarding European, North American, and other continents' nations (and, as Millie recognizes, it is increasingly called into question), religion at least implicitly informs modern notions of justice, mercy, punishment, and restoration that are embedded in the criminal justice system. Previously, Frank Schmalleger (1991) observed that theological and religious perspectives play a role "in the mind of a person faced with making an ethical decision of relevance to the criminal justice system" (p. xx). The impact of religion on criminal justice thus may be found in both the macro, or systemic and structural, level and the micro, or individual and personal, level. Undoubtedly, in nations where the line distinguishing between religion, culture, and society is more porous—such as Israel and Saudi Arabia—the impact of religion, such as Judaism or Islam (or Buddhism, Hinduism, etc.), on criminal justice may be just as, and perhaps even more, pronounced and, thus, merit further study (Millie, 2021b, p. 4).

Moreover, although the police are part of the criminal justice system, most research on the relationship between religion and criminal justice limits itself to trials and the courts, incarceration and prison reform (or abolition), and punishment and retribution (or restoration). The police prong of the criminal justice system tends to be overlooked. This narrow focus was evident several decades ago. In 1953, L. Harold DeWolf suggested, "If any people in the world ought to be interested in criminals, then Christians should have such an interest. As Christians we are the disciples of One who was convicted, sentenced, and executed for crime" (p. 188). Note that DeWolf did not mention Jesus' apprehension and arrest. So, too, Gerald Austin McHugh (1978), in his attempt to develop a "theology of criminal justice," claimed that criminal justice "is inextricably concerned with the same, vital, human issues which are so central to Christian belief," presupposing as well a "particular conceptualization of the human person" and their dignity and rights (pp. 1, 3). The scope of his analysis, however, remained limited to punishment, along with prison chaplaincy and ministry. McHugh also neglected giving due attention to religion and the police.

To their credit, some recent scholarly treatments of religion, theology, and criminal justice incorporate consideration of the police. In addition to the volume *Religion and Criminal Justice*, in which Keenan's chapter appears as the only one, out of 20, about the police, there is *Criminology and Public Theology: On Hope, Mercy and Restoration*, edited by Millie, which contains a chapter by Anglican theologian Alistair McFadyen, who is also a police officer, about theology and policing, although 13 other chapters continue to delve into the other components of criminal justice. McFadyen, too, observes that in the various subfields of theology "we can find some occasional, passing and indirect mention of policing, but almost no sustained or substantive discussion where policing is the direct focus" (2021, p. 217). McFadyen states that this absence is "curious" (2021, p. 218), a word that I have used for this state of affairs (Winright, 2018, p. 244). The police, after all, are the most visible prong of the criminal justice system, but they have been invisible, until recently, in religious studies and theology. Plus, the rest of the system depends initially on the police. McFadyen notes that in the United Kingdom, in the wake of the 7/7 bombings of the London transport system in 2005, "religion and faith communities have achieved greater significance in relation to policing," but this "is a development that has gone largely unnoticed in the academic disciplines of either criminology [...] or of theology and religious studies" (2021, p. 220). One of the reasons why more substantive analysis of the police may not be occurring, McFadyen suggests, is that punishment and penal policy attract theologians' and religious scholars' attention, since these spheres of criminal justice "are widely perceived by Christians to be closely correlated with core, foundational and fundamental aspects of Christian faith" (2021, p. 222). These deeper theological and religious commitments include love, mercy, forgiveness, redemption, restoration, and caring for the vulnerable, the marginalized, the outcast, and the undeserving. There is, however, some interest in true crime and detective stories I would note amongst theologians (Hauerwas, 1999; Vasko and Ferrara, 2022). McFadyen worries, though, that the predominant attention given to post-conviction treatment of offenders not only downplays what is due to the police, but also may neglect "the interests of the victim, of appropriate justice and so also of the community" (2021, p. 225). His constructive proposal of a theology for (and from) policing will be considered in section three of this chapter.

I would add one more basic reason why the police may have been neglected in theological scholarship and religious studies. Although violence has been a perennial problem in this literature, mostly in connection with war, personal self-defense, or the death penalty, the police as an institution did not appear historically until 1829 by Sir Robert Peel, when he created the New Police of Metropolitan London (Ascoli, 1979). Prior to this, the "police" function of providing community safety existed: in Plato's ancient Greece, there were the "guardians"; in ancient Rome, there were the *vigiles*; with the Norman Conquest by William in 1066 there came the shire reeve (sheriff); and there were night watches, constables, and the hue and cry. So, perhaps it should not be surprising that the police, arriving more recently on the historical scene, have not been addressed. Still, similar historical contextualization could be applied to detention, confinement, and punishment, all of which have undergone institutional development over the centuries, too. Thus, the deeper theological and religious reasons that McFadyen suggested for the predilection of theological and religious scholars towards penology rather than policing may indeed be on the mark.

Otherwise, it should be noted that a handful of studies examine how spiritual practices, such as prayer and meditation, might help police officers respond to stress in their work with more resilience (Ursitti, 2011; Smith and Charles, 2010). Some attention has also been given to spirituality, police culture and leadership (Moran, 2017; Feemster, 2007). These authors, too, acknowledge the lack of scholarship in this area. In an article included in an entire issue of the *FBI Law Enforcement Bulletin* devoted to the topic of spirituality and law enforcement, police sergeant Ginger Charles remarks, "The theme of spirituality remains relatively unexplored in law enforcement" (2009, p. 22; Charles, 2005). She adds that a book published in 1992 by Judith A. Kowalski and Dean J. Collins, containing reflections from several police officers, though not in any sense a serious scholarly study, "provided the first glimpse into police work and the topic of spirituality" (Charles, 2009, p. 22). It is to this and other similar anecdotal accounts that I now turn to show the need for sustained scholarly attention to the police and religion.

Reflections from Police regarding Religion

The book by Kowaski and Collins, *To Serve and Protect: Law Enforcement Officers Reflect on Their Faith and Work*, mentioned by Charles, was one of the few resources I found when I first began my own research (Winright, 2002, p. 18). Although such publications are not scholarly treatments of the impact of religion on policing, they offer a peek into the ways the police officers themselves attempt to make these connections between their religion, faith, or spirituality and their work in law enforcement. Common themes and concerns also become apparent in this literature.

Prominent psychologist Robert Coles (1971) once wrote about a police sergeant who confesses his anger about protesters to a priest: "Father, if you know what we're trying to do, I wish you'd let me know, and that would be two of us" (p. 73). This question about meaning and purpose, especially when addressing social strife and conflict, for many police officers ushers them into the realm of religion and theology. Related questions arise amongst the police officers interviewed in Kowalski and Collins' book. Each officer shares their story with an eye toward ways their religious faith informs their work and, on the other hand, how policing affects their religious commitments. All the officers identify as Christians, including Catholics, Lutherans, and Episcopalians.

Some, such as Jerome Stark, highlight how officers go beyond what is expected of them from supervisors and departmental policies by sharing clothes, toys, and other donations with persons in need. Benevolence, compassion, and love motivates them (Kowalski and Collins, 1992, pp. 15, 84). For another officer, Joseph Reyes, God inspires his efforts "to help other people in the community" (Kowalski and Collins, 1992, p. 69). Officer Natalie Aikins includes, as an example of the connection between her religious faith and her work in law enforcement, making death notifications, attempting to stop suicide, and assisting families in crisis (Kowalski and Collins, 1992, p. 78). Some officers point out their willingness to put their "lives on the line" during each shift (Kowalski and Collins, 1992, p. 15). A few mention that officers attend Mass or worship instead of taking a lunch break, and they attest that doing this and other similar spiritual practices helps them with what they experience during a difficult shift (Kowalski and Collins, 1992, pp. 16, 64, 75, 87). The tragedies and evils they see sometimes make them ask big questions, such as, Why would a loving God allow this to happen? (Kowalski and Collins, 1992, p. 100). Officer Allen Van Haute admits that once, while wrestling with a suspect and falling down a flight of stairs, "The only thing that came to mind was the Lord's Prayer. It wasn't that I was directly asking for help. I just remember saying the Lord's Prayer" (Kowalski and Collins, 1992, p. 37). Similar prayers are said while driving to the scene of an accident or kneeling next to a dying person. Undercover work, too, is occasionally broached, because it includes activities some religious police officers normally will not do, such as drinking alcohol (Kowalski and Collins, 1992, pp. 46–47, 61). In this connection, curiously, no one brings up possible religious qualms over using deception. Officer Reyes highlights the use of force, though only to downplay its occurrence: "Police life is mostly helping people out rather than fighting or shooting people" (Kowalski and Collins, 1992, p. 67). He does not express moral qualms about the use of force, but he rightly notes that police resort to it much less than as portrayed on television shows and in movies. Other officers confess how shootings affected them, even when their use of lethal force was justified (Kowalski and Collins, 1992, pp. 93–94, 112–118). A few police officers refer directly to passages from the Bible, such as Romans 13, which they reckon relevant for their work to "serve and protect" the community (Kowalski and Collins, 1992, pp. 39, 109). Some use the word "ministry" to describe their job, and say it is a "vocation" rather than a career (Kowalski and Collins, 1992, p. 83). In his own chapter, Kowalski, who is both a police deputy inspector and a Catholic deacon, emphasizes "the service ideal, both in law enforcement and in the diaconate" (Kowalski and Collins, 1992, p. 107).

In their reflections on these interviews, Kowalski and Collins note that religious beliefs and teachings "seem to have permeated" the officers' spiritual lives in ways that are practiced in their work (1992, p. 20). Like some of the officers they interviewed, Kowalski and Collins observe that there may be aspects of departmental expectations and police culture—for example, the competitive, military-like, or "them-against-us" mentality—that are in tension with some religious officers' beliefs and ethics (1992, pp. 13, 57, 93). Kowalski and Collins state: "True faith is so much a part of one's identity that it cannot be laid aside when a person goes to work, like changing from leisure clothes into a uniform" (1992, p. 83). For them, integrity requires consistency between one's spiritual life and profession (1992, p. 121). They highlight "concepts" that bridge law enforcement and religion: justice ("But let justice roll down like waters," Amos 5:24), caring for victims of crime (the "Good Samaritan," Luke 10:30–37), and protecting the peace ("Blessed are the peacemakers, for they will be called children of God," Matthew 5:9). In sum, most of what these police officers share has to do with moral values that, though religiously motivated, correlate with good police work: "they save people, they comfort people, they bring justice and peace to society, and they do so with care and confidentiality twenty-four hours a day" (Kowalski and Collins, 1992, p. 123). Their morality, anchored and formed in religious texts, beliefs, and practices, is a value-added dimension to their work as police officers. Moreover, these religious elements provide meaning and solace for when they encounter grave situations, horrific acts, and terrible tragedies.

Similarly, in a chapter included within a similar book, John A. Eterno (2002) writes about being a Catholic police officer. He notes that police officers who are Catholics "take with them into the streets, homes, offices, workplaces, and all other areas of the city the lessons given to us by faith" (p. 43). For him, Jesus' teaching "You shall love your neighbor as yourself" (Matthew 22:39), is the basis for a Catholic police officer's service to the community, including his daily interactions with persons, be they victims, offenders, or anyone. At times, instead of calling it "love," Eterno uses "respecting the dignity of all people, including those who are hurting others or not respecting others" (2002, p. 43). He admits that doing so can be challenging, not only when dealing with difficult persons but also in a "police culture" that can be negative (2002, pp. 44, 46, 48). On the use of force, he describes when a suspect in a crowded area pointed a gun at him, but Eterno did not shoot. Indeed, he approached the suspect, instructing him to remain still, until Eterno grabbed the gun from him. Highly unusual, especially in the United States, where most police officers' threat assessment would probably have led them to shoot the suspect (remember, too, as Eterno notes, "It all happened so quickly, in less than a minute."), he expresses his belief that "what made the difference between shooting and not shooting the armed man was respect for human life, both the suspect's and the crowd's" (2002, pp. 45–46). Eterno also mentions police officers' willingness to risk their lives to protect others, but he does well to explain that they are "rigorously trained to use the minimum amount of force necessary and to use deadly force (that is, to shoot) only when one's own life or the life of another is in danger" (2002, pp. 47–48). His religious beliefs and moral values as a Catholic, especially as "reinforced" during Mass and the celebration of the Eucharist, strengthen his respect for human life (2002, p. 48).

When Eterno refers to love and respect for others, these are not merely values or principles. They are virtues and character traits. James Keenan likewise writes about the virtues of his father, Francis A. Keenan, who was a sergeant-detective in New York City. Actively involved in his neighborhood, Keenan cared for those who depended on him, off the job as well as on it. He demonstrated discretionary prudence, relationality, and integrity. He had a sense of humor and humility, as well as vulnerability given how "he felt he was always close to the life of the beggar, the drunk driver, or the sex worker. We were, after all, working class, and bad fortune was just around the corner" (Keenan, 2016, p. 278). Although wherever he went, Keenan had his gun, he was pleased to be able to tell those who were curious about it, "I have never used my gun" (2016, p. 278). As his theologian son adds, sergeant-detective Keenan "liked not having to harm anyone" (2016, p. 278).

By attending to these accounts, it becomes apparent that religion can indeed have an impact on police officers' lives and work. These officers are attempting to establish and maintain integrity between their beliefs, such as that God created humans who possess a dignity that should be respected, and their moral values and virtues, such as service, love, peacemaking, justice, and caring for those in need. For these police officers, sustaining such integrity can be challenging in the face of what they encounter on the streets, especially when it is antagonistic and dangerous, and even within their department's culture. Much of what they share resonates with my own experience, although their lack of explicit reference to the moral issue of overt as well as "unconscious racism" in individual police officers or within the culture of policing in the United States is curious to me, especially given that the teachings of their religious traditions have become clear that racism is an individual and social sin poisoning persons and institutions (Massingale, 2010, pp. 24–33, 73, 103). Nevertheless, the efforts of these police officers to be consistent in their attitudes and actions, whether at home, in their place of worship, or on the job, displays moral integrity.

Further Theological and Religious Considerations, and the End of the Police

Most of what we have reviewed thus far has been descriptive of what it is like to be religious and a police officer, although more prescriptive suggestions about how police ought to be and to act have been suggested or implied. This latter is the domain of ethics, including religious and theological ethics. A half century ago, Ralph Potter (1973) observed,

> Seldom have American Christian scholars [...] addressed themselves seriously to the task of helping public officers reflect upon the mode of reasoning appropriate to their office that would guide them in determining when they should act, how they should act, and why.
>
> *p. 60*

Potter believed that police officers need ethical guidance for their work, especially concerning the use of force. From a Jewish religious perspective, Stephen M. Passamaneck, a professor of Rabbinic literature who also served as a chaplain and a reserve deputy for the Los Angeles County Sheriff's Department, begins his book *Police Ethics and the Jewish Tradition* by writing:

> No other inquiry of this type exists; in fact the meager bibliography on police and policing in Jewish materials, except for a few brief articles, virtually never touches upon any substantive tactical, operational, or administrative aspects of actual police work and there is nothing at all on the ethical implication of law enforcement or the ethical principles that are involved in it.
>
> *2003, p. 3*

Such is the present state of affairs, although the police, especially in the United States but also elsewhere, are under more scrutiny today, including from religious leaders and scholars, theologians, and ethicists. Indeed, in response to the grave and systemic injustices of police racism, brutality, and excessive force, many are calling for the "defunding" or "abolition" of the police.

Yet, as I suggested earlier, the police *function*, if not the *institution* as it has developed in, for example, the United States, seems to be a universal phenomenon and practice, historically and culturally, even if it goes by other names (e.g., constables, hue and cry). In ancient Jewish communities, there were the *shotrim*, who were public officers charged with enforcing the law, especially in marketplaces and shops as inspectors, bringing before a magistrate anyone who violated the law (Passamaneck, 2003, pp. 11–13). As Gerald W. Schlabach (2012) remarks, "No community can do without some kind of police function. No Christian community. No human community" (p. 67). Significantly, Mohandas Gandhi supposed that "even under a Government based primarily on non-violence a small police force will be necessary" (Palaver, 2021, p. 14). And former chief superintendent with the Royal Canadian Mounted Police Angela Workman-Stark warns, "The problem with these proposals [abolition and defunding] is that they're presented as solutions to police abuse without an appreciation that some element of coercive authority will still be required in society" (2021). More than ever, further scholarly study—critical, imaginative, and constructive—is needed.

An example of what I have in mind is the work of a theologian who is also a police officer, Alistair McFadyen. He proposes Jesus' instruction to love both neighbor and enemy as central to Christian faith and life within the context of "love of neighbour*hood*" (McFadyen, 2021, p. 228). Taking seriously the evils that human beings can do toward others, McFadyen (2021) also recognizes the "danger in any criminal justice system (and in all policing) of demonizing and dehumanizing offenders, of constructing systems and making decisions that are not transformative, hope bearing, forgiving, restorative; that are not loving" (p. 227). For him, Jesus' parable of the Good Samaritan (Luke 10:25–37) calls for "the active orientation towards the wellbeing of someone who crosses one's path" (McFadyen, 2021, p. 229). It extends to all who are vulnerable and marginalized, within or passing through the neighborhood. Policing as a proactive and dynamic presence and practice serves and protects the community, protecting persons from harm but also identifying and addressing conditions that contribute to the exploitation of others, as well as carrying out investigations to apprehend those who victimize others. These police responsibilities are aimed at "the constructive work of repairing neighbourhood" (McFadyen, 2021, p. 233).

As for the neighbor who attempts to harm, or has harmed, others in the neighborhood, McFadyen writes, "Policing is in fact where I have learned what it might mean to love enemies" (2021, p. 236). That is, the police officer's encounter with suspects is directed by the hope that the offender will be placed upon a trajectory toward restoration into the community. In this approach to policing, the use of force will be limited to "what is necessary, reasonable and proportionate in the circumstances (minimum level to achieve a lawful purpose) and in the interests of the neighbourhood" out of respect for "the wellbeing of the suspect—and their humanity" (McFadyen, 2021, p. 237). It also entails caregiving after force, such as an incapacitant spray, has been employed against an offender by the officer. In my view, McFadyen proposes a helpful theological and ethical account of policing that holds together many of the considerations and concerns shared and experienced by religious police officers. What McFadyen suggests is consonant with my own efforts to reimagine those who perform the police function as "peace officers" and, as in the Republic of Ireland, *garda siochona*, or "guardians of the peace" (Winright, 1999; Winright, 2020a).

In his widely read *The End of Policing*, Alex S. Vitale (2018) appears to urge the abolition (i.e., "the end") of policing altogether, but in actuality he calls for the rethinking of the "basic role," "orientation," "mindset," "mission," and "culture" of the police, indeed toward a "larger vision that questions the basic role of police in society and asks whether coercive government action will bring more justice or less" (pp. 27, 51, 65, 221–222, 226). Vitale turns attention to what others earlier in this chapter saw to be ultimate questions about the police, their function or, in the language of ethics, their end—not as in elimination but, rather, their *purpose* (i.e., *telos*)—within society. I believe that religion may have an impact here, too. Of course, none of this is to say that one must necessarily be religious to view and practice policing these ways. As Millie (2021a) maintains, religious beliefs and values about human dignity, compassion for others, restorative justice, service, and peacemaking "all ought to translate" into a secular criminal justice system, applying "to the religious and secular [practitioners] alike" (pp. 322, 327).

References

Alexis-Baker, Andy. 2021. "The Police." In *T&T Clark Handbook of Christian Ethics*, edited by Tobias Winright, 269–276. Bloomsbury T&T Clark.

Anonymous. 1963. "In This World: By a Policeman." *Student World* no. 56: 247–253.

Ascoli, David. 1979. *The Queen's Peace: The Origins and Development of the Metropolitan Police 1829–1979*. Hamish Hamilton.

Cahill, Lisa Sowle. 1994. *Love Your Enemies: Discipleship, Pacifism, and Just War Thinking*. Fortress Press.

Charles, Ginger. 2005. "How Spirituality Is Incorporated in Police Work: A Qualitative Study." Ph.D. dissertation. Saybrook Graduate School and Research Center.

Charles, Ginger. 2009. "How Spirituality Is Incorporated in Police Work: A Qualitative Study." *FBI Law Enforcement Bulletin* 78(5), 22–25.

Coles, Robert. 1971. "A Policeman Complains." *The New York Times Magazine* (June 13, 1971): 11, 73–80.

Davis, Angela J. 2017. *Policing the Black Man: Arrest, Prosecution, and Imprisonment*. Vintage Books.

Delattre, Edwin J. 2011. *Character and Cops: Ethics in Policing*, 6th edition. The American Enterprise Institute Press.

DeWolf, L. Harold. 1953. "The Church in the Prevention and Treatment of Crime." In *The Church and Social Responsibility*, edited by J. Richard Spann, 172–192. Abingdon-Cokesbury Press.

Eterno, John A. 2002. "Justice from a Higher Power: On Being a Catholic Police Officer." In *Professions of Faith: Living and Working as a Catholic*, edited by James Martin, S.J. and Jeremy Langford, 41–54. Sheed & Ward.

Feemster, Samuel L. 2007. "Spirituality: The DNA of Law Enforcement Practice." *FBI Law Enforcement Bulletin* 76(11), 7–8.

Forster, Greg. 1982. *"To Live Good"—The Police and the Community*. Grove Publications.

Hauerwas, Stanley. 1983. *The Peaceable Kingdom: A Primer in Christian Ethics*. University of Notre Dame Press.

Hauerwas, Stanley. 1999. "McInerny Did It: or, Should a Pacifist Read Murder Mysteries?" In *Recovering Nature: Essays in Natural Philosophy, Ethics, and Metaphysics in Honor of Ralph McInerny*, edited by John O'Callaghan and Thomas Hibbs, 163–175. University of Notre Dame Press.

Holdaway, Simon. 1983. "Policing and Consent." *Modern Churchman* 25(3), 30–39.

Jaycox, Michael. 2020. "A Catholic Case for Police Defunding and Abolition." Catholic Theological Ethics in the World Church. June 29, 2020. https://catholicethics.com/forum/police-abolition/.

John Paul II. 1999. "Homily in St. Louis, Missouri." January 27, 1999. Retrieved from: www.vatican.va/content/john-paul-ii/en/travels/1999/documents/hf_jpii_hom_27011999_stlouis.html.

Keenan, James F. 2016. "Religion and Virtues in the Lives of Police Officers." In *Religion and Criminal Justice*, revised first edition, edited by William J. Cook, Jr., 273–280. Cognella Academic Publishing.

Kleinig, John. 1996. *The Ethics of Policing*. Cambridge University Press.

Kowalski, Judith A., and Dean J. Collins. 1992. *To Serve and Protect: Law Enforcement Officers Reflect on Their Faith and Work*. Augsburg.

Massingale, Bryan N. 2010. *Racial Justice and the Catholic Church*. Orbis Books.

McCarthy, Eli. 2020. "Defunding Police: Human Dignity and Black Lives Matter." Catholic Theological Ethics in the World Church. October 1, 2020. Retrieved from: https://catholicethics.com/forum/defunding-police/.

McFadyen, Alistair. 2021. "Loving the Neighbourhood, Loving Enemies: Towards a Theology for (and from) Policing." In *Criminology and Public Theology: On Hope, Mercy and Restoration*, edited by Andrew Millie, 217–246. Bristol University Press.

McHugh, Gerald Austin. 1978. *Christian Faith and Criminal Justice: Toward a Christian Response to Crime and Punishment*. Paulist Press.

Millie, Andrew. 2021a. "Conclusions." In *Criminology and Public Theology: On Hope, Mercy and Restoration*, edited by Andrew Millie, 319–329. Bristol University Press.

Millie, Andrew. 2021b. "Introduction: Public Criminology Meets Public Theology." In *Criminology and Public Theology: On Hope, Mercy and Restoration*, edited by Andrew Millie, 1–18. Bristol University Press.

Moran, Ramon. 2017. "Workplace Spirituality in Law Enforcement: A Content Analysis of the Literature." *Journal of Management, Spirituality & Religion* 14(4), 343–364.

Palaver, Wolfgang. 2021. "Gandhi's Militant Nonviolence in the Light of Girard's Mimetic Anthropology." *Religions* 12(988), 1–22. https://doi.org/10.3390/rel12110988

Passamaneck, Stephen M. 2003. *Police Ethics and the Jewish Tradition*. Charles C. Thomas Publishing.

Potter, Ralph B. 1973. *War and Moral Discourse*. John Knox Press.

Reiner, Robert. 1992. *The Politics of the Police*, 2nd edition. University of Toronto Press.

Schlabach, Gerald W. 2012. "Must Christian Pacifists Reject Police Force?" In *A Faith Not Worth Fighting For: Addressing Commonly Asked Questions about Christian Nonviolence*, edited by Tripp York and Justin Bronson Barringer, 60–84. Cascade Books.

Schmalleger, Frank. 1991. *Criminal Justice Ethics: Annotated Bibliography and Guide to Sources*. Greenwood Press.

Sherman, Lawrence. 1982. *Ethics in Criminal Justice Education*. The Hasting Center.

Smith, Gregory A. 2021. "About Three-in-Ten U.S. Adults Are Now Religiously Unaffiliated." Pew Research Center, December 14. Retrieved from https://www.pewresearch.org/religion/2021/12/14/about-three-in-ten-u-s-adults-are-now-religiously-unaffiliated/.

Smith, Jonathan, and Ginger Charles. 2010. "The Relevance of Spirituality in Policing: A Dual Analysis." *International Journal of Police Science & Management* 12(3), 320–338.

United States Catholic Bishops. 1979. *Brothers and Sisters to Us: Pastoral Letter on Racism*. National Conference of Catholic Bishops. Retrieved from: www.usccb.org/committees/african-american-affairs/brothers-and-sisters-us.

Ursitti, Antoinette M. 2011. "A Quantitative Assessment of Spirituality in Police Officers and the Relationship to Police Stress." Ed.D. dissertation. Olivet Nazarene University.

Vasko, Elizabeth T., and Lyndsie Ferrara. 2022. *True Crime and the Justice of God: Ethics, Media, and Forensic Science*. Orbis Books.

Vitale, Alex S. 2018. *The End of Policing*. Verso.

Winright, Tobias. 1995. "The Perpetrator as Person: Theological Reflections on the Just-War Tradition and the Use of Force by Police." *Criminal Justice Ethics* 14(2), 37–56.

Winright, Tobias. 1999. "From Police Officers to Peace Officers." In *The Wisdom of the Cross: Essays in Honor of John Howard Yoder*, edited by Stanley Hauerwas, Mark Nation, and Harry Huebner, 84–114. Eerdmans.

Winright, Tobias. 2002. "The Challenge of Policing: An Analysis in Christian Social Ethics." Ph.D. dissertation. University of Notre Dame.

Winright, Tobias. 2018. "Faith, Justice, and Ferguson: Insights for Religious Educators from a Law Enforcement Officer Turned Theological Ethicist." *Religious Education* 113(3), 244–252.

Winright, Tobias. 2020a. *Serve and Protect: Selected Essays on Just Policing*. Cascade Books.

Winright, Tobias. 2020b. "White Privilege: A Confession." *The Tablet* 274, no. 9356 (June 13, 2020): 4–5.

Workman-Stark, Angela. 2021. "Defund the Police? Instead, End Toxic Masculinity and 'Warrior Cops.'" *The Conversation* (April 6, 2021). Retrieved from: https://theconversation.com/defund-the-police-instead-end-toxic-masculinity-and-warrior-cops-157106.

4

PROFESSIONALISATION AND POLICING RELIGIOUS COMMUNITIES

From Police Recruit to Police Management

Andrew McInnes

Introduction

Policing continues to develop as a profession to become more responsive to the needs of its citizens. A key element of this drive to achieve professionalism, is for police organisations to ensure that their frontline officers have the training and development that they need to deliver a professional service to all communities. Meeting the needs of citizens from all communities has posed some significant challenges for police leaders, and the development of community policing principles and practices remains at the heart of policing agencies across the world. The movement of people across countries and regions has changed the demographics of communities, including those with a religious background, and understanding how these changes impact on key issues for policing such as legitimacy, trust, and confidence has become an increasingly important strategic and operational imperative.

This journey towards a new paradigm of professionalism in policing has seen an increasing focus on the education and training that are provided to police recruits to enable them to fulfil the complex and challenging functions of their role. How police officers understand the needs of religious communities is key, as is how they manage their own perceptions of these communities and understand how their own background and previous experiences shape their decision-making on the ground.

Changes in the profile of religious communities in society place an obligation on leadership within policing to constantly review and develop their approach to the delivery of services to these communities. There are several strategic and operational imperatives that indicate that this is a critical element of the delivery of successful and responsive policing. Maintaining public trust and confidence is key in building positive relationships between the police and their communities, especially when considering the needs of those from different religions.

DOI: 10.4324/9781003276593-6

This chapter will critically evaluate the challenges facing policing from the perspective of religion. It will explore how policing has adapted to meet the needs of communities in a way that maintains and builds on levels of trust and credibility. It will also critically examine the development of police education and training, and will focus on the experience of policing in Northern Ireland. This provides an interesting example of how policing has had to adapt to changing political and religious circumstances. Training, and the awareness raising of new recruits, was adapted in order to build trust and confidence in the police from within diverse religious communities. The current developments with the delivery of recruit training in the UK and Australia will also be examined.

Professionalisation

The development of policing as a profession has led to significant changes to how police recruits are trained, developed, and deployed within their communities. The impact of a more professional approach to policing has had a positive impact on how the police are perceived and on the levels of engagement between the police and the people that they serve. Professionalism at its core indicates trust and expertise, and is the transformation of an occupation into a profession (Higgs, McAllister, & Whiteford, 2009).

Defining characteristics of a profession are self-regulation; the development of a body of knowledge; a role in serving society; dynamism; the provision of a code of ethics; and an appropriate qualification for entry. Each of the four elements of the 'New Professionalism' of Accountability, Legitimacy, Innovation and National Coherence has something to offer the police and the communities in which they work (Stone & Travis, 2013).

Sklansky (2013) highlights a practical meaning of professionalism as meaning high standards. How these high standards translate to policing is open to debate. This has been a significant challenge for how police officers view their communities. With the increased levels of accountability and oversight in policing, there has been a sea change in how forces manage, lead, and train their personnel. The provision of responsive policing and a community-based approach will be explored later in this chapter. The more professional an officer is, the more sophisticated he or she is in responding to people of all backgrounds and the more successful he or she is in cross-cultural contact (Shusta et al., 1995).

Individual officers benefit from respect and community trust in their expertise, so there is a clear operational and strategic advantage for policing in developing a more professional approach to how diverse communities are engaged with. Building levels of reassurance in policing with communities is key. Positive engagement with communities can help close any gaps in reassurance (Ratcliffe, 2019). Police leaders will recognise that these benefits are crucial at a strategic level in helping to address issues of crime and disorder in communities. This will include the establishment of policing priorities and objectives that will inform the allocation of resources, and crimes affecting communities can be more readily addressed through closer partnerships with communities.

There is a clear link between professionalism and community trust in policing. Hardin comments: "To say we trust you means we believe you have the right intentions towards us and that you are competent to do what we trust you to do" (Hardin, 2006, p.17). A further benefit to the professionalism of policing is to establish clear regulatory and accountability standards. These standards are used for oversight as well as a benchmark to establish whether police conduct adheres to the highest professional standards, and whether officers should face misconduct proceedings internally. Communities also benefit from the open publication of clear standards of behaviour through Codes of Ethics and Standards of behaviour for officers. In respect of openness and transparency, the publication of standards also acts as a link between the police and religious communities and enhances professionalism, trust, and confidence (Westmarland & Rowe, 2018).

The drive for professionalism in policing has led to an increase in the focus placed on the training and education of recruits as well as for the organisation. There is a clear responsibility on professions and professionals to maintain high standards of knowledge and education, not only as a way of increasing standards of performance but also for maintaining the status of the role as a profession. Professional policing, in this sense, means policing that is reflective and knowledge-based, a matter of expertise rather than common sense, intuition, or innate talent (Sklansky, 2013).

Academic education and an emphasis on lifelong learning are critical to ensure the police are equipped to deal with the changing dynamics of complex societies (Blakemore & Simpson, 2010). Keeping up with changes in the professional environment is an important element of the role of training and education for the police professional. This is the case with the religious construct of communities, and having a detailed knowledge of the specific needs of religious communities as well as an enhanced level of self-awareness is critical to how these communities are engaged with and how relationships can be developed over time.

Recruits

The initial training of new recruits into policing has a major role to play in distilling the main aims and visions of community policing, and in properly understanding and engaging with communities. Community policing has been viewed as the most effective way for policing confidence and trust to be developed. The recent history of political conflict and violence in Northern Ireland has served to exacerbate division and mistrust along religious lines. In this chapter, I have already explored how policing has developed into a profession, and how this new professionalism is a critical element of how the police can more effectively build positive community-focused relationships with diverse religious communities. The training and development that are provided to new recruits into policing, have changed significantly over recent years. These changes have included the development of a close relationship between higher education and police training. These more formal links with higher education and initial training, career progression, and academic qualifications further the police professionalisation agenda (Paterson, 2011).

The training curricula for police recruit programmes have changed in line with the new professional and academic approach. The traditional focus on physical training, rote learning, and legal theory and definitions has not been preparing new police officers for how they deal with the communities that they serve (Green, 2015). The introduction of simulated exercises and a focus on the development of interpersonal skills and communication have enabled recruits to better engage with citizens and to add value to the development of a more community-focused policing service. The advancement of policing as an academic discipline within higher education has created the requirement for the university sector to employ police practitioners to design and deliver police-specific higher education programmes (Green, 2015).

Those responsible for managing police education need to clearly identify how society changes, responding to strong currents within a given society (Rogers & Wintle, 2020). The raising of awareness of the needs and fears of religious communities has also become a critical element of successful recruit training programmes. There is now widespread acknowledgement that new forms of education are important to prepare police officers to respond to new, contemporary (technical or structural) challenges, as with the changing needs of religious communities (O'Shea & Bartkowiak-Theron, 2019).

The increased emphasis on training, education, and development of police recruits has led to an increased focus on practice-based education, which, as outlined by Higgs, is situated within practice-relevant contexts. It involves a process of "socialisation into professional, disciplinary and occupational worlds, roles, identities, and career paths and involves engagement, through industry partnerships, in practice-based teaching and learning activities" (Higgs, 2011, p.12). Higgs also argues that effective practice-based education should be relevant to the given occupation's practice, be grounded in and engaged with practice communities, and satisfy the needs, interests, and expectations of relevant stakeholders (Higgs, 2013). Policy changes driven by government, or in some cases by the practitioner body, have mandated higher education programmes be established as the prerequisite training and education for a wide range of occupational groups (Green, 2015). Marenin (2004) expands upon the issue of occupational complexity by suggesting that police officers must continually reflect on decisions, values, and rights, including the demands for effectiveness, while still protecting individual human rights. The style of policing that a society requires often reflects the relationship between the state and its citizens, and this process invariably begins with the education and training of those police officers (Rogers & Wintle, 2020). When diversity training and the diversity agenda are extended to other constructs of identity, such as religion, race arguably provides the paradigm or lens through which reference to these is incorporated (McFadyen & Prideaux, 2011).

There has been a new direction for curriculum development within police recruit training and development in the UK. One of the key objectives of the new approach has been to provide some consistency in how police learning for recruits is delivered. Achieving consistency of recruit training and development can be particularly problematic with 43 police services, each with different Police Crime Commissioners (PCCs) and chief officers and services that may have different approaches to police work and different local problems requiring a variety of solutions and skills (Rogers & Frevel, 2018). Recruit training should be a positive experience for student officers overall, with deeper knowledge and understanding, critical thinking, time management, and writing skills identified as benefits. As part of the new approach to recruit training, a total of 19 forces have introduced the Police Constable Degree Apprenticeship (PCDA), seven forces have gone live with the Degree Holder Entry Programme (DHEP), and 25 higher education institutions (HEIs) are currently delivering the pre-join Degree in Professional Policing (College of Policing 2019, p.9).

As a further example, from Australia, relationships between the police and higher education (HE) have been developed to provide a recruit training programme for new recruits into New South Wales Police (NSWP) through a collaborative higher education programme with Charles Sturt University (CSU). The programme has a focus on policing skills and knowledge, as well as the application of what has been learnt through a series of simulated practice and assessments that include a range of events that are typical of day-to-day general duties policing. (NSW Police, 2022). The curriculum is delivered in an integrated model which reinforces learning and develops critical thinking, decision-making, ethical behaviour, and provides ample opportunity for "practice" (Rogers & Frevel, 2018). On completion of their recruit training programme, students are awarded an Associate Degree in Policing Practice qualification (ADPP) from CSU. The ADPP is the only recruitment pathway into the NSWPF, and is therefore mandatory for all new recruits (Rogers & Frevel, 2018).

There are a number of important lessons that can be drawn from the history of recruit training in Northern Ireland. In 1998, after a series of difficult and protracted negotiations between major political parties, the signing of the Belfast Agreement was completed. As well as addressing a number of key constitutional questions, this landmark Agreement set out the Terms of Reference for a Commission on Policing for Northern Ireland (CPNI), with proposals designed to ensure that "policing arrangements, including composition, recruitment, training, culture, ethos and symbols were such that Northern Ireland could have a police service that could enjoy widespread support from, and be seen as an integral part of, the community as a whole" (Government for Northern Ireland 1998, p.23). The CPNI produced its final report entitled 'A New Beginning: Policing in Northern Ireland' in September 1999. A key recommendation encompassed the further development of a community awareness approach to the training and development of new entrants to policing:

> We therefore recommend that community awareness training for police recruits be developed to include representatives of all the main political and

> religious traditions in Northern Ireland. Moreover, community awareness should not be a stand-alone element of recruit training; it should be integrated into all aspects of training. People from each of the main communities should have ample opportunity to learn about the history, traditions and outlook of the other.
>
> *Government for Northern Ireland, 1999, p.94*

The recommendation provided renewed impetus for the innovative developments in police training and education that had been implemented prior to the publication of the report of the CPNI. A Community Awareness Programme (CAP) had been designed and delivered to new recruits in partnership with an independent consultant, Mediation Northern Ireland. The primary focus of the programme was first of all to suggest to the recruits that all citizens in Northern Ireland are formed by families from local communities, and that the nature of country is that families tend to be Catholic or Protestant, and local communities are Catholic, Protestant, or mixed, and that these in turn affect the outlook of the recruits (Byrne, 1997).

One of the main challenges was to encourage recruits to understand themselves as people who are on the one hand citizens, formed in our divided community, but on the other people engaged to do something above that, which is the role of the professional police officer (Byrne, 1997). The objectives of the CAP, were that on completion, recruits will have knowledge of community religious practice in Northern Ireland, will have reflected on their social and cultural backgrounds, and will have a deeper understanding of the complexity of policing in a divided society (Byrne, 1997).

Practical scenarios in applying learning are critical to the building of knowledge and awareness of religious communities. Allowing recruit learners to develop the communication and decision-making skills required to be an effective officer are an essential element of successful training. An important element of the change in approach to recruit training was to continue to focus on key elements of legal knowledge, but to deliver sessions that would encourage students to recognise their own backgrounds and identities. This would be a way of the recruits considering how their actions as a police officer could impact on those living in communities with a different religious background to their own, and how religious traditions could impact on the execution of their duty

Developing opportunities for experiential learning including listening to the views of members of diverse religious backgrounds is key (Byrne, 1997). It is only by listening to these views and in raising awareness of the needs of religious communities that police recruits can be prepared to deliver the community-based policing services that their role as a police professional demand. It is only perhaps in the context of exposure to the experiential world of the operational officer, and only then with the specific issue in mind, that the researcher might come to understand the breadth of the significance of religion in contemporary policing (McFadyen & Prideaux, 2011).

Earlier in this chapter, it was suggested that responsiveness, self-awareness, and a community focus are essential for the future of a community-based policing model that seeks to always align the police with the community. The operational response to policing situations and to the calls for assistance from members of the public can have a profound impact on how diverse religious communities both view the police and how they engage with police officers (Ratcliffe, 2019). For every police recruit, their initial training and education provide a starting point for their careers and engaging with students from an experiential and self-awareness level has been identified as critical to the success of policing at a community and professional level. Demands for change in policing are often frequent and compelling, and in the context of community policing and religious communities, it is important that training and development programmes can be responsive and sensitive to these changes.

Training should go beyond transference of facts and procedures and, as demonstrated from the experience of policing in Northern Ireland, it should also focus on personal growth and development. Recruits must be able to reflect on their own experiences as a citizen and as a member of a religious group (or of none), and more fully understand past and personal development and family influences (Byrne, 1997). There is therefore a greater responsibility on police leaders in developing their training and development curricula to consider how they can shape the behaviour of police officers and raise their awareness of the needs of diverse religious communities. The attitude of the organisation towards religious awareness will be a key factor in the success of developing community policing, with genuine proactive relationships with religious communities.

Management and Leadership

The imperative for police leaders to understand fully the needs and concerns of communities is embedded in the need to deliver effective public safety and crime prevention strategies. Given the dynamic and ever-evolving nature of policing, leaders must be able to adapt in meeting the demands of the complex public safety challenges, and changes in their communities. "Today, innovation is essential for police agencies in the development of the strategies, tactics, and technologies they employ to prevent crimes and solve problems of public safety" (Stone & Travis, 2011, p.84).

The role of police leadership is ensuring that the professionalism of policing demanded by religious communities from recruit officers, is delivered through training strategies and programmes. Strategic decision-making and strong governance and oversight at local level are essential factors in progressing implementation. Both are key to ensuring that sufficient resources are invested in the implementation of training strategies, and all relevant stakeholders are involved, including workforce planning, procurement, and in operational and training development. It is paramount that the curriculum is managed, maintained, and reviewed in line with changes in demographic, including that of religious communities (Walsh & Gennaro, 2019).

Police leaders must ensure that a proactive approach is adopted to understand the changes in religious communities, and that lessons are learnt from engagement with these communities. Leading a police organisation that is responsive and can develop processes where lessons are learnt from challenges that arise, and where mistakes are made, is key. Being a "learning organisation" allows for the identification and analysis of the driving forces that are affecting service delivery, and to be able to effectively evaluate their response to interactions with communities. Aligned with this, from a training perspective, is the ability to be able to adapt recruit training programmes so that changes can be embedded into operational practice at an early stage (DiBella & Nevis, 1998).

Police services in the UK must effectively plan for and manage engagement with religious communities. Listening effectively to community stakeholders in setting local policing objectives is important in building trust and confidence (Ratcliffe, 2019). There are many lessons that can be drawn upon from the policing experience in Northern Ireland. There have been huge strides to move from a policing model dominated by political violence, to one where community policing is much more aligned to what would be expected in the rest of the UK.

While the threat from political violence has diminished significantly, there remains the issue of communities that are divided on religious grounds, and parts of towns and cities in Northern Ireland remain segregated based on religion (Gregory et al., 2013). There are still significant political disagreements, and the devolved government in Northern Ireland remains fragile and frequently subject to crises and disruption. This has not helped the police develop better community relationships (Mulcahy, 2006). The role that the police have in delivering effective policing services to divided communities is key. The reforms delivered through the CPNI review of policing have gone a good distance in providing a police service that is more representative across the religious background of its officers. The change of name from Royal Ulster Constabulary to the Police Service of Northern Ireland has also contributed to higher levels of trust and confidence. In this cultural shift, faith and religion have come to be recognised as significant issues for recruit training that impinge on, and shape behaviour and experience, interacting with other facets of identity (McFadyen & Prideaux, 2011).

Application to Policing Religious Communities

Community policing has been at the forefront of the vision for policing in major democratic policing societies such as the UK, Australia, and Canada. Several characteristics describe effective community policing; however, police leaders should not assume that there is a single model that can fit every situation and every community. This is particularly the case when considering the specific needs of religious communities. An assessment determines the type or style that satisfies the intended and articulated purpose (Verma et al., 2012). The policing of visible minority groups is one of the most contentious issues in criminal justice. These groups find themselves disproportionately ensnared in the justice systems of most, if not all, of those countries with ethnically diverse populations (Hough, 2020).

Communities can be defined in several ways, and it is imperative that police leaders have a clear understanding of the range of religious communities that exist within their jurisdictions when seeking to develop a community-based policing approach. The landscape of "communities" has significantly departed, worldwide, from its original meaning. From a localised and geographically confined concept, communities are now understood as much more complex entities (Brogden & Nijhar, 2005). Reisig and Parks (2004) indicate the feelings of safety for residents and police officers increased when there was greater interaction between the groups.

A sense of community can be defined as a feeling that members have of "belonging, a feeling that members matter to one another and to the group, and a shared faith that members' needs will be met through their commitment to be together" (McMillan and Chavis, 1986, p.9). Reassurance is important given the gulf between fear of crime and actual crime. People can worry about their safety so much that it affects their behaviour and is a barrier to meaningful engagement between the police and religious communities (Ratcliffe, 2019).

Influence is also a key element of successful policing. Those within religious groups must feel that they can influence their local policing priorities and can shape the relationships that exist between the police and their community members. Influence is defined by the significant positive relationships between cohesiveness, and a community's influence on members indicates the strength of the bond (McMillan & Chavis, 1986). Police officer perceptions of the neighbourhood are key in the implementation of successful community crime prevention programmes (Terpstra, 2009). One of the lessons learnt from the Northern Ireland experience was the lack of awareness amongst officers of the practices and traditions of religions other than their own (Byrne, 1997). This lesson was addressed through changes made to the recruit training programme through the CAP already outlined (Byrne, 1997).

Community policing strategies are designed to consider the needs of citizens; however, police officers need to take the lead if the programmes are to be effective. Engagement with established and emerging community groups and organisations, including from faith communities, is a key element of success. When engagement is effective, community organisations across the religious spectrum have demonstrated that they can play major roles with great effectiveness, including organising and mobilising people to press for improvements, creating self-help programmes to provide community services and develop housing and economic development projects (Mott, 1992).

Some see community policing as originating from the Peel "community" principles whereby crime prevention and the relationship between the police and the public became epitomised in the words "the public are the police and the police are the public" (Peak & Glensor, 2002, p.2). The principles are perennially held up as the embodiment of community policing (Lentz & Chaires, 2007), So, community policing in the twenty-first century is seen as "a common point of reference" (Brogden & Nijhar, 2005, p.21), and a return in many ways to the Peel principles (Peak & Glensor, 2002). Community policing is designed not only to prevent criminal activity, but to reduce the conditions under which deviant behaviour is encouraged (Sarre, 2016).

At the heart of community policing is understanding the range of needs and concerns of the communities that are served. Adopting a stakeholder approach to how community policing is managed and the co-delivery of policing services with a stakeholder approach to how citizens and communities are viewed is key (Ratcliffe, 2019). Trust and confidence in law enforcement do not stem from just tackling crime. Modern policing is about delivering a service that "addresses harm, social disorder, community safety and reassurance, all in a framework that instils confidence in the police and is procedurally just" (Ratcliffe, 2019 p.5).

The shift towards neighbourhood policing in the UK over the last decade has required new forms of community engagement and partnership working, focused on the key outcomes of public reassurance, confidence, and satisfaction (McFadyen & Prideaux, 2011). Engaging with religious communities is a critical element of community engagement, consultation, and partnership that should not just be taken forward by community policing teams but by all police officers, including those who have only recently completed their recruit training. In part that is because all neighbourhoods will contain people who self-identify at least partly in terms of religion. That is evidenced through formal and informal religious groups that meet, worship, and organise in service of the community (McFadyen & Prideaux, 2011). The role that frontline officers have in building positive relationships is clear, as is the alienation and mistrust that can develop when there are issues with police relations with religious communities. Public approval will enable the police to exercise their powers and to secure the willing cooperation of the public in the task of ensuring observance of laws, and also to maintain the respect of the public (Lentz & Chaires, 2007).

Public confidence in the police is secured and developed when communities see their treatment by police officers as being fair, even-handed, and delivered from an approach that is based on principles that were espoused by Peel. Fundamentally, the identification of criminals, the providing of information informally or through the process of informant handling are important aspects of the delivery of policing services to communities. These elements of successful policing are predicated on the existence of a professional policing approach, allied with communities that have trust in how they are being kept safe by officers. When people express their trust in police, it suggests people view police officers as motivated, sincerely helpful, and caring, giving priority to the best interests of the community (Tyler, 1990).

Impact and Consequences

One of the key consequences of this new approach to recruit training is that there is a focus on developing the professionalism of police officers and thereby enhancing the service provided to religious communities. Public trust and confidence are also a key element of successful policing. Religious communities that feel marginalised in society look to the police for help and support, and trust and confidence are essential to develop this two-way relationship. To secure compliance with the law, voluntary cooperation and support from the public will be required and will need to draw on people's feelings of obligation and responsibility (Hough, 2020). Religious communities deserve effective and responsive policing and to engage with good police officers who treat those with whom they have contact fairly and respectfully, accord them dignity, and listen to what they have to say. However, this raises the question of whether good police officers simply have to perform fairness and respect, or whether they are required to hold and internalise the values that underpin legitimate policing (Hough, 2020).

The impact on police organisations has been to enhance the importance of leadership, and in setting appropriate strategies for community engagement as well as training of recruit officers. This also includes how curricula for recruit training are managed and delivered. Leaders must ensure that training for police recruits goes beyond the delivery of knowledge and skills and focuses on raising awareness of the needs of religious communities. Training programmes must also challenge new recruits on their opinions, behaviours, and attitudes when considering religious communities. In considering the new approach to recruit training developed in Northern Ireland after the publication of the CPNI report, efforts have been made to raise awareness and knowledge of different religious communities and to be able to internalise the core values of policing. The CAP sought for the first time not only to enhance the community awareness of recruits to help professionalise their policing practice, but also to build confidence in policing and engagement amongst all communities.

Conclusion

This chapter has examined the complex issues associated with the need for professional policing to be aware of, and fully responsive to, the needs of diverse religious communities in their areas of responsibility. Policing, by its very nature, is often faced with new and unforeseen challenges. Police recruits need to be fully equipped to deal with these challenges and to act in a way that supports the achievement of safe and secure religious communities.

What is more of a challenge is the recognition and understanding of the sensitivity of how religious communities must be engaged with and supported. The Northern Ireland experience demonstrates that recognising the diversity of experiences of new recruits and helping them understand how their religious background and community affiliations can affect their professionalism, is a critical success factor for any training strategy.

The support from the police organisation at strategic leadership and management levels is key. Training strategies must reflect the need for a more practice-based approach to be developed, along with the raising of awareness of the policing needs of religious communities. Frequent reinforcement of key messages relating to community policing and responsive curriculum development will enable knowledge, skills, and self-awareness to be enhanced.

This should be supported by proactive environmental scanning of changes in the needs of religious communities, at both strategic and operational levels. Religious communities evolve as does society, and for the police to continue to develop as a profession, the links between community needs, training, and officer conduct must be maintained and strengthened. Trust, and confidence in the police cannot be taken for granted, and the needs of religious communities should be a priority for police leaders across the world.

References

Blakemore, B., & Simpson, K. (2010). A comparison of the effectiveness of pre-and post-employment modes of higher education for student police officers. *The Police Journal*, 83:1, 29–41.

Brogden M., & Nijhar P. (2005). Community-oriented policing: The Anglo-American model, in M. Brogden & P. Nijhar (Eds.), *Community policing: National and international models and approaches*. Willan Publishing, pp. 23–45.

Byrne, L. (1997). *Without fear or favour*. MBA thesis, University of Ulster.

College of Policing. (2019). *Policing Education Qualifications Framework Initial entry routes; Learning to date: development and implementation, 2016 to 2019*. Retrieved from: https://assets.college.police.uk/s3fs-public/2021-02/peqf-learning-to-date.pdf.

DiBella, A., & Nevis, E. (1998). *How organizations learn: An integrated strategy for building learning capacity*. Jossey-Bass.

Government for Northern Ireland. (1998). *Belfast Agreement*. Retrieved from: www.gov.uk/government/publications/the-belfast-agreement.

Government for Northern Ireland. (1999). The Independent Commission on Policing for Northern Ireland. A New Beginning: Policing in Northern Ireland. *The Report of the Independent Commission on Policing for Northern Ireland*. Retrieved from: https://cain.ulster.ac.uk/issues/police/patten/patten99.pdf.

Green, T.A. (2015). *Becoming a Police Academic: From Practitioner to Educator*. MA Social Science (Equal Opportunities). Northumbria University.

Gregory, I.N., Cunningham, N.A., Lloyd, C. D., Shuttleworth, I.G., & Ell, P.S. (2013). *Troubled geographies: A spatial history of religion and society in Ireland*. Indiana University Press.

Hardin, R. (2006). *Trust*. Polity Press.

Higgs, J. (2011). *Professional and practice-based education at Charles Sturt University*. Paper presented at the Education for Practice Institute, CSU.

Higgs, J. (2013). Practice-based education pedagogy: Professional pedagogy for professional education, in J. Higgs, D. Sheehan & B. Currens (Eds.), *Realising exemplary practice-based education*. Sense Publishers, pp. 6–10.

Higgs, J., McAllister, I., & Whiteford, G. (2009). *Understanding and researching professional practice*. Sense.

Hough, M. (2020). *Good policing, trust, legitimacy and authority*. Policy Press.

Lentz, S., & Chaires, R.H. (2007). The invention of Peel's principles: A study of policing 'textbook' history. *Journal of Criminal Justice* 35:1, 69–79.

McFadyen, A., & Prideaux, M. (2011). *Effective community policing: Negotiating changing religious identities*. CI Project.

McMillan, D.W., & Chavis, D.M. (1986). Sense of community: A definition and theory. *Journal of Community Psychology* 14 (January), 9–16.

Mott, A.H. (1992). The decades ahead for community organisations, in M.J. Palmiotto (Ed.). *Community policing: A police-citizen partnership*. Routledge, 113–116.

Mulcahy A. (2006). *Policing in Northern Ireland, conflict, legitimacy, and reform*. Willan.

New South Wales Police. (2022). *Associate Degree in Policing Practice*. Retrieved from: www.police.nsw.gov.au/recruitment/the_training/associate_degree_in_policing_practice

O'Shea, B., & Bartkowiak-Theron, I. (2019). Being a topic expert is not sufficient': A mixed-method analysis of teaching dynamics at the Tasmania police academy. *Police Practice and Research*, 20: 3, 288–299.

Paterson C. (2011). Adding value? A review of the international literature on the role of higher education in police training and education. *Police Practice and Research*, 12: 4, 286–297.

Peak, K., & Glensor, R. (2002). *Community policing and problem-solving: Strategies and practices*. Prentice Hall

Ratcliffe, J. (2019). *Reducing crime. A companion for police leaders*. Routledge.

Reisig, M.D., & Parks, R.B. (2004). Community policing and the quality of life. in W. G. Skogan (Ed.), *Community policing: Can it work?* Wadsworth, pp. 207–227.

Rogers, C., & Wintle, E. (2020). Police education in Australia, in P. Birch, M. Kennedy & E. Kruger (Eds.), *Australian Policing: Critical Issues in 21st Century Policing*. Routledge, pp. 7–22.

Rogers, C., & Frevel, B. (Eds.) (2018). *Higher education and police: An international view*. Springer.

Sarre, R. (2016). Ten 'big bangs' in theory and practice that have made a difference to Australian policing in the last three decades. *Salus Journal*, 4:2, 1–18.

Shusta, R.M., Levine, D.R., Harris, P.R., & Wong, H.Z. (1995). *Multicultural law enforcement: Strategies for peacekeeping in a diverse society*. Prentice Hall.

Sklansky, D.A. (2013). The promise and the perils of police professionalism, in J.M. Brown, (Ed.). *The future of policing*. Routledge, pp. 343–352.

Stone, C., & Travis, J. (2011). *Toward a new professionalism in policing*. National Institute of Justice.

Stone, C., & Travis, J. (2013). Toward a new professionalism in policing. *Australasian Policing*, 5:1, 23–32. Retrieved from: https://search-informit-org.ezproxy.csu.edu.au/doi/10.3316/informit.494353916466180.

Terpstra, J. (2009). Citizen involvement in local security networks. *Security Journal*, 22, 156–169.

Tyler, T. (1990). *Why people obey the law*. Princeton University Press.

Verma, A., Dilip, D., & Manoj, A. (2012). *Global community policing: problems and challenges*. CRC Press.

Walsh, W., & Gennaro, F. (2019). *Police leadership and administration: A 21st century strategic approach*. Routledge.

Westmarland, L., & Rowe, M. (2018). Police ethics and integrity: Can a new code overturn the blue code? *Policing and Society*, 28:7, 854–870.

5

POLICE LEGITIMACY IN DIVIDED SOCIETIES

Exploring the Interface of Religion and Social Cohesion

Conor Murray, Brian Payne and Philip Birch

Introduction

This chapter explores the legitimation of policing in diverse contexts, focusing on the challenges and issues raised when attempting to apply policing models and practices in divided societies. Academic research continues to pay significant attention to police legitimacy in divided societies where state authority can often be widely disputed, leading to a series of concerns expressed by those who perceive state power to be disproportionately levelled against them (see, for example, Smith, 2016; Van Damme, 2017; Holland, 2021).

Drawing on examples from two jurisdictions, Israel and Northern Ireland, the chapter will explore the difficulties faced in maintaining police legitimacy in 'divided societies'. In this instance, 'divided societies' refers to societies in which overt and covert forms of division exist, and where structural impediments to effective policing are based primarily on religious differences. The chapter also highlights the continued importance of police reform in diverse contexts as a means for improving police legitimacy, particularly within divided societies that are historically polarised and lacking social cohesion. Such reforms include the strict application of external police accountability mechanisms, an emphasis on education and training, and ensuring the police are reflective of all the communities that they serve.

Police Legitimacy in Contrast

Research has consistently identified that police legitimacy can provide social order and ensure the police enjoy the necessary levels of cooperation and compliance needed to perform their roles (Murphy, 2008; Goodman-Delahunty, 2010; Mazerolle et al., 2012; Jackson et al., 2012). Moreover, it is argued that public belief

DOI: 10.4324/9781003276593-7

in a legitimate police force results in a moral obligation to conform to and accept directives from that authority (Sunshine and Tyler, 2003; Tyler, 2006). As a legal authority, the legitimacy of a police service therefore depends on its ability to demonstrate to the public why its exercise of powers is rightful (Reisig et al., 2007).

Noteworthy studies conducted in the USA (Sunshine and Tyler, 2003; Tyler, 2006) and the UK (Bradford et al., 2009; Bradford, 2011; Martin and Bradford, 2021), as illustration, support the argument that perceptions of fair police conduct can improve relations and legitimacy. Fairness is often achieved in two forms: first, procedural fairness, achieved by fair decision-making, using discretion fairly, remaining impartial and being considerate of the views and values of those who are being policed; second, distributive fairness, which is achieved by equal outcomes and treatment for those who are policed (Pehrson et al., 2017; also see Tyler, 2006).

Similarly, procedural justice is often argued to be a central tenet to fair policing, and one of the 'most important antecedents of police legitimacy' (Mazerolle et al., 2012: 344). Procedural justice refers to the fair and respectful treatment of citizens by the police (Mazerolle et al., 2012; Galovic et al., 2016). When citizens feel they are treated respectfully and fairly, they are more likely to view the police as legitimate. As a result, they are more likely to cooperate with the police and comply with the law (Tyler, 2003; Reisig et al., 2007). Consequently, police come to be viewed as legitimate when they are frequently present in communities managing conflicts, solving problems, and building relationships (also see Birch, 2011; Tyler, 2011; Jackson et al., 2012).

However, in societies where significant social division exists, for example in the context of religious conflict, or though structural factors such as those linked to inequality, poverty, and other forms of discrimination, an enhanced set of challenges exist for policing amidst a broader need to bring about social and political integration of disparate groups within a climate of structural exclusion and socio-economic deprivation (see, for example, Loader and Mulcahy, 2003; Hearty, 2018; Holland, 2021). In this context, groups who have traditionally been polarised against the police, or even those who feel estranged from policing as it moves through a reform process can experience a perceived legitimacy deficit, further impeding effective policing and deepening associated deficits. By considering the impact of religion on policing and police legitimacy, this chapter reflects on policing in Israel and Northern Ireland, each providing an exploration of some of the issues which characterise this fraught and conflicted relationship and providing the foundation for an examination of police legitimacy in divided societies.

Policing Sectarian Conflict

Religion is a significant catalyst for sectarian conflict; as a consequence, policing in such contexts is typically characterised by a militarised approach in which sectarian bias is present (Weitzer, 1985). It is therefore understandable how police legitimacy is questioned, and social cohesion is jeopardised under such conditions. The experience of both Israel and Northern Ireland are examples that illustrate this vexed context, while also providing insights into ways of mitigating the sectarian conflict.

Israel in Focus

The formation of the Israeli state can be traced back to post–World War I, the collapse of the Ottoman Empire, and colonial powers taking control of the Middle East (Kamrava, 2005). Under the Mandate for Palestine, Britain formally took control of the Palestinian region in 1920. While there was a single government in place, Arabic (also referred to in the chapter as Palestinians) and Jewish communities and economies developed separately. It was during the period 1920–1948 that the social, political, and economic foundations for an Israeli state were formed through external investment in the Jewish economy and a mass influx of Jewish immigration to the region. During this period the Jewish population grew exponentially from approximately 56,000 to 630,000, with many Zionists moving to the region as they believed the Jews needed their own state to exist freely and peacefully (Halevi, 2008).

After the mandatory period of British control, the State of Israel was formed in 1948 amidst protest and conflict; many neighbouring states believed the Jews did not belong in Palestine (Connolly, 2018). The Arab League invaded Israel, and while Israel won the conflict, Egypt captured the Gaza Strip and Jordan captured the West Bank – annexing two Palestinian territories within the Israeli state. The conflict displaced over 700,000 Palestinians, who became refugees (Hammad and Tribe, 2021). Another period of mass immigration followed between 1948 and 1951, which saw the Jewish population double in only three years (Shvarts et al., 2005). At the conclusion of the Six Day War (1967), Israel took control of the Gaza Strip and West Bank. In the succeeding years, Jewish settlements were developed in the territories causing continuous hostilities and conflict, particularly as investment in infrastructure and local economies benefited Jews (Halevi, 2008).

The social and political divisions between the Jews and Arabs continue today (Ben-Porat, 2021). Arabs make up approximately 20 per cent of the population (Ramadi et al., 2019), rendering them an ethnic minority. Israel is a Jewish state, and the national symbols, such as the flag and national anthem, are founded upon Judaism and protected by a strong political majority and legislature that prevents major changes (Ben-Porat, 2021), leading some scholars to suggest that 'the state privileges the ethnic majority and discriminates against the minority' (Ben-Porat, 2021: 261). Indeed, inequalities are conspicuous: Arabs experience discrimination in housing, employment, and education (Ben-Porat, 2021). Discussions regarding state security and policing of the Arab community are prevalent. The ongoing Israeli–Palestinian conflict positions Arabs in a state of suspicion, regarded by the state as a prospective threat, and has resulted in political activists, NGOs, schoolteachers, and principals being placed under the surveillance of the state (Ben-Porat, 2021). Strained relationships between police and Palestinians are a chronic issue. Compared to their Jewish counterparts, Arabs are less likely to trust police, less likely to feel safe in police–citizen encounters, and less likely to report crimes to the police (Hasisi and Weitzer, 2007).

In deeply divided societies, it is common for ethnic minorities to have a tempestuous relationship with police (Hasisi and Weitzer, 2007), as the police are tasked with the protection of 'a sectarian regime and the maintenance of a social order based on institutionalized inequality between dominant and subordinate communal groups' (Weitzer, 1995: 5). This has led some scholars to suggest that Israel's approach to policing the Palestinian minority constitutes characteristics of 'sectarian policing' (Boulos, 2020: 174). In addition to the police perceiving Palestinians to be a threat to national security, as discussed above, other characteristics of sectarian policing seen elsewhere that may apply to Israel include the excessive use of force, the over-policing of political activities, and the under-policing of ordinary crime (Weitzer, 1995) – each of which will be discussed below.

Incidents of unnecessary or excessive use of force have plagued the Israeli police. In 1956, Israel Border Police shot dead 48 unarmed Arab citizens who were returning from work unaware of the implementation of a new curfew. Yet despite originally being imprisoned, the officers were later pardoned (Robinson, 2003). In 1976, six Palestinians were killed during protests against the planned expansion of Jewish settlements in northern Israel (Hawari, 2018). In 2000, police shot dead 13 unarmed Palestinian protesters and injured hundreds of others (Dalal, 2003). The events prompted a public inquiry. The Investigation Committee headed by Supreme Court Justice Theodor Or (The Or Commission) criticised the Israeli government for decades of discrimination, stating that the:

> Government handling of the Arab sector has been primarily neglectful and discriminatory [...] The state did not do enough or try hard enough to create equality for its Arab citizens or to uproot discriminatory or unjust phenomenon [...] serious distress prevailed in the Arab sector in various areas. Evidence of the distress included poverty, unemployment, a shortage of land, serious problems in the education system and substantially defective infrastructure.
>
> *Or Commission 2003, para. 3*

In specific relation to policing, it stated there was a need 'to uproot prejudice, which exists even among officers who are experienced and admired. The police must learn to realize that the Arab sector in Israel is not the enemy and must not be treated as such' (Or Commission 2003, para. 27). Despite the report's condemnation of the government and police, Arab citizens criticised the Commission for its failure to indict the police officers responsible for the murders (Adalah, 2020). Following the report's recommendations, some of the police's training has been revised, but armed force is still used, and between 2000 and 2019, 56 Palestinian citizens were murdered by police (Boulos, 2020). Over-policing also remains an issue, as evidenced by the joint letter, signed by over 40 human rights organisations, sent the chief of police and the minister of interior protesting the over-policing of, and institutional bias against, minority groups in Israel (ACRI, 2020).

Arguably in Israel, the focus on state security and policing political activities is prioritised above the rights of citizens, which has resulted in the benign neglect of policing ordinary crime in Arab towns (Hasisi and Weitzer, 2007). A focus on securitisation – in combination with institutional discrimination leading to high levels of poverty and unemployment – has resulted in a sharp increase in crime in Arab communities in the last decade (Boulos, 2020). The neglect of policing these ordinary crimes is not attributed to resourcing or incompetence but to discriminatory under-policing. That is, police officers display greater endeavour when Jewish victims are involved (Gurr, 2015). Between 2000 and 2017, 1,236 Arabs died from violent crimes (Boulos, 2020). The rate of unsolved homicides with Arab victims is disproportionately high (approximately 50 per cent), compared to their Jewish counterparts (approximately 33 per cent) (Arraf, 2020). Arraf (2020) estimates there are approximately 400,000 illegal weapons dispersed amongst criminal organisations operating in Palestinian communities, including guns, grenades, and explosives, the majority of which have been stolen from the Israeli army. In a response to the prevalence of gun crime in Palestinian communities, the State Comptroller (2018) investigated the issue and reported that 95 per cent of shootings occur in Palestinian communities, while only a small portion of these are prosecuted. Zoabi (2017) also identified the low prosecution rate in cases with Palestinian victims, reporting that during some investigations, police neglected interviewing key witnesses, at times encouraging them not to provide statements, and failed to collect crucial evidence.

The distrust of the Israeli police by Palestinian citizens, a product of the over-policing of political activities and the under-policing of ordinary crime, has led to a lack of police legitimacy in Palestinian communities. For Palestinians, the Israeli police force represents the coercive power of a sectarian state to which they feel no allegiance. They are the physical symbolisation of institutional discrimination and the unequal distribution of resources. These issues are exacerbated by Israeli state symbols, the legislature, and a strong political majority, which contribute to ensuring the subjugation of the Palestinian identity, and the cultural domination of Judaism. To address issues of police legitimacy in Israel – if this is what the state truly desires – then a wider process of separating policing from the state would likely be required. While this will not solve all the issues of a contested state, it will contribute to the diffusion of identity politics by disassociating policing from wider questions on governance and focusing instead on integrating the police into all the communities it serves. However, shifting policing away from issues of state security, towards an approach based on an adherence to shared values and equality will always be difficult in the absence of wider societal reform. The Israeli experience of sectarian conflict, whilst unique in many ways, therefore, has many similarities to our second case study, the 'troubles'[1] of Northern Ireland, which has experienced a notable drive for peace underpinned by root-and-branch reform of policing as a fundamental part of a broader process of societal change.

Northern Ireland in Focus

For a considerable period, Northern Ireland has occupied a prominent position in global debates on police reform (Mulcahy, 2008; Ellison et al., 2012). This is in part due to the history of policing in Northern Ireland and its intrinsic link to both the conflict – a protracted period of civil disobedience and paramilitary activity based on political/religious fault lines spanning 1968–1998 – and the sustained efforts to resolve it since the later 1990s (Ellison and Smyth, 2000; McGarry and O'Leary, 2004). The transformation of policing from the former Royal Ulster Constabulary (RUC) into the Police Service of Northern Ireland (PSNI) is central to such debates and was premised, in large part, on placing community policing at the core of efforts to promote peace by developing relations with previously estranged communities (McEvoy et al., 2002; Ellison, 2007; Ellison and O'Rawe, 2010).

The RUC was created following the partition of the island and the disbandment of the Royal Irish Constabulary (RIC) which had previously policed Ireland as a whole (Brewer, 1991). Policing in Ireland in many ways provided a framework for the development of policing in Britain itself based on its priorities of responding to riots, crime, and class control (Brogden, 1987). In addition, the colonial model of policing employed in Ireland was also exported throughout the British Empire. A central element of the Irish and other colonial models of policing, therefore, was the use of the police as a mechanism to suppress agrarian and political unrest (O'Donnell and O'Sullivan, 2001; Kilcommins et al., 2004).

While there was a deliberate and sustained attempt to establish the legitimacy of the police in England by 'depoliticising' the nature of policing (Reiner, 2000: 9), the police in Ireland were often confronted with explicitly political disputes with certain sections of the population that were essentially hostile to colonial rule. That tradition of suppressing nationalist dissent was accompanied by significant support from Loyalists and Unionist sections of the population (most commonly in the north) who largely (but not universally) approved of British rule. As Smyth (2002) notes, if the minimum requirement for police legitimacy is the full support of the population, then this did not apply to Ireland as a whole prior to 1922, or indeed in Northern Ireland after partition where the police became widely viewed as the 'armed wing of Unionism' (see also Farrell, 1983).

The partition of Ireland between the six north-eastern counties of Ireland and the rest of the island took place on the third of May 1921, creating two entities on the island. The partition of the northern six counties occurred at a time of severe political violence and was designed to produce a majority in one section of the population over another (Brewer and Magee, 1991). The Northern Irish parliament was established as a miniature version of the Westminster system employed in Great Britain itself. Under this system, the party (or parties) that enjoyed a majority in the legislature had untrammelled executive and legislative power. This policy ensured that the Unionist parties dominated the Northern Ireland Parliament for the next 50 years (McGarry and O'Leary, 2004).

From its establishment, the Northern Ireland government saw the maintenance of security and the protection of the fledgling state as its central responsibility. Initially, there was a plan to simply divide the existing (all Ireland) RIC between Northern Ireland and the Irish Free State, but continuing negotiations and violence deemed that notion unworkable (McGloin, 2003). Instead, the RIC remained intact until the establishment of the RUC on 1 June 1922 when almost 1,000 RIC officers were absorbed into the new force (Ellison and Smyth, 2000). As noted above, a substantial minority of Catholics remained living in the six counties which now comprised Northern Ireland, and periodically their rejection of the legitimacy of partition, and consequently the authority of the RUC, led to eruptions of violence against the British state and its representatives (Brewer and Magee, 1991).

Throughout its history the RUC remained a largely Protestant police force. Recruitment of Catholics peaked at 21 per cent in 1923 (Ellison and Smyth, 2000), and had decreased to 11 per cent by 1969 (Farrell, 1983). In the period from 1968 to 1969, street demonstrations and riots over sectarian dominance overwhelmed the under-resourced RUC (Brogden and Nijhar, 2005).[2] The role of the RUC during this period led to three Royal commissions, Cameron (1969), Hunt (1969), and Scarman (1972), with each criticising the conduct of the RUC. The report of the Hunt committee was particularly influential as it recommended an end to what it saw as the dual role of policing in Northern Ireland, that is, performing all the normal roles expected of a police force in the United Kingdom while, on the other hand, undertaking security duties of a military nature.

As Gordon (2008) notes, the historical and political context of policing in Northern Ireland became a fundamental obstacle to achieving institutional legitimacy. The tendency to utilise a style of policing that appeared both excessive and intrusive had obvious implications for the relationship between the RUC and the Nationalist community. Writing on this issue, Weitzer (1995) suggested that the counterinsurgency methods employed by the state made the legitimation of the police impossible. He argues that the mechanisms of police accountability were fundamentally weakened by such measures, and attempts to uphold accountability were interpreted by police and their supporters as being weak on terrorism. In this regard, the need to maintain a dual system of policing ensured that the public support that the police required to carry out their normal policing duties became compromised, providing the conditions to instil a legacy of fear and distrust (Mulcahy, 2006). This analysis became an important plank in the subsequent reform of policing in Northern Ireland.

In September 1999, the Independent Commission on Policing in Northern Ireland (ICP), chaired by Chris Patten, published its recommendations. The commission was established in the aftermath of the Good Friday agreement that ushered in a road map for the end of the conflict and also offered the potential for a 'radical reconceptualization of how policing in Northern Ireland would be conceived and structured' (Mulcahy, 2006, 4).

Throughout the Northern Ireland peace process, the question of police reform has been a central element of political negotiations. As in other contexts, 'the police' was both an imagined and a material representation of the state (Ellison and Smyth, 2000). For many Protestants and Unionists, the police represented loyalty and service to the British crown. For many Catholics and Nationalists, the police represented the coercive embodiment of a state to which they owed no allegiance, as well as the 'sharp end' of sectarian and politically discriminatory policing tactics (Ruane and Todd, 1995; Mulcahy, 1996). This perceived absence of legitimacy of policing in many parts of the Northern Ireland jurisdiction created a context in which police reform became a central plank, both real and symbolic, in the constitutional redesign of the state of Northern Ireland itself (Hillyard and Tomlinson, 2000; Gordon, 2008).

When the ICP, chaired by Patten, published its recommendations, the final report was developed around a golden thread, which he interpreted as comprising two principal strands: 'the importance of local knowledge and capacity and a post-factum view of the appropriate relationship between scrutiny and direction' (Shearing, 2001: 261). More specifically, Kempa and Shearing (2005) identify two distinct, but overlapping, strands of reform that underpin the document: 'conventional' reforms to the 'system of police'; and reforms that sought to shift the emphasis from the 'police' to 'policing'.

The 'conventional' reforms to the 'system of police' in Northern Ireland have involved the enhancement of oversight structures, training, recruitment, and cultural change (Ellison, 2007). The ICP recognised that, to gain legitimacy, the police service needed to be representative of the community it was policing. One outcome from this was the reformation of the controversial recruitment policy, with the aim that the new intake of police officers should comprise 50 per cent Catholic and 50 per cent Protestant or others. Colloquially known as the '50/50 rule', this ran from 2001 to 2011, by which stage the proportion of Catholic officers had reached almost 30 per cent.

The Commission also argued that 'every neighbourhood (or rural area) should have a dedicated policing team with lead responsibility for policing in its area' (ICP, 1999: 43), which would be 'empowered to determine their own local priorities and set their own objectives, within the overall Annual Policing Plan and in consultation with community representatives' (ICP, 1999: 45).

In the context of a shift in emphasis from the 'police' to 'policing', the Commission intended to connect programmatically to the idea that the police should no longer monopolise crime prevention (Bayley, 1994). As Shearing (2000) notes, the ICP envisaged policing as a regulated network of participatory 'nodes', each with the authority, capacity, and knowledge to provide for the governance of security. This ethos is particularly relevant to Northern Ireland, given the involvement of non-state organisations in the governance of security in their local communities throughout the conflict, including paramilitary groups (Kempa and Shearing, 2005). Consequently, the ICP was faced not with the problem of how to construct new justice participants, but rather, how to encourage and involve the diverse networks that were already in existence, and to do so in ways that guaranteed non-violence and the protection of human rights.

The idea that policing should involve the active participation of community members has been far from straightforward, and Northern Ireland continues to face a number of structural impediments to successful police working, such as the continued security threat to police and issues relating to legitimacy and procedural justice (Deglow, 2016). This is exacerbated by the continued involvement of non-state organisations, including paramilitaries, in the governance of security in their local communities (McGarry et al., 2017). Most recently, a series of social media-fuelled public protest and rioting have followed incidents where the PSNI were perceived in some quarters to have operated in a way that appeared to prioritise the policing of one section of the community over the other (Lawther and Hearty, 2021). Each has served to highlight the impact of a continued inability to deal with the legacy of Northern Ireland's past and the subsequent tightrope that the police in Northern Ireland must walk as they navigate an inherently complex political and social environment.

Certainly, the experience of Northern Ireland suggests that 'Policing with the Community' can continue to build impressions of a modern accountable police service that belongs to no one group. However, some commentators have pointed to a move away from this key ambition of the ICP as being a factor in the continued struggles the PSNI faces to cope with the challenges brought by intercommunal tensions (Caparini and Hwang, 2019). Nevertheless, while ideological views of the role and nature of the police present a considerable challenge in scenarios where deep divisions remain, areas of commonality can be found. Reinforced, they will help foster a shared ethno-nationalist ideal of a reformed police service that attracts enduring support as it adapts to and helps counter the structural impediments of a post-conflict society and prevent the appropriation of the symbolic power of the police by groups external to the organisation (Hearty, 2018; Holland, 2021).

Conclusion

Policing divided societies is a complex issue driven by many facts, with religion being a common catalyst. A fallout of such division is the sectarian bias that typically occurs through police practice. This is illustrated in this chapter through the consideration of both Israel and Northern Ireland as case examples. The impact of such social division through policing is the question of legitimation of the police in which police practices are scrutinised through a lens of representativeness, prescriptiveness, fairness, inclusiveness, and above all accountability to all sections of society. The need for the police to respond in a positive manner to the structural impediments resulting in the lack of social cohesion brought about by both political division and social exclusion is a common theme that runs through each of the examples used to explore police legitimacy in divided societies.

Both Israel and Northern Ireland continue to occupy global interest with respect to the police reform debates, in which both the history and the perceived legitimacy of policing are intrinsically linked to the conflict and the sustained efforts to maintain peace within the contemporary landscape. This chapter, therefore, has considered the continued and evolving impact of sectarianism on policing set against the police reform process, focusing on the complex interaction between religion and social cohesion; exploring the impact of religion on key strands of policing reform, such as achieving a police service that is representative; instilling effective community policing and partnership structures; and on the potential for the transformation of the legitimacy of the police. A central argument put forward in this chapter is that historical challenges to police legitimacy have evolved along religious and sectarian lines to present new and sustained difficulties for policing in police forces within Israel and Northern Ireland contemporaneously. While debates on policing, religion, and sectarian conflict are advanced, policing continues to be beset by the challenges of policing intercommunal conflict and division. However, there is scope for optimism, as evidenced in this chapter, by reflecting on how policing might respond to these challenges in order to fully integrate religious differences and ensure community cohesion. Arguably, the common denominator for such integration is through embracing police practices that bring the police closer to the public they serve and that incorporate a series of values designed to increase perceptions of fairness, procedural justice, and most importantly, the impression that the police belong to every section of society. Only then can the police achieve that illusive ideal of being perceived as a legitimate entity that has the confidence of all.

Notes

1 The 'Troubles' refer to the sectarian conflict in Northern Ireland between 1968 and 1998 (see: www.britannica.com/event/The-Troubles-Northern-Ireland-history)

2 The Civil Rights Movement emerged in the 1960s to address the perceived discrimination of the nationalist population. The movement featured an organised and motivated nationalist organisation, 'The Northern Ireland Civil Rights Association', which presented several demands including an end to electoral gerrymandering, the repeal of emergency legislation, and the abolition of the B specials (a part-time militia force) (Mulcahy, 2006).

References

Adalah. (2020). 'The October 2000 Killings'. *Adalah*. Retrieved from: www.adalah.org/en/content/view/10127.

Arraf, S. (2020). 'Organised Crime within the Palestinian Community in Israel'. *Israeli Affairs*, 77, 23–33.

Association for Civil Rights in Israel (ACRI). (2020). Letter to The Minister of Interior and the Acting Chief of Police. Retrieved from: https://01368b10-57e4-4138-acc3-01373134d221.usrfiles.com/ugd/01368b_9022121cba2d475ca50c7e67081eb320.pdf.

Bayley, D. (1994). *Police for the Future*. Oxford: Oxford University Press.

Birch, P. (2011). 'Working with Communities: Social Inclusion and Policing Practice', in *Policing in Practice*, P. Birch and V. Herrington (eds.). Palgrave, pp. 10–26.

Boulos, S. (2020). 'Policing the Palestinian National Minority in Israel: An International Human Rights Perspective'. *Journal of Holy Land and Palestine Studies*, 19(2), 151–174.

Bradford, B. (2011). 'Voice, Neutrality and Respect: Use of Victim Support Services, Procedural Fairness and Confidence in the Criminal Justice System'. *Criminology and Criminal Justice*, 11(4), 345–366.

Bradford, B., Jackson, J., and Stanko, E. (2009). 'Contact and Confidence: Revisiting the Impact of Public Encounters with the Police'. *Policing and Society*, 19(1), 20–46.

Brewer, J. D. (1991). 'Policing Divided Societies: Theorising a Type of Policing'. *Policing and Society*, 1(3), 179–91.

Brewer, J. D., and Magee, K. (1991). *Inside the RUC: Routine Policing in a Divided Society*. Clarendon Press.

Brogden, M. (1987). 'An Act to Colonize the Internal Lands of the Island: Empire and Origins of the Professional Police'. *International Journal of the Sociology of Law*, 15, 179–208.

Brogden, M., and Nijhar, P. (2005). *Community Policing: National and International Models and Approaches*. Willan.

Cameron Report. (1969). *Disturbances in Northern Ireland: Report of the Cameron Commission*. HMSO.

Caparini M.A., and Hwang J. U. (2019). *Police Reform in Northern Ireland: Achievements and Future Challenges*. Oct 28. Stockholm International Peace Research Institute.

Connolly, M. (2018). *The Founding of Israel: The Journey to a Jewish Homeland from Abraham to the Holocaust*. Pen and Sword.

Dalal, M. (2003). *October 2000: Law and Politics before the Or Commission of Inquiry*. The Legal Center for Minority Rights in Israel.

Ellison, G. (2007). 'A Blueprint for Democratic Policing Anywhere in the World? Police Reform, Political Transition and Conflict Resolution in Northern Ireland'. *Police Quarterly*, 10(3), 243–269.

Ellison, G., and O'Rawe, M. (2010). 'Security Governance in Transition: The Compartmentalising, Crowding Out and Corralling of Policing and Security in Northern Ireland'. *Theoretical Criminology*, 14(1), 1–27.

Ellison, G., Shirlow, P., and Mulcahy, A. (2012). 'Responsible Participation, Community Engagement and Policing in Transitional Societies: Lessons from a Local Crime Survey in Northern Ireland'. *The Howard Journal of Criminal Justice*, 51(5), 488–502.

Ellison, G., and Smyth, G. (2000). *The Crowned Harp*. Pluto Press.

Farrell, M. (1983). *Arming the Protestants: The Formation of the USC and the RUC 1920–27*. Dingle, Ireland.

Galovic, S., Birch, P., Vickers, M., and Kennedy, M. (2016) 'Procedural Justice and Frontline Policing: The Effects of the Police Complaints System'. *Journal of Forensic Practice*, 18(2), 1–12.

Goodman-Delahunty, J. (2010). 'Four Ingredients: New Recipes for Procedural Justice in Australian Policing'. *Policing: A Journal of Policy and Practice*, 4(4), 403–410.

Gordon, J. (2008). 'Post-Conflict Transformation: The Process of Institutional Legitimation of the Police in Northern Ireland'. *Ethnopolitics*, 7(1), 137–157.

Gurr, T. (2015). *Why Men Rebel*. Routledge.

Halevi, N. (2008). 'A Brief Economic History of Modern Israel', in *EH.Net Encyclopaedia*, R. Whaples (ed.). Retrieved from: http://eh.net/encyclopedia/a-brief-economic-history-of-modern-israel/

Hammad, J., and Tribe, R. (2021). 'Culturally Informed Resilience in Conflict Settings: A Literature Review of Sumud in the Occupied Palestinian Territories'. *International Review of Psychiatry*, 33(1–2), 132–139.

Hasisi, B., and Weitzer, R. (2007). 'Police Relations with Arabs and Jews in Israel'. *The British Journal of Criminology*, 47(5), 728–745.

Hawari, Y. (2018). 'Palestine Land Day: A Day to Resist and Remember'. *Al Jazeera*, 30 May. Retrieved from: www.aljazeera.com/opinions/2018/3/30/palestine-land-day-a-day-to-resist-and-remember

Hearty, K. (2018). 'Discourses of Political Policing in Post-Patten Northern Ireland'. *Critical Criminology*, 26(1), 129–143.

Hillyard, P., and Tomlinson, M. (2000). 'Patterns of Policing and Policing Patten'. *Journal of Law and Society*, 27(3), 394–415.

Holland, C. (2021). 'Identity, the Politics of Policing, and Limits to Legitimacy in Northern Ireland, Innovation'. *The European Journal of Social Science Research*, 34(1), 44–68.

Hunt, Lord. (1969). *Report of the Advisory Committee on Police in Northern Ireland*. HMSO.

Independent Commission on Policing (ICP). (1999). *Report of the Independent Commission on Policing in Northern Ireland A New Beginning: Policing in Northern Ireland*. The Patten Commission Report. NIO/HMSO.

Jackson, J., Bradford, B., Hough, M., Myhill, A., Quinton, P., and Tyler, T. (2012). 'Why Do People Comply with the Law? Legitimacy and the Influence of Legal Institutions'. *British Journal of Criminology*, 52(6): 1051–1071.

Kamrava M. (2005). 'Democracy and Democratisation', in *Palgrave Advances in Development Studies*, J. Haynes (ed.), 67–88. Palgrave Macmillan.

Kempa, M., and Shearing, C. (2005). *Post-Patten Reflections on Patten. Public Lecture 8th June*. Queens University Belfast.

Kilcommins, S., O'Donnell, I., O'Sullivan, E., and Vaughan, B. (2004). *Crime, Punishment and the Search for Order in Ireland*. Dublin Institute of Public Administration.

Lawther, C., and Hearty, K. (2021). 'Through the Looking Glass: Memory, Myth and Policing the Past'. *Policing and Society*, 32(7),1–15.

Loader, I., and Mulcahy, A. (2003). *Policing and the Condition of England: Memory, Politics and Culture*. Oxford University Press.

Martin, R., and Bradford, B. (2021). 'The Anatomy of Police Legitimacy: Dialogue, Power and Procedural Justice'. *Theoretical Criminology*, 25(4), 559–577.

Mazerolle, L., Bennett, S., Antrobus, E., and Eggins, E. (2012). 'Procedural Justice, Routine Encounters and Citizen Perceptions of Police: Main Findings from the Queensland Community Engagement Trial'. *Journal of Experimental Criminology*, 8(4), 343–367.

McEvoy, K., Gormally, B., and Mika, H. (2002). 'Conflict, Crime Control and the "Re"-construction of State/Community Relations in Northern Ireland', in *Crime Prevention and Community Safety*, G. Hughes, E. McLaughlin, and J. Muncie (eds.) 183-212, Open University Press.

McGarry, J. (2004), 'The Politics of Policing Reform in Northern Ireland', in *The Northern Ireland Conflict*, J. McGarry and B. O'Leary (eds.). Oxford University Press.

McGarry, J., and O'Leary, B. (2004). *The Northern Ireland Conflict*. Oxford University Press.

McGarry, K., Redmill, D., Edwards, M., Byrne, A., Brady, A., and Taylor, M. (2017). 'Punishment Attacks in Post-Ceasefire Northern Ireland: An Emergency Department Perspective'. *The Ulster Medical Journal*, 86(2), 90–93.

McGloin, J. M. (2003). 'Shifting Paradigms: Policing in Northern Ireland'. *Policing: An International Journal of Police Strategies and Management*, 26(1), 118–143.

Mulcahy, A. (2006). *Policing Northern Ireland: Conflict, Legitimacy and Reform*. Willan Publishing.

Mulcahy, A. (2008). 'Community Policing in Contested Settings: The Patten Report and Police Reform in Northern Ireland', in *The Handbook of Knowledge-Based Policing: Current Conceptions and Future Directions*, T. Williamson (ed.), 371-403. Wiley-Blackwell.

Murphy, S. (2008). 'The Role of Emotions and Transformational Leadership on Police Culture: An Autoethnographic Account'. *International Journal of Police Science and Management*, 10(2), 165–178.

O'Donnell, I., and O'Sullivan, I. (2001). *Crime Control in Ireland: The Politics of Intolerance*. Cork University Press.

Or Commission. (2003). Official Summation of the Or Commission Report. *Jewish Virtual Library*. Retrieved from: www.jewishvirtuallibrary.org/the-official-summation-of-the-or-commission-report-september-2003

Pehrson, S., Devaney, L., Bryan, D., and Blaylock, D. (2017). 'Beyond Group Engagement: Multiple Pathways from Encounters with the Police to Cooperation and Compliance in Northern Ireland'. *PLoS ONE*, 12(9), 1–20.

Ramadi, K. B., Srinivasan, S., and Atun, R. (2019). 'Health Diplomacy through Health Entrepreneurship: Using Hackathons to address Palestinian-Israeli health concerns'. *BMJ Global Health*, 4(4), 1–7.

Reiner, R. (2000). *The Politics of the Police*, 3rd edition. Harvester Wheatsheaf.

Reisig, M., Bratton, J., and Gertz, M. (2007). 'The Construct Validity and Refinement of Process-Based Policing Measures'. *Criminal Justice and Behavior*, 34(8), 1005–1028.

Robinson, S. (2003). 'Local Struggle, National Struggle: Palestinian Responses to the Kafr Qasim Massacre and Its Aftermath, 1956–66'. *International Journal of Middle East Studies*, 35(3), 393–416.

Ruane, J., and Todd, J. (1996). *The Dynamics of Conflict in Northern Ireland*. Cambridge University Press.

Scarman, Lord. (1972, April). *Violence and Civil Disturbances in Northern Ireland in 1969*, Cmd. 566. HMSO.

Shearing, C. (2000). 'A New Beginning for Policing'. *Journal of Law and Society*, 27(3), 386–393.

Shearing, C. (2001). 'A Nodal Conception of Governance: Thoughts on a Policing Commission'. *Policing and Society: An International Journal*, 11(3–4), 259–272.

Shvarts, S., Davidovitch, N., Seidelman, R., and Goldberg, A. (2005). 'Medical Selection and the Debate over Mass Immigration in the New State of Israel (1948–1951)'. *Canadian Bulletin of Medical History*, 22(1), 5–34.

Smith, D. (2016). 'New Challenges to Police Legitimacy', in *Transformations of Policing*, A. Henry and D. J. Smith (eds.), 273–305. Routledge.

Smyth, J. (2002). 'Community Policing and the Reform of the Royal Ulster Constabulary'. *Policing: An International Journal of Policing Strategies and Management*, 25(1), 110–124.

Sunshine, J., and Tyler, T. (2003). 'The Role of Procedural Justice and Legitimacy in Shaping Public Support for Policing'. *Law and Society Review*, 37(3), 513–548.

Tyler, T. (2003). 'Procedural Justice, Legitimacy, and the Effective Rule of Law'. *Crime and Justice*, 30(1), 283–357.

Tyler, T. (2006). *Why People Obey the Law*. Princeton University Press.

Tyler, T. (2011). 'Procedural Justice Shapes Evaluations of Income Inequality: Commentary on Norton and Ariely'. *Perspectives on Psychological Science*, 6(1), 15–16.

Van Damme, A. (2017). 'The Impact of Police Contact on Trust and Police Legitimacy in Belgium'. *Policing and Society*, 27(2), 205–228.

Weitzer, R. (1985). 'Policing a Divided Society: Obstacles to Normalization in Northern Ireland'. *Social Problems*, 33(1), 41–55.

Weitzer, R. (1995). *Policing under Fire: Ethnic Conflict and Police–Community Relations in Northern Ireland*. State University of New York Press.

Zoabi, H. (2017). *Crime in the Arab Society: Negligence in Police Work*. A Report Presented to the State Comptroller.

6

CHURCH–STATE RELATIONS IN US PRISON RELIGION

An Update with Recommendations

Michael Hallett

Introduction

This chapter offers a summary of the changing role of religion in US prisons. While religious programs offer powerfully transformative access to social capital for many prisoners, the growing prominence of religious volunteers with program authority over inmates warrants further study and deliberation. As under-resourced correctional facilities come to increasingly rely upon religious volunteers for delivering services to prisoners, research on the constitutionality of faith-based programs in prisons has not kept pace with the growing diversity of programs. Drawing from site-based research, this chapter explores how religion may serve as an emancipatory resource for prisoners as opposed to one that is oppressive, colonialist, and full of paternalism. To profile these concerns, the growing role of religious penal voluntarism in maximum security prisons is highlighted and a response to four constitutional concerns is offered: lack of state neutrality toward religion, excessive state entanglement with religious service providers, inadequate solicitation of alternative programming, and a de facto measure of coercion in delivery of services. The chapter concludes with recommendations for helping assure religion in prisons serves as an emancipatory resource for prisoners.

Angola: America's Largest Maximum-Security Prison

That America's largest maximum-security prison is still named after the former slave plantation upon which it stands, is a fact not lost upon many of its self-proclaimed Christian inmates. Louisiana State Penitentiary at Angola is an encampment of five separate prisons nestled upon 18,000 acres of fertile delta farmland, made so by the centuries of Mississippi River mud water that regularly floods its terrain. Surrounded along its northern, western, and southern boundaries by the

DOI: 10.4324/9781003276593-8

Mississippi River and closed off along its eastern perimeter by the Tunica Hills, correctional officers from Angola's "escape team" boast that "if we don't catch 'em, the snakes and the gators will." Despite having thought deeply about the connections between state religion and the history of American slavery, many Angola prisoners fervently embrace Christianity.

Today, over 85% of Angola's inmates are Black. The prison retains its name from an era when slaves from the western region of Africa known as "Angola" plowed its fields. The name stuck. Today, the plantation's plowing is done by Angola's adjudicated prisoners, a practice legally authorized by the 13th Amendment, which abolished slavery and indentured servitude, literally "except as punishment for a crime." Angola is not only America's largest maximum-security prison complex, it is also arguably America's toughest prison, at least in terms of sentence length: 90% of Angola's inmates die on-site while serving natural life terms. Louisiana's 2020 incarceration rate of 1,094 per 100,000 citizens makes Angola part of a state prison system that confines roughly double the national average of 664 citizens per 100,000. Louisiana's incarceration rate is the nation's highest (Prison Policy Initiative, 2020).

Many of Angola's prisoners come to embrace religion while incarcerated, particularly what they refer to as a "Bapticostal" hybrid version of nondenominational Christianity. Religion has long been practiced at Angola, with prisoner-built churches on its grounds dating back to convict leasing and before. Today Angola hosts a unique Christian seminary inside its gates, founded by religious volunteers in the aftermath of the federal government's revocation of Pell Grant eligibility for convicted felons in 1994. After visiting the Angola compound and learning about the vibrant religious lives of many of its prisoners, New Orleans Baptist Theological Seminary (NOBTS) responded to a call from Angola's warden, who sheepishly invited them to "come on campus" to offer some courses. NOBTS faculty today describe Angola's seminary students as among their most dedicated and talented (Hallett et al., 2017). This chapter offers an account of the religious lives of Angola's long-term prisoners and how religious practice can be emancipatory for inmates.

Religion as a Structural Charity

While prisoners retain their constitutional right to practice the religion of their choosing and to express themselves in religious ways, prison administrators are constrained from promoting a religious orthodoxy within their institutions (Hallett et al., 2019). A fine balance must be maintained between the religious sentiments of prisoners on-site and the constitutional rights of staff and diverse inmates. As a result of these strictures, individual prison facilities maintain highly place-bound and ecumenical religious identities. Due to the fiscal and other constraints facing most prisons today, however, religious volunteers and private religious parachurch organizations have gained novel levels of access to and influence over daily prison life. Programs designed, funded, and operated by religious volunteers are now routinely administered inside American prison facilities, funded by private religious organizations. Volunteers make decisions over program admission, content, terms of participation, and enrollment. Many correctional facilities remain so seriously challenged by staff turnover and lack of resources, that prison administrators are eager to invite religious volunteers inside their facilities to do so. In many prisons it is not uncommon for outside religious organizations and volunteers to offer the only sustained programming available to prisoners (Johnson, Hallett, & Jang, 2021).

While having faded from national prominence since the heyday of faith-based programming during the administration of President George W. Bush, prison administrators enduring sustained budget cuts have happily continued to accept resources from private religious organizations including everything from musical instruments to ceiling fans to educational programming inside prisons (Hallett, 2006). That religious voluntarism has today become a prominent staple of correctional budgeting is well documented, as correctional administrators and state legislators capitalize upon religious volunteers as a means of reducing correctional budgets and achieving cost savings (Hackworth, 2012; Corcoran, 2014). As noted by the *Washington Post* in 2004 regarding the transformative budgetary impact of Florida's faith-based correctional agenda:

> As Florida has slashed spending for prison rehabilitation programs, money is not flowing from the state to religious groups. It is flowing from religious groups to the state. Enthusiastic state officials believe this novel arrangement will reduce recidivism and save taxpayer money. While touting its faith-based approach, Florida has chopped funds for chaplaincy, eliminating 13 full-time chaplains and 60 support staff from its 52 prisons last year.
>
> *Cooperman, 2004*

Disrupting the "Failed State" Prison Model

As a result of the growing centrality of religious voluntarism in American prisons, new questions about church–state relations have also emerged (Sullivan, 2009). Meanwhile, conditions and safety inside prison institutions have continued to deteriorate. It would be hard to overstate the challenges currently facing the American prison system. Rampant violence, extremely high levels of offender recidivism, mounting taxpayer cost, and difficulty retaining employees typify recent headlines from the world of American "corrections" (Kaufman, 2019; Alper et al., 2018; USDOJ, 2020). It is also clear that prisons do little to meaningfully correct offenders' past behavior, nor do they deter future offending (Alper et al., 2018; USDOJ, 2020). Many American prisons have become so violent that they comprise what Cambridge University prison scholar Alison Liebling calls "failed state" institutions. In "failed state" institutions, not even the most basic levels of safety and security can be provided by authorities (Liebling, 2017). "Failed state" institutions not only cause more human damage than they prevent, but they produce emotionally crippled citizens and elevate the likelihood of reoffending after release

(Gilligan & Lee, 2004). New research from the non-partisan Sentencing Project in Washington, DC, moreover, highlights the likelihood that "mass incarceration" will remain a permanent feature of American society (Ghandnoosh, 2020). In short, the American prison system is badly broken and in need of both new resources and new paradigms. Over the past 20 years, religious volunteers have been actively providing both of these, while gaining new levels of access as well. In the midst of the challenges described above, a new, more collaborative model of correctional programming is quietly taking hold in the United States. This model draws upon innovative work inside some of America's largest and most violent prison environments, established through new partnerships with religious voluntary organizations and groups of volunteers (Johnson, Hallett, & Jang, 2021). These new approaches are being developed primarily at maximum-security prisons, which have long remained under-resourced until lethal violence boils over and costly litigation gleans new funding.

Put differently, in the face of the realities facing them, prison administrators have become increasingly open to "outsourcing" rehabilitation programs such as drug treatment and education to religious volunteers as a form of de facto correctional privatization (Hallett, 2006; Hallett, 2001). In the process, new stakeholders are helping prison administrators redefine correctional practice. In an increasingly large number of prison facilities, religious programming offered by unpaid volunteers is now the dominant source of inmate programming. In what is fast becoming a nationwide model, religious educators and faith-motivated volunteers are now operating in at least 27 states and over 70 US maximum-security prisons nationwide (Johnson, Hallett, & Jang, 2021). Such religious voluntarism promotes an alternative model of penal help – "restorative corrections" – one that strategically deploys the lived experience of carefully selected prisoners under the nomenclature of the "wounded healer," with the goal of cooperatively transforming American corrections to be more transparent, effective, and collaborative. Research documents an overwhelming desire among citizens serving time in prisons to achieve redemption and who harbor a genuine willingness to follow a path toward earned forgiveness and social acceptance only to encounter a profound lack of opportunities for achieving these goals (Stansfield & Mowen, 2018).

The Complexities of Religious Establishment in US Prisons

> The "establishment of religion" clause of the First Amendment means at least this: Neither a state nor the Federal Government can set up a church. Neither can it pass laws which aid one religion, aid all religions, or prefer one religion over another. Neither can it force nor influence a person to go to or to remain away from church against his will or force him to profess a belief or disbelief in any religion. No person can be punished for entertaining or professing religious beliefs or disbeliefs, for church attendance or nonattendance. No tax in any amount, large or small, can be levied to support any religious activities or institutions, whatever they may be called, or whatever form

> they may adopt to teach or practice religion. Neither a state nor the Federal Government can, openly or secretly, participate in the affairs of any religious organizations or groups and vice versa.
>
> *Justice Hugo Black, Everson v. Board of Education, 1947*

Despite robust evidence of their programmatic effectiveness for lowering misconduct and improving mental health, previous litigation over religious programming in prisons has resulted in the closure of faith-based programs on constitutional grounds (Sullivan, 2009). Volunteer religious partnerships with prison administrators have proliferated faster than research can be conducted. While religious programs in US prisons offer powerfully transformative access to social capital for many prisoners, religious programs have also been found to be unconstitutional, containing programmatic elements judged to be exclusionary, coercive, and to violate strictures against governmental "establishment" and "endorsement" of religion (Sullivan, 2009; Ward, 2006). This chapter discusses related concerns regarding how religious programs in prisons can become emancipatory resources for prisoners while avoiding coercion, lack of neutrality, excessive state entanglement, and inadequate solicitation of a diverse range of religious volunteers.

"Working with what we've got": Navigating Pitfalls of Religion in US Prisons

A complex matrix of factors helps determine religious practices in individual prisons, including but not limited to statutory differences governing inmate programming, the doctrinal beliefs of available volunteers, and levels of staffing in relation to overcrowding. Because of this substantial variation, exacerbated by the federated nature of the American criminal justice system featuring one federal and 50 different state departments of correction, "the devil is in the details" regarding the constitutionality of faith-based programs (Branham, 2008). In short, religious programming in prisons is by no means a "one-size-fits-all" proposition, with correctional leaders having to work with what they have got. A broad disparity in institutional readiness and access to resources for religious programming has created a correspondingly wide variation in types of religious voluntarism. As with other forms of correctional privatization, little oversight and a system of ad hoc contracting structures a wide variety of efforts. While keeping diverse beliefs and available resources in mind, wardens must navigate many pitfalls when seeking to capitalize upon religious voluntarism. Prison administrators may, under certain circumstances, place limitations upon inmates' religious practices, specifically those over which "legitimate penological interests" are served (i.e., protecting safety). While there are obvious compelling governmental interests in prohibiting some practices associated with religious worship in prisons—for example, not allowing Sikhs to obey a commandment that they carry daggers—the US Constitution also sets limits on how restrictions over worship may be imposed by correctional authorities.

When religion is restricted, a two-pronged test is used to safeguard the religious liberty of prisoners: first, demonstration of a compelling state interest to justify any restriction; and, second, an assessment of whether these means are the *least restrictive* available for doing so (Branham, 2004). Unless a compelling state interest can be demonstrated, prisons must not "unreasonably" interfere with or substantially burden a prisoner's right to free exercise of religion when there are reasonable means of accommodating it (Kosiak, 2021). Prison administrators must not be "arbitrary or irrational" when seeking to balance legitimate penological objectives with inmates' religious freedom, while also being mindful of the impact policies have on staff and other inmates (Anderson, 2007). Administrators must accommodate a wide range of religious practices and beliefs, including allowing religious intermediaries from the outside, material articles of faith such as prayer beads and sacred texts, as well as requests from practitioners for resources from non-mainstream faiths. Given that available resources for accommodating divergent religious practices among prisoners are often limited, however, and given that a central dimension of religious worship is that it is often corporate in nature, correctional administrators often find themselves accused of having unduly restricted and/or having privileged one religion over another. Allegations of privileging access to locally or even culturally dominant religious groups are commonplace from inmates (Branham, 2008). While "free exercise" suits brought by prisoners are the most common, alleging unconstitutional restrictions upon inmate worship, Establishment Clause suits challenging prison administrators' "establishment" and "endorsement" of religion are also on the rise (Kosiak, 2021).

When seeking to provide meaningful worship opportunities for prisoners, wardens often face irreconcilable circumstances of too few volunteers amid simultaneous allegations of favoring one faith over another. For example, the US Supreme Court has ruled that correctional administrators must assure Buddhist prisoners have comparable opportunities for religious practice as their Christian peers, that prison administrators must meet the "exceptionally demanding" standard of consistently using the "least restrictive means" when prohibiting inmates' religious practice, and that accommodations must be provided to meet the religiously motivated dietary and grooming proclivities of inmates holding disparate religious beliefs (Kosiak, 2021). Thus, while religion provides prisoners and prisons great benefits, religion in prison also introduces burdens and legal risks.

Testing for Religious Establishment and Free Exercise of Religion in US Prisons

With regard to governance of religion inside correctional settings, "what has proven to be an arduous struggle" for the US Supreme Court has culminated in the adoption of three distinct but overlapping tests of Establishment Clause parameters: the Lemon Test, the Endorsement Test, and the Coercion Test (Branham, 2004; Cates, 2005). In the Supreme Court case *Lemon v. Kurtzman, 403 U.S. 602* (1971), exploring the issue of government funding of religious schools as an Establishment Clause concern, three requirements for assessing religious establishment were articulated as the *Lemon Test*. Elements of the Lemon Test also figure prominently in evaluating the constitutionality of religion in public prisons. Statutes providing for religious practice in public institutions face three tests and, by dictum, help set standards for religious programming in prisons:

1. The statute must have a secular legislative purpose (Purpose Prong).
2. The principal or primary effect of the statute must not advance nor inhibit religious practice (Effect Prong).
3. The statute must not result in an "excessive government entanglement" with religious affairs (Entanglement Prong) (Kosiak, 2021, 139).

Endorsement Test

While in *Lemon* the Supreme Court established boundaries for governmental engagement with religious activity, subsequent litigation placed further limitations upon the extent to which governmental authorities can "endorse" religious activity. In the *Endorsement Test*, "actions that would be perceived by the reasonable observer as reflecting governmental endorsement of religion contravene the Establishment Clause" (Branham, 2004; Cates, 2005). According to this test, a government action is invalid if it creates a perception in the mind of a reasonable observer that the government is either endorsing or disapproving of religion. As Justice Sandra Day O'Connor put it, "at the heart of this test is a revulsion for state-created orthodoxy in religious matters," particularly one that may positively or negatively be "relevant to a person's standing in the political community" (Branham, 2004).

Coercion Test

Finally, a subsequent elaboration of Establishment Clause jurisprudence occurred with the *Coercion Test*. In the context of litigation over administrator-led prayer in public schools, the Coercion Test "proscribes governmental compulsion to adhere to or disavow certain religious tenets or to engage in or refrain from engaging in certain religious practices" in what a reasonable observer may conclude is "state-created orthodoxy" of religion or nonreligion (Branham, 2004). "Courts employing the coercion test analyze state action to determine whether it subtly or directly coerces individuals to participate in religious activity"(Fields, 2005, 546). While some have interpreted the Coercion Test as redundant to the intention of the Establishment Clause, coerciveness is a widely cited concern among critics of faith-based correctional programs (Anderson, 2007). Combined with the Lemon Test and Justice Sandra Day O'Connor's endorsement or disapproval criteria, the Coercion Test examines the presence of *undue pressure* in specific contexts to either participate or not participate in religious activity. Importantly, the jurisprudence surrounding coerciveness in Establishment Clause cases relies upon a contextual analysis of "all options available to the relevant actors" and their ability to make a "true private choice" to participate (or not) in religious activities (Anderson, 2007). Such "true private choices" require a diversity of programs from which to choose, rather than only a limited number of well-resourced but narrowly sectarian programs. Administrative inducements to openly pray at a school assembly, for example, have been interpreted by the US Supreme Court as unduly coercive (Kemp, 2007). A lack of freely available and equivalent alternative programs for US prisoners has also figured prominently in previous litigation over prison religion.

> There are three ways in which faith-based prisons or prison units may unconstitutionally coerce inmates to participate in religious exercise: 1) offering inmates a safer environment; 2) offering participants better opportunity for parole; 3) offering inmates a much higher quality of life than available alternatives provide. If inmates lack a 'genuine alternative choice' among relatively adequate substitutes, courts should hold that the faith-based prison unit violates the Establishment Clause. *Fields, 2005, 541*

In using volunteer hours and donations of time, money, clothing, food, educational materials, and program delivery, many US prisons have, in practice, become dependent upon religious volunteers as a form of structural charity (Hallett et al., 2017). As state legislatures continue to underfund prisons, leaving them in often dysfunctional condition, religious volunteers have increasingly stepped in to serve prisoners behind bars (Johnson, Hallett, & Jang, 2021). A growing number of programs modeled loosely after the Angola prison seminary have quickly developed in the United States, all featuring diverse uses of "inmate ministry," wherein training of prisoners in various aspects of ministry attempts to supplant laid-off chaplains and prison counselors. At no cost to prisons or prisoners, such programs have increasingly taken leading roles in many large American prisons. As a result of these innovations, however, and on the basis of the religious credentials provided to them within the prison, many US prisoners find themselves directly involved in constitutionally untested forms of "inmate ministry" that have yet to surface in the courts (Johnson, Hallett, & Jang, 2021).

Prisons are regulated spaces of public life, in constant evolution from within and without. Overreliance upon religious structural charity, however, especially for providing access to rehabilitative services for prisoners, has uniquely privileged Christian educational institutions for lack of other volunteers. It was congressional revocation of Pell Grant eligibility for convicted felons in 1994, however, that caused this innovation, and Pell Grant revocation is still the most frequently cited rationale used by prison administrators to justify on-site installation of religious education programs (Hallett, 2019). Such heavy reliance upon religious voluntarism poses new challenges for correctional administrators in regard to their constitutionality. While it appears many programs are quietly being shut down or stripped of religious content prior to full implementation due to concerns about religious

Establishment or Endorsement, this leaves prisoners themselves with few if any resources for personal development and arguably violates the religious freedom rights of inmates desirous of religious education in prison and who voluntarily make a "true private choice" to enroll in the programs (Fields, 2005). While more research is needed to confirm the constitutionality of religious programs within prisons, a number of steps can be taken to help assure that they conform to legal strictures against Establishment and Endorsement of religion.

Making Religion Emancipatory in Prison: Adequately Fund Prison Operations

As mentioned above, much of contemporary innovation in religious programming in US prisons stemmed from the revocation of Pell Grant eligibility for convicted felons by Congress in 1994. Fearing increased violence in his prison due to the loss of collegiate education as an incentive for good behavior, then-Angola warden Burl Cain actively sought out religious volunteers to help manage his prison. Each of the constitutional concerns mentioned above can be remedied by the provision of adequate secular programming and rehabilitative care by the state. Eager to bring resources to their prisons, correctional leaders often find themselves in the position of being beggars, not choosers. Wardens must take what they can get in terms of volunteers willing to assist, resulting in a de facto "privileging" of some faith groups over others in ways that are perceived to be biased and not "neutral" toward religion. As authorities strive to assist their religious volunteers in running programs that are safe and effective, they invariably also become "entangled" in religious activity in such a way that literally constitutes both "establishment" and "endorsement" of religion. Adequate provision of alternative resources can help assure that religious programs are only some among many and that they do not come to dominate inmate programming by default. More importantly, as a result of having multiple program options provided by the state, prisoners will be less likely to experience informal pressure to adopt religion.

Publish Annual "Report Cards": Documenting Religious and Rehabilitative Neutrality

As a de facto form of prison privatization, religious voluntarism in US prisons now frequently involves direct supervision of prisoners by volunteers who are not correctional employees. Like other forms of correctional privatization, this "outsourcing" of inmate programming to non-state actors includes no meaningful oversight and very little transparency. To facilitate transparency in religious programming and robust solicitation of ecumenical religious and secular rehabilitative programming, departments of corrections should publish the items listed in Table 6.1 below. These report cards should include an annual religious climate survey soliciting inmate feedback, a full listing of programs and budgets, as well as annual "confirmation reporting."

TABLE 6.1 Annual reporting requirements for religious programmes in prisons

Item Published and Reported per Facility	*Annual Status Reporting Requirement*
Annual Survey of Prison Religious Climate Completed/Published	Yes/No
All Religious Prison Sponsors/Programs/Enrollment Published	Yes/No
All Secular Prison Sponsors/Programs/Enrollment Published	Yes/No
All New Prison Programs Solicited/Sponsors Published	Yes/No
Annual Report of Program Enrollment/Dropout Rate Published	Yes/No
Description of Inmate Religious Work Activity Published	Yes/No
Annual Confirmation Reporting Published	
Religious Work Requirement of Religious Graduates?	Yes/No
Confirm Full List of Active Prison Voluntary Organizations Published	Yes/No
Confirm No Doctrinal Affiliation Required for Enrollment/ Practice Published	Yes/No
Confirm No Loyalty Oath Required for Enrollment/Practice Published	Yes/No
Confirm No Sexuality Oaths Published	Yes/No

Prison Religion as Ecumenical, Multicultural, and Multigenerational

> I think it is one of the tragedies of our nation, one of the shameful tragedies that 11:00 am Sunday morning is one of the most segregated hours if not the most segregated hour in American life.
>
> *Dr. Martin Luther King Jr.*

For many prisoners, religious practice not only provides a momentary escape from prison life, but it offers help for redefining and reclaiming their lives, even under oppressive conditions. The most striking feature of "church in prison" is the robustly interracial character of the "congregation." As Dr. Martin Luther King Jr. pointed out in 1960, American religious practice is nothing if not racially segregated. By necessity, religious worship in prison, however, is both racially integrated and remarkably ecumenical. To witness the sign of the cross and hear a call-and-response during one and the same ceremony—sometimes even from the same practitioner—is not uncommon. For long-time inmate religionists, cross-fertilization of worship becomes a normalized practice, with inmate lifers often referring to themselves as "Bapticostal" or "Catholipalean." Religion in prison is characterized by an enforced non-hierarchical ecumenism amid diverse forms of religious practice in what must be a doctrinally neutral space. In many respects, religion in prison is practiced more openly and ecumenically than in the outside world. In part because of the above-mentioned strictures prohibiting establishment of a religious orthodoxy, divergent practitioners and non-believers intermix and are regularly accommodated amid faithful inmates. Perfectionism in faith and the performative gestures that often accompany corporate worship on the outside, are simply nonexistent in prison. By definition, everyone here has fallen and often confesses as much. Indeed, confessional practice is a central part of the successful treatment of addiction (LeBel et al., 2015). Religion can also be anti-colonial:

> *For a long time I thought there were two systems of justice. But in studying the Bible in prison—especially in this particular prison, Angola—I have come to see there are not two systems of justice, but one system of injustice. While this system treats everyone differently, it treats no one properly. Empires divide people so they can't see how much they have in common. That's their method. I came to this understanding through reading the Bible, which is all about empire. But Jesus took personal responsibility for fixing a broken Empire, through His own unique method: face to face lovingkindness. I had to learn that lesson for myself. That love matters most. So I decided that's what I'm going to do. I'm going to do what the Empire cannot possibly do: I'm going to live out of love and not fear. As a result of that, even though I'm still incarcerated, I left prison many years ago.*
>
> *Graduate, Angola Prison Seminary*

Religion in Prison Encourages Starting Over

Religious practice in prison emphasizes religion's private dimension. Steeped in the 12-step theologies of addiction recovery programs, in which *finding God as one understands God* is the task, many prisoners adopt surprisingly tolerant views concerning the religious doctrines of their peers. Prison religion is preoccupied with the meeting of immediate spiritual and sometimes physical needs. Prisoner prayer groups, Bible studies, outside church volunteer groups, yoga practitioners, Buddhist meditation leaders, and many others all sometimes combine to create uniquely intensive religious environments. Unfortunately, however, many religiously motivated volunteers fear going inside prisons, leaving predominantly Evangelical volunteers to the task.

But participation in voluntary religious communities in prisons sponsored by outside organizations infuses the lives of prisoners with social capital that would otherwise be inaccessible to them (Lafferty et al., 2015). Small-group prayer in prison, for example, has been shown to be highly prosocial and highly transformative in practice (Maruna et al., 2006). Decades of criminological research document the salutary benefits of religious programming for both prisoners and prisons. Religious programs in prison reduce social isolation and shame among prisoners, offering emotional and network pathways that help support re-biographing and fresh starts. Even modest interventions such as attending volunteer-led Bible studies in prison have been found to be associated with significant recidivism reduction following release from prison (Johnson et al., 2021).

Perhaps the most important key to success of religious volunteers' rehabilitation efforts is their embrace of the "wounded healer" model, which prioritizes peer-to-peer relationships in counseling and rehabilitation. Since the 1950s, criminologists have recognized the particular effectiveness of previously convicted citizens helping offenders reform. Faith-based and addiction-focused programs have been especially active in utilizing peer-based rehabilitative programming. Former addicts are often recognized by those in recovery as the most effective drug treatment counselors, not because they have academic credentials in addiction therapy, but because they possess direct experience in overcoming the challenges of addiction (LeBel et al., 2015). Inmate peer ministry programs view the offending pasts of prisoners as only one aspect of a prisoner's entire life story—as a place to start over. Cultivating holistic understandings of personal biographies that highlight positive aspects of inmates' past lives, introduces new opportunities for shaping prosocial self-identities while mitigating the shame and isolation common to prison life. Importantly, the benefits of peer counseling are also recognized as being *bi-directional*, that is, bearing fruit for both those receiving help as well as for those offering it. Indeed, peer-mentors often view themselves as the real beneficiaries in their relationships with offenders.

Conclusion: Accompaniment versus Indoctrination

Perhaps one of the most illuminating settings to observe the power of religion in American life is from within its sprawling prison system. Insofar as prisons are state-run institutions and religion is also regulated by the state, prisons offer a unique vantage point from which to consider the function of religion in American life. This chapter suggests the boundaries and uses of prison religion are important to explore, both to gain understanding of its impact upon prisoners as well as to highlight its lessons for prison reform. To profile concerns about constitutionality and religious freedom in prison amid the rapid growth of religious programming in prisons, however, the growing role of religious penal voluntarism in maximum security prisons has been highlighted. A response to the four constitutional concerns discussed above was offered, suggesting that robust reporting and oversight of religious activity in prison can help assure it remains truly voluntary and effective.

In a prison system that has become an irrationally punitive and unimaginative human dumping ground, correctional leaders have turned to religious volunteers. Many institutions today offer services to fewer than 10% of their prisoners. American corrections is in a state of crisis, bankrupt in its results, and failing both society and American taxpayers. Inmates emerge from America's prisons only to reoffend at higher rates than before, with the majority being reincarcerated within five years. Put simply, America's prison system not only fails to be "correctional," but it is in fact criminogenic. Today, religious volunteer service organizations are once again becoming mainstay components of correctional operations. Not only is cost-free religious programming a growing feature of prison life, but correctional administrators find it useful for reasons of accessibility, ease of use, and appeal to inmates. "An enormous variety of religion is everywhere in US prisons," writes Winnifred Sullivan. "Religion facilitated by prison chaplains, various external organizations, and groups attached to large conglomerates of the world religious traditions, as well as every form of small-scale and new religious movement" (Sullivan, 2009, 14). As a result of this religious privatization of prisons, more robust reporting and oversight requirements are necessary. Religious volunteers are transforming American corrections, but questions remain about the constitutionality of how they are doing so. Improved transparency can mitigate these concerns.

References

Alper, M., Durose, M. R., & Markman, J. (2018). 2018 Update on Prisoner Recidivism: A 9-Year Follow-Up Period (2005–2014). US Department of Justice, Office of Justice Programs. Bureau of Justice Statistics.

Anderson, M. (2007). The constitutionality of faith-based prison programs: A real world analysis based on New Mexico. *University of New Mexico Law Review, 37*(3), 487–532.

Branham, L. (2004). Go and sin no more: The constitutionality of governmentally funded faith-based prison units. *University of Michigan Law Review, 37*, 291–352.

Branham, L. (2008). The devil is in the details: A continued dissection of the constitutionality of faith-based prison units. *Ave Maria Law Review, 6*(2), 409–444.

Cates, P. (2005). Faith-based prisons and the establishment clause: The constitutionality of employing religion as an engine of correctional policy. *Willamette Law Review, 41*, 777–826.

Cooperman, A. (2004, April 25). An infusion of religious funds in Florida prisons. *The Washington Post*. Retrieved from: www.washingtonpost.com/archive/politics/2004/04/25an-infusion-of-religious-funds-in-fla-prisons/

Corcoran, M. (2014). The trajectory of penal markets in an age of austerity: The case of England and Wales. *Sociology of Crime, Law and Deviance, 19*, 53–74.

Cullen, F.T., Jonson, C., & Nagin, D.S. (2011). Prisons do not reduce recidivism: The high cost of ignoring science. *The Prison Journal, 91*(3), 48S–65S.

Erzen, T. (2017). *God in captivity: The rise of faith-based prison ministries in the age of mass incarceration*. Beacon Press.

Fields, R. (2005). Perks for prisoners who pray: Using the coercion test to decide Establishment Clause challenges to faith-based prison units. *University of Chicago Legal Forum, 2005*(I), Article 15, 541–567.

Ghandnoosh, N. (2020). *US prison decline insufficient to undo mass incarceration*. Sentencing Project.

Gilligan, J., & Bandi, L. (2004). Beyond the prison paradigm: From provoking violence to preventing it by creating "anti-prisons" (residential colleges and therapeutic communities). *Annual Review of the New York Academy of Science Journal, 2004*, 1036–1065.

Hackworth, J. (2012). *Faith based: Religious neoliberalism and the politics of welfare in the United States*. University of Georgia Press.

Hallett, M. (2001). Faith-based corrections as symbolic crusade. *Humanity & Society, 25*(3), 219–238.

Hallett, M. (2006). *Private prisons in America: A critical race perspective*. University of Illinois Press.

Hallett, M. (2019). Confronting Christian penal charity: Neoliberalism and the rebirth of religious penitentiaries. *Social Justice, 45*(1), 99–119.

Hallett, M., & Bookstaver, M. (2017). "We serve forgotten men": Structural charity vs religious freedom in serving ex-offenders. In: K. Kerley (ed.) *Religion in prison, 58-72*. Praeger.

Hallett, M., Hays, J. Johnson, B., Jang, S.J., & Duwe, G. (2017). *The Angola Prison Seminary: Effects of faith-based ministry on identity transformation, desistance, and rehabilitation*. Routledge.

Hallett, M., Johnson, B., Hays, J., Jang, S.J., & Duwe, G. (2019). US prison seminaries: Structural charity, religious establishment, and neoliberal corrections. *The Prison Journal, 99*(2), 150–171.

Johnson, B., Hallett, M., & Jang, S.J. (2021). *The restorative prison: Essays on inmate peer ministry and prosocial corrections*. Routledge.

Kaufman, C. (2019). Solutions to a national problem: Correctional officer turnover in the U.S. *Policy Perspectives: George Washington University's Online Policy Journal*. Dec 18, 2019.

Kemp, M. (2007). Blessed are the born again: An analysis of Christian fundamentalists, the faith-based initiative, and the establishment clause. *Houston Law Review, 43*, 1523–1561.

Kosiak, D. (2021). *Legal aspects of corrections*. Jones & Bartlett Publishing.

Lafferty, L., Chambers, G.M., & Guthrie, J. (2015). Indicators of social capital in prison: A systematic review. *Health Justice, 3*, 7.

LeBel, T.P., Richie, M., & Maruna, S. (2015). Helping others as a response to reconcile a criminal past: The role of the wounded healer in prisoner reentry programs. *Criminal Justice and Behavior, 42*(1), 108–120.

Liebling, A. (2017). Appreciative inquiry, generative theory, and the "failed state" prison. In J. Miller and W. Palacios (Eds). *Qualitative research in criminology: Advances in criminological theory*. Transaction Publishers, pp. 251–269.

Maruna, S., Wilson, L., & Curran, K. (2006). Why God is often found behind bars: Prison conversions and the crisis of self-narrative. *Research in Human Development, 3*, 161–184.

Prison Policy Initiative. (2020). *Louisiana Profile*. Retrieved from: www.prisonpolicy.org/profiles/LA.html

Stansfield, R., & Thomas, M. (2018). Religious involvement, moral community and social ecology: New considerations in the study of religion and reentry. *Journal of Quantitative Criminology, 35*, 493–516.

Sullivan, W.F. (2009). *Prison religion: Faith-based reform and the Constitution*. University of Chicago Press.

US Department of Justice (USDOJ). (2020). US Justice Department Files Lawsuit against the State of Alabama for Unconstitutional Conditions in State's Prisons for Men. Press Release: USDOJ Dec 9 2020. Retrieved from: www.justice.gov/opa/pr/justice-department-files-lawsuit-against-state-alabama-unconstitutional-conditions-states

Vera Institute of Justice. (2017). The price of prisons. Retrieved from: www.vera.org/publications/price-of-prisons-2015-state-spending-trends;

Ward, C. (2006). Coercion and choice under the Establishment Clause. *William & Mary Law School Scholarship Repository, 39*, 1621–1667.

7

"BELIEVING" IN YOUTH JUSTICE

Gary Manders

Introduction

A world-view perspective is proposed in this chapter as a potent tool for effective practice within youth justice, based on research from an examination of the belief systems of 40 children in conflict with the law in two youth offending teams (YOTs) located in the Midlands area of England. The purpose of this research was to explore how the interplay between beliefs and values and behaviour generates possibilities for change away from offending. It was specifically focused on the importance of an engagement with the perceptions and values of young offenders in seeking to work effectively with them towards rehabilitation and desistance, with its application for improving practice in youth justice. This approach corresponds with the priorities of YOTs to effectively support the desistance, safety and well-being needs of children and young people through personalised and coordinated implementation and delivery of services (YJB, 2014; Hampson, 2018). It places centrally the significance of listening to the voices of children especially when they are expressing their beliefs and values about how they see the world and in them seeking meaningful change (Haines and Case, 2015, p.45).

This chapter will first explore how an appreciative inquiry of a young person's world view can be framed as a fusion of horizons, arising from a good quality of conversation about their beliefs and values. It then turns to examine the concept of world view, followed by how this can be applied to open up the conversation about the nature of a good life, the future self and the influence of good role models. These themes are illustrated through some narratives of young offenders.

Appreciatively Seeing the World through the Eyes of the Other

The world-view perspective involves both the fusion and expansion of horizons, drawing on Nielson's (2013) interpretation of Gadamer's dialogical model of

DOI: 10.4324/9781003276593-9

understanding to explore the relational dynamics between a practitioner and a child in trouble with the law under statutory supervision. A young person's horizon refers to their culturally and historically formed interpretative grid through which they see and navigate the world, which is not fixed but fluid and mutable (Nielsen, 2013, p.2). The process of perceiving the other's experience and view of the world involves a dialogical encounter of openness, what Taylor (2002, p.127) describes as a "coming to an understanding with an interlocutor". Through empathic listening and discussion, "we allow the other person to enrich and expand our own horizon" (Nielsen, 2013, p.22). There is an expansion of vistas created from the fusion of two people's horizons. Each person's view of the world can be delicately examined, their horizon and prejudices laid bare, opening up possibilities for change. This is achieved through practitioners' growing religious literacy, "the[ir] ability to engage in a good quality of conversation about religion and belief [or the child or young person's Worldview]" (Dinham, 2012, p.6). Religious literacy means possessing "the knowledge and skills to recognise religious faith as a legitimate and important area for public attention" (Dinham & Jones, 2010, p.16) in a pluralistic society. It should not exclude the non- religious or secular (see Lee, 2015). There is a need to acknowledge the complexity of religions, how internally diverse they are, and that they evolve and change over time and religious influences are embedded in all dimensions of human experience (Moore, 2016, p.37).

The competencies of religious literacy are beneficially realised through taking an adapted appreciative inquiry approach (AAI), which examines both the positive and the negative aspects of religion, spirituality and world views more comprehensively. Traditionally, appreciative inquiry is a positive, strengths-based change approach usually applied to organisations and their development and extended to research (Cooperrider, Whitney, & Stavros, 2008). AAI takes a middle path between the extremes of rejecting religion tout court and embracing an idealistic and extreme dogmatism. After all, a partial view of religion or spirituality will lead to a distorted and misleading perspective, which does not do justice to the complexities involved. It does not mean ignoring the shadow side of religion or the criticisms of religious faith. Additionally, AAI avoids a sectarian or anti-religious bias. A more beneficial encounter and balanced view of reality is being endorsed, taking a lead from the positive criminology perspective of Ronel and Elisha (2011). Spirituality has often been framed as the positive construct (Wolfer, 2012) in contrast to the negative idea of religion (Wong & Vinksy, 2009), whereas Bernard Moss (2012) seeks a rebalancing of the assumption that religion is primarily bad, advocating that the "dark side" of both religion and spirituality is balanced and contrasted with the positive, or "Wow!" side. While religion has been implicated in oppressive practices, it can also be a resource for positive change (Thompson & Moss, 2021).

An AAI approach promotes authentic and respectful dialogue, what has been termed "moral conversations" (Manders, 2015). This means listening carefully to the young person or practitioner's lived experience of religious faith and then being able to gently challenge their perceptions. This would be conducted as part of the supervisory relationship for young people or as part of the research process for both young people and practitioners. There needs to be space to tune into what religion means for the children and young people supported in youth justice. Supervisees need to be encouraged to examine their own perspectives and biases, and to reflect and grow in awareness. In James Fowler's (1995) *Stages of Faith* research, he found that people move through a journey of faith, involving an early stage of certainty often espoused in fundamentalism, to more critical and open-minded belief systems as time progresses/with the passage of time. It is also worth considering how practitioners' religiosity and beliefs inform their professional practice. Our own sense of "self-location" is important in critical practice because who we are and where we come from, affects our values, assumptions and perspectives.

Thompson and Moss (2021, p.11) delineate spirituality as "what we do to give expression to our chosen Worldview". This chapter views religion, spirituality, faith and belief as coterminous with the broader concept of world view containing a person's "beliefs and values about life" (Sheldrake, 2013). It employs the notion of "lived religion" with its focus on how it is practiced and how religion is experienced and encountered in different environments; and its starting point for analysis is the activities and interpretations of individuals (McGuire, 2008).

The Concept of a World View

Everyone has a world view that they inhabit because it is a shared human phenomenon, requiring an understanding of how world views operate in human life. This is the position adopted by the Commission on Religious Education (CoRE/RE) in their proposal for reframing the study of RE in UK schools (CoRE, 2018) with a world-view paradigm as opposed to the world religion paradigm. CoRE's definition is:

> A Worldview is a person's way of understanding, experiencing and responding to the world. It can be described as a philosophy of life or an approach to life. This includes how a person understands the nature of reality and their own place in the world. A person's worldview is likely to influence and be influenced by their beliefs, values, behaviours, experiences, identities and commitments.
>
> *CoRE, 2018, p.4*

It is an eminently sensible proposition, given the pluralistic world in which we live, although it has caused some objections, deftly confronted in Cooling, Bowie and Panjwani's (2020) report *Worldviews in Religious Education*. They advance a fluid and open understanding of world views in contrast to a sealed box and strictly propositional conception. There are identifiable world views, but personal experience of being part of a particular world view may be very diverse. A young person's world view constitutes their underlying system of basic assumptions, "beliefs and values" about their view of life and the nature of being and reality (Koltko-Rivera, 2004). Naugle (2002) has provided a seminal history of the development of this concept, where a world view incorporates: an interpretation of reality, a view of the nature of being, an ideal for living, and a sense of one's immersion in the world. World views are both personal and organised. Cooling et al. (2020, p. 44) define a personal world view as "an individual's own way of understanding and living in the world, which may or may not draw from one, or many, institutional worldviews".

A recent multi-site study of religious conversions to Islam in prison, comprising 279 Muslim prisoners in England, Switzerland and France, has used a world-view construct to understand different types of Islam and Islamism. World views are defined in their study as "integrated ways of being in and knowing the world" (Wilkinson et al. 2021, p.5). Drawing on the work of Naugle (2002), "A Worldview represents the aspiration of the person to form a consistent idea of the self and its relationship to the world together with a concomitant way of behaving in the world" (Wilkinson et al. 2021, p.5). World views involve a dynamic and evolving process of complex conceptual construction; they can shift and change with ongoing lived experience and across the lifespan as people grow and interact with the world.

Schiltz et al. (2011) describe a world view as "the ways in which we make sense and meaning of the world around us" grounded in our values and beliefs. These are the filters through which young people see, know and sense the world and their place in it. As Schlitz et al. (2011) state: "A Worldview combines beliefs, assumptions, attitudes, values, and ideas to form a comprehensive model of reality. In our Worldviews, we construct complex conceptual frameworks to organize our beliefs about who we are and about the world we live in" (Schlitz et al., 2011, n.p.). These function in similar ways to internal working models elaborated by Bretherton and Mullholland (1999) and affect our perceptions and behaviour. While a distinction can be made between religious and non-religious world views, a world view is here considered inclusive of both positions, because the dialectic relationship between the two is fundamental. The approach taken here is to learn about young persons' world views with reference to the lived experience of these adherents.

Research Methodology

This research made use of a narrative-biographical approach, similar to a life story and a life history methodology (Atkinson, 1998). The interview schedule was created using an adapted version of Crossley's (2003) *Narrative Psychology*, drawing on the work of McAdams (1997). It was augmented with aspects of Fowler et al.'s (2004) faith development model. Both purposive and convenience sampling were used to obtain the cohort of research participants. Interviews were conducted between 2009 and 2010 with 40 young offenders in two YOTs in the Midlands area of England. The interviews were transcribed and coded thematically to identify key issues in exploring young people's world views (Braun & Clarke, 2006). Names and places were pseudonymised to ensure anonymity and confidentiality. Ethical approval was received from both local authorities involved and from the University of Birmingham ethics committee. While some years have elapsed since my initial research was undertaken, there have not been any similar studies conducted in youth justice, which supports the validity of the research findings.

Future Orientation and the Knack of Leading a Good Life

One of the functions of a world view is to provide "an ultimate vision of what people should be striving for in their lives" (Pargament & Parks, 1995, p.15) and the strategies to reach those ends. A world-view perspective will examine perceptions about future orientation, identifying specific factors that can encourage and motivate change away from offending and the adoption of positive values. It will also explore factors that will mitigate against positive change. It is contended that an understanding and acceptance of what constitutes a "good life" as a life worth living can provide a focus and motivation for change in attitudes and behaviour. The aim is to help young people in conflict with the law cultivate the knack of leading a good life, which means "to develop more personally meaningful and fulfilling lives by attending to their individual interests, abilities, and aspirations" (Fortune, 2018, p.24). The interrelationship of identity, beliefs and values and behaviour generates possibilities for change. Identity refers to the type of person a young offender perceives themselves to be and wishes to become, and the kind of life they are leading and see themselves leading. A good life relates to Markus and Nurius' (1986; 1987) concept of possible selves as representations of one's self in future states: how young offenders see themselves in the future. This is based on the distinction between the current existing identity of an individual and the person they would like to be and not be in the future. It incorporates an awareness of how young people tend to frame their motivation to change, indicating the kinds of selves to be approached or avoided.

The change process involves contemplation of a possible self as a non-offender as the initial impetus for change in contrasting a bleak future of further offending. An offender's increasing dissatisfaction with their life provides the initial impetus for change. According to these authors, the notion of "possible selves represent[s] individuals' ideas of what they might become, what they would like to become, and what they are afraid of becoming" (Markus & Nurius, 1987, p.157). The feared self refers to the fear of further offending, committing more violence and the attendant negative consequences of going to prison, fear about getting back on drugs alongside negative perceptions of the self/negative self-concepts. There are real concerns that young people in conflict with the law may not be able to find meaningful work because of criminal records, and whether it will be possible to achieve success and make a change in their lives. Young offenders' aspirations to achieve positive goals are related to bringing their current lives more in alignment with their hoped-for selves (Islelin et al., 2012). There are some indications that positive self-identity inhibits crime and assists with efforts to desist from crime. As Hunter and Farrall (2018, p.292) assert, "a 'blue-print' of a non-offending future self assists desistance by providing a goal towards which the individual can work (Giordano et al., 2002;

Hunter, 2010)". It makes them aware of the possibilities for change, offering a "goal to be striven for and a guide to behaviour" (Hunter & Farrall, 2018, p.304).

Matthew is a 14-year-old white male who attends Boy's Brigade, a Christian youth organisation and admits that he drifts into offending because of boredom, messing around, mischief and nuisance. His peer group also heavily influences him. Matthew believes the good life is about avoiding crime, social harm and about doing good:

> *Take out all bad things and that would be a good life. Take out like crime, drugs, just got to believe things can be better. If done something bad, you're not gonna start crying about it, you just gotta get on and fix what you have done wrong and make it correct.*
>
> *Matthew, 14/Christian*

It is also about self-improvement and putting things right by acknowledging and working to resolve what a person has done wrong. He also expresses hope that things can be improved.

Young offenders display a sense of wanting to achieve primary human goods, that is: "valued aspects of human functioning and living" (Ward & Mann, 2004, p.600). This refers to a core assumption of the good lives model as a strengths-based rehabilitation framework (Ward & Maruna, 2007); that is, all human beings strive to meet and accomplish similar basic needs and aspirations in their life (Emmons, 1999; Deci & Ryan, 2000). These include 11 primary goods: life (healthy living and functioning), knowledge, excellence in work (mastery experiences), excellence in play (autonomy and self- directedness), inner peace (freedom from emotional turmoil and stress), friendship (relationships, intimate and family relationships), community, spirituality (in the broad sense of finding meaning and purpose in life), pleasure and creativity (Ward and Gannon, 2006, p.79). The process of change involves assisting the young person to acquire the capacities (skills, knowledge, opportunities and resources) to fulfil these needs through prosocial means, without causing harm to others or themselves. This is based on an understanding of criminal behaviour as a young person's attempt to meet these primary needs through inappropriate or maladaptive means. Ultimately, the good life is about achievement and goal attainment. Goals are a concrete expression of future orientation and life purpose. There is a need to help young people revise their goals, standards and priorities as a strategy for human flourishing (Frisch, 1998).

Joshua is a 17-year-old black male from a Christian background, who highlights the contradictions at the heart of the idea of a good life. What is the source and nature of the good that is being envisaged?

Joshua: See me, if I was to take up a religion, you know what religion I would take up? I would turn Muslim, that is a strong religion. Everyone just lives a good life in that religion.

What is a good life?

> *A normal life, I dunno [...] People just have a nice life, no trouble innit. For some people, it's doing crime-gangsta life. Living smartly. My idea of a good life would be getting a good job. I want to get into construction or one of them things, have my own plumbing company or something, a van.*
>
> *Do you want to have a family?*
>
> *Joshua: Them kind of things I don't really think about. I just make sure that I am alright at the moment. Until I am alright then I can start thinking about them other things. I have got to make sure I have money to look after myself, got somewhere to live, got somewhere to sleep, something to eat and if I can do that for myself, then I can aim for higher. I could provide for my kids, provide for my girlfriend. Provide for whoever. (Joshua, 17/Christian background)*

A good life can be a religiously motivated life or a standard law-abiding or conventional life, but arguably, a "gangsta life" despite the perception of it being a "good" is not a virtuous or worthwhile life. On what basis do we make such judgements in a pluralistic context? This invites a thoughtful conversation based in moral philosophy and the cultivating of conscience; building a moral compass and understanding of what is morally good and worthwhile. This requires encouraging the development of "[young people's] ability to refine and evaluate their telos [goal or purpose/ evolving aspirations], their conception of what it means to be live excellently" (Bohlin, 2005, p.20). Joshua is being supported to reflect critically on imperfect versions of the telos and inspired to a clearer understanding of what that moral vision ought to be. It involves deliberate ethical evaluation about certain actions being objectively right and wrong, better or worse than others. The process enables the young person to contemplate "where they are headed and why?", to acquire "the internal disposition to see and choose well among competing claims or appeals," in order to consider what is the best possible life to lead (Bohlin, 2005, p.18). A moral framework including our beliefs about right and wrong forms part of one's world view. An ethical explanation of crime appreciates that both internal and external factors have a role to play in influencing people's criminality.

The Necessity of Good Role Models

Role models are a central means of helping young people achieve the good life (Lockwood et al., 2002). They serve as moral exemplars for the young person to follow and look up to as an example of how to be a good person. These are people who live out a certain lifestyle that is inspirational in some way, reflecting a possible self they could become. They display care for the young person and believe in them, something that is reciprocated by the young person. This could be a family member, a religious leader like an imam or even a youth justice practitioner. Ronel and Elisha (2011, p.310) underline how exposure to positive values for adolescents at risk of deviance expanded their egocentric world view after meeting volunteers who offered them help. The crux of the moral life is to see the good with a clear vision because one's egotistical desires are contained, thus allowing a more wholesome response to the world (Murdoch, 2007, 376–7). These are the glimpses of goodness observed by the young people through their relationships and interactions with their role models. A distinction needs to be made between someone a young person admires and someone they wish to emulate (Ben Ze'ev, 2003) if transformation is to take place, as Kristjánsson (2006) demonstrates. Harpreet is a 17-year-old currently placed in local authority care because of issues of domestic violence at home and having committed an offence of robbery. She is from a Sikh background but has converted to Islam through a partner with whom she committed this offence. She commented:

> *I feel strongly about working with people who need help and I feel strongly about people on drugs, they need someone they can speak to like an advocate. Like people like me they need someone like my manager [manager of the residential home]. I want to be one of them type of people. If I believe I can do that and believe that within myself that I am that person to be like her then I am gonna do it. I know I believe in myself. She just listens and is here for the kids and not for the money. I have never met anybody like her. She is just amazing, everything she does, she has done so much for us. She can suss out when I am upset even if I don't cry or say anything. She can suss when I am really tired. She knows me really well and has only been here about three months. I think she knows me better than my mum.*
>
> *Harpreet, 17/Sikh-Muslim*

Here is a residential social worker who is embodying a positive lifestyle and attitude, representative of moral virtue in Aristotelian terms – a moral exemplar. The idea of a moral exemplar is to waken oneself to one's higher self, a higher ideal to which to aspire, to enable Harpreet "to arrive at an articulate conception of what [she] values and wants to strive towards and help [her] find realistic means to that end" (Kristjánsson, 2006, p.41). The manager possesses an ethic of care, empathy and an ability to engage with young people through building authentic relationships, someone whom this young person desires to emulate rather than learning to merely imitate an ideal person. Harpreet is expressing more than admiration. She articulates a desire to be like her manager in some way, but without enviously wishing to take anything away from her. The manager is somebody whose qualities she wishes to instantiate in her own life. Harpreet wants to find herself deserving of the goods she desires. She wants to "be like her" in her ethic of care to become an advocate for other young people, but "not to be exactly like [her] but in the capacity to be provoked by [her] example [...] of how a fulfilling life can be lived and what it involves" (Kristjánsson, 2001, p.7). It is an example of generativity, a concern and commitment for promoting the development and well-being of others. Harpreet fervently believes she can actualise the qualities she sees embodied in the life of the manager of her residential home, but she cannot just do this without making an effort to acquire the admired qualities. This involves self-understanding and rational self-persuasion to move towards achieving these goods. It makes it easier for people to become virtuous (a good person) if they are exposed to virtuous people (McNeil & Farrall, 2013).

Kai is a 17-year-old mixed-race young person with some Christian religious involvement while growing up, who started to enquire about Islam in prison through the influence of his cousin who was serving a long custodial sentence for armed robbery and had recently converted to Islam. He was encouraged by the imam to attend Koranic classes and shown how to pray. This could be seen to be the inception of creating a new pious, non-criminal self (van Nieuwkerk, 2014) and the desire to give up criminal behaviour.

> *I don't pray five times a day, not all the time. Sometimes I do [...] Most of the time I did when I was inside [...] I do know the prayers in Arabic, taught from other inmates, Muslim brothers innit. I know about prayers and wuzu [ritual cleansing].*

Kai talked about his religious practice in prison, such a prayer offering a reflexive management of the self as a method of dealing with the pains of imprisonment. This concurs with recent research that people chose to practice Islam in prison for reasons of piety, emotional coping and for good company (Wilkinson et al., 2021).

> *It is a bit scary [in prison][...] people turn to religion in prison to have someone to speak to, like when they feel down and out, so you go to someone to speak to and ask for forgiveness and them things.*
>
> *Kai, 17/Muslim*

The regular performance of these practices requires concerted effort and demonstrates it is difficult to sustain without the support of like-minded others and the right environment, underlining the effects of good company. This raises the issue of how faith communities can support the reintegration of ex-prisoners back into society and their journey of desistance (Kotzé, 2013).

Discussion and Conclusion

A world-view perspective allows children in conflict with the law to understand their emerging identity: "who am I?", and to evaluate how they show up and relate to the world around them: "how am I living?" and "what matters to me?" It provides a framework to explore young peoples' underlying beliefs and values, and the connections between beliefs and behaviour. Practitioners are encouraged to explore the actual belief structures of young people, in order for them to answer two fundamental questions as key components of their world view: "who do I want to be?" and "how do I want to live?" The young person is sensitised to the process of change through imagining "possible selves" and envisaging a better future without crime in the exercise of what constitutes a good life. This enables adolescents "to make sense of, their past in order to move forward with a clearer sense of how they would ideally like to live their lives" (Deering & Evans, 2021, p.3175). It is a process of instilling hope that change is both possible and beneficial. Exposure to positive human values through interactions with role models promoting goodness, empathy and care leads to constructive outcomes for young people. It can result in changes in self-identity and growth in virtue (Ronel & Elisha, 2011).

Barbara Wintersgill (2019, pp.2–3) offers a useful summary of world views. She identifies six big ideas for use in religious education that are pertinent to an understanding of how world views develop and function in human life and can be extended to the youth justice context. They are: 1. Continuity, Change and Diversity; 2. Words and Beyond; 3. A Good Life; 4. Making Sense of Life's Experiences; 5. Influence and Power; 6. The Big Picture. World views of young people "involve interconnected patterns of beliefs, practices and values. They are also highly diverse and change in response to new situations and challenges" (Wintersgill, 2019, p.2). It is often difficult for young people to express their deepest beliefs and feelings using everyday language, and they may use figurative language and non-verbal forms of communication such as art, music and drama to seek to explain or illustrate their ideas or experiences. Young people strive to live according to what they understand as a good life, and religious and non-religious world views provide guidance on how to be a good person and live a good life. World views help individuals interpret their experiences. World views mutually "interact with wider societies and cultures" (Wintersgill, 2019, p.2) both simultaneously affecting and affected by each other. World views often provide a grand narrative about how and why the world is as it is and offer a critique and vision of a good society. Making use of organised world views, young people often interpret, construct and apply the constituent elements of world views personally.

An examination of a young person's beliefs and values opens up the possibilities for transformation, which corresponds with a core concern of youth justice to influence and support change away from offending. It enables a deeper appreciation of how religion or belief can inform and develop young people's sense of identity and increase their desire for a better way of being or of living. Indeed, this valuable tool for change endorses the promotion of a good life as a life lived well in a positive and pro-social direction and examines how this is to be built in practice.

References

Atkinson, R. (1998) *The Life Story Interview*. SAGE.

Ben-Ze'ev, A. (2003) Aristotle on emotions toward the fortune of others. In D. Konstan & N.K. Rutter (Eds) *Envy, spite, and jealousy: the rivalrous emotions in ancient Greece*. Edinburgh University Press, pp.99–121.

Bohlin, K.E. (2005) *Teaching Character Education through Literature*. Routledge Falmer.

Braun, V., & Clarke. V. (2006) Using thematic analysis in psychology, *Qualitative Research in Psychology*, 3(2), 77–101. www.tandfonline.com/doi/abs/10.1191/1478088706qp063o

Bretherton, I., & Munholland, K.A. (1999) Internal working models in attachment relationships: A construct revisited. In J. Cassidy & P.R. Shaver (Eds) *Handbook of attachment theory, research and clinical applications*. Guildford Press, pp.89–114.

Commission on Religious Education (2018) *Religion and worldviews: The way forward.* Retrieved from: www.commissiononre.org.uk/wp-content/uploads/2018/09/Final-Report-of-the-Commission-on-RE.pdf

Cooling, T., Bowie, B., & Panjwani, F. (2020). Worldviews in Religious Education. Retrieved from: www.theosthinktank.co.uk/cmsfiles/Worldview-in-Religious-Education---FINAL-PDF-merged.pdf

Cooperrider, D. Whitney, D., & Stavros, J. (2008) *Appreciative Inquiry Handbook: For Leaders of Change* (2nd ed.). Crown Custom Publishing.

Crossley, M. (2003) *Introducing Narrative Psychology: Self, Trauma and the Construction of Meaning.* Open University Press.

Deci, E.L., & Ryan, R.M. (2000) The "what" and "why" of goal pursuits: Human needs and the self-determination of behavior. *Psychological Inquiry*, 11, 227–268. https://doi.org/10.1207/S15327965PLI1104_01

Deering, J., & Evans, J. (2021) Lost in translation or a work in progress? Developing Desistance-informed youth justice practice in the Welsh context. *The British Journal of Social Work*, 51(8), 3172–3189. https://doi.org/10.1093/bjsw/bcaa209

Dinham, A. (2012) A public role for religion: On needing a discourse of religious literacy. *International Journal of Religion and Society*, 2(4), 1–12; 291–302.

Dinham, A., & Jones, S. (2010) Religious Literacy Leadership in Higher Education: An Analysis of Challenges of Religious Faith, and Resources for Meeting them, for University Leaders, Religious Literacy Leadership in Higher Education Programme, York. Retrieved from: https://research.gold.ac.uk/id/eprint/3916/1/RLLP_Analysis_AW_email.pdf

Emmons, R.A. (1999) *The Psychology of Ultimate Concerns.* Guilford Press.

Fortune, C.A. (2018) The Good Lives model: A strength-based approach for young offenders. *Aggression and Violent Behaviour*, 38, 21–30. https://doi.org/10.1016/j.avb.2017.11.003

Fowler, J. (1995) *Stages of Faith: The Psychology of Human Development and the Quest for Meaning.* Harper Collins.

Fowler, J., Streib, H., & Keller, B. (2004) *Manual for Faith Development Research.* Emory University.

Frisch, M.B. (1998) Quality of life therapy and assessment in health care. *Clinical Psychology: Science and Practice*, 5(1), 19–40. https://doi.org/10.1111/j.1468-2850.1998.tb00132.x

Haines, K., & Case, S. (2015) *Positive Youth Justice: Children First, Offenders Second.* Policy Press.

Hampson, K.S. (2018) Desistance approaches in youth justice – The next passing fad or a sea-change for the positive? *Youth Justice*, 18(1), 18–33. https://doi.org/10.1177/1473225417741224

Hunter, B., & Farrall, S. (2018) Emotions, future selves and the process of desistance. *The British Journal of Criminology*, 58(2), 291–308. https://doi.org/10.1093/bjc/azx017

Iselin, AM.R., Mulvey, E.P., Loughran, T.A. et al. (2012) A longitudinal examination of serious adolescent offenders' perceptions of chances for success and engagement in behaviors accomplishing goals. *Journal of Abnormal Child Psychology*, 40, 237–249. https://doi.org/10.1007/s10802-011-9561-z

Koltko-Rivera, M.E. (2004) The psychology of worldviews. *Review of General Psychology*, 8(1), 3–58. https://doi.org/10.1037/1089-2680.8.1.3

Kotze, J. (2013) Developing collaborative and sustainable networks of social support – Community chaplaincy, faith communities and the successful reintegration of ex-prisoners. *International Journal of Community Chaplaincy*, 2(1), 3–13.

Kristjánsson, K. (2001) The didactics of emotion education. *Analytic Teaching*, 21(1), 5–15. https://citeseerx.ist.psu.edu/viewdoc/download?doi=10.1.1.484.7138&rep=rep1&type=pdf

Kristjánsson, K. (2006) Emulation and the use of role models in moral education. *Journal of Moral Education*, 35(1), 37–49. https://doi.org/10.1080/03057240500495278
Lee, L. (2015) *Recognizing the Non-religious: Reimagining the Secular.* Oxford University Press.
Lockwood, P., Jordan, C. H., & Kunda, Z. (2002) Motivation by positive or negative role models: Regulatory focus determines who will best inspire us. *Journal of Personality and Social Psychology*, 83(4), 854–864. https://doi.org/10.1037/0022-3514.83.4.854
Manders, G. (2015) Moral conversations and askesis as tools for change within youth justice. *Safer Communities*, 14(2), 69–79. https://doi.org/10.1108/SC-05-2015-0015
Markus, H., & Nurius, P. (1986) Possible selves. *American Psychologist*, 41(9), 954–969. https://doi.org/10.1037/0003-066X.41.9.954
Markus, H., & Nurius, P. (1987) Possible selves: The interface between motivation and the self-concept. In K. Yardley & T. Honess (Eds), *Self and identity: Psychosocial perspectives.* John Wiley & Sons, pp. 157–172.
McGuire, Meredith B. (2008) *Lived Religion: Faith and Practice in Everyday Life.* Oxford University Press.
McNeill, F., & Farrall, S. (2013) A moral in the story? Virtues, values and desistance from crime. In M. Cowburn, M. Duggan, A. Robinson, & P. Senior (Eds) *Values in criminology and community justice.* Policy Press, pp.147–164.
Moore, D.L. (2016) Diminishing religious literacy: Methodological assumptions and analytical frameworks for promoting the public understanding of religion. In A. Dinham & M. Francis (Eds) *Religious literacy in policy and practice.* Policy Press, pp. 27–38.
Moss, B.R. (2012) The pedagogic challenge of spirituality: A "co-creative" response. *Journal of Social Work*, 12(6), 595–613.
Murdoch, I. (2007) *The Sovereignty of the Good.* Routledge.
Naugle, D.K. (2002) *Worldview: The History of a Concept.* Eerdmans.
Nielsen, C.R. (2013) Hearing the other's voice: How Gadamer's fusion of horizons and open-ended understanding respects the other and puts oneself in question. *Otherness Essays and Studies*, 4(1), 1–25. Retrieved from https://otherness.dk/fileadmin/www.othernessandthearts.org/Publications/Journal_Otherness/Otherness__Essays_and_Studies_4.1/Gadamer_on_Hearing_the_Other_s_Voice.pdf
Pargament, K.I., & Park, C.L. (1995) Merely a defense? The variety of religious means and ends. *Journal of Social Issues*, 51(2), 13–32. https://doi.org/10.1111/j.1540-4560.1995.tb01321.x
Ronnel, N., & Elisha, E. (2011) A different perspective: Introducing positive criminology. *Internal Journal of Offender Therapy and Comparative Criminology*, 55(2), 305–325.
Schlitz, M., Vieten, C., Miller, E.M., Homer, K., Peterson, K., & Erickson-Freeman, K. (2011) The Worldview Literacy Project: Exploring new capacities for the 21st century student. John's Hopkins University School of Education. *New Horizons for Learning* 9(Winter)(1).
Sheldrake, P. (2013) *Spirituality: A Very Short Introduction.* Oxford University Press.
Taylor, C. (2002) Gadamer on the human sciences. In R.J. Dostal (Ed) *The Cambridge companion to Gadamer.* Cambridge University Press, pp. 126–142.
Thompson, N., & Moss, B. (2021) *The Spirituality and Religion Practice Manual.* Avenue Media Solutions.
van Nieuwkerk, K. (2014) "Conversion" to Islam and the construction of a pious self. In L. Rambo & C.E. Farhadian (Eds). *The Oxford handbook of religious conversion.* Oxford University Press, pp. 667–686.
Ward, T., & Gannon, T.A. (2006) Rehabilitation, etiology, and self-regulation: The comprehensive good lives model of treatment for sexual offenders. *Aggression and Violent Behavior*, 11(1), 77–94. https://doi.org/10.1016/j.avb.2005.06.001

Ward, T., & Mann, R. (2004) Good Lives and the rehabilitation of offenders: A positive approach to sex offender treatment. In P.A Linley & S. Joseph (Eds) *Positive psychology in practice*. John Wiley and Sons, pp. 598–616.

Ward, T., & Maruna, S. (2007) *Rehabilitation: Beyond the risk paradigm*. Routledge.

Wilkinson, M., Irfan, L., Quraishi, M., & Schneuwly Purdie, M. (2021) Prison as a site of intense religious change: The example of conversion to Islam. *Religions*, 12(3),1–24. https://doi.org/10.3390/rel12030162

Wintersgill, B., with Cush, D. and Francis, D. (2019) Putting Big Ideas into Practice in Religious Education. Retrieved from: http://www.reonline.org.uk/knowing/bigideas-into-practice/

Wolfer, T. A. (2012) Religion, spirituality, health, and social work. In S. Gehlert & T. Browne (Eds) *Handbook of health social work* (2nd ed.). John Wiley & Sons, pp. 263–290.

Wong, Y.L.R., & Vinsky, J. (2009) Speaking from the margins: A critical reflection on the "spiritual-but-not-religious" discourse in social work. *British Journal of Social Work*, 39, 1343–1359.

Youth Justice Board (2014) AssetPlus model document. Retrieved from: https://assets.publishing.service.gov.uk/government/uploads/system/uploads/attachment_data/file/364092/AssetPlus_Model_Document_1_1_October_2014.pdf

8

THE INFLUENCE OF RELIGION ON PROBATION

A Reflection on the Profession

Ioan Durnescu and Gabriel Oancea

Introduction

Although the probation service's place of birth is still in dispute, almost all scholars agree that its ideological roots are in the Christian religion. In its early days, the probation officer was a man of God, 'a man with experience and tact and full of the milk of human kindness' (Jarvis, 1972:8). Consequently, missionaries treated individuals as holders of the 'divine spark'. Moral characteristics of the probation officer were more important than his/her skills. However, compassion, acceptance, empathy and so on were often mentioned as important 'tools' of craft. Still, these 'tools' are found in the professional monographs as the core values of probation practice. This chapter argues that, despite its current secular ideology, probation activity is still animated by strong religious and spiritual values and beliefs such as forgiveness, compassion, acceptance and so on. It is argued that these values have metamorphosed into different principles and standards of practice but retained their core messages that place the individual and his/her uniqueness in the centre of attention.

To do that, we will take a chronological approach in trying to follow up on how this Christian ethos became reflected at different stages of the history of probation, focusing on the literature in the Anglo-Saxon countries. To a certain extent, these developments were mirrored in other global jurisdictions as ideas about probation have diffused globally.

Probation in the Early Days

One of the obligations of Christians is to have an active concern for those in conflict with the law, which is based on the New Testament. In the parable of the final judgment, Jesus tells his disciples to 'inherit the kingdom that has been prepared for

DOI: 10.4324/9781003276593-10

you since the foundation of the world! For I was hungry, and ye gave me meat: I was thirsty, and ye gave me drink: I was a stranger, and ye took me in: I was naked, and ye clothed me: I was sick, and you visited me, I was in prison, and you came to me'. 'The parable reveals the Christian perspective in relation to those incarcerated, who are not essentially seen as criminals but rather as people who need help, such as those who suffer from hunger or are sick' (Nicklas, 2016:51).

Problems related to crime and the rehabilitation of those in conflict with criminal law were to be one of the themes that marked the nineteenth century. The Revolution brought a series of major socio-economic changes, including accelerated urbanization. In a relatively short period of time, there was a massive transfer of population from rural to urban areas on both sides of the Atlantic. Most of the time, the living conditions of the newcomers were precarious, being characterized by overcrowding, unhealthy housing, pollution, lack of sewage systems or access to water so that health problems such as cholera or dysentery were common (Bryson, 2010; Schwarz, De Vries, Johnson, Smith, & Wrightson, 1992).

Also, the political, economic and social phenomena that underlie the process of industrialization required both of communities as well as individuals, often had a negative impact on the latter. Under these conditions, depression, anxiety, suicidal tendencies or substance abuse were common in nineteenth-century metropolises (Allen, 2009; Dooley & Catalano, 1980; Inkeles & Smith, 2013). Alcohol abuse was a social problem, given the technological advances that made it possible to produce alcohol on a large scale, so that alcohol became accessible as a direct consequence of the sharp rise in consumption, especially among the working class in urban areas (Mokyr, 1988; Room, 2013). Described in terms of a real 'social plague', alcohol consumption was presented at the time as being the cause of immoral conduct or crime (Lane, 1974; Levine, 2012). Beyond that, the problems generated by alcohol consumption were likely to cause concern for employers who needed disciplined workers, but also for authorities who were concerned with maintaining social order (Hands, 2018; Roberts, 2019). These are the preconditions for the emergence of the temperance movement in the United States in the early nineteenth century, which highlighted the negative effects of alcohol consumption, promoted abstinence and encouraged the state to adopt stricter regulations on the production and distribution of alcoholic beverages. Similar movements soon occurred in the United Kingdom, Germany, Australia and New Zealand (Gusfield, 1986; Levine, 1992; Murdach, 2009). Almost everywhere the movement had a strong religious foundation; the vectors through which it was promoted were represented by various Protestant churches (Calvinist, Evangelical or Methodist) (Gusfield, 1986).

Living in the new metropolises was also uncertain. Theft, robbery, the trafficking of stolen goods, and murder were commonplace. The authorities faced a rapid increase in crime, and traditional methods of identifying offenders proved ineffective. Thus, sanctioning methods such as flogging, infamy, public executions or penal transportation were subject to criticism and later abandoned (Emsley, 2013; Graff, 1977). The police become professional, and in 1829, the Metropolitan Police Service of London was established. The conditions of detention were re-examined as penitentiaries were overcrowded, failing to offer minimum hygiene conditions and without precise rules for the separation of detainees (McConville, 2015; Porter, 1995). What must be emphasized from the perspective of our approach is the fact that in most cases, reforms were promoted by individuals or charities with deeply religious motives. The pity felt for those who broke the law was the basis for change, whether we are talking about reforms undertaken by Quakers in the United States or by Elizabeth Fry in the United Kingdom (Cooper, 1979; Summers, 1995).

In its turn, the emergence of probation-related practices correlated with the aforementioned reformist ethos.

For some scholars, the origin of probation is found in the initiative of John Augustus, who provided the courts in Boston with the bailout option for petty offenders who were also alcohol abusers. The legal device used in 1829 was the 'binding over for good behaviour' that was a form of temporary release during which the offender had to prove himself worthy of pardon or other lesser sentences (Lindner & Jay, 2006; Panzarella, 2002).

Almost all historians agree that Augustus was a successful businessman in the boot-making industry (Lamar & Owens, 1994). However, what few may know is that he was also a prominent member of the Washington Total Abstinence Society which promoted alcohol abstinence. For the members of this society, alcohol was an obstacle that needed to be removed for the person to be open to God (McWilliams, 1983). It seems that Augustus' activity started in 1841 when he was attending police court to bail out 'common drunkards'. The plan was for the bailed person to appear in court after three weeks as a sober man, accompanied by Augustus, who would vouch for him. By 1858, Augustus had provided bail support for 1,946 persons. Only ten of them seemed to have breached their conditions. Not only that, Augustus provided direct services to the courts and people, but he is recognised as the main spokesman for probation. According to historians, he inspired others such as John Murray Spear in Massachusetts, Lucy Flower in Chicago and Samuel Barrow in New York to use these ideas and promote probation in practice and later in legislation (Lindner & Savarese, 1984).

Soon these generous ideas travelled from the United States to the European continent where the end of the nineteenth century was dominated by what Mair (1997) has called a moral panic about the drinking problem. Following the example of the Washington Total Abstinence Society, the Church of England Temperance Society started to work with police court missionaries to 'save the souls' of those 'drunkards whose foot has once slipped' (Jarvis, 1972:2). The mission of the police court missionaries was exclusively based on 'Christian charity and humanitarian concern' (Jarvis, 1972:1), and their activities were mostly based on visits, the organizing of temperance meetings, restoration, reclamation but also exhortation, persuasion and confrontation (Jarvis, 1972; Vanstone, 2004). These activities, however, were not performed with all 'drunkards'. On the contrary, candidates were selected among those who appeared successful for probation, based on character, age, peers and so on (Auerbach, 2015). That does not mean that missionaries had no hope for all individuals but that different people needed to be exposed to intervention methods in order to find their way back to God. One of the most important beliefs of these missionaries was that every single individual is unique and shares the 'divine spark'.

They All Deserve to Be Saved

As mentioned in one of the London Police Court Mission documents, a man can become a missionary if he is 'a man of God, a man with vocation, a man of character, a man with experience and tact and full of the milk of human kindness' (Jarvis, 1972:8).

Therefore, the origin of probation is very much linked with the religious fervour and the humanistic pressure where missionaries were animated by Christian values of good and bad, abstinence, a second chance for those whose 'foot once slipped', and the firm belief that all people are fundamentally good and share the same 'divine spark'. In this normative context, compassion and acceptance were at the core of any salvation mission (Auerbach, 2015).

Professionalization of Probation

The end of the nineteenth and the beginning of the twentieth century marked a major paradigm shift in social work. Thus, the concern for providing support began to be doubled by an activity to identify the underlying causes of social problems. Also, social work activity was professionalized, and the first educational institutions in the field of social work were created. Although not abandoned, philanthropy now took a back seat. All these changes were based on a change in vision. The economic laissez-faire approach that had dominated the previous period was abandoned, and the socio-economic problems created by the industrial expansion of the nineteenth century forced governments to intervene more actively in infrastructure development, to alleviate social tensions or redistribute wealth. Under these conditions, poverty, for example, was no longer approached from a moral perspective. It was revealed that its causes were a lack of opportunity or how wealth is distributed (Handman et al., 1931; Woodard, 1962).

All these changes from sociology, psychology and criminology were integrated into the practice of social work (Hagood, 1937; Kadushin, 1959).

These transformations were also reflected in the field of probation. Therefore, in 1878, the first public probation service was established in Massachusetts. This trend was maintained at the beginning of the twentieth century, so that in 1925 the National Probation Act was adopted. In the case of the United Kingdom, the drafting of probation legislation took place earlier, with the adoption in 1907 of the Probation of Offender Act (Evjen, 1975; Gard, 2007).

However, this professionalization of the work carried out by missionaries would not bring an immediate change in the specifics of the actual activity carried out by the new professionals. The 'missionary ideal' of the previous century would exert a strong influence, primarily because probation officers hired under the 1907 act were recruited from among former missionaries. Also, the religious beliefs as well as the missionary spirit of the person occupied a central place in the evaluation of the candidate who aspired to occupy the position of probation officer (Whitehead, 2016:154).

Another factor that contributed to the perpetuation of the missionary spirit was the fact that the wage of probation officers was modest, so that the motivation to become a probation officer was the desire to help those in conflict with criminal law (Nellis, 2007).

Although a number of debates began to take place in the probation system regarding the training of probation officers and the scientific basis of their work, the influence of missionaries was maintained until the 1930s, the impact of these measures being questioned. Thus, as mentioned in a report by the Departmental Committee on the Training, Appointment and Payment of Probation Officers, the need for academic training was placed in the background, and considered as much more important were issues related to personal qualities and the following of Christian principles (Bochel, 1976; Whitehead, 2016).

It should also be noted that the law of 1907 subsumed the practice in the probation field of proving the principle of 'advise, assist and befriend'. The ways in which new probation officers worked with those entrusted to their oversight and guidance were not fundamentally different from those of missionaries. They continued to assist those in conflict with the law in court, to visit their homes or to guide them in finding a job (Gard, 2007).

The establishment of the National Association of Probation Officers (NAPO) in 1912 would mark the beginning of a period of shaping the professional identity of probation officers and removing probation from the influence of the Church of England and the temperance movement. From the very beginning, NAPO set out to incorporate scientific advances in the field of practice, these processes culminating in the establishment of the *Probation Journal* in 1929 (Bochel, 1976; Tidmarsh, 2021).

These developments were consolidated after 1925 with the drafting of the Criminal Justice Act, leading to the extension and professionalization of probation, with the new changes (central control, the training of probation officers and the introduction of an inspection system) being likely to raise several concerns about the removal of probation from the missionary ideal. In response to these concerns, Clark Hall, president of NAPO, pointed out in a 1931 article in the *Probation Journal* that: 'it would be the greatest possible disaster to the system were at any time divorced from the religious and idealistic spirit [...] Probation work must be idealistic in spirit' (p.116).

The 1930s, however, were marked by a gradual reduction in the influence of the 'missionary ideal', amid criticism of the 'dual control' exercised over probation officers who were funded by both the state as well as by religious organizations.

In addition, the progress made after 1925 contributed to the creation of probation as a public service, integrated into Home Office structures, so that the involvement of London Police Court Mission missionaries was no longer seen as useful in the new context (Gard, 2012).

This phenomenon of removing probation from its missionary origins was noted in most jurisdictions where probation had arisen as a result of the zeal of philanthropic organizations in rehabilitating those who were in conflict with the law.

The Missionaries' Legacy

Contemporary probation systems have little in common with the probationary work of missionaries. Through a process of 'diffusion and imitation' (Timasheff, 1943), probation spread out to different jurisdictions, amid the challenges that the states were facing in trying to identify sustainable ways to manage crime. This expansion of non-custodial sanctions and their importance in criminal justice systems led to the development of international instruments aimed at establishing a minimum set of rules for member states on issues such as respect for human dignity and the protection of human rights of probationers, staff training, the importance of ensuring adequate funding by states and the importance of a scientifically sound practice.

Given that most probation systems are funded from the public budget, they have had to subsume their activity to some political imperatives (Raynor, 2020; Teague, 2016). Probation systems have therefore had to deal with fundamental changes over the last few decades, including a change in vision, with the rehabilitation of people in conflict with the law subsuming the imperative of strengthening public safety (Dickey & Smith, 1998; Nellis, 1995). The words that seem to describe probation activity in the new context are 'control', 'public safety' and 'intervention'. Also, as a result of the emergence of a managerial vision, probation systems must be subject to a 'vision', their activity being based on 'business strategy'. In these new circumstances, 'advise, assist and befriend' is replaced by 'assess, protect and change' (Ainslie, 2021).

However, we appreciate that the ethos of the early missionaries continues to exist in various forms appropriate to the new context, in the current practice of probation. First, as mentioned (Annison, Eadie, & Knight, 2008; Deering, 2016), despite the efforts of the political factor to make probation an institution focused on 'criminal management', and control of offenders and professional training, there is no conclusive evidence of a fundamental change in the practice of probation staff in current probation activity.

The central element on which intervention in the direction of rehabilitation is based, is the belief in a person's ability to make changes (Mawby & Worrall, 2013). Moreover, the changes made in probation systems in the above-mentioned directions seem to have a rather demoralizing effect, given that bureaucratic activities are perceived as having rather the role of limiting the quality of interaction and intervention with probationers (Farrow, 2004). Under these conditions, a large part of supervision activity is allocated by the probation staff to discussions on ways to improve the lives of supervised persons or to the need to stop criminal behaviour (Brown, 1998). Also, what motivates individuals in choosing a career in the field of probation is primarily their desire to 'help people change'. Issues such as the desire to work in the justice system or to contribute to public safety are subsidiary (Knight, 2007:60).

The first missionaries' desire to help is found again in contemporary probation and volunteer work. They are still considered an important resource in probation systems, and their important role is also emphasized by a number of international probation regulations. For example, Recommendation (2010) 1 regarding probation rules developed by the Council of Europe contains several provisions on how to involve volunteers, emphasizing the importance that should be given to supporting, selecting and allocating resources to volunteer activity. In some systems (e.g. Japan), volunteer work is an essential component in the operation of probation (Akashi, 2018; Watson, 2019).

An important activity developed by volunteers, similar to that of the nineteenth-century missionaries, is their involvement in mentoring programmes. Sometimes mentors may even be people who have previously had problems with criminal law, which they have managed to solve, and thus their personal experience being able to give the people they work with hope that the problems they face can be solved, serving as sources of inspiration in the process of change. This is because people who are on probation often feel powerless, unsuccessful within a group of friends or family, or blamed for the problems they are faced with (Kavanagh & Borrill, 2013). Moreover, mentors can sometimes have more credibility in relation to the people they work with, their authority being much more consistent. Another advantage of mentoring is that mentors typically more time with the people they work with than do the probation staff (Brown & Ross, 2010). Similar to the 'advise, assist and befriend' model, the mentoring relationship involves 'caring, listening and encouraging small steps' (Buck, 2018:14). In these conditions, there is a series of evidence (Jalain & Grossi, 2020; Reingle Gonzalez, Rana, Jetelina, & Roberts, 2019; Sells et al., 2020) that highlights the success of mentoring programmes, in terms of reducing recidivism, solving of problems and so on.

On the other hand, it should be noted that religious organizations continue to play an important role in probation. An example of this is the Salvation Army Church, which cooperates with probation systems in various jurisdictions, providing support services for people released from prison and support for those facing homelessness or addiction problems. In the Netherlands, the Salvation Army Church is even an integral part of the probation system (Aarten, 2019). Faith-based programmes run by churches or religious organizations can also be found as a direct continuation of the efforts of the early missionaries involved in the rehabilitation of those in conflict with the law (Duwe & Johnson, 2013; Duwe & King, 2013).

Another aspect of the practice of contemporary probation that has its roots in missionary activity is the importance of the professional relationship in the process of change. At a time when community resources were limited, as was understanding about the process of changing behaviour, missionaries, through their one-to-one relationship with offenders, were the main drivers of change. Subsequently, this model of practice was marginalized (Burnett & McNeill, 2005), being replaced with structured programmes, motivational interviews, approaches focused on the risk-need-responsiveness model and so on. The last decades, however, have been marked by an emergence of the importance of the professional relationship as a fundamental element of the desistance process. Several studies (Ansbro, 2008; McNeill, 2006; McNeill & Weaver, 2010) have shown that a humane approach, based on empathy, respect for the clarification of roles, a careful approach to the relationship between sanctions and rewards, and confidence in the individual's capacity for changing are fundamental aspects that support the process of change (Trotter, 2015). Research has highlighted the central role of empathy in the rehabilitation process of offenders, an approach that integrates an empathic dimension with a low recidivism rate (Trotter, 1990).

The old/new approaches reinforced in probation a spiritual dimension. When discussing the spiritual dimension, it is considered that, beyond current criminogenic needs related to homelessness, addiction, problems connected to low educational level and so on, it is important for probationers to acquire a meaningful life. Under these conditions, the importance of including in the practice of correctional services a spiritual dimension based on religion, or originating in psychology or psychiatry (for example, logotherapy) is emphasized (Whitehead & Braswell, 2000). One model of practice that integrates the need for meaning in life is represented by the Good Lives Model, according to which problems with criminal law derive from the obstacles that the offender faces in obtaining primary human goods, represented by happiness, skills, friendships and by gaining satisfaction in professional activity. The probation officer must consider in the evaluation and intervention process what are the elements that the offender considers to be primary human goods for him, and failure to take these into account can create frustration and lead to recidivism (Ward & Brown, 2004; Ward, Mann, & Gannon, 2007). More recently, various spiritual elements have been introduced into probation work, such as yoga or mindfulness (Holt, 2015; Kerekes, Fielding, & Apelqvist, 2017)

It should be noted that there is also a reiteration of the importance of the Christian value of forgiveness that should characterize correctional practices. Former offenders are often kept in a situation of marginalization and exposed to the risk of committing offences through a series of provisions relating to the maintenance of unjustifiably long criminal records or exclusion from a role in the labour force market (Lacey & Pickard, 2015).

Conclusion

Probation has its roots in the philanthropic movement that characterized the nineteenth century amid accelerated correlative industrialization and urbanization. As a result of a policy of laissez-faire and a quasi-non-involvement of power in solving social problems, religious organizations were the ones to take the initiative to 'save the souls' of the marginalized. In these circumstances, problems related to alcoholism, crime, lack of shelter and so on were viewed from a moral perspective, which determined that the activity these persons or organizations carried out should take the form of missionary work, the modalities of intervention thus having a strong religious foundation.

These approaches changed at the beginning of the twentieth century amid the involvement of governments in solving social problems but also in the development of the social sciences, which gradually replaced the missionary discourse.

Probation, in turn, went through a process of professionalization and institutionalization, with missionarism being abandoned. However, this did not mean giving up on a series of values and practices that marked the beginnings of probation.

Although the last few decades have been marked by a number of important changes in probation practice (managerialism, risk-based approaches, a focus on community safety etc.), what drives people to pursue a career in probation is still the desire to help those who have broken the law. Contemporary probation systems also continue to benefit from the ethos of community members to get involved in helping offenders through volunteer or mentoring programmes. Moreover, the last decades have witnessed a reversal in the importance of the professional relationship that is established between the probation officer and the offender. Although the mercy of the first missionaries has been replaced by empathy, there is solid evidence that the way the probation officer handles his/her individual interaction with the offender is a key element of the rehabilitation process.

The importance of the spiritual element in the process of change that marked the activity of the first missionaries has in turn been reaffirmed, as the need for a meaning in life is fundamental to each and every individual.

References

Aarten, P. G. (2019). Exploring probation supervision compliance in the Netherlands. *Law & Contemporary Problems, 82*, 227–251.

Ainslie, S. (2021). Probation: what next and who decides? *Probation Quarterly, 21*, 42–45.

Akashi, F. (2018). The role of volunteer probation officers in Japan-Recent challenges and responses. *International Journal of Law, Crime and Justice, 54*, 121–132.

Allen, R. C. (2009). *The British industrial revolution in global perspective*: Cambridge University Press.

Annison, J., Eadie, T., & Knight, C. (2008). People first: Probation officer perspectives on probation work. *Probation Journal, 55*(3), 259–271.

Ansbro, M. (2008). Using attachment theory with offenders. *Probation Journal, 55*(3), 231–244.

Auerbach, S. (2015). 'Beyond the pale of mercy': Victorian penal culture, police court missionaries, and the origins of probation in England. *Law and History Review, 33*(3), 621–663.

Bochel, D. (1976). *Probation and after-care: Its development in England and Wales*: Scottish Academic Press Edinburgh.

Bryson, B. (2010). *At home: A short history of private life*: Transworld.

Brown, I. (1998). Successful probation practice. In D. Faulkner & A. Gibbs (Eds.), *New politics, new probation?* (Probation Studies Unit Report No. 6, pp. 57–76): Centre for Criminological Research, University of Oxford.

Brown, M., & Ross, S. (2010). Mentoring, social capital and desistance: A study of women released from prison. *Australian & New Zealand Journal of Criminology, 43*(1), 31–50.

Buck, G. (2018). The core conditions of peer mentoring. *Criminology & Criminal Justice, 18*(2), 190–206.

Burnett, R., & McNeill, F. (2005). The place of the officer-offender relationship in assisting offenders to desist from crime. *Probation Journal, 52*(3), 221–242.

Cooper, R. A. (1979). The English Quakers and prison reform 1809–23. *Quaker History, 68*(1), 3–19.

Deering, J. (2016). *Probation practice and the new penology: Practitioner reflections*: Routledge.

Dickey, W. J., & Smith, M. E. (1998). *Rethinking probation: Community supervision, community safety*. US Department of Justice.

Dooley, D., & Catalano, R. (1980). Economic change as a cause of behavioral disorder. *Psychological Bulletin, 87*(3), 450.

Duwe, G., & Johnson, B. R. (2013). Estimating the benefits of a faith-based correctional program. *International Journal of Criminology and Sociology, 2*, 227–239.

Duwe, G., & King, M. (2013). Can faith-based correctional programs work? An outcome evaluation of the Innerchange Freedom Initiative in Minnesota. *International Journal of Offender Therapy and Comparative Criminology, 57*(7), 813–841.

Emsley, C. (2013). *Crime and society in England: 1750–1900*: Routledge.

Evjen, V. H. (1975). The federal probation system: The struggle to achieve it and its first 25 years. *Federal Probation, 39*(2), 3–15.

Farrow, K. (2004). Still committed after all these years? Morale in the modern-day probation service. *Probation Journal, 51*(3), 206–220.

Gard, R. (2007). The first probation officers in England and Wales 1906–14. *The British Journal of Criminology, 47*(6), 938–954.

Gard, R. (2012). The creation of a 'fully public service' Probation in England and Wales between the wars. *Probation Journal, 59*(4), 323–338.

Graff, H. J. (1977). Crime and punishment in the nineteenth century: A new look at the criminal. *The Journal of Interdisciplinary History*, 7(3), 477–491.

Gusfield, J. R. (1986). *Symbolic crusade: Status politics and the American temperance movement*: University of Illinois Press.

Hagood, M. J. (1937). Some contributions of psychology to social case work. *Social Forces, 15*(4), 512–519.

Hall, W.C. Religion in probation. *Probation Journal*, July 1931, 1(8), 116.

Handman, M., Usher, A. P., Stocking, G. W., Bladen, V., Mitchell, B., Jaffé, W., … Goodrich, C. (1931). Economic history – The decline of laissez faire. *The American Economic Review, 21*(1), 3–10.

Hands, T. (2018). *Drinking in Victorian and Edwardian Britain: Beyond the spectre of the drunkard*: Springer Nature.

Holt, R. W. (2015). *Investigating the utility of a mindfulness-based intervention with men on probation or parole*: University of Missouri-St. Louis.

Inkeles, A., & Smith, D. H. (2013). *Becoming modern*: Harvard University Press.

Jalain, C. I., & Grossi, E. L. (2020). Take a load off Fanny: Peer mentors in veterans treatment courts. *Criminal Justice Policy Review, 31*(8), 1165–1192.

Jarvis, F. (1972). *Advise, assist and befriend: A history of the Probation and Aftercare Service*: National Association of Probation Officers London.

Kadushin, A. (1959). The knowledge base of social work. In Alfred J. Kahn (Ed.), *Issues in American social work* (pp. 39–79): Columbia University Press.

Kavanagh, L., & Borrill, J. (2013). Exploring the experiences of ex-offender mentors. *Probation Journal, 60*(4), 400–414.

Kerekes, N., Fielding, C., & Apelqvist, S. (2017). Yoga in correctional settings: A randomized controlled study. *Frontiers in Psychiatry, 8*, 1–11.

Knight, C. (2007). Why choose the probation service? *British Journal of Community Justice, 5*(2), 55–69.
Lacey, N., & Pickard, H. (2015). To blame or to forgive? Reconciling punishment and forgiveness in criminal justice. *Oxford Journal of Legal Studies, 35*(4), 665–696.
Lamar, H. R., & Owens, K. N. (1994). John Augustus Sutter, wilderness entrepreneur. *California History, 73*(2), 98–113.
Lane, R. (1974). Crime and the industrial revolution: British and American views. *Journal of Social History, 7*(3), 287–303.
Levine, A. (2012). Alcohol use and policy formation: An evolving social problem. *Social Work in Public Health, 27*(6), 604–615.
Levine, H. G. (1992). Temperance cultures. In M. H. Lader, G. Edwards, & D. C. Drummond (Eds.), *The nature of alcohol and drug related problems* (pp. 16–36): Cambridge University Press.
Lindner, C., & Jay, J. (2006). John Augustus, father of probation, and the anonymous letter. *Federal Probation, 70*, 77–78.
Lindner, C., & Savarese, M. R. (1984). The evolution of probation-early salaries, qualifications, and hiring practices. *Federal Probation, 48*, 3–10.
Mair, G. (1997). Community penalties in England and Wales. *Federal Sentencing Report, 10*, 263–267.
Mawby, R., & Worrall, A. (2013). *Doing probation work: Identity in a criminal justice occupation*: Routledge.
McConville, S. (2015). *A history of English prison administration*: Routledge.
McNeill, F. (2006). A desistance paradigm for offender management. *Criminology & Criminal Justice, 6*(1), 39–62.
McNeill, F., & Weaver, B. (2010). *Changing lives? Desistance research and offender management*. SCCJR Project Report, No. 03/2010. Retrieved from www.sccjr.ac.uk/wp-content/uploads/2012/10/Report%202010_03%20-%20Changing%20Lives.pdf.
McWilliams, W. (1983). The mission to the English police courts 1876–1936. *The Howard Journal of Criminal Justice, 22*(1–3), 129–147.
Mokyr, J. (1988). Is there still life in the pessimist case? consumption during the industrial revolution, 1790—1850. *The Journal of Economic History, 48*(1), 69–92.
Murdach, A. D. (2009). The temperance movement and social work. *Social Work, 54*(1), 56–62.
Nellis, M. (1995). Probation values for the 1990s. *The Howard Journal of Criminal Justice, 34*(1), 19–44.
Nellis, M. (2007). Humanising justice: The English probation service up to 1972. In In L. Gelsthorpe, & R. Morgan (Eds.), *The handbook of probation* (pp. 25–58): Willan.
Nicklas, T. (2016). Ancient Christian care for prisoners: First and second centuries. *Acta Theologica, 36*: 49–65. Retrieved from: www.scielo.org.za/scielo.php?script=sci_arttext&pid=S1015-87582016000200004.
Panzarella, R. (2002). Theory and practice of probation on bail in the report of John Augustus. *Federal Probation, 66*, 38–42.
Porter, R. (1995). Howard's beginning: Prisons, disease, hygiene. In R. Creese, W. F. Bynum y J. Bearn (Eds.), *The Health of Prisoners* (pp. 5–26): Brill.
Raynor, P. (2020). Evidence versus politics in British probation. *Forensic Science International: Mind and Law, 1*, 100029.
Reingle Gonzalez, J. M., Rana, R. E., Jetelina, K. K., & Roberts, M. H. (2019). The value of lived experience with the criminal justice system: A qualitative study of peer re-entry specialists. *International Journal of Offender Therapy and Comparative Criminology, 63*(10), 1861–1875.
Roberts, J. S. (2019). *Drink, temperance and the working class in nineteenth century Germany*: Routledge.

Room, R. (2013). Sociocultural aspects of alcohol consumption. In P. Boyle, P. Boffetta, A.B. Lowenfels, H. Burns, O. Brawley, W. Zatonski and J. Rehm (Eds.), *Alcohol: Science, Policy, and Public Health* (pp. 38–45):Oxford University Press.

Schwarz, L. D., De Vries, J., Johnson, P., Smith, R., & Wrightson, K. (1992). *London in the age of industrialisation: Entrepreneurs, labour force and living conditions, 1700–1850*: Cambridge University Press.

Sells, D., Curtis, A., Abdur-Raheem, J., Klimczak, M., Barber, C., Meaden, C., … Emigh-Guy, M. (2020). Peer-mentored community reentry reduces recidivism. *Criminal Justice and Behavior, 47*(4), 437–456.

Summers, A. (1995). Elizabeth Fry and mid-nineteenth century reform. In Richard Creese, Wm. Randolph Bynum, and J. Bearn (Eds.), *The Health of Prisoners* (pp. 83–101): Brill.

Teague, M. (2016). Probation, people and profits:The impact of neoliberalism. *British Journal of Community Justice, 14*(1), 133–138.

Tidmarsh, M. (2021). *Professionalism in probation: Making sense of marketisation*: Routledge.

Timasheff, N. S. (1943). *One hundred years of probation, 1841–1941…: Probation in Continental Europe, Latin America, Asia and Africa*: Fordham University Press.

Trotter, C. (1990). Probation can work: A research study using volunteers. *Australian Social Work, 43*(2), 13–18.

Trotter, C. (2015). *Working with involuntary clients: A guide to practice*: Routledge.

Vanstone, M. (2004). Mission control:The origins of a humanitarian service. *Probation Journal, 51*(1), 34–47.

Ward, T., & Brown, M. (2004). The good lives model and conceptual issues in offender rehabilitation. *Psychology, Crime & Law, 10*(3), 243–257.

Ward, T., Mann, R. E., & Gannon, T. A. (2007). The good lives model of offender rehabilitation: Clinical implications. *Aggression and Violent Behavior, 12*(1), 87–107.

Watson, A. (2019). Probation and volunteers in Japan. *Advancing Corrections Journal,* 7:46–59.

Whitehead, J. T., & Braswell, M. C. (2000). The future of probation: Reintroducing the spitual dimension into correctional practice. *Criminal Justice Review, 25*(2), 207–233.

Whitehead, P. (2016). *Transforming probation: Social theories and the criminal justice system*: Policy Press.

Woodard, G. (1962). Reality and social reform:The transition from laissez-faire to the welfare state. *Yale Law Journal, 72*, 286–328.

9

"YES, MY LORD"

Examining the Impact of Religion on the Legal Profession

Michael Quinlan

"Let justice flow like water and uprightness like a never-failing stream."
New Jerusalem Bible, 1994, p. 1536

Introduction

Religion has had a fundamental impact on the development of the Western legal tradition and on the legal profession in the Western world. There have been periods of stress and conflict between the religious convictions of some lawyers and the laws of the state. As religious belief has declined and become more variegated, the relationship between the laws of the state and the religious beliefs of lawyers is experiencing a new era of friction. This chapter considers what this means for legislative responses to criminal law, criminal justice policy and practice in the contemporary Western world. As Christian traditions have been the majority religious faiths in the Western world, this chapter focuses on those traditions. It concentrates on the countries within the common law tradition and in particular England, America, Canada and Australia. Whilst Christianity arrived in different circumstances in each of those countries and each has its own specific laws, judicial system and constitutional framework, there is sufficient commonality to warrant this approach. In this chapter the legal profession is considered broadly to include practising lawyers (solicitors, barristers, legal counsel) and the judiciary. The chapter examines the role of religion on the legal profession by considering the particular role that Christianity has played in the actions of some pre-eminent Christian lawyers. A number of lawyers are referred to by name as "Christian lawyers" in this chapter. These lawyers have self-identified as Christian or within one of the Christian traditions. The chapter does not exclude lawyers from that characterisation by applying any doctrinal or denomination test. It argues that, whilst there is likely to be continued drift away from legislative recognition of traditional Christian positions in an increasing

DOI: 10.4324/9781003276593-11

number of areas, the legal profession must be open to, and supportive of, membership by lawyers from Christian and other religious backgrounds to maintain public confidence and to remain representative.

The Impact of Religion on the Western Legal Tradition and the Legal Profession

The Western Tradition

Whilst some may quibble with Parkinson's view that "Christianity was to the formation of the Western legal tradition as the womb is to human life" (Parkinson, 2013, p.29), Christianity has had a profound impact on the Western legal tradition and the legal profession (Dreisbach, 2019). Concepts such as the right to life, homicide, private ownership, theft, defamation, equality before the law, human rights including freedom of religion, speech and thought, the enforceability of contractual promises, individual responsibility for actions, the need to establish intention (mens rea) for criminal liability, equity, the separation of powers, perjury, trial by jury and probate have all been traced to this source (Blinka, 2019; Hill and Helmholz, 2017; Lindsay and Hudson, 2021b; Murphy, 2019; Paley, 1966; Phang, 2017; Vincent, 2017; Webster, 2021; Wilken, 2019; Williams, 2017; Zimmermann 2018a). Whilst not accepted today, Chief Justice Matthew Hale's assertion, in the seventeenth century, that Christianity was "parcel of the laws of England" was a view repeated by many English, Australian and American jurists up to the twentieth century (Williams, 2008). It was the view, for example, of William Blackstone (author of the seminal *Commentaries on the Laws of England*), Sir James Martin (chief justice of New South Wales (1873–1886)), Simon Greenleaf (founder of Harvard Law School), and US Supreme Court Justices James Wilson and Joseph Story (Blinka, 2019; Drakeman, 2019; Helmolz and Hill, 2017; Lindsay and Hudson, 2021a; Prest, 2017; Stoner, 2019).

Historically, laws relating to moral issues generally reflected the answers on those matters to be found within mainstream Christianity. States in the Western world recognised "marriage" as exclusive to one man and one woman relationships, permitted divorce only under prescribed conditions, and proscribed suicide, the aiding and abetting of suicide, sexual activity between persons of the same sex, contraception, abortion and euthanasia. The leading American work on criminal law and medical jurisprudence in the nineteenth century was not only written by an ordained Episcopal priest, but it quoted St Paul to explain that sin and crime were acts of personal choice (Przbyszewski, 2019b). The influence of Christianity has not however resulted in laws or societies which have fully reflected Christianity. As Blackstone observed, lying, although contrary to Christian morality, was liable to punishment under the law only in limited and specific circumstances (Prest, 2017). Similarly, whilst Lord Atkin was a devout Christian, when he formulated the "neighbour principle" and revolutionised tort law in his judgement in *Donoghue v Stevenson*, he identified much more limited obligations than the Biblical call to love one's neighbour (Deagon, 2017). The fact that Lord Atkin specifically referred to the parable of the Good Samaritan in his judgement did not result in a legal principle which really reflected that parable. As Sir Gerard Brennan, former chief justice of Australia's High Court observed in 2006, "Our laws and policies do not reflect the Christian value of the Good Samaritan. The outcasts are, by definition, denied their dignity" (Brennan, 2006 as cited in Keyzer, 2021, p.230).

Lawyers, parliamentarians and judges who have called themselves Christians have also been responsible for passing and enforcing some deeply unjust laws. Whilst Christians were heavily involved in the emancipation movements, which ultimately resulted in the abolition of slavery in the English Empire and later in America, injustices such as slavery, religious intolerance and persecution; the claiming of sovereignty over lands lived in for millennia by First Nations peoples; the stigmatisation of unmarried mothers and children born out of wedlock; miscegenation laws; and the limiting of the teaching of history and science in conflict with particular readings of scripture were all justified on claimed Christian foundations (Byrd, 2021; Harris, 2018; Hill and Helmholz, 2017; Lindsay and Hudson, 2021b; *Loving v Virginia* 1966; McGarvie, 2016; Smith, 2017). However, as Lindsay and Hudson have observed, speaking of Australia but their point might equally be made for the other nations the focus of this chapter, Christianity may have influenced the law and the actions of lawyers in respecting the human dignity of each person and in expecting more from government than rules and the exercise of power (Lindsay and Hudson, 2021b). Indeed, they argue that:

> According to its own lights, Christianity has long served as the nation's conscience; the Christian scriptures have long provided a corrective for errant behaviour; and a Judeo-Christian ethic has long informed law and legal practice. At its best, it restrains unbridled pursuit of self-interest and elevates concerns for others.
>
> *Lindsay and Hudson, 2021b, p.24*

The Legal Profession

Christianity has been a major influence on the legal profession. Many of the most pre-eminent English, Australian and American lawyers have been practicing and professing Christians including Sir Edward Coke, Hale, Lord Mansfield, Blackstone, Lord Denning, Greenleaf, John Jay (the first chief justice of the United States), John Marshall Harlan, Antonin Scalia, Lord Atkin and Australian High Court judges Victor Windeyer, Ronald Wilson, Gerard Brennan, William Deane, Murray Gleeson and Michael Kirby (Hill and Helmholz, 2017; Dreisbach and Hall, 2019a; Lindsay and Hudson, 2021a). Some of these lawyers considered Christianity to be a key attribute of good lawyers. Greenleaf, for example, told his students that the duty of lawyers was "to employ their influence of the side of virtue, patriotism and religion" (Greenleaf, 1846, as cited in Binka, 2019, p.172). Denning held a similar view:

> Lawyers should be men of religion and speaking generally that has always been the case in this country. It is the reason why the common law of England is so great. The law has been moulded for centuries by judges who have been brought up in the Christian faith. The precepts of religion, consciously or unconsciously, have been their guide in the administration of justice.
>
> *Denning, 1943, as cited in Phang, 2017, pp.325–326*

The brief list of eminent lawyers above demonstrates the breadth and variety of contribution and the range of thought of even distinguished Christian lawyers living at the same time. Christian lawyers have taken contrasting positions on such matters as the proper role of judges and on doctrine and emphasis within their religious faith.

Judicial Approach and Theory

Prominent Christian lawyers have included advocates of natural law theory, positivists, constitutional originalists and judicial activists. There is no single Christian approach to the role of judges engaged in interpreting texts (Berg, 2019). Some Christian lawyers (such as Henry of Bratton (Bracton), Hale, John Selden, Blackstone and Jay) have embraced natural law. Even here their approach has not been uniform. Some have emphasised reason and others divine revelation in their thought. Some have considered fidelity to natural law as a criterion against which positive, domestic laws can be judged and, if found wanting, properly considered 'void' or not obligatory (Berman and Witte, 2017; Bird, 2019; Sytsma, 2017; Vincent, 2017). Not all would accept Hale's view that in such a circumstance a citizen who failed to obey a law in conflict with natural law could still legitimately be punished (Sytsma, 2017). Other Christian lawyers, including Story and Scalia, have respected precedent and parliamentary supremacy to the extent that they would not entertain the possibility of undermining either even if a law offended natural law or their Christian faith (Berg, 2019; Stoner, 2019). Story rejected slavery as contrary to Christianity and morality and said so in his 1822 judgement in *La Jeune Eugenie*. He decided that case on factual grounds and reached an outcome consistent with his own faith. However, he stayed silent in *The Antelope*, which recognised that slavery was not forbidden by the law of nations and his fidelity to the then-text of the Constitution saw him support the recapture of fugitive slaves in *Prigg v Pennsylvania* (Stoner, 2019). Scalia adopted a positivist approach focusing on the text to be interpreted (Berg, 2019). He rejected appeals to "fundamental" moral or social values as leaving too much scope for judges to impose their personal views (Berg, 2019). Scalia said that he tried "mightily to prevent my religious views or my political views or my philosophical views from affecting my interpretation of the laws, which is what my job is about" (Scalia, 2002 as cited in Berg, 2019. p.250). Scalia and some other Christian US Supreme Court judges, have embraced constitutional originalism. Stoner describes the aim of an originalist as being "to arrive at the objective account of the Constitution's meaning, uncorrupted by an individual judge's (or professor's) personal religious faith" (Stoner, 2019, p.144). This approach might coincide or conflict with an outcome consistent with a judge's Christian beliefs. In cases dealing with abortion, same sex marriage or the death penalty, for example, originalist judges do not ground their reasoning on Christianity or natural law but claim to be searching for the intention of the writers or ratifiers of the Constitution and its amendments. As Stoner opines, "Being a Christian and being a constitutionalist, in short, are to a modern originalist unrelated; if one is both, it is a mere coincidence" (Stoner, 2019, p.145). Scalia made the same point in 2010, observing that despite his personal and religious views about abortion, he would rule that there was a constitutional right to abortion "[i]f I genuinely thought that the Constitution guaranteed a woman's right to abortion." (Scalia, 2010 as cited in Berg, 2019, p.246). He said that he would resign were a conflict between his religious faith and the Constitution to arise (Berg, 2019).

Some Christian lawyers, such as Lords Selborne, Mansfield and Kenyon, were clearly influenced by their Christian faith in their judgements (Hill and Helmholz, 2017b; Poser, 2017). Mansfield's judgements reflected his belief that "morality was an essential part of the English common law" (Poser, 2017, p.210). Whilst severe in punishing criminals, such as gang leaders, Mansfield helped the weak and vulnerable and was creative to avoid the impact of anti-Catholic laws (Poser, 2017). Mansfield's successor as chief justice of the Court of King's Bench, Lord Kenyon, was also public about his Christian faith and shared the view that the law has a key role in enforcing public morals. Kenyon referred to his faith in his directions to juries so frequently he could be said to have engaged in "preaching from the bench" (Oldham, 2017. p.239). Whilst Kenyon stated in *Ellah v Leigh* in 1794 that it was for the legislature to change the law if new manners or customs were to be reflected in the law, this reticence to develop the law seems not to have been evident in his directions to the jury in *Howard v Bigham* in the same year. There he said: "I had not been long on the Seat of Justice before I felt I should best discharge my duty to the public by making the law of the land subservient to the laws of morality and religion" (Kenyon, 1794, as cited in Oldham, 2017, p.250). In more recent times, Denning was not only very public about his Christian faith, including in his extra-judicial writing, but had a passion for justice in individual cases and a desire to develop the law more generally. Whilst Denning never expressly referenced his religious belief in his judgements, "his vision of the law was premised on a unified and objective basis rooted in his Christian faith" (Phang, 2017, p.319). Kirby, arguably Australia's most famous recent activist judge, was similarly willing to ignore or creatively distinguish precedents in favour of achieving justice (Sanson and Anthony, 2019). Kirby described the idea of judicial function as being "purely mechanical, strictly formal, and wholly predictable" as a fairy tale, which was dishonest and "fundamentally incompatible with the creative element of the common law" (Kirby, 1992 as cited in Sanson and Anthony, 2019, p.446). Christian lawyers on the bench who profess neutrality will find it elusive in practice. This is because judges have to decide on the rules to apply, limit, distinguish or overlook and, whether they do so internationally or not, they will be influenced or guided by their own moral systems in doing so (Reid, 2019, p.219). This is why Catholic judge and jurist John T. Noonan rejected the idea that "a neutral universe [...] governed by rules exists" (Noonan, 2002 as cited in Reid, 2019, p.219).

Differences in Doctrine and Influence

Christian lawyers on the bench will reach their conclusions only by applying differing judicial approaches, such as those discussed above. Whether in a judicial or other role, Christian lawyers, whether intentionally or not, will also be influenced by their Christianity in differing ways. This should be expected given that, whilst most Christians identify with a particular denomination or tradition, Selden's seventeenth-century observation about the ultimately personal and individual nature of religious belief is no doubt even more true today:

> Religion is like the fashion, one man wears his doublet slash'd, another lac'd, another plain; but every man has a doublet. So every man his religion. We differ about the trimming. Men say they are of the same religion for quietness sake; but if the matter were well examin'd, you would scarce find three anywhere of the same religion in all points.
>
> *Selden 1689, as cited in Berman and Witte, 2017, p.147*

Whilst most Christians in any age might have held to the permanence of the Ten Commandments and the admonition against murder, for example, and there remain some fixed points, there have always been differences in emphasis, perspective and doctrine among those considering themselves "Christians" (Helmholz and Hill, 2017). Those differences are increasing. Even among devout traditional Christian lawyers the dominant view as to the extent to which the criminal law, for example, should reflect traditional Christian moral dictates such as proscriptions on blasphemy, working on the Sabbath, suicide, adultery and other sexual conduct between consenting adults (not married in a form recognised as such within many Christian denominations) have changed significantly over the centuries. Helmholz and Hill suggest that this may be the result of a growth in human understanding and of a fuller understanding of the intention of the Gospel rather than "simply changes of mind" (Helmholz and Hill, 2017, pp.9–10). McGarvie argues that, whilst Christianity has been the majority religious faith since the early days of the United States, this has not produced consistency "regarding the doctrine, morals, values of Christianity" (McGarvie, 2016, p.xiv). His point is equally valid among Christians certainly across the Western world. As he notes, there is no single Christian position on questions such as the following:

> Is salvation or the social good the primary goal of the church? Can homosexuals marry or be ministers? To what degree does Christianity condone extreme inequalities of wealth within its community or even its own congregation.
>
> *McGarvie, 2016, p.xiv*

Even where there may not be significant differences in doctrinal belief, Christian lawyers may still act quite differently. Some Christian lawyers, including John Dickinson and Hale, refused to act for potential clients or to take cases which they considered immoral (Calvert, 2019; Sytsma, 2017). Others, whether bound by the "cab rank rule" (which obliges some lawyers to act in certain circumstances) or not, see it as their duty as a lawyer to represent all who seek their aid as "all defendants are entitled to legal representation, no matter how unsavoury or dangerous they are" (Creyke, Hamer, O'Mara, Smith and Taylor, 2021, p.141). Some Christian lawyers, including Lord Mansfield, have sought to keep their faith private and not to talk or write about their religious faith (Poser, 2017). Others, such as Harlan, David J. Brewer and Scalia, have been very open to doing so (Przbyzcewski, 2019a; Przbyzcewski, 2019b; Berg, 2019). As Berg explains, Christian judges do not all approach Constitutional issues in the United States, in the same way:

> Scalia's particular Catholic formation and outlook may have helped make him sceptical of judicial discretion. But justices formed by a more philosophical version of natural law may be inclined to think that constitutionally recognized general concepts such as equality or private property have a moral logic capable of elucidation in particular cases. And justices formed by a Christian concern for the vulnerable may be inclined to emphasize the Constitution's guarantees of protection and equality for minority groups and unpopular perspectives.
>
> *Berg, 2019, p.261*

A New Era of Friction

As the execution of St Thomas More in 1535 evidences, stress and conflict between the religious convictions of some lawyers and the laws of the state are not a new phenomenon. Tensions with traditional Christian thought were already emerging in America prior to its independence even though early colonial laws were often explicitly based on Christianity and the Bible (Dreisbach and Hall, 2019b). Challenges by rationalist, church–state separationists and secularists were being made in the West during the nineteenth century, and these principles were being used to argue for the exclusion of legal arguments and opinions informed by Christian or Biblical principles by the twentieth century (Dreisbach and Hall, 2019). These conflicts began in a context in which the central themes of Christianity and its sacred texts were well known and, in a sense, proponents and opponents of Christianity and of its continuing influence spoke the same language. Such challenges have continued and now occur in a climate of greatly diminished religious literacy and in an era of decline in which the proportion of people professing Christianity is experiencing serious decline (Sheridan, 2021).

By the 1970s, the "culture wars" had begun in America and differing "conceptions of and policies regarding family, education, morality, art, law and political leadership" were being fought over (McGarvie, 2016, p.161). These conflicts have found their own form throughout the Western world and show no sign of abating, with growing and broader challenges in legislation, judicial determinations and public opinion to the influences of Christianity on the law (Dreisbach, 2019). Rather than the positive endorsement of Christianity's place and influence in the law, expressed by jurists such as Hale, the Canadian Supreme Court in 2018 found that Trinity College, a Christian university in Canada, could not require its law students and staff to abide by a Community Covenant Agreement because, among other things, it set a strict code of Christian sexual morality (Walsh, 2021). As de Freitas has documented, the judiciary regularly dismisses religion as irrational, nonsensical, illogical and bizarre (de Freitas, 2021). These changes are occurring in societies in which the law intrudes more frequently into areas which might once have been considered matters of personal choice. For example, the state is involved in determining: the manner in which children are educated; the appropriate distribution of an intestate's property; challenges to wills which inadequately provide for family members; whether certain medical procedures can be performed on children, with or without the support of both parents; and in ensuring that a "[p]erson can no longer avoid legal obligations of 'family' by living indefinitely unmarried" (Lindsay and Hudson, 2021b, pp.14–15). Whilst there are dimensions beyond a hardening attitude against strongly held religious views which might explain the opposition to presidential judicial nominees who are professing Christians in the United States, there has been a ratcheting up of that opposition over the last half-century. Whilst Catholic pro-life nominees, such as President Ronald Reagan's nominees Noonan and Scalia faced opposition, each received unanimous approval from the Senate Judiciary Committee and easy confirmation to the bench (Reid, 2019; Berg 2019). This can be contrasted with the experiences of recent Supreme Court appointees who did not receive bipartisan support (Frey, 2020; Helering, 2018).

Impact on Legislative Responses to Criminal, Criminal Justice Policy and Practice

As noted above, historically, criminal, criminal justice policy and practice reflected traditional understandings of Christian morality. There is a greater variety of views within Christian traditions on such matters, and state laws are much more likely to vary from traditional Christian positions today. This trend is likely to continue. In 2003, the US Supreme Court found that a Texas law which criminalised sodomy violated the right of privacy and could not be justified on the basis that such behaviour might cause offence to many Christians. The minority judges expressed concern about the Court's prohibition on "laws based on moral choices," observing that that approach also challenged "laws against bigamy, same-sex marriage, adult incest, prostitution, masturbation, adultery, fornication, bestiality and obscenity" (*Lawrence v Texas,* 2004 as cited in McGarvie, 2016, p.187). In 2016, McGarvie noted that "[n]o doubt many liberals would argue that, but for the bestiality laws protecting innocent animals, those laws regarding private behavior by sole or consenting adults should be repealed" (McGarvie, 2016, p.187). If they remained law in 2003, in many parts of the Western world many of those laws, with the possible exception of bestiality, have since been repealed, amended or are under review. Every law, including laws proscribing bestiality, ultimately involves a moral choice. Given the falling proportion of the populations of the countries which are the focus of this chapter, that identify as Christian, and the variety of approaches within that broad tradition discussed earlier, it might be expected that a default to traditional Christian moral positions would not continue to be a guide for the law. However, today arguments for the maintenance of positions grounded on traditional Christian moral positions are likely to be rejected even if there is a rational foundation for them. As the grounding of such laws on Christian tradition is rejected, there is a greater reliance on statistical, empirical and scientific arguments and evidence in support of law reform. In criminal justice there is a greater understanding of socio-economic conditions, upbringing, genetics and heredity as influences on human behaviour (Przbyszewski, 2019b). It is important to recognise that there are limits to the value of empirical evidence and that not every scientific study is of equal worth (Ritchie, 2020). An uncritical over-reliance on studies can result in the acceptance of small biased or erroneous research lacking in rigour as foundations for law reform. Each approach to law reform has its own challenges. The legal profession has a key role in assisting contemporary Western societies to navigate these challenges.

The Need for the Profession to Welcome Membership by Lawyers of Religious Faith

The role of a legal professional is not simply a matter of technical proficiency. It is not limited to knowing and explaining the law accurately but extends to seeking to amend the law when it is irrational, unfair or unjust (Marinac, Hart, Chisholm, Nielsen, Wood, Evans and McKibbin, 2021). These are criteria on which reasonable people may disagree. As discussed above, the judiciary regularly dismisses religion as irrational, nonsensical, illogical and bizarre (de Freitas, 2021). Many other contemporary lawmakers would share this view. This puts understandings of fairness and justice grounded on traditional religious understandings at a disadvantage in discussions about the law and law reform. Western societies as democracies share pluralism as an essential characteristic (Taylor, 2020). For a democratic society to develop laws which respect pluralism requires consideration of some complex questions. These include the extent to which the state should demand equal compliance with all laws, notwithstanding the differing impact that a given law may have on particular groups or persons within society, and the extent to which the state will respect difference and allow for differential operation of laws to accommodate difference. As former Australian High Court judge Sir William Deane observed when governor general of Australia:

> The challenge and the responsibility to ensure that religious and cultural diversity is a source of advantage, benefit and good rather than a cause of disharmony, conflict and evil lie close to the heart of the quest for happiness, fulfilment and survival of our kind [...] the key to real success in relation to

> that challenge and responsibility lies in mutual and genuine understanding, tolerance and respect of and for different cultural and religious traditions, practices and beliefs. The real difficulty lies in the identification and effective implementation of the best means of fostering and maintaining such understanding, respect and tolerance particularly in circumstances of actual or perceived completion, inconsistency or antipathy.
>
> *Deane, 2002, pp.62–63*

Writing in a US context, Stoner puts the task in these terms:

> To my mind, the liberty guaranteed by the Constitution is political liberty, and that entails the right of citizens of every faith to bring their witness to the public square in the making of laws and so inevitably as well in their application, together with their responsibility, often learned through bitter defeat in the political process, to explore possibilities for shared understanding and tolerable working arrangements in public and civic life, even when these cut against what one might wish for on the basis of one's religion's ideal.
>
> *Stoner, 2019, p.199*

As lawyers have such a significant role in the development of the law, as judges who settle questions about its meaning and as advocates for particular interpretations of the law, to achieve this goal in any nation requires a legal profession which is not monochromatic. It requires a profession drawn from a diverse range of religious beliefs and other viewpoints. For some lawyers, religious belief remains an important source of identity and of understanding fairness and justice. As the discussion above demonstrates, even for such lawyers, Christian faith does not equate to a uniform position on matters as diverse as whether to act for a client; the extent to which their faith has been public; the proper role of judges; and doctrine and emphasis within their religious faith. However, as The Law Society of New South Wales Commission of Inquiry (2017) recognised, religious faith is a factor which holds lawyers back from full participation in the legal profession.

Conclusion

This chapter has demonstrated that Christianity has had and continues to have a significant influence on the legal systems and legal professions of the countries considered in this chapter. Whilst Christians in the legal profession are not easily characterised, they include those public and those private about their faith, subscribers to natural law theory, conservatives and liberals, positivist and activist judges, judges who have been demonstrably influenced by their religious faith in their judgements and those for whom that influence is less obvious. Whilst Christianity is declining in the Western world and the divergence between traditional Christian moral precepts and the law is continuing to expand, the legal profession should continue to welcome Christian lawyers, together with lawyers from all religious traditions and from none. This will not only assist the profession to maintain public confidence and to remain representative, by reflecting the diversity found in these pluralist nations, but also provide a link to their foundational traditions.

References

Berg, T.C. (2019). Antonin Scalia: Devout Christian, worldly judge? In D.L. Dreisbach and M.D. Hall (Eds.). *Great Christian Jurists in American History* (pp. 245–264). Cambridge University Press.

Berman, H.J., and Witte, J. Jr. (2017). The integrative Christian jurisprudence of John Selden. In M. Hill and R.H. Helmholz (Eds.), *Great Christian Jurists in English History* (pp. 139–161). Cambridge University Press.

Bird, W. (2019). John Jay: The first chief justice. In D.L. Dreisbach and M.D. Hall (Eds.). *Great Christian Jurists in American History* (pp. 112–129). Cambridge University Press.

Byrd, J.P. (2021). *A Holy Baptism of Fire and Blood*. Oxford University Press.

Blinka, D.D. (2019). Harvard's evangelist of evidence: Simon Greenleaf's Christian common sense. In D. L. Dreisbach and M. D. Hall (Eds.). *Great Christian Jurists in American History* (pp. 161–178). Cambridge University Press.

Calvert, J.E. (2019). The friendly jurisprudence and early feminism of John Dickinson. In D. L. Dreisbach and M. D. Hall (Eds.). *Great Christian Jurists in American History* (pp.72–89). Cambridge University Press.

Creyke, R., Hamer, D., O'Mara, Patrick, Smith, B., and Taylor, T. (2021). *Laying Down the Law*. LexisNexis.

Deagon, A. (2017). *From Violence to Peace: Theology, Law and Community*. Hart Publishing.

Deane, W. (2002). *Directions A Vision for Australia*. St Pauls.

de Freitas, S. (2021). Law, judges and the exclusionary nature of inclusion. In M. Quinlan and A.K. Thompson (Eds.). *Inclusion, Exclusion and Religious Freedom in Contemporary Australia* (pp. 47–71). Shepherd Street Press.

Drakeman, D.L. (2019). James Wilson. In D.L. Dreisbach and M.D. Hall (Eds.). *Great Christian Jurists in American History* (pp. 130–143). Cambridge University Press.

Dreisbach, D.L. (2019). Introduction: Christianity and American law. In D.L. Dreisbach and M.D. Hall (Eds.). *Great Christian Jurists in American History* (pp. 1–15). Cambridge University Press.

Dreisbach, D.L., and Hall, M.D. (Eds.). (2019a). *Great Christian Jurists in American History*. Cambridge University Press.

Dreisbach, D.L., and Hall, M.D. (2019b). Preface. In D.L. Dreisbach and M.D. Hall (Eds.). *Great Christian Jurists in American History* (pp. xvii–xxii). Cambridge University Press.

Frey, J.A. (2020, 15 October). "Like Amy Coney Barrett, I'm a professional woman criticized for my big, Catholic family." *USA Today*. Retrieved from: www.usatoday.com/story/opinion/voices/2020/10/15/amy-coney- barrett-catholic-big-family-religion-bias-column/3642952001/

Harris, J. (2018). *One Blood*. Australians Together.

Helering, B. (2018, 17 July). Could anti-Catholic bias sink Kavanaugh's Supreme Court nomination? *Courier Journal*. Retrieved from: www.courier- journal.com/story/opinion/columnists/bob-heleringer/2018/07/17/supreme-court- anti-catholic-bias-sink-brett-kavanaugh-heleringer/781447002/

Hill, M., and Helmholz, R.H. (Eds.). (2017). *Great Christian Jurists in English History*. Cambridge University Press.

Keyzer, P. (2021). Francis Gerard Brennan (1928–). In G. Lindsay and W. Hudson (Eds.). *Australian Jurists & Christianity* (pp. 228–239). The Federation Press.

Law Society of New South Wales Commission of Inquiry. (2017). *FLIP: The Future of Law and Innovation in the Profession*. Retrieved from: www.lawsociety.com.au/sites/default/files/2018-03/1272952.pdf

Lindsay, G., and Hudson, W. (Eds.). (2021a). *Australian Jurists & Christianity*. The Federation Press

Lindsay, G., and Hudson, W. (2021b). Spirit in the temporal. In G. Lindsay and W. Hudson (Eds.). *Australian Jurists & Christianity* (pp. 1–31). The Federation Press.

Loving v Virginia 206 Va. 924, 147 S.E.2d 78 (1966).

Marinac, A., Hart, C., Chisholm, R., Nielsen, J., Wood, A., Evans, A. and McKibbin, S. (2021). *Learning Law*. Cambridge University Press.

McGarvie, M.D. (2016). *Law and Religion in American History*. Cambridge University Press.

Murphy, A.R. (2019). Friendly laws: William Penn's Christian jurisprudence. In D.L. Dreisbach and M.D. Hall (Eds.). *Great Christian Jurists in American History* (pp. 54–71). Cambridge University Press.

New Jerusalem Bible Study Edition. (1994). Darton Longman & Todd.

Oldham, J. (2017). Lord Kenyon. Preaching from the bench. In M. Hill and R.H. Helmholz (Eds.). *Great Christian Jurists in English History* (pp. 237–251). Cambridge University Press.

Paley, R.S. (1966). The position of the law school in the university. *Catholic University Law Review* 16, 34–52.

Parkinson, P. (2013). *Tradition and Change in Australian Law*. LawBook.

Phang, A. (2017). A passion for justice. Lord Denning, Christianity and the law. In M. Hill and R.H. Helmholz (Eds.). *Great Christian Jurists in English History* (pp. 319–338). Cambridge University Press.

Poser, N.S. (2017). Lord Mansfield. The reasonableness of religion. In M. Hill and R.H. Helmholz (Eds.). *Great Christian Jurists in English History* (pp. 187–211). Cambridge University Press.

Prest, W. (2017). William Blackstone's Anglicanism. In M. Hill and R.H. Helmholz (Eds.). *Great Christian Jurists in English History* (pp. 213–235). Cambridge University Press.

Przybyszewski, L. (2019a). Judicial conservatism and Protestant faith: The case of Justice David J. Brewer. In D.L. Dreisbach and M.D. Hall (Eds.). *Great Christian Jurists in American History* (pp. 194–207). Cambridge University Press.

Przybyszewski, L. (2019b). John Marshall Harlan the Elder. In D.L. Dreisbach and M.D. Hall (Eds.). *Great Christian Jurists in American History* (pp. 179–193). Cambridge University Press.

Reid, C.J. Jr. (2019). John T. Noonan, Jr.: Catholic jurist and judge. In D.L. Dreisbach and M.D. Hall (Eds.). *Great Christian Jurists in American History* (pp. 208–229). Cambridge University Press

Ritchie, S. (2020). *Science Fictions*. The Bodley Head.

Sanson, M., and Anthony, T. (2019). *Connecting with Law*. Oxford University Press.

Sheridan, G. (2021). *Christians*. Allen & Unwin.

Smith, D.C. (2017). Sir Edward Coke. Faith, law and the search for stability in Reformation England. In M. Hill and R.H. Helmholz (Eds.). *Great Christian Jurists in English History* (pp. 93–113). Cambridge University Press.

Stoner, J.R. Jr. (2019) Was Justice Joseph Story a Christian constitutionalist? In D.L. Dreisbach and M.D. Hall (Eds.). *Great Christian Jurists in American History* (pp. 144–160). Cambridge University Press.

Sytsma, D.S. (2017). Matthew Hale as theologian and natural law theorist. In M. Hill and R.H. Helmholz (Eds.). *Great Christian Jurists in English History* (pp. 163–185). Cambridge University Press

Taylor, P.M. (2020). *A Commentary on the International Covenant on Civil and Political Rights.* Cambridge University Press.

Vincent, N. (2017). Henry of Bratton (alias Bracton). In M. Hill and R.H.Helmholz (Eds.). *Great Christian Jurists in English History* (pp. 19–44) Cambridge University Press.

Walsh, G. (2021). Trinity Western University and the future of conservative religious education. In B.W. Bussey and A.J.L. Menuge (Eds.). *The Inherence of Human Dignity Law and Religious Liberty*, Vol. 2 (pp.185–202). Anthem Press.

Wilken, R.L. (2019). *Liberty in the Things of God.* Yale University Press.

Williams, I. (2017). Christian St .German. Religion, conscience and law in Reformation England. In M. Hill and R.H. Helmholz (Eds.). *Great Christian Jurists in English History* (pp. 69–91). Cambridge University Press.

Williams, R. (2008) *God Actually.* ABC Books.

Zimmermann, A. (2018a). *Christian Foundations of the Common Law.* Vol. 1: *England.* Connor Court Publishing.

Zimmermann, A. (2018b) *Christian Foundations of the Common Law*, Vol. 2: *The United States.* Connor Court Publishing.

10

WHAT DOES GOD REQUIRE OF US? THE CALLING OF LAWYERS IN THE CRIMINAL JUSTICE SYSTEM[1]

Isabelle R. Gunning and Russell G. Pearce

Introduction

Religious lawyers can and should bring their religion into their work in the criminal justice system consistent with their professional obligations. In doing so, they will develop resources both for finding reward in their work and for making a greater contribution to the public good. In Part A, we consider how bringing one's religion into one's work as a lawyer challenges the belief that lawyers should embrace a stance of neutrality toward moral objectives in their professional role. Not only is the aspiration to bleach out unachievable, but it denies lawyers resources important to fulfilling their professional roles. We draw upon Micah's teaching (Micah 6:8, Sefaria Tanakh (Bible)) that we should do justly, love mercy, and walk humbly, which offers a basic guide for lawyers in the criminal justice system. In Part B, we explore ways in which religious lawyers should take a leadership role in two crucial controversies facing the criminal justice system—restorative justice and reparations.

In offering this analysis, we provide a perspective that we share despite our different religious and spiritual commitments. One of us is a New Thought Christian. One of us is Jewish. We will try to broaden the reach of our chapter by alluding to other religious perspectives, including Muslim, Buddhist, and Hindu. In these ways, our chapter seeks to promote dialogue among lawyers of all religions who seek to determine the relevance of their religion in their work in the criminal justice system. Nonetheless, we acknowledge that even in our Christian, and Jewish traditions, as well as in those traditions the authors do not share, many will take different views. For those who disagree, our goal is to encourage further dialogue along lines that many lawyers have not previously considered. We believe that taking religion seriously can open new doors for lawyers as they seek meaning in their work and guidance in their public leadership.

DOI: 10.4324/9781003276593-12

A Religious Lawyering as a Criminal Justice Resource

At the core of the dominant conceptions of role in the modern legal system is the concept of neutrality, generally understood as the belief that lawyers should "bleach out" their identity from their work as a lawyer. (Levinson, 1993) Applicable to criminal defense lawyers is the ideology of the neutral partisan—lawyers who are extreme partisans with no moral accountability for their conduct as lawyers so long as they act as extreme partisans within the bounds of the law. The neutral partisan concept requires lawyers to "bleach out" elements of their identity, including their values. The rationale for bleaching out is twofold. First, it rests on the assumption that lawyers can only achieve the extreme partisanship and amorality required of the neutral partisan by bleaching out their identity and values. Second, from a systemic perspective, equal justice relies on equal representation and, the argument goes, defendants can only receive equal representation if lawyers are fungible, a condition that can only be achieved if lawyers bleach out their identity and values. (Levinson, 1993; Pearce, 1996, p. 1261; Wilkins, 1998). Commentators have similarly argued that prosecutors should take a neutral stance toward their duties (Zacharias & Green, 2004). Although Zacharias and Green have identified a range of meanings of neutrality for prosecutors, one of those meanings offers an analog to bleaching out—"excluding personal beliefs." (Zacharias & Green, 2004, pp. 24–25).

Beginning with the work of Thomas Shaffer in the late 1970s, the Religious Lawyering movement has emerged as one of numerous critiques arguing that neutrality and bleaching out are fictions and that even as aspirations, they deny lawyers meaningful guidance either in their daily practice or in their public leadership (Pearce, 1998). Individual lawyers find they are unable to satisfactorily reconcile their personal and professional aspirations with the realities of their work (Pearce, 1998). Most people are not capable of the compartmentalization of their lives that bleaching out requires. Moreover, neutrality or amorality provides little inspiration in representing clients or in providing public leadership. Neutrality offers no foundation for building trust, connection, and interpersonal relationships (Gunning, 2015). It similarly provides no vision of justice and leaves lawyers adrift in the face of systemic injustices that often result from superficially neutral procedures imposed on a society built on inequity and racism, much like the American "justice" system (Gunning, 2015).

Shaffer posited that for Christians their faith commitment should be the primary point of reference for decisions about their professional life (Pearce & Uelmen, 2004). Shaffer's work has led to the development of a significant body of scholarship and discussion on the part of legal scholars, lawyers, and theologians from myriad faith backgrounds (Pearce, 1998; Gunning, 2015). Today, the Religious Lawyering movement focuses on ways in which religious values and perspectives may provide a completely different structural framework for an approach to professional life within the context of liberal democracy (Pearce & Uelmen, 2004).

We offer Micah's teaching as one path because a wide range of religious perspectives embrace the commitment to justice, mercy, and walking humbly—not only our Christian and Jewish traditions but also Buddhism, Hinduism, Islam, and most other religions. Micah's teaching transforms a lawyer's religion from a barrier to be bleached out to a strength that a lawyer can draw upon in her work. In contrast to the neutral prosecutor whose professional task is to bleach out her identity, the religious prosecutor looks to her faith to reinforce her professional commitment to justice and to mercy (Levine, 1996; Skeel & Stuntz, 2006). From a Jewish perspective, Samuel Levine reflects that:

> as a prosecutor, I have a unique opportunity to integrate my religious principles with my professional life. [...] If I am successful, I help return order to society, benefiting the members of society while at the same time helping further the purpose of God's creation.
>
> *Levine, 1996, p. 1209*

And Zulkifli Hasan notes that Islam requires lawyers "to uphold justice without fear and favor" (Hasan, 2015, p. 10).

In contrast to the neutral partisan criminal defense lawyer struggling to separate her religious and professional selves, the religious lawyer finds in justice and mercy, obligations to represent the accused because both a just legal system and the lawyer's personal compassion compel her to do so. Shaffer, for example, relies in part on the insights of a Jewish theologian to argue that the religious obligation to represent even a guilty defendant is more powerful than that of professional duty. He writes that:

> It would involve a more generous response than our official rules allow for; it would involve even a loving relationship, an I–Thou relationship, as Martin Buber put it. The gospel seems to say that we have to do that; we are commanded to do it. The Christian system for approaching outcasts is manifestly a system for, above all, being with them.
>
> *Shaffer, 1981, p. 55*

Micah's third instruction, walking humbly with God, is integral to doing justice and to providing loving mercy for both a prosecutor or criminal defense attorney. It frames how we see ourselves and how we see others. Isabelle Gunning recounts how lawyers in a multifaith dialogue found a connection to faith through the "love of thy neighbor" or "the dignity and worth of all individuals" (Gunning, 2015, p. 231). Peter Gabel applies these insights to both justice and mercy, noting that recognizing the other as created in God's image produces empathy and compassion (al-Hibri et al., 1999). Dr. Martin Luther King Jr. defines "justice as love correcting that which revolts against love" (Al-Hibri et al., 1999, p.128). Lenn Goodman, discussing love's connection with equality, states that "mutuality is a moral implication of equality, treating the other as another self [...] What the mitzvah ordains is that one deem all of another's concerns as weighty as one's own" (Goodman, 2008, p. 13). From a Buddhist perspective, Kinji Kanazawa identifies *dana*, or the selfless giving of love and time to all (Kanazawa, 1998). The eminent Buddhist thinker Thich Nhat Hanh describes "the world [as] a place webbed by interconnectedness, not a place full of individuated and separated beings and processes" (Nhat Hanh, 2001, p. 56).

We have presented a general framework based on religious commitments the two of us share. We realize, however, that not all religious people will share those commitments or our view of the inadequacy of the "bleached out" neutral partisan and neutral prosecutor models (but see Reza, 1999; Freedman, 1990; Freedman, 1966). In the next Part, we will further apply Micah's framework to two policy areas where prosecutors and criminal defense lawyers have an obligation to provide public leadership.

B The Public Leadership of the Religious Lawyer

1 Restorative Justice

As it exists today, the United States carceral system—accounting for over 20 percent of the world's prison population (ACLU, 2022) and disproportionately impacting Black and Latinx communities (Davis et al., 2015)—is built around a retributive framework (Wetstone, 2022). This punitive approach narrowly focuses on finding the "perpetrator" of a legally defined crime and punishing them. It also leads to stigmatization and dehumanization, seeks little involvement from such "perpetrator" in finding a resolution to harm done, and often prevents the "perpetrator's" successful reintegration into the community (Wetstone, 2022; McCold & Wachtel, 2003, pp. 1–2; Lanni, 2021, p. 646).

Restorative justice diverges from retributive practices. Restorative justice practices look at "crimes" as "harms" that impact a range of stakeholders connected to both the individual harmed and the individual committing the harm (McCold & Wachtel, 2003). Restorative justice practices are designed to acknowledge the roles, relationships, and needs of stakeholders involved, and to generate opportunities for the healing of the primary stakeholders—both the person harmed as well as the person committing the harm (McCold & Wachtel, 2003).

A restorative justice approach seeks to identify the following: (i) the harm caused by an act, (ii) what must be done to correct that harm, and (iii) who is responsible for this correction (Lerman, 2000, p. 1665). Further, restorative justice is predicated on several core principles, including (but not limited to) that crime is an offense against human relations, that community must be restored to the degree attainable, and that stakeholders share responsibilities through partnerships for action (Lerman, 2000, p. 1665). Ultimately, the goal of restorative justice practices is for the person who has committed harm to be "reconciled" back into the larger community and to allow for greater social unity through the focus on healing (McCold & Wachtel, 2003).

The restorative justice movement, as it is known in Western legal discourse today, originated in the 1970s under the strong influence of both Indigenous traditions and Mennonite-led reconciliation initiatives (Davis, 2019; Beaty Chiste, 2007; Beaty Chiste, 2013; Greenwood, 2001). Restorative practices have existed throughout history, are rooted in various Indigenous cultures and, most pertinent to this discussion, are identifiable in thousands of years of spiritual religious traditions, practices, and religious law (Clark, 2001; Braithwaite, 1999, Beaty Chiste, 2007; Beaty Chiste, 2013).

The most recognizable of such restorative tenets is the Golden Rule. A concept espoused across religions like Hinduism (Brihaspati, Mahabharata 13.113.8.) philosophies of Buddhism and Taoism (Udanavarga 5:18; Tao Te Ching, ch. 49), and the Abrahamic religions of Islam (Kitab al-Kafi, p. 146), Judaism (Leviticus 19:18, 34), and Christianity (Revised Standard Edition Bible, 2022, Matthew 7:12; Luke 6:31), it teaches reciprocity in our treatment of others. More simply put, "do unto others as you would have them do unto you" (Luke 6:31).

In addition to reciprocity of treatment, unity is a concept critical to restorative justice practices. Unity, too, is shared across religions. For example, in Judeo-Christian teachings this can be seen in one of the oldest tenets: the creation of humankind in the image of God (Genesis 1:1–27). In other religions and philosophies, such as Buddhism or New Thought, the concept of unity comes in the form of "oneness" (Garfield et al., 2014, p. 357; Holmes, 1998, p. 332).[2] This concept, regardless of name, is implicitly grounded in the interrelation and interconnection of all humans, whether in kinship as the children of God or as threads of the same spiritual cloth.

The restorative justice approach also acknowledges the relational nature of all people—even in the context of the commission of some harm. Interconnection means that neither the person nor the act can be isolated from the web of relationships that preceded the act, nor the possibilities that could proceed from the act, as well as the importance of addressing and healing harms as a means of maintaining unified communities.

The process of restorative justice focuses on the interplay and interrelation of stakeholders. The primary stakeholders include the person harmed and their family, who all must regain a sense of empowerment, and the person who has committed the harm, who must regain the trust of the community through an assumption of responsibility for their actions (McCold & Wachtel, 2003). When the greater community has played a role in creating environmental conditions that make harm likely (e.g., traumatic conditions created by domestic violence, familial incarceration, poverty, etc.), the community must also be included in this primary justice response, having the responsibility to fulfill its obligations to the harmed and the person committing the harm Davis, 2015). Secondary stakeholders, such as officials or the wider community, have the duty to make room for and facilitate the restorative process, actions that exemplify the concepts of reconciliation and peacemaking (Davis, 2015)—concepts that also are grounded in religious teachings.

In the Abrahamic religions, the concept of reconciliation is a common theme, manifesting through various redemptive rites and rituals around sin and repentance (Sarre & Young, 2011). In Judaism, the holiest day of the calendar is Yom Kippur, the Day of Atonement (Sarre & Young, 2011; Leviticus 23:26–27). In Islamic law, which emphasizes the dignity of the individual and supports opportunities for the rehabilitation and healing of harmed parties (Hascall, 2011), one aspect of *qisas*, or capital punishment, encourages the family of the victim to forgive the wrongdoer completely or to accept reparation payment in lieu of capital punishment; this option for forgiveness lies solely with the wronged party (Humayun, 2021). In Christian scripture, there are also teachings of forgiveness: turn the other cheek (Matthew 5:38–42), repay no evil and live at peace with everyone (Matthew 5:38–42; Romans 12:17–18), forgive the sinner (2 Corinthians 2:6–8). God is depicted in Jewish and Christian teachings as compassionate and capable of forgiveness (Psalm 103:8–10), a sentiment illustrated in the Book of Micah, "Who is a God like you [...] You do not stay angry forever but delight to show mercy" (Micah 7:18).

Relying on the shared spiritual values of unity, reciprocity, reconciliation, and forgiveness, the religious lawyer then would be called to do "justice" in the criminal legal context by facilitating restorative justice principles, as opposed to acquiescing or remaining complicit in the retributive, and racially unjust (Davis, 2015), criminal system currently in place.

For example, religious lawyers practicing in the field of criminal justice would be required to aid in the restorative processes: to identify harms done, to help clients ascertain what must be done to correct these harms and who is responsible for such correction, and to facilitate dialogues working toward repairing these harms (McCold & Wachtel, 2003). Where possible, religious lawyers should advocate for policy in line with restorative justice, and aid with shifts away from retribution and punishment (Reza, 1999). Further, a religious take on the restorative justice process might also call for a transformation of the role of the prosecutor as it exists in today's criminal justice system—that is, as the driving force behind charging decisions and thus the driving force behind the posture a defendant may take in their case (to plead or to litigate) (Reza, 1999). This role of the prosecutor in the criminal justice system not only impedes the overall secular process of restorative justice practice (Reza, 1999), but also obstructs the potential for unity and reconciliation of the community and is fundamentally contrary to the expectation of religious lawyers to "do justice," "love mercy," and "walk humbly with [their] God."

Ultimately, if there is an inherent form of divinity in each person (i.e., a "oneness" or unity through divine interconnection), such a God-created and placed essence cannot be undone by humans. While that unchangeable essence can be ignored, reviled, or rejected, it can never be eradicated. It means that there is always the possibility for "redemption," that is, for any individual to reclaim that essence of interconnection. The foundational tenets of restorative justice practices, that healing is possible for all, are most consistent with these spiritual values.

2 Reparations

One dictionary definition of reparation is "making amends for a wrong one has done, by paying money to or otherwise helping those who have been wronged."

Reparations connects to the spiritual value of "justice by repairing a wrong." Justice requires a penitent attitude that reflects a genuine shift in viewpoint and understanding, a heartfelt pain at the wrong done, and an authentic decision to be and do things differently going forward.

Three moral bases for reparations establish a national debt owed to formerly enslaved people and their descendants as well as immigrant Black/African people who have also endured the damaging effects of structural racism within American institutions. One, enslaved people performed labor for more than 265 years without pay or wealth to pass down to their descendants. Two, after the Civil War, the U.S. government did not uphold its promise to provide equal citizenship and treatment to formerly enslaved people. Last, state-sanctioned economic, political, and racial oppression excluded all Blacks—whether formerly enslaved, free peoples during slavery, or immigrants after the formal legal abolition of slavery—from full self-determination and prosperity. Reparations will help eliminate the racial wealth gap and further the needed efforts to dismantle the vestiges of slavery.[3]

The call for reparations for African Americans in the United States has recently gained some momentum.

The Commission to Study and Develop Reparation Proposals for African Americans Act, H.R. 40 (117th Congress, 2021), has been reintroduced to the U.S. Congress. The Commission would address the fundamental injustice and inhumanity of slavery in the United States between 1619 and 1865. After a fact-finding period, the 13-person commission would hold hearings, submit findings to Congress, and recommend appropriate remedies including a possible national apology. Yet, the commission would not execute any financial reparations (Summers, 2021).[4] The lack of national policies with tangible effects reflects the country's hesitancy to address slavery reparations for African Americans fully.[5]

The history of reparations in the United States too often involves failure and, in cases of those few successes, inadequate if symbolic compensation. The first successful reparations act in the United States was not to repair the harm done to formerly enslaved people, but rather to compensate the enslavers for the loss of their "property." On April 16, 1862, President Abraham Lincoln signed the District of Columbia Compensated Emancipation Act (Craemer, 2021; McDaniel, 2021). The U.S. government paid enslavers $300 per person who was set free. Some 3,100 enslaved individuals were made free through these payments at "a total cost of $930,000—almost $25 million in today's money" (Craemer, 2021; McDaniel, 2021). The formerly enslaved received no money under this Act unless they agreed to leave the United States permanently (Craemer, 2021; McDaniel, 2021).[6]

When the U.S. government did start to address reparations for formerly enslaved people, those promises were broken. As one example, in 1865 Special Field Order No. 15 (Myers, 2020) was issued, granting formerly enslaved people an army mule and not more than 40 acres of land. Although some African Americans received land, President Andrew Johnson returned this Confederate land to former enslavers if they upheld the abolition of slavery, paid off their war debt, and swore loyalty to the Union (LDHI, 2022).

African Americans acted on their own behalf by bringing individual private suits for reparations. While some were successful, these cases failed to create viable legal precedents. As one example, the first private case of reparations occurred in 1783, when Belinda Sutton (Royall House Association, 2022), enslaved in Massachusetts, was legally awarded a pension from the estate of her former enslaver, Isaac Royall. Sutton's case resulted in an annual pension of 15 pounds and 12 shillings; however, subsequent pension payments decreased in amount and then ceased. Moreover, Sutton's momentary success did not create a precedent for other formerly enslaved persons because Royall's status as a Loyalist absentee allowed Massachusetts to provide monetary support out of her former enslaver's confiscated property (Royall House Association, 2022).

African Americans also have demanded reparations—through lawsuits or petitions to local or state governments—for the damage done by the vestiges of slavery, that is, for state-sanctioned attacks on their communities, persons, and properties that occurred after the legal abolition of slavery. Again, the results have been mixed. As one example, in 1921, a white mob, deputized by the City of Tulsa, killed 300 African Americans and left thousands homeless in the wealthy and predominately Black Greenwood community (Ogletree, 2004). Eighty years later, the *Tulsa Race Riot Commission Report* was issued on February 28, 2001, and it documented that the city, state, and county governments were all complicit in the riot. Many of the commissioners declared that reparations were due to the historic Greenwood community and they

> recommended courses of actions to include direct payments to riot survivors and descendants, a scholarship fund to students affected by the riot, establishment of an economic development enterprise zone in the historic Greenwood district and a memorial for the riot victims.
>
> *Francis-Smith, 2022*

Yet in 2004, a U.S. court refused to provide reparations to Tulsa riot victims or their descendants, citing the expiration of the statute of limitations (*Alexander v. Oklahoma*, 2004). Due to the persistence of an Oklahoma state legislator, Rep. Regina Goodwin, the Oklahoma legislature did pay some reparations in the form of low-income student scholarships (Francis-Smith, 2022). At the end of 2021, the Justice for Greenwood Foundation started a lawsuit seeking further reparations. The case is still pending (Jones, 2021).

There have been some successes in suits that African Americans have brought for other state-sanctioned injustices done to them. The Tuskegee Experiment survivors, Black men who had been unwitting subjects of untreated syphilis by the U.S. Public Health Service and the Centers for Disease Control, received $10 million in an out-of-court settlement (CDC, 2022). Living survivors of the 1923 Rosewood Massacre—another instance where a self-sufficient predominantly Black town was destroyed by rioting white men in 1923—received $2.1 million from the Florida state government in 1994 (D'orso, 1997). Additionally, Black farmers received a consent decree against the U.S. Department of Agriculture after a court found systematic racial discrimination in allocating farm loans from 1981 to 1996 (111th Congress, 2010).

The H.R. 40 Act represents the possibility for the United States to start the process of true reparations. Reparations must be tangible because they seek to repair a history of enslavement, apartheid laws, and systemic racism directed at all African Americans.[7] Legislative apologies are only performative. Community dialogues are more meaningful and involve the sharing of the painful truth of American history around slavery and race. These conversations can allow those community members of all races who participate to feel authentic pain and remorse for past wrongdoings. Additionally, community dialogues on reparations assist "rememory" or the process of remembering one's cultural past and reclaiming accurate historical memory (Sundquist, 2001, p. 659).

True reparations must include all facets of slavery's and colonization's legacy. Reparations should cover the wrongs of unpaid labor and the wrong of forced religious conversion. Laws required the newly enslaved to convert to Christianity and prohibited the practice of other religions, particularly African-based religions (Boaz, 2007).[8] Whites justified Black enslavement through the negative portrayals of African-based religions as barbaric, primitive, and immoral (Boaz, 2007). The forced reimagining of African-based religions and the fear of persecution prevented African practitioners from religious expression (Boaz, 2007). The historical existence of religious oppression should also be included in the dialogue on reparations.

True reparations must also include some actual "repayment" to African Americans and some processes to dismantle racism embedded in the current structures of American society. The demolition of structural racism is essential to any authentic decision to be different from the past. This demolition asks us to make white privilege visible and to "displace whiteness as the dominant norm" (Sundquist, 2001, p. 660).

The religious lawyer's obligations regarding reparations are rooted in the same spiritual values as those stated regarding restorative justice: unity or oneness, reciprocity, reconciliation, and forgiveness since reparations is also a part of the criminal legal context. In this case the criminal context is international law (Allain, 2017).

Just as the religious lawyer is called to do "justice" domestically based upon and within the domestic criminal system, she/he/they are also called to do "justice" domestically based upon international law and to stand for the repair of the harms of slavery and its continuing vestiges through support of reparations for those who were and continue to be harmed. This same restorative justice framework compels the religious lawyer to overcome one common objection to reparations: How can people who never personally owned human beings be required to part with any money or benefits? For the religious lawyer and the restorative justice framework, "who is responsible for the correction of the harm" includes a broad range of stakeholders—including the larger community and those members who benefited from the institutional structures created by slavery and intended to support white supremacy at the expense of African Americans (Craemer, 2021; Allain, 2017).[9]

This obligation is a prophetic one. Conversations and debates around reparations can stumble, fall, and fail around the pragmatic issue of cost. But we rest our support on the shared spiritual belief that all are made in God's image and that certain acts can never be committed against a child of God. Once heinous harms are committed against a child of God, then repair of those harms must occur. There is no moral ground to claim it would cost too much money to repair and heal these harms, especially in a world where enormous military budgets are routinely proposed and passed with little debate (Democracy Now, 2022).[10] Consequently, the goal for religious lawyers must be to support reparations that are designed to fully repair and heal the harms that have been and continue to be done.

Conclusion

In this chapter, we explore the question of what it means for the religious lawyer to do justice, love mercy, and walk humbly in the context of criminal law. For the religious prosecutor and criminal defense lawyer, these are moral imperatives in their daily work. Religious lawyers from many traditions see the connections to and interconnected nature of all people and peoples. In their public leadership role, these shared values dictate that the religious lawyer prefer a restorative justice framework over a retributive one. They understand that harm always occurs within the context of relationships and must be repaired within that same context—with all stakeholders involved in accountability and healing. These same values further call upon the religious lawyer to support reparations for the evil of slavery and its continuing vestiges. Of course, the analysis in this chapter is only a beginning. The framework we propose for religious lawyers has far broader implications for addressing systemic wrongs in the criminal justice system.

Notes

1 The authors would like to acknowledge the contribution of Janae Barrett and Samantha Guzman to the research work that supported the development of this chapter.

2 Holmes, "The Unity of Good is a revelation of the greatest importance for it teaches us that we are One with the whole and One with each other."

3 In the United States there is debate within the "pro-reparations" community. Some reparations advocates only support reparations for people who are descended from people formerly enslaved in the United States. Others support the view that all African Americans living in the United States, even those who emigrated from other countries, should also qualify for reparations. See e.g. Taryn Luna, *Reparations Panel OKs Lineage Approach: State task force votes 5–4 to tie potential compensation for slavery to ancestry, LA Times*, March 31, 2022. (California is on track to be the first state in the nation to approve statewide reparations for slavery.) We support this latter position.

4 Summers, J., "It is not the study of getting a check. It is not giving you a check. It is not the bill on a check," Jackson Lee said. "It is to study slavery and develop reparations proposals, which would create, first of all, the platform for understanding."

5 Providing reparations for the victims of racial prejudice and violence is not without precedent in the United States. In 1988, President Ronald Reagan signed into law the Civil Liberties Act of 1988, which officially apologized for the internment of Japanese Americans on behalf of the U.S. government and authorized a payment of $20,000 to each former internee who was still alive when the act passed. Densho Encyclopedia Densho.org.

6 The "emigration incentive" was less than what the enslavers received: any formerly enslaved person who would leave was given "$100 or around $2,283 in 2021 dollars."

7 Native Americans and Indigenous peoples also suffered enslavement, apartheid laws, and systematic racism in the United States and U.S. colonies. On September 8, 2000, "the Bureau of Indian Affairs' 175th anniversary, Assistant Secretary-Indian Affairs Kevin Gover apologized for the ethnic cleansing and cultural annihilation the BIA had wrought against American Indian and Alaska Native people in years past." *See* Darling, N., 2000. Gover Apologizes For BIA's Misdeeds | Indian Affairs. [online] Bia.gov. [Accessed March 25, 2022].

8 Boaz, D., African-based religions such as Voodoo, Santeria, Obeah, Candomble, and Orisha worship.

9 This approach of having the larger community and future generations take responsibility for debts for which they are not personally responsible has been done in the reparation contexts in other countries—only not for the benefit of formerly enslaved people. Craemer, T. (2021), Citing the fact that Haiti was forced by France to repay its enslavers 150 million francs over a total of 122 years and that the British government paid "reparations totaling 20 million pounds (equivalent to some 300 billion pounds in 2018) to slave owners " and "serviced [the loans it had to take out] for 182 years" (emphasis in the original).

10 Democracy Now, noting that the Biden White House proposed $5.8 trillion budget would boost military spending by 10 percent to an unprecedented $813 billion.

References

111th Congress (2010). H.R. 4783.

117th Congress (2021). H.R. 40.

Al-Hibri, A.Y., Carter, S., Gabel, P., and O'Hare, J. (1999). Remarks: Panel Discussion: Does Religious Faith Interfere with a Lawyer's Work? *Fordham Urban Law Journal*, 26, 985–1017.

Allain, J. (2017). Introductory Note: Slavery Convention, Protocol Amending the Slavery Convention, Supplementary Convention on the Abolition of Slavery, the Slave Trade, and Institutions and Practices Similar to Slavery, *United Nations Audiovisual Library of International Law*. Retrieved from: https://legal.un.org/avl/ha/sc/sc.html.

Alexander v. Oklahoma, 382 F.3d 1206 (10th Cir. 2004).

American Civil Liberties Union (ACLU). (2022). Mass Incarceration, ACLU. Retrieved at: www.aclu.org/issues/smart-justice/mass-incarceration.

Beaty Chiste, K. (2007). Faith-Based Organizations and the Pursuit of Restorative Justice, *Manitoba Law Journal*, 32(1), 27–28.

Beaty Chiste, K. (2013). Origins of Modern Restorative Justice: Five Examples from the English-Speaking World, *UBC Law Review*, 46(1) 33–80.

Boaz, D. (2007). Religious Reparations from the Trans-Atlantic Slave Trade: Forming Demons, Cults, and Zombies to Justify Black Enslavement, *St. Thomas Law Review*, 20, 604–621.

Braithwaite, J. (1999). Restorative Justice: Assessing Optimistic and Pessimistic Accounts, *Crime and Justice*, 25, 1–107.

Brihaspati. *The Mahabharata* 13.113.8. Sacred Texts. Retrieved from: https://sacred-texts.com/hin/m13/index.htm.

Centers for Disease Control and Prevention (CDC). (2021). The U.S. Public Health Service Syphilis Study at Tuskegee. Retrieved from: www.cdc.gov/tuskegee/timeline.htm.

Clark, P. (2001). Restorative Justice and ADR: Opportunities and Challenges, *Advocate (Idaho State Bar)*, 44(11), 13–16.

Craemer, T. (2021, March). There was a Time Reparations Were Actually Paid Out—Just Not to Formerly Enslaved People, *UConn Today*. Retrieved from: https://today.uconn.edu/2021/03/there-was-a-time-reparations-were-actually-paid-out-just-not-to-formerly-enslaved-people/

Davis, F.E. (2019). *The Little Book of Race and Restorative Justice: Black Lives, Healing and US Social Transformation*. Good Books.

Davis, F.E., Lyubansky, M., & Schiff, M. (2015). Restoring Racial Justice. In Scott, R. A., & Kosslyn, S. M. (Eds.), *Emerging Trends in the Social and Behavioral Sciences: An Interdisciplinary, Searchable, and Linkable Resource*. John Wiley & Sons, pp. 1–16.

Democracy Now. (2022, March 29). Biden Budget Plan Calls for Record Military Spending, $32 Billion for Police. Retrieved from: www.democracynow.org/2022/3/29/headlines/biden_budget_plan_calls_for_record_military_spending_32_billion_for_police.

Dharmatrata, Prajnavarman, Vidyaprabhkara, Vasubandhu, and Rockhill, W.W. (1883). *Udanavarga: A Collection of Verses from the Buddhist Canon*, Trubner & Co.

D'orso, M. (1997). Revisiting Rosewood, *The Virginia Pilot*. Retrieved from: https://scholar.lib.vt.edu/VA-news/VA-Pilot/issues/1997/vp970216/02140719.htm

Francis-Smith, J. (2022, February 22). A Century Later, Reparations for Greenwood Still Elusive, *Journal Record*. Retrieved from: https://journalrecord.com/2022/02/22/a-century-later-reparations-for-greenwood-still-elusive/.

Freedman, M.H. (1966). Professional Responsibility of the Criminal Defense Lawyer: The Three Hardest Questions, *Michigan Law Review*, 64, 1469–1484.

Freedman, M.H. (1990). *Understanding Lawyers' Ethics* (4th ed.). LexisNexis.

Garfield, A.M. et al. (2014). The Oneness Beliefs Scale: Connecting Spirituality with Pro-Environmental Behavior, *Journal for the Scientific Study of Religion*, 53(2), 356–372.

Goodman, L.E. (2008). *Love Thy Neighbor As Thyself*. Oxford University Press.

Greenwood, J.E. (2001). Restorative Justice and the Dynamics of Faith, *The Clergy Journal*, 3–5.

Gunning, I.R. (2015). Lawyers of All Faiths: Constructing Professional Identity and Finding Common Ground, *The Journal of the Legal Profession*, 39(2), 231–272.

Hasan, Z. (n.d.). Ethical Principles of Lawyers in Islam, 1–13. Retrieved from: https://zulkiflihasan.files.wordpress.com/2008/10/shariah-law-report-ethics1.pdf.

Hascall, S. C. (2011). Restorative Justice in Islam: Should Qisas Be Considered a Form of Restorative Justice? *Berkeley Journal of Middle Eastern & Islamic Law*, 4, 35–78.

Holmes, E. (1998). *The Science of Mind: A Philosophy, a Faith, a Way of Life*. Tarcher Putnam.

Humayun, N. (2021). The Islamic Position on Capital Punishment: A Restorative Justice Model Which Aligns with International Law and Inspires Reasoning for Prison Industrial Complex Abolition in the U.S., *Berkeley Journal of Middle Eastern & Islamic Law*, 12, 9–29.

Jones, C. (December 21, 2021). Lawsuit: Race Massacre Survivors Call for Financial Investment into Greenwood, *Tulsa World*. Retrieved from: https://tulsaworld.com/news/local/racemassacre/lawsuit-race-massacre-survivors-call-for-financial-investment-into-greenwood/article_d3fc0116-6268-11ec-a3ea-a3470606e19f.html.

Kanazawa, K. (1998). Being a Buddhist and a Lawyer, *Fordham Law Review*, 66, 1171–1175.

Kitab al-Kafi. (2022). *Abrahamic Study Hall*, vol. 2, p. 146. Retrieved from: www.abrahamicstudyhall.org/2016/11/22/the-golden-rule/#Islam.

Lanni, A. (2021). Taking Restorative Justice Seriously, *Buffalo Law Review*, 69, 635–681.

Lerman, D.M. (2000). Forgiveness in the Criminal Justice System: If It Belongs, Then Why Is It So Hard to Find? *Fordham Urban Law Journal*, 27, 1663–1675.

Levine, S. (1996). The Broad Life of the Jewish Lawyer: Integrating Spirituality, Scholarship and Profession, *Texas Tech Law Review*, 27, 1199–1210. Retrieved from: https://digitalcommons.tourolaw.edu/cgi/viewcontent.cgi?article=1026&context=scholarlyworks.

Levinson, S. (1993). Identifying the Jewish Lawyer: Reflections on the Construction of Professional Identity, *Cardozo Law Review*, 14, 1577–1612.

Lowcountry Digital History Initiative (LDHI) (May 29, 1865).. 2. President Johnson Offers Amnesty to Former Confederates. Retrieved from: https://ldhi.library.cofc.edu/exhibits/show/after_slavery_educator/unit_one_documents/document_two

McCold, P., and Wachtel, T. (2003). In Pursuit of Paradigm: A Theory of Restorative Justice, *Restorative Practices*, 1–3. Retrieved from: www.iirp.edu/pdf/paradigm.pdf.

McDaniel, W.C. (2021, September 4). The Former Slave Who Sued for Reparations, and Won, *The New York Times*. Retrieved from: www.nytimes.com/2019/09/04/opinion/henrietta-wood-reparations-slavery.html.

Myers, B. (2020). Sherman's Field Order No. 15, *New Georgia Encyclopedia*. Retrieved from: www.georgiaencyclopedia.org/articles/history-archaeology/shermans-field-order-no-15/.

Nhat Hanh, T. (2001). *Essential Writings*, Robert Ellsberg (Ed.). Orbis Books.

Ogletree, C.J. Jr. (2004). Tulsa Reparations: The Survivors' Story, *Boston College Third World Law Journal*, 24(1), 13–30.

Pearce, R.G. (1996). The Jewish Lawyer's Question, *Texas Tech Law Review*, 27, 1259–1270.

Pearce, R.G. (1998). Forward, Symposium, The Religious Lawyering Movement: An Emerging Force in Legal Ethics and Professionalism, *Fordham Law Review*, 66, 1075–1082.

Pearce, R.G., and Uelmen, A.J. (2004). Religious Lawyering in a Liberal Democracy: A Challenge and An Invitation, *Case Western Reserve Law Review*, 55, 127–160.

Revised Standard Version Bible. (2022). Retrieved from: www.biblegateway.com/versions/Revised-Standard-Version-RSV-Bible/

Reza, S. (1999). Religion and the Public Defender, *Fordham Urban Law Journal*, 26, 1051–1067.

Royall House Association. (2022). Belinda Sutton and Her Petitions, *Royal House and Slave Quarters*. Retrieved from: https://royallhouse.org/slavery/belinda-sutton-and-her-petitions/.

Sarre, R., and Young, J. (2011). Christian Approaches to the Restorative Justice Movement: Observations on Scripture and Praxis, *Contemporary Justice Review*, 14(3) 345–355.

Shaffer, T.L. (1981). *On Being a Christian and a Lawyer*. Brigham Young University Press.

Skeel, D.A, and Stuntz, W.J. (2005). Christianity and the (Modest) Rule of Law, University of Pennsylvania, *Journal of Constitutional Law*, 8, 809–839.

Summers, J. (2021, November 12). A Bill to Study Reparations for Slavery Had Momentum in Congress, But Still No Vote, *NPR*. Retrieved from: www.npr.org/2021/11/12/1054889820/a-bill-to-study-reparations-for-slavery-had-momentum-in-congress-but-still-no-vo

Sundquist, C. (2001). Critical Praxis, Spirit Healing, and Community Activism: Preserving a Subversive Dialogue on Reparations, *New York University Annual Survey of American Law*, 58, 659–698.

Tanakh (bible). Sefaria Tanakh Online. Retrieved from: www.sefaria.org/Tanakh.

Wetstone, K. (2022). Breaking Out of a Broken System: America's Fixation on Retribution, Punishment, and Incarceration, *Berkeley MDP*. Retrieved from: https://mdp.berkeley.edu/breaking-out-of-a-broken-system-americas-fixation-on-retribution-punishment-and-incarceration/.

Wilkins, D.B. (1998). Identities and Roles: Race, Recognition, and Professional Responsibility. *Maryland Law Review*, 57 (4/5), 1502–1594.

Zacharias, F.C., and Green, B. (2022). Prosecutorial Neutrality, *Wisconsin Law Review*, 2004(3), 837–904. Retrieved from: www.researchgate.net/publication/279717619_Prosecutorial_Neutrality.

PART 3

Appraisal of Contemporary Issues

11

HUMAN RIGHTS, RELIGION AND THE CRIMINAL JUSTICE SYSTEM

Roadblocks, Diversions and Repairs

Jonathan Kearney

Introduction

'And as you wish that others would do to you, do so to them' (English Standard Version Bible, 2001, Luke 6:31). This teaching of Christ has been grouped with the teaching of other world religions and ethical systems under the title of the Golden Rule (Blackburn, 2016). But in an age that for the West has become increasingly secular, how can this teaching be applied in circumstances where the *you* and the *others* have significantly differing expectations, beliefs or opinions? It seems that the level of common intersection between the religious and secular liberal spheres is diminishing, with clashes rather than coexistence becoming the narrative. The religious perspective adopted in this chapter will be primarily that of Christianity. In terms of human rights instruments, the greatest focus will be on the European Convention of Human Rights.

The progress and development of human rights protections have been variously charted through the likes of the Cyrus Cylinder, the Magna Carta, the United States Declaration of Independence and the French Declaration of the Rights of Man (Youth for Human Rights International, 2010). However, the more universal approach of the contemporary era of human rights has its foundation in the Universal Declaration of Human Rights (UDHR) proclaimed by the United Nations General Assembly in 1948. The UDHR formed the basis not only for the subsequent International Covenants on Civil and Political Rights, and Economic and Social Rights but also for the variety of regional rights' documents (Steiner & Alston, 2000). Holland (2019, 505) suggests that the human rights propounded by the United Nations are essentially a repackaging of Christian concepts for non-Christian audiences, necessitated by a desire to obscure their origins amongst the canon law of medieval Europe, so enabling their claim to global rather than Western jurisdiction. Certainly, the notion of the freedom to choose and change

DOI: 10.4324/9781003276593-14

religions, has been considered unacceptable by a number of Islamic states, and their responses have ranged from expressing specific reservations in relation to Article 18 of the International Covenant on Civil and Political Rights (ICCPR) to working from the basis that the wording has always meant different things to different states (Khaliq, 2012, 191–192). Shortall and Steinmetz-Jenkins (2020, 2–5) unpack the main historical analyses that vie for position in explaining the modern human rights movement – Judeo-Christian tradition, the Enlightenment's revolt against religion and, more recently, a project of the Christian right rather than the secular left. Regardless of whether or not the origin of human rights lies within Christian thought and practice, 'freedom of religion and belief is one of our most cherished and contested rights [...] [which] occupies a unique and complex space in international human rights law' (Gunatilleke, 2020, 20–22).

Part of the complexity derives from the inevitable debates emanating from the perceived lack of fit between on the one hand, faith, doctrine and progressive human rights interpretations, and on the other hand, questions over the appropriateness of freedom of religion even being part of the human rights canon (Evans, 2013, 565–566). Tiedemann (2015, 87) explores this perspective regarding the right to freedom of religion as a subtype of other higher rights. Thus, he regards the general right to freedom of thought and freedom of speech as adequately capable of covering the thoughts and expressions of religion (Tiedemann, 2015, 88). Using this reasoning, freedom of assembly or association would also connect with aspects of religious freedom.

To a large extent, arguments regarding the appropriateness or usefulness of the right to religious freedom within the human rights corpus might be considered as effectively redundant or purely academic. The simple fact is that the right has been codified and accepted, and states parties have agreed to be bound by the human rights instruments. Religion is not going away, and a growing body of jurisprudence has arisen. In fact, despite the propensity for religion to be a polarising influence within human rights law (Khaitan & Norton, 2020, 111), it has experienced a comeback to the extent that many societies are grappling with religious pluralism, religious conflicts, religious terrorism and lower-scale religious hostility (2019, 1126).

Religion and Human Rights

Article 18 of the UDHR sets out the tenets of freedom of thought, conscience and religion – the right includes freedom to change religion or belief, and freedom, either alone or in community with others and in public or private, to manifest religion or belief in teaching, practice, worship and observance (United Nations, 1948). Article 18 of the International Covenant on Civil and Political Rights (ICCPR) drew upon the terminology of the UDHR but also introduced the potential for limitations to the right that were considered to be legal and necessary. Article 9 of the European Convention on Human Rights codifies freedom of thought, conscience and religion.

Whilst other regional rights instruments exist – the American Convention on Human Rights 1969, the African Charter on Human and Peoples' Rights 1981 and the Arab Charter on Human Rights 2004 – the jurisprudence in relation to freedom of religion is most clearly developed within the UN's Human Rights Committee and the European Court of Human Rights, with the latter's jurisprudence being the most voluminous (Khaliq, 2012, 202). The past two decades have witnessed increasing numbers of Article 9 cases being examined by the European Court of Human Rights, with an increasingly rich and richly controversial jurisprudence having resulted (Evans, 2013, 569).

There are three aspects to the freedoms of Article 9 (See Figure 11.1); the first two aspects (freedom of thought, conscience and religion, and the freedom to change religion or belief) are absolute rights in that 'any action by the state to coerce or compel people's thinking, or to make them reveal their beliefs is contrary to the Convention and cannot be justified by considerations relating to the public interest' (Starmer, 1999, 131). Conversely, the third aspect (freedom to manifest one's religion or beliefs) is not an unfettered right. It is qualified by a restriction that 'has some basis in domestic law [...] sanctioned by reasonably clear legal rules which are accessible to potential victims (Starmer, 1999, 130). Necessity within a democratic society indicates that there is a pressing social need for the restriction, with the restriction in question being a proportionate response to that need – going no further than is necessary (Starmer, 1999, 130). Thus, any interference with the right must be prescribed by law, have a legitimate purpose and be necessary in a democratic society (Schabas, 2015, 420).

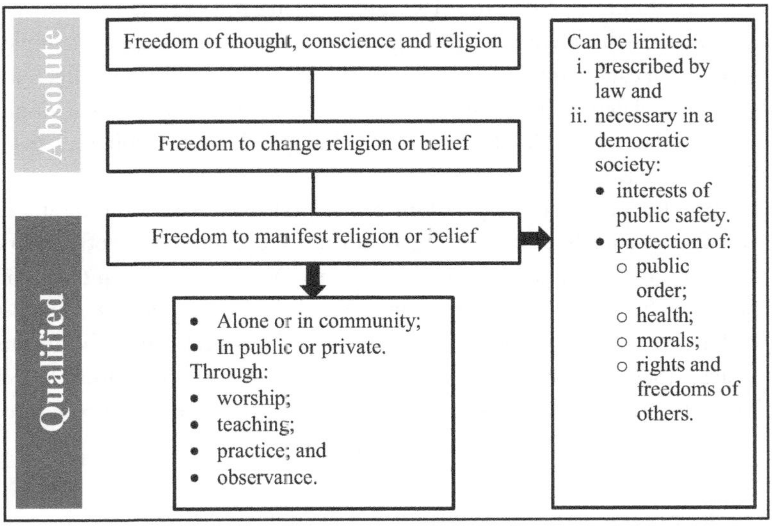

FIGURE 11.1 Aspects of Article 9 of the ECHR – Freedom of thought, conscience, and religion

Allied Freedoms

As with freedom of thought, conscience and religion, the unfolding of freedom rights in respect of expression and association are represented in the Universal Declaration (Articles 19 and 20), the ICCPR (Articles 19 and 21), and the ECHR (Articles 10 and 11). In tandem with his observations concerning the necessity of religious freedom as a right, Evans (2013, 563–64) notes that other human rights, such as thought, expression, association, equality and non-discrimination tend to find their outworking in the context of religious belief and belief systems. Unlike freedom of thought, conscience and religion with its absolute and qualified portions, freedom of expression and freedom of assembly and association are qualified rights in toto.

Articles 8 to 11 of the ECHR all contain restrictions or limitations, but Article 10 (Freedom of Expression) is the only one of the suite of four that specifically mentions duties and responsibilities in connection with the exercise of the right. Of the human rights described so far, exercising freedom of expression rights can have a significant impact on the rights and freedoms of others (Davis, 2014, 126). In exercising freedom of expression there is a heightened likelihood of offence being taken, reputational damage being experienced, private and confidential information being published, defence and national security being undermined, or the rule of law being compromised. Thus, given the potential for damage to be inflicted on individuals and institutions, it follows that reasonable restrictions on this particular freedom are considered to be both desirable and necessary; and limiting them can be perfectly consistent with a well-functioning democratic society (Davis, 2014, 126). But it must be remembered that the impact of freedom of expression being used in a pillorying manner varies depending on the context and circumstances. Feinberg (cited in Van Noorloos, 2015, 165–166) differentiates the experiences of harm and taking offence – the former is unacceptable, and the latter is simply unpleasant. Experiencing harm results in the victim's interests being adversely affected, with rights being violated. While being unpleasant, shocking or sometimes disgusting, there is no violation of individual interests in being offended (Feinberg, 1984–88 as cited in Van Noorloos, 2015, 165–166).

Litigation under Article 11 (freedom of assembly and association) has tended to focus on three main categories of organisation – religious groups, political parties and trade unions (Schabas, 2015, 499). So, whilst Article 11 has some significance in relation to the practice of religion, in the main, those rights have tended to be regarded as being closely related to the exercise of political rights within modern democracies (Schabas, 2015, 483). It might even be argued that within the sphere of religion, the freedom of assembly and association rights tend to be engaged less frequently than those of freedom of expression.

A Shift in Focus

Much of the European jurisprudence in relation to freedom of expression and religion has manifested itself in the freedoms of the non-religious to criticise, attack or inflame churches or religious groups. The United Kingdom has witnessed a reversal to some extent, with individuals from faith groups being challenged in terms of freedom of expression and what they can legitimately say about those who differ from them in terms of world view. Recently, this has manifested itself most notably in the areas of LGBTQI+ freedoms that conflict with religious teaching and interpretation.

A Case Study in Enforcement

Freedom of religion and freedom of expression rights have come into sharper focus over recent years as far as some members of faith communities have been concerned. In one case, Dale McAlpine, a street preacher, was arrested on two different occasions. In 2010, having been engaged in preaching in a public place in the centre of the English town of Workington, McAlpine was approached by a Police Community Support Officer (PCSO). Although McAlpine had not mentioned the subject of homosexuality whilst preaching, the PCSO (who identified as being gay) told him if he had mentioned the subject whilst preaching, he would be arrested. In the conversation, McAlpine told the PCSO that according to the Bible, homosexuality was a sin (Petre, 2010). Police officers were called to the scene (PCSOs have no powers of arrest) and after a conversation with McAlpine, he was arrested by virtue of Section 5 of the Public Order Act 1986.

The case was eventually dropped by the Crown Prosecution Service due to a lack of evidence and McAlpine was subsequently awarded £7,000 plus costs from Cumbria Police following a claim of wrongful arrest, unlawful imprisonment and breach of his human rights (Christian Institute, 2019). The *Keeping the Peace* police manual of guidance issued in 2010 by the Association of Chief Police Officers, its Scottish counterpart (ACPOS) and the National Policing Improvement Agency examined S.5 of the Public Order Act 1986, highlighted the need to prove action, intention and impact, and made the point that

> police officers are expected to display a degree of fortitude and for an officer to be caused harassment, alarm or distress, the conduct complained of must go beyond that which he or she would regularly come across in the ordinary course of police duties. *ACPO/ACPOS/NPIA, 2010, 30–31*

In 2018, McAlpine was again approached by three police officers in the English town of Kendal following an allegation by two security guards that he had preached against Allah, spread hate and insulted people.

On this occasion, McAlpine was arrested by virtue of S.4A of the Public Order Act 1986. S.4A differs from S.5 in that the alleged offender is deemed to have intended to cause harassment, alarm or distress rather than the experience occurring as a consequence of his actions. He was released after six hours and was notified a number of months later that police would be taking no further action. Again, a claim against Cumbria Constabulary for wrongful arrest and false imprisonment resulted in compensation to McAlpine of £4,000 plus costs.

Lightning rarely strikes in the same place twice, yet in the case of Dale McAlpine, the same police force seems to have fallen foul of its officers resorting to courses of action which ultimately gave rise to claims for unlawful arrest and false imprisonment. The decision-making processes used on each occasion might reasonably be questioned. This is not to diminish the often-invidious nature of the positions in which police officers find themselves when responding to the wide variety of calls that they deal with constantly. There can be a variety of determining factors driving officers in their responses and decision-making – pressure to produce results, fears of complaints from dissatisfied callers or the necessity of being seen to be acting resolutely, to name but a few. Therefore, it is critical that officers have recourse to adequate resources and guidance in making their operational decisions.

The National Decision Model

The National Decision Model (NDM) is regarded by the United Kingdom's College of Policing as being suitable for all (policing) decisions and a tool that ought to be used by everyone in policing (See Figure 11.2). Its universal appropriateness for policing decisions means that it can be applied to spontaneous incidents

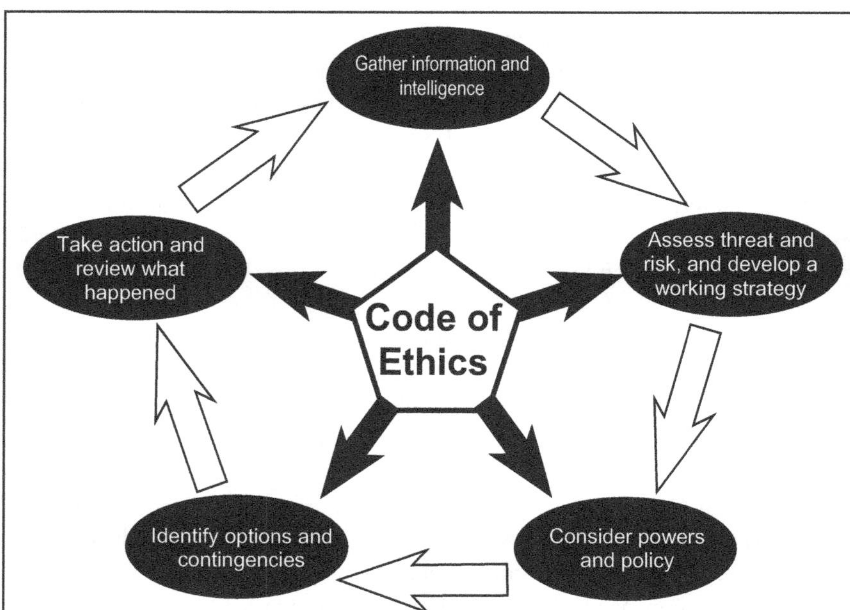

FIGURE 11.2 The National Decision Model used by all United Kingdom police forces (Contents © College of Policing Ltd re-used and licensed under the Open Government Licence v3.0.)

or planned operations; by an individual or a team; in both operational and non-operational situations (College of Policing, 2014, National Decision Model).

The central core of the model is the Code of Ethics – a ten-point list of principles and standards of professional behaviour that apply to police officers and police staff. This ethical core is expected to inform the five peripheral activities at every stage as they are considered in sequence. Initial action in relation to any police response will involve the gathering of intelligence and information; the expectation is that such information will be obtained and handled in a manner that is consistent with the Code of Ethics.

The second stage involves analysis of the information that has been gathered to consider possible threats, risks and benefits in order to develop a strategy for addressing the issue. Again, this is done with reference to the Code of Ethics before progressing to the third stage – considering the powers that are available and the policies that are pertinent to the situation. This allows the options and contingencies to be considered commensurate with the available information, time constraints, available resources (bearing in mind knowledge, experience and skills), and the impact of potential action; all the while considering the proportionality, legitimacy and necessity of the planned actions. The final aspect of the model relates to taking action and being in a position to review the outcome. Again, the Code of Ethics is intrinsic to this final stage of the model, although given the potential for cyclical use of the model within a developing or ongoing scenario, it may not be the final stage as much as the completion of a particular phase of an operation or response.

The NDM was launched in 2011, albeit in a slightly different format, but the intent and process were the same. The NDM replaced three other decision-making models – the Conflict Management Model (to which it closely approximates), the SARA (Scanning, Analysis, Response and Assessment) problem-solving model and a Values-Based Decision-Making model (F. Pike, personal communication, March 14, 2022). Certainly, the officers involved in each of the McAlpine cases would have had access to useful decision-making models, although the actual degree to which frontline officers involved in local policing would have been exposed to some of the models is moot. Perhaps the nomenclature of the Conflict Management Model could have masked the degree to which it could be applied to non-conflict situations, given that the first incident had no overtones of disorder or conflict. Likewise, the second incident had no such defining characteristics, but officers would have had sufficient information to be able to use the NDM. Use of a model such as the NDM need not be attended by an elaborate bureaucratic procedure or time-consuming analysis – its self-declared universal utility renders it applicable in a range of interactions from the apparently mundane to the noticeably spectacular.

Closely tied to police decision-making is the notion of the critical incident. A critical incident is 'any incident, where the effectiveness of the police response is likely to have a significant impact on the confidence of the victim, their family and/or the community' (College of Policing, 2013). Thus, inappropriate police responses can transfer routine or ongoing incidents into the domain of the critical incident. The doctrine guiding police responses to critical incidents is largely a consequence of the 1999 public enquiry into the investigation conducted by the Metropolitan Police Service into the murder of Stephen Lawrence in 1993 (College of Policing, 2013). Given the nature of the faith communities involved, the arrests of Dale McAlpine would have been unlikely to cause widespread disaffection, but it is not inconceivable that the police handling of such incidents could have a serious impact on community confidence. Single factors or the actions or inactions of one person rarely cause a critical incident (College of Policing, 2013), but a series of events can diminish trust in the police, producing circumstances where a community or minority may sense that their interests are very much at odds with enforcement and response trends. Consequently, the necessity of making well-judged and reasoned decisions is paramount.

An examination of the arrests of United Kingdom-based street preachers shows that the allegations and reasons for arrest centre for the greater part on what is regarded as mainstream Christian teaching on LGBTQI+ issues, particularly around the introduction of same-sex marriage. At the time of writing, it would appear that the battle lines are being drawn around Christian ministry or church activities and the definition of conversion therapy – a clash that is likely to engage a wider swathe of the Christian church within the United Kingdom than a small number of individuals engaged in public preaching.

A New Front

The primary issue in this debate is the actual understanding of what constitutes conversion therapy. At the level of the United Nations, Madrigal-Borloz describes conversion therapy as falling into three categories – psychotherapeutic, medical and faith-based (2020, 10–13) – which seek to change non-heteronormative sexual orientations and non-cisnormative gender identities (2020, 2). It is, in effect,

> an umbrella term to describe interventions of a wide-ranging nature, all of which are premised on the belief that a person's sexual orientation and gender identity, including gender expression, can and should be changed or suppressed when they do not fall under what other actors in a given setting and time perceive as the desirable norm, in particular when the person is lesbian, gay, bisexual, trans or gender diverse. Such practices are therefore consistently aimed at effecting a change from non-heterosexual to heterosexual and from trans or gender diverse to cisgender. Depending on the context, the term is used for a multitude of practices and methods, some of which are clandestine and therefore poorly documented.
>
> *Madrigal-Borloz, 2020, 4*

In Australia, whilst Queensland was the first state to ban conversion therapy, the legislation focused on health providers (Health Legislation Amendment Act 2020). The State of Victoria has extended the impact of its conversion therapy legislation to all of society through Section 5(1) of the Change or Suppression (Conversion)

Practices Prohibition Act 2021, referring to practice or conduct directed towards a person with a view to changing or suppressing that person's sexual orientation or gender identity. In Canada, the Act to amend the Criminal Code (conversion therapy) (S.C. 2021, c. 24) refers to a practice, treatment or service designed to bring about a change to sexual orientation or gender identity. The language used in the cases of the State of Victoria and Canada could be regarded as being broad in its scope and vague in its target, but as with all new legislation, the interpretive tests will ultimately be applied in the courts in order to define what actually constitutes a practice, conduct, treatment or service and the extent, if any, to which the legislation engages the views on sexual ethics and mores advocated by Christian doctrine.

As the United Kingdom and its various devolved legislatures consider legislating in relation to conversion therapy, the definition of what constitutes conversion therapy and what might therefore be banned is exercising the minds of many constituencies. The Equality and Human Rights Commission has demonstrated sensitivity to the breadth of considerations in its response to the UK government's consultation on the banning of conversion therapy –

> the legislation must be carefully drafted in order not to catch legitimate and appropriate counselling, therapy or support which enables a person to explore their sexual orientation or gender dysphoria, and to avoid criminalising mainstream religious practice such as preaching, teaching and praying about sexual ethics.
>
> *Equality and Human Rights Commission, 2022, 6*

Another advocacy group regards the potential for prayer to be exempted from the definition of conversion therapy as being 'a significant loophole that would be open to abuse, and [...] misguided given that a great number of conversion practices are prayer-based and given that they are often conducted in a religious context and environment' (Ban 'Conversion Therapy' Legal Forum, 2021, 8). Contrast that perspective with the views of the 2,500 signatories of a letter presented to Downing Street (the UK prime minister's residence and office) calling for ordinary Christian activity to be excluded from any forthcoming ban and making the point that although they were 'the last people in the world who want to be criminalised', they would 'rather go to prison for five years' than neglect the full teaching of the Christian faith (Christian Institute, 2022). With such disparate views, it is not unrealistic to see the police being placed in a position where they could come into contact with a broader section of the Christian populace and be faced with the demands of balancing the interpretation of the law with the freedom of religion and freedom of expression rights.

Add to that the view that faith is being marginalised in the public realm (Carey & Carey, 70), a view that appears to be resonating in the United Kingdom and beyond. There is a sense that churches are absolutely dependent upon the limited tolerance of a largely religiously illiterate and disinterested state (Carey & Carey, 73), and Dreher observes that dissenters from prevailing secular world views

> can find their businesses, careers and reputations destroyed. They are pushed out of the public square, stigmatized, cancelled and demonized as racists, sexists, homophobes and the like and they are afraid to resist, because they are confident that no one will join them or defend them.
>
> *2020, 9*

How might this difficult territory be negotiated?

Quo Vademus?

For the police there may be an operational need to engage with faith communities to better grasp their heritage, understanding and world view. One Christian human rights barrister has suggested that because of the arrests of a number of street preachers over recent years, it would be prudent for the College of Policing to agree a

> Street Preacher's Charter – a set of guidelines which makes clear the law on freedom of speech – both to street preachers, and police officers on the beat who, increasingly, have little understanding of the Christian faith or, why Christians might want to share the gospel.
>
> *Diamond, 2022*

A not dissimilar suggestion by a former Archbishop of Canterbury urging the Court of Appeal to create a small panel of judges who had training in or understanding of religious faith, to rule in the appeal court on issues of religious freedom and liberty, where they clashed with other rights, was roundly rejected as being deeply unprincipled (Carey & Carey, 101).

The College of Policing exists to, among other things, 'set standards for key areas of policing which help forces and individuals provide consistency and better service for the public' (College of Policing, n.d.). With regard to community engagement and tension, the College states that, 'failing to engage will undermine community confidence in law enforcement and make positive policing outcomes more difficult to achieve' (College of Policing, 2020). Freedom of information enquiries with all of the United Kingdom's territorial police forces asked the following question:

> Has [named force] interacted or engaged with any faith communities, organisations or denominations in relation to preaching and teaching in situations where the subject matter may potentially engage the criminal law?
>
> *Personal FOI communications, February 21, 2022*

None of the responses indicated any such engagement, but a number of responses referred to the College of Policing's Authorised Professional Practice (APP) which provides operational guidance for the investigation of hate crime. The APP has been the subject of judicial review in the High Court and subsequent appeal. Following a complaint made to Humberside Police that a number of gender-critical tweets posted by him were transphobic, Mr. Harry Miller was notified that a non-crime hate incident had been recorded and several conversations ensued between him and the investigating officer, the facts and content of which were disputed.

The designation of an incident as being motivated by hate or hostility has its roots in the Macpherson report, published as a consequence of the Metropolitan Police Service's handling of the investigation into the murder of Stephen Lawrence. Recommendation 12 defined a racist incident as 'any incident which is perceived to be racist by the victim or any other person' (Macpherson, 1999). The perception-based recording of crime and non-crime incidents motivated by hate was a valuable and necessary introduction to UK policing, yet one with certain risks, although as originally propounded, the likely benefits outweighed the potential costs. Perception-based recording was widened by the College of Policing to include incidents relating to race, religion, disability, sexual orientation or transgender identity. The victim does not have to justify or provide evidence of their belief for the purposes of reporting, and police officers or staff should not directly challenge this perception ([2020] EWHC 225 (Admin), para. 200).

Miller challenged the legality of the Hate Crime Operational Guidance and the manner in which Humberside Police dealt with him under the policy ([2020] EWHC 225 (Admin), paras. 16 & 115), claiming that his freedom of expression rights had been interfered with unlawfully. The judgement endorsed the operational guidance but questioned the action taken by Humberside Police. Although not the substance of the review, the judge entertained considerable doubt whether Miller's tweets were properly recordable under the operational guidance at all ([2020] EWHC 225 (Admin), para 281). In response to the findings, the College of Policing made some revisions to the guidance, with a greater emphasis on proportionality, in an attempt to meet the criticisms made of the police conduct in the case ([2021] EWCA Civ 1926, para. 122). On appeal, the Court agreed with Miller's arguments in relation to interference with his freedom of expression and lack of proportionality in the police response. It was noted that the type of interference experienced had a chilling effect on expression and debate. In terms of the procedures, the absence of any means to exclude irrational complaints and those devoid of any evidence of hostility created an obvious weakness.

Consequently, the College of Policing is examining its best practice guidance on the investigation of hate crime. Aligning the McAlpine and Miller experiences in relation to investigative decision-making highlights the contested nature of the territory and the difficulty experienced when a prescribed course of action may satisfy the needs and desires of one victim but actually creates other victims as a result of a process which may no longer be fit for the purpose for which it was intended. An algorithmic approach to the interpretation of powers and policy will always be fraught with difficulty and there will be circumstances that fall between the gaps. The judicial thinking revealed in two recent judgements has effectively highlighted the chilling effect of a zealous interpretation of guidance that appears to discourage a rational and reasoned analysis consonant with the circumstances. This moment may offer a golden opportunity for the College of Policing to engage with a broad swathe of Christian denominations and advocacy groups to ensure that a constituency that could easily be labelled by means of existing and anticipated legislation, has the opportunity to shape its own understanding and that of others.

References

ACPO/ACPOS/NPIA. (2010). *Keeping the Peace*. National Policing Improvement Agency.

Ban 'Conversion Therapy' Legal Forum. (2021). *Recommendations on legislating effectively for a ban on conversion practices*. Ozanne Foundation.

Blackburn, S. (2016). Golden rule. In *A Dictionary of Philosophy*. Oxford University Press. Retrieved from: www.oxfordreference.com/view/10.1093/acref/9780198735304.001.0001/acref-9780198735304-e-1399.

Carey, G., & Carey, A. (2012). *We don't do God*. Monarch.

Christian Institute. (2019). Christian street preacher vindicated in £4,000 police payout following wrongful arrest. Retrieved from: www.christian.org.uk/press_release/christian-street-preacher-vindicated-in-4000-police-payout-following-wrongful-arrest/.

Christian Institute. (2022). Church leaders present 'conversion therapy' letter to Downing Street. Retrieved from: www.christian.org.uk/news/church-leaders-present-conversion-therapy-letter-to-downing-street/.

College of Policing. (n.d.). About us. Retrieved from: www.college.police.uk/about.

College of Policing. (2013). Critical incident management. Retrieved from: www.app.college.police.uk/app-content/critical-incident-management/types-of-critical-incident/.

College of Policing. (2014). National decision model. Retrieved from: www.app.college.police.uk/app-content/national-decision-model/the-national-decision-model/.

College of Policing. (2020). Major investigation and public protection: Community engagement and tension. Retrieved from: www.app.college.police.uk/app-content/major-investigation-and-public-protection/hate-crime/community-engagement-and-tension/.

Davis, H. (2014). *Beginning human rights law*. Routledge. https://doi-org.ezproxy.csu.edu.au/10.4324/9781315815367

Diamond, P. (2022). Street preachers keep being arrested. I have a plan to stop this from happening. Retrieved from: www.premierchristianity.com/opinion/street-preachers-keep-being-arrested-i-have-a-plan-to-stop-this-from-happening/6047.article

Dreher, R. (2020). *Live not by lies: A manual for Christian dissidents*. Sentinel.

English Standard Version Bible. (2001). Crossway.

Equality and Human Rights Commission. (2022). *Banning conversion therapy: Response submitted to United Kingdom Government consultation*. EHRC.

Evans, M. (2013). The relationship of religion and human rights. In S. Sheeran & N. Rodley (Eds), *Routledge handbook of international human rights law*. Taylor & Francis Group, pp. 563–579.

Gunatilleke, G. (2020). Criteria and constraints: The Human Rights Committee's test on limiting the freedom of religion or belief. *Religion and Human Rights, 15*, 20–38. https://doi:10.1163/18710328-bja10002

Holland, T. (2019). *Dominion*. Abacus.

Home Office. (1999). *The Stephen Lawrence Inquiry*. Cm 4262-I. HMSO.

Khaitan, T., & Norton J.C. (2020). Religion in human rights law: A normative restatement. *International Journal of Constitutional Law, 18*(1), 111–129. https://doi:10.1093/icon/moaa008

Khaliq, U. (2012). Freedom of religion and belief in international law: A comparative analysis. In A. M. Emon, M. Ellis, & B. Glahn (Eds), *Islamic law and international human rights law: Searching for common ground?* Oxford University Press, pp. 563–579.

Madrigal-Borloz, V. (2020) *Report of the Independent Expert on protection against violence and discrimination based on sexual orientation and gender identity: Practices of so-called 'conversion therapy'*. United Nations. Retrieved from: https://documents-dds-ny.un.org/doc/UNDOC/GEN/G20/108/68/PDF/G2010868.pdf?OpenElement.

Petre, J. (2010, December 18). 'Homosexuality is a sin' street preacher wins £7k from police. *Daily Mail*. Retrieved from: www.dailymail.co.uk/news/article-1339843/Homosexuality-sin-street-preacher-wins-7k-police.html.

Schabas, W.A. (2015). *The European Convention on Human Rights: A Commentary*. Oxford University Press.

Shortall, S., & Steinmetz-Jenkins, D. (2020). Introduction. In S. Shortall & D. Steinmetz-Jenkins (Eds), *Christianity and human rights reconsidered* (Human Rights in History). Cambridge University Press, pp. 1–16.

Starmer, K. (1999). *European human rights law: The Human Rights Act 1998 and the European Convention on Human Rights*. Legal Action Group.

Steiner, H., & Alston, P. (2000). *International human rights in context* (2nd ed.). Oxford University Press.

Tiedemann, P. (2015). Is there a human right to freedom of religion? *Human Rights Review, 16*(83–98), https://doi.org/10.1007/s12142-014-0342-2

United Nations General Assembly. (1948). *Universal Declaration of Human Rights*. United Nations. Retrieved from: www.un.org/en/development/desa/population/migration/generalassembly/docs/globalcompact/A_RES_217(III).pdf.

United Nations General Assembly. (1966). *International Covenant on Civil and Political Rights*. United Nations. Retrieved from: www.un.org/en/development/desa/population/migration/generalassembly/docs/globalcompact/A_RES_2200A(XXI)_civil.pdf.

VanLoon, K. (Designer). (2000). The Golden Rule poster [Online Image]. Retrieved from: www.scarboromissions.ca/golden-rule/golden-rule-across-the-worlds-religions.

Van Noorloos, M. (2015). Extreme speech in a religious context: A legal theoretical perspective on the case law of the European Court of Human Rights. In A. Ellian & G. Molier (Eds), *Freedom of speech under attack*. Eleven International Publishing, pp. 163–183.

Youth for Human Rights International. (2010, January 9). *What Human Rights Are* [Video]. YouTube. Retrieved from: www.youtube.com/watch?v=e2NuwF_xlE4.

12

RELIGION, ABORTION AND THE CRIMINAL JUSTICE SYSTEM IN NORTHERN IRELAND

Emma Campbell, Maureen Mansfield and Fiona Bloomer

Introduction

Religiosity dominates discourse on abortion law and policy globally. In Western societies, restrictions typically stem from a conservative right-wing Christian ethos, impacting law, policy and provision of abortion services (Bloomer et al., 2018). Globally, where societies reify motherhood, abortion is erroneously seen as challenging this norm, and is regarded with hostility by moral conservatives (Bloomer and O'Dowd, 2014; Bloomer et al., 2017; Lowe and Page, 2019; Pierson, 2022). In this chapter we seek to unpack the influence of religion on abortion within the criminal justice system (CJS) in Northern Ireland.

Global statistics reveal the enormous scale of the issue of abortion access. Around 73 million induced abortions take place worldwide each year (World Health Organisation, WHO, 2021). Approximately 40% of the world population lives in countries where abortion is heavily restricted, and 25% reside in countries which either prohibit abortion entirely or permit it only to save a woman's life. These countries are mostly located in the Global South (El Salvador, the Dominican Republic and Nicaragua). Malta is the only European country which bans abortion in all cases. Liberal legislation, however, does not guarantee access to abortion, as demonstrated in South Africa, where inherent problems within the health system and abortion stigma limit access to safe abortion (Bloomer et al., 2018). Globally, around 45% of all abortions are unsafe, and are a leading cause of maternal deaths and morbidities. This results in physical and mental health complications and social and financial burdens for girls, women, pregnant people, communities and health systems (WHO, 2021).

The evidence base is clear that illegality and other barriers to accessing abortion present a challenge to abortion seekers, including the risk of criminality, but do not prevent anyone from seeking abortions.

DOI: 10.4324/9781003276593-15

In examining such legislative restrictions, scholars have studied the influence of the Christian right at international policy and individual country levels. The Christian right, embedded with the value base of supporting pro-natalist, anti-abortion policies, have engaged in alliances with unlikely partners, such as conservative Islamic countries, to influence international policy on sexual and reproductive health (SRH). As a result of these alliances, consideration of SRH was weakened in global policy, with funding of programmes directly affected. One impact was the absence of reproductive health within the 2001 Millennium Development Goals (MDG). Whilst the absence was addressed in 2005, it had a detrimental impact on a range of indicators including: maternal health, child mortality, access to education, gender equality, and reducing sexually transmitted diseases including HIV rates (Hulme, 2009). Later programmes such as the United Nations Sustainable Development Goals have paid particular attention to maternal health and specifically reproductive health; however, progress has been hampered by the Global Gag Rule, a US anti-abortion policy first enacted during the Christian right presidency of Ronald Reagan, which prevented foreign non-governmental organisations (NGOs) from providing abortion services, information, counselling, referrals or advocacy (Bloomer et al., 2018). This has resulted in a hostile context for both global governance of abortion and the larger field of SRH (McGovern et al., 2020), impacting on 12 billion dollars of aid (Ahmed, 2020). Whilst the US policy has been reversed by President Joe Biden, the legacy of the Global Gag Rule remains.

At country-specific levels, the Christian right have operated to restrict legal access to abortion. This is exemplified within the Northern Ireland context whereby we see faith-based opposition impact on policy and lawmaking.

Law, Policy and Religiosity in Northern Ireland

Abortion was decriminalised in Northern Ireland on 22 October 2019, following introduction of the Northern Ireland Executive Formations Act, which had been informed by an international inquiry, conducted by the United Nations Committee on the Elimination of Discrimination Against Women (CEDAW) (Aiken and Bloomer, 2019). This historic legal achievement was long and complex, involving those with lived experience, activists, politicians, health professionals, academics, artists, trade unionists, students and many others (Bloomer and Campbell, 2022a, 2002b). Prior to decriminalisation, abortion in Northern Ireland was restrictive, with on average less than 20 abortions per year conducted in the National Health Service, compared to an average of 1,000 women who travelled elsewhere and hundreds who risked criminalisation by self-managing their abortion at home using abortion medication (Aiken and Bloomer, 2019).

The law in Northern Ireland prior to decriminalisation was the 1861 Offences Against the Person Act (OAPA), with case law permitting abortion in case of immediate threat to life or long-term health of the woman. This law was implemented conservatively, dependent on the interpretation of individual doctors to the phrase in case law of abortion being permitted on the grounds of 'grave and long-term ill-health' (Enright, 2022). The limited interpretation was ascribed to stigma and fear of criminalisation amongst health professionals (Bloomer et al., 2018). It is of note that OAPA remains active in England and Wales, with the 1967 Abortion Act providing exceptions under which abortion can be provided; abortion outside of these exceptions is a criminal act. In the last decade several prosecutions have been brought in England including: Gurpreet Kaur, who was sentenced to 27 months in prison for supplying abortifacients to clients; Natalie Towers, who was sentenced at Newcastle Crown Court to two-and-a-half years in prison for unlawfully procuring her own miscarriage (BMA, 2017). In March 2022, a woman in Oxford was charged under similar circumstances and her case referred to the Crown Court (Oxford Mail, 2022).

In the years leading up to decriminalisation, several attempts were made through the courts to overturn the archaic law in Northern Ireland. This culminated in a case brought to the UK Supreme Court in 2018, which included the observation:

> It is clear that there exists in Northern Ireland a considerable body of religious or moral opinion that places great weight on the interests of the unborn child and believes that, even in the situations in issue on this appeal, those interests deserve such protection as the present legislative prohibition affords.
> *Hale, Mance, Kerr, Wilson, & Reed, 2018, section 105, Article 8*

Yet despite the religious pressure, the judges reflected on the lack of effect this exerted on the thousands of people who travelled to England for abortions, even in a context where the dominance of a faith-based narrative resulted in legal restrictions.

Since 2000, within the Northern Ireland Assembly, there have been several attempts to revise abortion law. Pierson and Bloomer's 2018 study of political discourse identified that anti-abortion politicians relied on religiosity and abortion myths in these debates, such as abortions causing mental health conditions, breast cancer and fertility problems. Typical of the interventions which invoked religiosity, is that from the then-equality minister, Jonathan Bell of the Democratic Unionist Party (DUP), within a debate about the newly established Marie Stopes International (MSI) reproductive health clinic in Belfast. Bell, upon realising that the attempt in the Assembly to shut the clinic had failed, stated, 'may God forgive us for what we have done in this House today – the God who said he knew us and formed us in our mother's womb' (Hansard, 2013, p.25). The prominence of religiosity in political discourse was ascribed to politicians' personal views and also to the influence of anti-abortion lobby groups. One such group, Precious Life, provided the secretariat to the All-Party Prolife group, which operated at the Northern Ireland Assembly from 2007 through to 2015 with membership including representatives from Protestant unionist parties such as the DUP and the Ulster Unionist Party (UUP), and the Catholic nationalist party, the Social Democratic and Labour Party (SDLP). Pierson and Bloomer (2018, p.287) asserted that 'the discourse used by Precious Life, indicated through its policy consultation responses and website articles, has been mirrored in political discourse'. A prominent example of Precious Life's influence is when it called for protests against the dominant DUP, after their leader, Peter Robinson, stated he would permit members a free vote on any upcoming bill allowing abortion on grounds of foetal abnormality. Permitting a free vote would have resulted in a significant change in party policy. Within a week Robinson retracted his offer of a free vote, stating that he believed the upcoming bill was doomed. It is significant to note that preceding the retraction, Precious Life had used social media to demand that those who opposed the change should contact DUP politicians and provided the phone number for party headquarters to enable direct contact (Irish News, 2015).

In addition to anti-abortion lobby groups, church leaders have almost exclusively taken an anti-abortion position and have lobbied politicians to support their view. In 2008, for instance, when there was an opportunity in the UK Parliament to extend the 1967 Abortion Act to Northern Ireland, leaders of the four main churches (Catholic, Church of Ireland, Presbyterian, Methodist) wrote to all members of parliament (MPs) asking them not to intervene (Bloomer et al., 2018). Similar public declarations occurred during key points including in advance of decriminalisation in 2019 (Moriarty, 2019).

Examination of policymaking reveals the religiosity influencing access to abortion. From 2003 to 2016, a lengthy legal battle was undertaken by the Family Planning Association NI (FPANI) to force the Department of Health to issue guidelines for medical professionals to advise on interpretation of case law (Rowan and Simpson, 2022). The draft guidelines issued in 2013 were criticised as flawed and anti-abortion in tone. The document, for instance, suggested sharing of information on abortion was not allowed, despite this contravening Article 10 of the European Convention, which stipulated sharing of information on abortion access was permitted in settings were abortion was restricted. Consultation responses from anti-abortion lobby groups dominated in number and it would seem influenced the content of the document. Revised guidelines issued in 2016 were viewed as more appropriate. Of particular note is consideration of the availability of the abortion pill from online providers. This is highly significant, as it was the first time the Department of Health had acknowledged that women in Northern Ireland were risking criminalisation and self-aborting at home (Bloomer et al., 2018).

Institutionally, the Department of Health alongside the Northern Ireland Assembly has been regarded as anti-abortion, as evidenced by the delays on issuing appropriate guidelines for health professionals (Bloomer et al., 2018). It has also adopted delaying tactics to prevent reform. Following decriminalisation, the department failed to commission abortion services, meaning that no funding was provided to allow the full scope of services to be implemented. Despite a lengthy consultation process following decriminalisation, the minister for health stated he wished to invoke another consultation process. The minister is well known as being anti-abortion, and notably attended an anti-abortion protest framed as the 'Darkest Day' in the weeks preceding decriminalisation (Black, 2019). This event was led by Dr Paul Coulter, who described himself as a man of deep faith and evangelical ministry (Coulter, n.d.).

The use of delaying tactics, combined with hostile, religious discourse from anti-abortion politicians, mirrors similar settings elsewhere, wherein new policies that challenge conservative morality policies are hindered from full implementation by introducing new mechanisms such as consultation processes and advisory groups (Engeli et al., 2013).

From 2012 onwards, a changing political and public discourse was evident. This was partly prompted by the opening of an MSI clinic in Belfast (October 2012) which began offering abortions within the restricted legal framework. The opening of the clinic brought about significant political and international media attention, and challenged the widespread assumption that abortion was completely illegal in Northern Ireland (Enright, 2022). The tragic and unnecessary death of Savita Halappanavar in Galway (Republic of Ireland), was painfully described by her husband, Praveen, as featuring a restrictive religious element. Whilst experiencing a miscarriage, she was refused a requested termination. Praveen stated Savita was told no, not only because the foetal heartbeat was still present but also that 'this is a Catholic country' (Houston, 2012). This tragic incident was one of the sparks that lit legislative change in Ireland. Her death justifiably caused an international outcry and it amplified public discourse about abortion access across the island.

One year later in the North, Sarah Ewart was denied an abortion following a fatal foetal abnormality diagnosis. Her widely publicised ordeal shifted public and political debate towards the idea of abortions being permitted in exceptional circumstances, which was aided greatly in the public debate, by her married and church-going status, exemplifying a woman who was performing Christian womanhood correctly (Lowe & Page, 2019). This case resulted in a consultation process to change the law on those restrictive grounds only. The proposed change, led by the minister for justice, failed in the Northern Ireland Assembly not long before the devolved government collapsed for three years (Pierson, 2022).

Policing

Throughout this time anti-abortion protests continued outside the FPANI clinic, which provided counselling services for those experiencing crisis pregnancies, and during its time of operation (2012–2017), outside the MSI clinic. Standard anti-abortion and religious practices such as prayer vigils (Lowe & Hayes, 2018) were used, as well as the targeting of any woman of childbearing age entering the premises of both organisations. Clinic escorts, who guided and protected those using the MSI clinic, were subjected to hostile verbal and physical abuse, filming, as well as performances of prayer and the throwing of holy water. In the first three years of MSI's operation in Belfast, 183 reports were made to police about protesters, including intimidation, verbal harassment, physical abuse and assault (Hughes, 2015). An abundance of written testimony and video evidence gathered by clinic escorts and submitted to the police failed to result in any prosecutions regarding protests outside MSI. This has been ascribed to the police mirroring the position of the state regarding reluctance to deal constructively with the clinic protests (Biernat and Johnston, 2022). Charges were brought against Bernie Smyth of Precious Life but later dropped on a technicality. Fellow protester Moira Brennan was prosecuted in relation to an incident outside FPANI's offices, but the resulting fine did little to deter further protests and harassment. In another instance, the lengthy testimony of a clinic escort who had been physically assaulted was lost by the police and the case later failed to result in court proceedings (Biernat and Johnston, 2022).

The lack of prosecutions regarding clinic protests rests in sharp contrast to high-profile prosecutions regarding abortion medication which occurred in 2013 and 2016 (PPSNI, 2018). In 2013, a woman was charged under the OAPA for procuring abortion pills for her 15-year-old daughter (though she denied the charges). The moratorium clause in the decriminalisation legislation meant the case was, thankfully, halted in October 2019, but not before she had been subject to six years of hearings, postponements and the ongoing threat of imprisonment (Irish Times, 2019). In 2016, a 21-year-old woman was charged under the same act with administering abortion pills. The woman had intended to legally travel to England for an abortion but failed to raise adequate funds, she pleaded guilty, and was given a three-month jail sentence, suspended for two years (*Belfast Telegraph*, 2016). Over 200 activists in a show of public support signed a letter stating that they had either take abortion medication or had helped procure abortion medication. The police did not pursue any activists regarding these declarations nor did they arrest three activists, Collette Devlin, Diana King and Kitty O'Kane, who had handed themselves in to the Strand Road Police Station in Derry, requesting that they too be prosecuted for procuring and distributing abortion pills (O'Dowd et al., 2022; O'Brien, 2022).

These two high-profile cases of 2013 and 2016 created a national furore and were recognised as huge moments by the local and international press, as well as the pro-choice movement. However, few people realised that the arrests were to become the tipping point towards decriminalisation, despite the ongoing work of researchers and grassroots organisations (Sheldon, 2016). Only a short time before this, legislators were quibbling about the difference between 'serious' or 'fatal' foetal anomalies. Attention was not being paid to the simple need to not be pregnant, nor was attention being paid to the fact that doctors were fearful of advising on matters such as access to abortion care in England, never mind providing abortions in Northern Ireland (Aiken et al., 2018). Then remarkably, as a result of the huge public well of support for the women involved in both cases, the decision makers began to grasp the full horror of what exactly the end result of making abortion a criminal offence meant – arresting women and pregnant people (Hewson, 2017).

Activists in particular were further horrified when on International Women's Day in 2017, the police raided the home of an activist and the workplace of another in search of abortion medication (McVicker and Crickard, 2022). Neither search resulted in arrests, however the timing of the searches, occurring at the exact same time as when internationally renowned feminist activist Angela Davis was speaking at a rally in Belfast City Hall, were regarded by those targeted and by activists as symbolic of a police service hostile to abortion activism (McVicker and Crickard, 2022).

Further, the PSNI's position on abortion demonstrates their lack of understanding of both human rights standards and legal jurisprudence in its response to a consultation on safe access zones outside abortion clinics, wherein it incorrectly cites the need to recognise the rights of the foetus: 'The over-riding "health" considerations of this Bill will inevitably draw it in to legal challenge with the competing rights of the unborn child which is the key area of ground for the protestors' (Jones, 2021:2).

Up until 2010, criminalisation of abortion in Northern Ireland had been more of a threat than a reality for those seeking to manage their own abortion via medication they had obtained from online providers. The use of criminal policy around abortion is often cited as protectionist for women who do not know better – yet the language of Northern Ireland politician Reverend Ivan Foster from a debate in February 1984 pinpoints the nexus of religion and control through criminality. He argued that most abortions were:

> carried out on unmarried girls between the ages of 16 and 24. These were therefore guilty of having had sexual relationships outside marriage, which was 'contrary to the Word of God', 'sinful and will be judged by Almighty God'.
>
> *Molinari, 2020*

When we evaluate the language of those who have opposed abortion in Northern Ireland, few are as demonstratively misogynist as the above false statement, which ultimately rests on Christian–patriarchal ideas of sexual purity, with additional misinformation on the commonality and need for abortion across all years of potential fertility. It is widely understood that people who are already parents are the largest cohort of abortion seekers and marriage has little to no effect when taken with other factors (Bloomer and Hoggart, 2016).

During this intense period, it is significant to note the attorney general for Northern Ireland, the most senior legal role in the country, was QC John Larkin, who has been open about his conservative Catholic views and their influence on his legal role (O'Brien, 2013). He made repeated attempts to block any progress for abortion access including providing disingenuous evidence to the UK Parliament's Women and Equalities Committee Inquiry into abortion in Northern Ireland (Coyne, 2019). Throughout his time as attorney general (2010–2020), Larkin was widely seen to overstep his role as attorney by intervening in cases (The Guardian, 2012). The BBC's political expert commented that:

> When Mr Larkin's 2008 radio interview emerged from the archive, in which he compared abortion to shooting a new born baby, it was natural that

questions would be asked about how much personal baggage he brings to his consideration of the issue.

Devenport, 2012

In 2021, after he was no longer attorney general, he continued his anti-abortion project, representing anti-abortion organisation SPUC, in a judicial review that questioned the legitimacy of the Northern Ireland secretary of state in his actions to direct the Northern Ireland Assembly to act on decriminalisation (The Christian Institute, 2021). Further, it was reported that he authored the bill that the DUP attempted to use to thwart the arrival of the decriminalisation legislation in 2019 (PA News, 2019).

Evolving Moralities

During the decade of 2010 onwards, early medical abortion remained taboo in mainstream media and politics (Aiken et al., 2018; McDonald, 2015), but campaigners began slowly raising public consciousness around self-managed abortion with pills and autonomy (O'Dowd et al., 2022). The anti-choice campaigns began to recognise the success of this and reappropriated, quasi-feminist language, veering away from previous campaigns steeped in biblical verse and relying on faith-based arguments. Consequently, 'Both Lives Matter', 'Love them Both' and 'Precious Life' attempted to rebrand their misogynist and anachronistic image into one of 'protecting' women who might have been pressured by a morally ambiguous culture (Ralph, 2022). However, despite their assertions of secularism, cursory glances at these organisational websites reveal a steadfast adherence to scripture and conservative Christian teaching. It is useful to understand many anti-abortion narratives use the teachings of Christianity to entwine womanhood and motherhood, even if the woman and not the foetus becomes the focus of their attention. This is likely why they often presume that someone choosing abortion is always reacting to pressure or coercion, as women would never 'naturally' choose abortion (Lowe & Page, 2019:172).

Indeed, attempts to contain the 'middle ground' by various pro-choice campaigns such as Together for Yes in Ireland, seemed to cede this gendered moral coding embraced by anti-choice groups. This left some of us struggling to understand why there was 'emphasis on women less as political agents than as vulnerable recipients of love, compassion and decent medical care' (Enright, 2018:1), which in turns denies the agency enshrined in a framework of justice, rights and responsibility, and can even paper over the cruellest aspects of any abortion ban. The dominance of anti-abortion narratives is evident in the discourse of the flatmates of the young woman who was arrested in 2016, who were then roundly criticised by the general public on social media following interviews with the press. It was clear that the false narrative of an anti-abortion majority had impacted the mindset of the flatmates. They repeatedly demonstrated their shock at the anger people showed towards them. One of the housemates describes a lack of regret and penitence as a reason for the woman deserving police, and not medical attention:

> This isn't anything to do with the rights and wrongs of abortion. I'm not anti-abortion. I believe there are circumstances, like rape, where it should be a woman's choice. This is about her attitude. It was as if she was getting rid of a piece of clothing, 'she stated'. There was absolutely no remorse. Even the way she was up and away out and doing her own thing a day after the abortion, while me and our other house-mate just walked around in shock.
>
> *McAleese, 2016*

Religious views did not only crop up in citizen narratives but were also acknowledged in the courts. In the case of the *Attorney General vs the Northern Ireland Human Rights Commission* in 2017, Lord Justice Gillen argued that

> the issue of abortion is a classic instance of the type of highly controversial issue touching on social, moral and **religious policies** on which there is no consensus either in Europe or for that matter in this jurisdiction.
>
> *British and Irish Legal Information Institute, 2017 author emphasis*

This problematic position largely ignored any of the minimum international human rights standards widely available at the time, including CEDAW and high-profile case precedent of *Tysiac vs Poland* (Centre for Reproductive Rights, 2005). Both Ireland and the UK had ratified CEDAW at that time, which was calling for access for severe foetal anomaly and sexual crimes. The ongoing unwillingness to accommodate for international human rights standards in the courts, which were also slowly but surely becoming more progressive and accommodating for abortion seekers, alongside a problematic eagerness to warrant religious belief a greater stake in the formation and application of the abortion law, was frustrating for abortion seekers and activists. This disconnect was also clear for the vast majority of the public to witness. The DUP as a party has a long history of entanglement with the Free Presbyterian church (Molinari, 2020). Their founder was a pastor, but in the 2000s and 2010s in Northern Ireland, it was increasingly clear that these particular religious foundations, of literal interpretations of scripture, did not motivate their electoral base. As Molinari, (2020:88) observes,

> Free Presbyterianism, while a very small Church, is greatly over-represented within the DUP and more particularly so among its elected representatives. 36.8% of Assembly members elected in 2011 belonged to it, a percentage which, prior to the Good Friday Agreement, amounted to 56%.

More recently, it was clear that sectarianism and a bipartisan forced coalition served to ensure their stay in power was because of their allegiance to a nation state rather than a god (Hayes & Nagle, 2018). The submission from the Centre for Bioethical

Reform (CBR) below on the serious Foetal Anomaly Bill, proposed by Paul Givan, DUP, to the Northern Ireland Assembly, demonstrates an attitude completely aligned with the core fundamental Christian values of the DUP. Yet such views would be widely understood as a niche opinion, contrasting with broad support for reform – reflected by multiple population level surveys (Gray et al., 2018).

> This Bill is [...] an iniquitous decree as outlined in Isaiah 10:1–2. The Bill was created without any consultation with organisations in Northern Ireland and falls far short of the Democratic Unionist Party, of whom the proposer is a member, pledge that full repeal of the abortion laws in Northern Ireland would be the first item on the agenda when the Assembly returned some 14 months ago.
>
> *CBR, 2021*

Drawing on a Foucauldian feminist framework, which examines how concepts of surveillance and disciplinary power, normalising gaze and resistance can be applied to elucidate an understanding of gendered oppression in society, Bloomer et al. (forthcoming) identify how anti-abortion values have been normalised in the apparatus of the state in Northern Ireland, despite this being a minority position. Activist organisations such as Alliance for Choice understand that niche religious opinions can keep barbaric laws intact for decades and work therefore to make both the law and the understanding of its fundamentalist religious basis untenable. A campaign for decriminalisation, including the moratorium on arrests suggested to the CEDAW committee in 2016, was the only way to ensure the most marginalised of those needing abortions still had access, from international NGOs such as Women on Web and Women Help Women, without risk of prosecution. This was specifically included in the decriminalisation legislation, applied by the UK Parliament, in recognition that anti-abortion members of the Northern Ireland Assembly would do everything in their power to erect barriers to statutory access in the region even after the primary legislation was passed.

Post-2019, even with the astounding and unprecedented CEDAW-based legislation, activists continued pushing hard on the outstanding issues: the ongoing protests outside clinics; the Safe Access Zones legislation, which is likely to face further legal action; ongoing lobbying and campaigning activities of anti-abortion organisations; a continued lack of easy-to-find information about the legal services which are available; a remaining lack of resourcing into UK-wide services which increases waiting times for those needing to travel; the lack of adequate relationship and sex education in schools, held back because of religious lobbying; and finally the remaining stigma around abortion, positioning it as something exceptional rather than useful and common. However, activists continue to grow their support as new generations of activists refuse to be dominated by religious patriarchy. "I am still so angry that it is always up to women to push every legal claim to its conclusion; that the legislative system, and the politics it recognises, never concede anything on their own" (Enright, 2018:12).

Whilst in this chapter we have focused on the impact of religion and moral conservatism in legislation, policy and policing, it is also imperative to acknowledge that within the CJS we need to account for provision of abortion services for women and pregnant people in prison and other forms of state detention. At present in Northern Ireland, regulations do not include a pathway to access abortion services in prison. At the time of writing (March 2022), in the two years since decriminalisation, abortion services have not been requested by any inmates. This is not anticipated to remain as a service that is not required, as elsewhere figures for pregnancy and abortion remain congruent inside and outside of prison. It is significant to note that as highlighted by Mansfield et al. (2022), UK-wide, women who are criminalised and in prison seeking abortions is an area that is under-considered, aside from the ongoing advocacy work of Birth Companions and BPAS to ensure that issues of reproductive justice and equivalency of care are raised in relation to healthcare provision for women in prison. This dearth of knowledge presents a considerable gap in understanding of this context. Evidence related to healthcare generally in prisons has identified a series of issues including: delays in booking appointments; inability to find information and take charge of the process oneself; logistics around prison staff being available to escort prisoners to clinic appointments; and cancellation due to staff shortages. These all have an added layer of urgency when a woman is pregnant and does not wish to continue. Having to be escorted to abortion clinics raises the issue of confidentiality, and it is unknown whether the prison environment, culture and attitudes (of both prisoners and those working there) have an impact on decisions and experiences of women who seek to access abortions while in prison. The role of support services is also unknown in relation to crisis pregnancies in prison settings (Mansfield et al., 2022). It is clear that research is needed that will provide evidence related to policy, practice and experience of women and pregnant people not only in Northern Ireland but across the UK as a whole.

Conclusion

On 24 March 2022, three key pieces of progressive legislation were passed by the Northern Ireland Assembly: the Period Products (free provision) Bill – making period products freely available in public buildings and schools; the Domestic Abuse (safe leave) Bill – providing ten days per year of paid leave to victims of domestic abuse; the Abortion Services (Safe Access Zones) Bill – banning anti-abortion protests outside health clinics and settings (BBC, 2022). The passing of this legislation serves as a marker of the waning of misogynistic, patriarchal and anti-abortion positions within the political domain. The Abortion Services Bill was historic as it achieved a notable majority, 55 votes to 27, and is illustrative of the lessening influence of anti-abortion lobby groups, as notably the minister for health, Robin Swann, voted in favour of the bill. Finally, the progressive views of the population regarding abortion are being evidenced within the apparatus of the state. However, caution should be exercised. As we have demonstrated, progress has been slow and those with niche religious morality anti-abortion perspectives remain visible. There remains a block from the DUP on enacting a commissioning paper for the Abortion Services Bill. We remain hopeful about the trajectory but cautious about a linear path of progress.

References

Ahmed, Z. (2020). The Unprecedented Expansion of the Global Gag Rule: Trampling Rights, Health and Free Speech. Guttmacher Institute. Retrieved from: www.guttmacher.org/gpr/2020/04/unprecedented-expansion-global-gag-rule-trampling-rights-health-and-free-speech

Aiken, A., & Bloomer F. (2019). Abortion decriminalised in Northern Ireland. *BMJ*, 367, l6330. https://doi.org/10.1136/bmj.l6330

Aiken, A.R.A., Padron, E., Broussard, K., & Johnson, D. (2018). The impact of Northern Ireland's abortion laws on women's abortion decision-making and experiences. *BMJ Sexual & Reproductive Health*, *45*(1), 3–9. https://doi.org/10.1136/bmjsrh-2018-200198

Barrhead News. (2019, November 25). Foster says DUP in talks with NI's attorney general on abortion legal challenge. *Barrhead News*. Retrieved from: www.barrheadnews.com/news/national-news/17994769.foster-says-dup-talks-nis-attorney-general-abortion-legal-challenge/ *News*. (2019, November 25). Foster says DUP in talks with NI's attorney general on abortion legal challenge. *Barrhead News*. Retrieved from: www.barrheadnews.com/news/national-news/17994769.foster-says-dup-talks-nis-attorney-general-abortion-legal-challenge/

BBC. (2022). As it happened: Six bills pass as Stormont adjourns, *BBC*. Retrieved from: www.bbc.co.uk/news/live/uk-northern-ireland-politics-60848842

Belfast Telegraph (2016, April 5). Editorial: Prosecution of woman who bought abortion drugs online "in public interest." *Belfast Telegraph*. Retrieved from: www.belfasttelegraph.co.uk/news/northern-ireland/prosecution-of-woman-who-bought-abortion-drugs-online-in-public-interest-34600144.html

Biernat, N., & Johnston, S. (2022). MSI clinic escorts, in Bloomer, F. and Campbell, E. (2022b). *Decriminalising Abortion in Northern Ireland*, Volume 2: *Allies and Abortion Provision, 195-208*. Bloomsbury.

Black, R. (2019, September 6). Silent demonstration at Stormont over planned liberalisation of abortion laws. *Belfast Telegraph*. Retrieved from: www.belfasttelegraph.co.uk/news/northern-ireland/silent-demonstration-at-stormont-over-planned-liberalisation-of-abortion-laws-38474602.html

Bloomer, F., & Campbell, E. (Eds.). (2022a). *Decriminalising Abortion in Northern Ireland*, Volume 1: *Legislation and Protest*. Bloomsbury.

Bloomer, F., & Campbell, E. (Eds.). (2022b). *Decriminalising Abortion in Northern Ireland*, Volume 2: *Allies and Abortion Provision*. Bloomsbury.

Bloomer, F., & Hoggart, L. (2016). Abortion Policy – Challenges and Opportunities, Briefing Paper, Northern Ireland Assembly, Knowledge Exchange Seminar Series. Retrieved from: https://pure.ulster.ac.uk/en/publications/abortion-policy-challenges-and-opportunities

Bloomer, F., MacNamara, N., & Bloomer, S. (forthcoming). Faith voices resisting anti-abortion norms. *Women's Studies International Forum*.

Bloomer, F., & O'Dowd, K. (2014). Restricted access to abortion in the Republic of Ireland and Northern Ireland: exploring abortion tourism and barriers to legal reform. *Culture, Health & Sexuality, 16*(4), 66–380. https://doi.org/10.1080/13691058.2014.886724

Bloomer, F., O'Dowd, K., & Macleod, C. (2017). Breaking the silence on abortion: The role of adult community abortion education in fostering resistance to norms. *Culture, Health & Sexuality, 19*(7), 709–722. https://doi.org/10.1080/13691058.2016.1257740

Bloomer F., Pierson, C., & Estrada, S.C. (2018). *Reimagining Global Abortion Politics*. Policy Press.

British and Irish Legal Information Institute. (2017). *The Attorney General for Northern Ireland & Anor v The Northern Ireland Human Rights Commission [2017] NICA 42 (29 June 2017)*. Bailii.org. Retrieved from: www.bailii.org/nie/cases/NICA/2017/42.html

British Medical Association (BMA). (2017). Decriminalisation of abortion: A discussion paper from the BMA. Retrieved from: www.bma.org.uk/media/1142/bma-paper-on-the-decriminalisation-of-abortion-february-2017.pdf

The Christian Institute. (2021, May 13). *Former NI Attorney General to front legal challenge to Westminster abortion 'power grab'*. Retrieved from: www.christian.org.uk/news/former-ni-attorney-general-to-front-legal-challenge-to-westminster-abortion-power-grab/

Collins, S. (2021). The impact of religion on gender, sexuality, and abortion politics: A comparative study of Northern Ireland and the Republic of Ireland. *College of Arts & Sciences Senior Honours Theses*. Retrieved from: https://ir.library.louisville.edu/honors/256/

Coulter, P. (n.d.). Paul B Coulter | Ministry. Paul B Coulter. Retrieved from: www.paulcoulter.net/ministry

Coyne, E. (2019, March 1). Abortion ban defended in dead baby case. *The Times*. Retrieved from: www.thetimes.co.uk/article/abortion-ban-defended-in-dead-baby-case-bwdb9f36r

Devenport, M. (2012, October 24). Attorney General John Larkin hits headlines for wrong reasons. *BBC News*. Retrieved from: www.bbc.co.uk/news/uk-northern-ireland-20054111

Dyer, C. (2017). Mother wins right to challenge prosecution for buying abortion pills in Northern Ireland. *BMJ*, j527. https://doi.org/10.1136/bmj.j527

Engeli, I., Green-Pedersen, C., & Larsen, L.T. (2013). The puzzle of permissiveness: Understanding policy processes concerning morality issues. *Journal of European Public Policy, 20*(3), 335–352. https://doi.org/10.1080/13501763.2013.761500

Enright, M. (2018). "The Enemy of the Good": Reflections on Ireland's New Abortion Legislation. *Feminists@Law, 8*(2). https://doi.org/10.22024/UniKent/03/fal.658

Enright, M. (2022). Alliance for Choice as Agents of Legal Change. In F. Bloomer & Campbell, E. (eds) (2022a). *Decriminalising Abortion in Northern Ireland, Volume 1 Legislation and Protest*. Bloomsbury, pp. 160–188.

Haidt, J. (2001). The emotional dog and its rational tail: a social intuitionist approach to moral judgment. *Psychological review*, 108(4), 814–834.

Hansard. (2013). Official Report of the Northern Ireland Assembly, Tuesday 12 March 2013, Volume 83, no 2.

Hewson, B. (2017, February 1). Why should abortion be governed by criminal law? *The Justice Gap*. Retrieved from: www.thejusticegap.com/abortion-governed-criminal-law/

Hulme, D. (2009). *The Millennium Development Goals (MDGs): A short history of the world's biggest promise*. Manchester: University of Manchester, Brooks World Poverty Institute.

Irish News. (2015, May 2). Robinson accused of abortion law U-turn. *The Irish News*.

Jones, M. (2021). Written submission from PSNI to Abortion Services (Safe Access Zones Bill). Retrieved from www.niassembly.gov.uk/globalassets/committee-blocks/health/2017---2022/police-service-of-northern-ireland.pdf

Love for Life. (n.d.). *What We Do*. Love for Life. Retrieved from: www.loveforlife.org.uk/what-we-do/

Lowe, P., & Hayes, G. (2018). Anti-abortion clinic activism, civil inattention and the problem of gendered harassment. *Sociology, 53*(2), 330–346.

Lowe, P., & Page, S.-J. (2019). Rights-based claims made by UK anti-abortion activists. *Health and Human Rights, 21*(2), 133–144. https://doi.org/10.1177/0038038518762075.

Mansfield, M., Campbell, E., & Bloomer, F. (2022) Abortion and Reproductive Justice in the Prison System. Briefing Paper.

McAleese, D. (2015, July 6). Pro-life campaigner guilty of hitting sexual health worker with clipboard. *Belfast Telegraph*. Retrieved from: www.belfasttelegraph.co.uk/news/northern-ireland/pro-life-campaigner-guilty-of-hitting-sexual-health-worker-with-clipboard-31356836.html

McAleese, D. (2016, April 6). Why we reported abortion pills girl to Northern Ireland police. *Belfast Telegraph*. Retrieved from: www.belfasttelegraph.co.uk/news/northern-ireland/why-we-reported-abortion-pills-girl-to-northern-ireland-police-34602857.html

McDonald, H. (2015, July 15). Pro-choice campaigners to picket police stations in Northern Ireland. *The Guardian*. Retrieved from: www.theguardian.com/world/2015/jul/15/northern-ireland-pro-choice-protest-police-stations

McGovern, T., Schaaf, M., Battistini, E., Maistrellis, E., Gibb, K., & Casey, S.E. (2020). From bad to worse: global governance of abortion and the Global Gag Rule. *Sexual and Reproductive Health Matters, 28*(3), 54–63. https://doi.org/10.1080/26410397.2020.1794411

McGuinness, E. (2015). *Subversive Swallowing: The Self-Help Abortion as a Site of Stigma and Resistance in the Anti-Choice State; The case of Northern Ireland* (H. Pereira De Melo, Ed.). Retrieved from: https://repository.gchumanrights.org/bitstream/handle/20.500.11825/192/ToC_Mc%20Guinnes.pdf?sequence=1&isAllowed=y

McVicker, A., & Crickard, H. (2022). The Women's Sector. In F. Bloomer, & Campbell, E. (eds) (2022a). *Decriminalising Abortion in Northern Ireland, Volume 2 Legislation and Protest*. Bloomsbury, pp. 284–311.

Molinari, V. (2020). The Northern Irish Assembly and the Abortion Issue, 1967–2017. *Études Irlandaises, 45*(2), 77–99. https://doi.org/10.4000/etudesirlandaises.10202

Moriarty, G. (2019, October 22). Christian leaders criticise Northern Ireland abortion law change. *Irish Times*. Retrieved from: www.irishtimes.com/news/ireland/irish-news/christian-leaders-criticise-northern-ireland-abortion-law-change-1.4059634

O'Brien, M. (2013, November 21). Keeping faith in the law [Interview]. In *The Irish Catholic*. Retrieved from: www.irishcatholic.com/keeping-faith-in-the-law/

O'Brien, M. (2022). Alliance for Choice Derry: Delivering decriminalisation: activism in the north-west, in F. Bloomer, & Campbell, E. (eds) (2022a). *Decriminalising Abortion in Northern Ireland,* Volume 2: *Legislation and Protest*. Bloomsbury, pp. 274–293.

O'Dowd, K., Cross, J., & Bloomer, F. (2022). Alliance for Choice new beginnings. In F. Bloomer, and Campbell, E. (eds) (2022a). *Decriminalising Abortion in Northern Ireland,* Volume 2: *Legislation and Protest* (pp. 201–225). Bloomsbury.

Oxford Mail. (2022, March 22) Woman in court charged with 160-year-old 'procuring miscarriage' offence. *Oxford Mail*. Retrieved from: www.oxfordmail.co.uk/news/20011511.woman-court-charged-160-year-old-procuring-miscarriage-offence/

Pierson, C. (2022). Power-sharing, devolution and patriarchy: An analysis of the role of the Northern Ireland Assembly in abortion law reform. In F. Bloomer, and Campbell, E. (eds) (2022a). *Decriminalising Abortion in Northern Ireland,* Volume 1: *Legislation and Protest* (pp. 28–48). Bloomsbury.

Pierson C., & Bloomer F. (2017). Macro- and micro-political vernaculizations of rights: Human rights and abortion discourses in Northern Ireland. *Health and Human Rights, 19*(1), 173–185.

Pierson C., & Bloomer F. (2018). Anti-abortion myths in political discourse. In C. McQuarrie, Pierson C., Bloomer F., & Shettner, S. (eds), *Crossing Troubled Waters: Abortion in Ireland, Northern Ireland, and Prince Edward Island,* (pp. 184–2013). Prince Edward University Press.

Public Prosecution Service Northern Ireland (PPSNI). (2018). FOI 524/ 18–19. (pp. 1–4). Retrieved from: www.ppsni.gov.uk/sites/ppsni/files/publications/FOI%2006%2018%20Abortion.pdf

Ralph, D. (2022). 'Between a whisper and a shout': Repealing the eighth and pro-choice Irish women's abortion testimonies. *Gender, Place & Culture*, 29(2), 201–221. https://doi.org/10.1080/0966369x.2020.1860911

Rowan, R., & Simpson, A. (2022). Dismantling the walls of silence surrounding abortion in Northern Ireland. In F. Bloomer, and Campbell, E. (eds) (2022a). *Decriminalising Abortion in Northern Ireland, Volume 1 Legislation and Protest* (pp. 294–317). Bloomsbury.

Sheldon, S. (2016). How can a state control swallowing? The home use of abortion pills in Ireland. *Reproductive Health Matters, 24*(48), 90–101. https://doi.org/10.1016/j.rhm.2016.10.002

Sheldon, S., O'Neill, J., Parker, C., & Davis, G. (2020). 'Too much, too indigestible, too fast'? The decades of struggle for abortion law reform in Northern Ireland. *The Modern Law Review, 83*(4), 761–796. https://doi.org/10.1111/1468-2230.12521

The Guardian (2012, October 25). Northern Ireland: Larkin with the law | Editorial. *The Guardian*. Retrieved from: www.theguardian.com/commentisfree/2012/oct/26/northern-ireland-abortion-larkin

The Guardian (2021, March 12). El Salvador abortion laws on trial in case of woman jailed after miscarriage. *The Guardian*. Retrieved from: www.theguardian.com/global-development/2021/mar/12/el-salvador-abortion-laws-on-trial-in-case-of-woman-jailed-after-miscarriage

Trinity Term. (2018). UKSC 27 On appeal from: [2017] NICA 42 JUDGEMENT In the matter of an application by the Northern Ireland Human Rights Commission for Judicial Review (Northern Ireland) Reference by the Court of Appeal in Northern Ireland pursuant to Paragraph 33 of Schedule 10 to the Northern Ireland Act 1998 (Abortion) (Northern Ireland), (United Kingdom Supreme Court July 2018). Retrieved from: www.supremecourt.uk/cases/docs/uksc-2017-0131-judgment.pdf

World Health Organization (WHO). (2021). Abortion: Key Facts. Retrieved from: www.who.int/news-room/fact-sheets/detail/abortion

13

THE DEATH PENALTY, RELIGION AND THE US CRIMINAL JUSTICE SYSTEM

Logan A. Yelderman and Matthew P. West

Introduction

Religion plays a critical role in the criminal justice system, from the development of law and policies to the delivery of justice and punishment. The current chapter discusses several ways religion has shaped or varied with the development of laws, the criminal justice system, and legal practices in the U.S. It focuses specifically on the role of religion in the death penalty.

Religion and Law

The First Amendment of the U.S. Constitution specifies both the separation of church and state and the right of religious exercise. The very first words of this Amendment acknowledge that, if left unaddressed, religion and law would come to occupy the same personal or behavioral domain, potentially causing conflict or confusion. Both religion and law inform morality in society (Hamburger, 1993), dictating how people ought to behave. Thus, people have moral obligations according to their religion and moral obligations according to law. Despite the ostensible separation of religion and government, it is likely that the framers of the U.S. Constitution and the founders of the country used their personal and religious views to shape the laws of the country and governmental structure (Berman, 1980). Moreover, much of the development of the legal structure of the U.S. can be credited to religious influences dating back hundreds of years prior to 1776 (Berman, 1983). Perhaps the most obvious overlap between religion and law is criminal law. Some of the most fundamental criminal laws regulate behaviors like theft, murder, and lying to incriminate others, embodying the Judeo-Christian "Ten Commandments."

DOI: 10.4324/9781003276593-16

Religions typically include moral dictates delineating right and wrong behavior, or good and bad characteristics. Similarly, the law includes "secular" moral dictates. The death penalty is one case in which the lines between these dictates are blurry. It is a punishment that is dealt to a person after a moral judgment is made about a person's behavior, and, at least implicitly, their character. The existence of factors that make a defendant more or less deserving of the death penalty is a matter of fact, but the relative weight of these factors is a matter of morality (e.g., *Ford v. Strickland*, 1983). Of course, not all laws imply morality (i.e., minor traffic violations), but the death penalty, and punishment in general, is used to encourage moral behavior and to deter immoral behavior (see Peterson, 2020 for discussion). Laws, in this regard, guide and convey morality, a morality that often aligns with religious morality.

Punishment in general, and the death penalty in particular, varies by religion and country. Predominantly Catholic countries are more likely to abolish the death penalty than predominantly Muslim countries (Mathias, 2013; see also Purba et al., 2020). Moreover, theistic religions appear to be more supportive of the death penalty than ethicalistic religions (Bornstein & Miller, 2009; Muryani & Rosyidah, 2020). Religion can shape people's death penalty attitudes and beliefs, and religions that underlie culture can influence the legal and political structures in societies, linking punitive religious doctrines to more active death penalty policies (Greenberg & West, 2008).

Origins and Evolution of the U.S. Death Penalty

The death penalty in the American colonies was imported from English Common Law (Latzer & McCord, 2011). There were numerous offenses punishable by death, and in the case of murder, the death penalty was mandatory. The death penalty often occurred as public beheading under English Common Law, to both punish the offender and deter others. Public hangings were the primary execution method in colonial America and throughout the early twentieth century (Espy & Smykla, 2016). These public hangings had the same goal as precolonial English beheadings, to punish and deter crime—"an emphatic display of power, a reminder of what the state could do to those who broke its laws" (Banner, 2002, p. 13). However, in colonial America, public hangings were also a chance for the criminals to repent for their sins and get their lives right with God. Despite qualitative and quantitative changes to the death penalty over time, the opportunity for repentance before execution remains (see *Dunn v. Smith*, 2021).

Methods of execution evolved (from hangings to primarily electrocution and now lethal injection), states began abolishing the death penalty, and the interpretation of the Eighth Amendment's "cruel and unusual" clause changed throughout the end of the nineteenth century to the modern day (Espy & Smykla, 2016; Paternoster et al., 2008; *Trop v. Dulles*, 1958; *U.S. v. Weems*, 1910). These changes established and shaped the modern death penalty, which we describe in the next section.

A Brief Case History of the Modern U.S. Death Penalty

In the landmark case, *Furman v. Georgia* (1972), the U.S. Supreme Court ruled that the capital trial scheme at the time permitted "wantonly" and "freakishly" imposed death sentences and was therefore unconstitutional. The decision in *Furman* led to a moratorium, which ended up being brief—because the problems were in the death sentencing and trial process (e.g., *McGautha v. California*, 1971), states simply changed the process. Although the revised capital trial scheme varied somewhat across states, the Supreme Court deemed the schemes in Georgia (*Gregg v. Georgia*, 1976), Florida (*Proffitt v. Florida*, 1976), and Texas (*Jurek v. Texas*, 1976) constitutional. These schemes had two important characteristics. First, the capital trial was bifurcated; there was a guilt phase and a penalty phase (addressing issues related to deciding guilt and punishment in the same trial). Second, the jury's discretion was circumscribed (addressing issues of unconstrained jury discretion). Thus, the modern, prototypical capital trial scheme involves a jury first determining whether a defendant is guilty or not guilty; if the defendant is found guilty, a jury must then endorse and weigh evidence in favor of a death sentence (aggravating circumstances) and evidence in favor of a sentence lesser than death (mitigating circumstances).

After the decision in *Gregg* and its companion cases, several themes in death penalty cases emerged. One theme was clarifying the role the judge and jury in sentencing procedures. Whereas states like Georgia revised their capital trial procedures to constrain jury discretion after the *Furman* decision, some states removed it all together. These mandatory death penalty schemes were struck down in short order (*Roberts v. Louisiana*, 1976; *Woodson v. North Carolina*, 1976). After *Gregg*, the Court initially approved of schemes that afforded judges discretion, for instance, in overturning a jury's sentencing recommendation (*Spaziano v. Florida*, 1984; *Walton v. Arizona*, 1990). However, the Court has repeatedly affirmed the jury's role as "fact Tfinders" in the past two decades. That is, the jury *alone* is responsible for finding every fact necessary to justify the imposition of a death sentence (*Hurst v. Florida*, 2016; *Ring v. Arizona*, 2002). Judges still have some degree of discretion in capital sentencing—especially so if a defendant waives their right to a jury trial—but the decision of whether a defendant should live or die largely rests with the jury.

A second theme that emerged was the consideration of evidence, specifically aggravating and mitigating circumstances. In *Lockett v. Ohio* (1978), the court established that *any* mitigating evidence could be introduced at trial (i.e., the defendant's character or record, as well as circumstances of the offense). Later, the U.S. Supreme Court ruled that the jury does not have to unanimously agree on mitigating evidence for it to be considered in reaching a sentencing decision (*McKoy v. North Carolina*, 1990). In contrast, aggravating evidence was and still is statutorily defined, and, in a series of cases, the Supreme Court emphasized that aggravating circumstances must meet the "narrowing requirement" (*Godfrey v. Georgia*, 1980; *Maynard v. Cartwright*, 1988; *Zant v. Stephens*, 1983). In essence, the courts expanded the range of evidence acceptable in favor of life in prison and reduced the range of evidence acceptable in favor of the death penalty.

A third theme emerged involving the extent to which the effectiveness of counsel was tied to the pursuit and presentation of mitigating evidence. The U.S. Supreme Court decided that presenting mitigating evidence to the extent of reasonable and professional standards would warrant effective counsel (*Strickland v. Washington*, 1984). However, failure to reasonably investigate and present mitigating evidence, which might influence a jury's decision, could be considered ineffective council (*Williams v. Taylor*, 2000; *Wiggins v. Smith*, 2003). These cases provided specificity as to how the discovery and presentation of "any mitigating evidence" (decided in *Lockett v. Ohio*, 1978) should be represented in capital trials.

A fourth important theme in the history of capital trials in the U.S. is the qualification and selection of jurors. In addition to the *Furman* and *Gregg* cases, the U.S. Supreme Court decided that it was constitutional to remove jurors during voir dire under challenges for cause if they would never vote for the death penalty under any circumstances, always vote for the death penalty upon a guilty verdict, or if jurors' attitudes and beliefs about the death penalty were strong enough to compromise their ability to be impartial (*Morgan v. Illinois*, 1992; *Wainwright v. Witt,* 1985; *Witherspoon v. Illinois*, 1968).

A fifth theme that emerged is the potential for racial discrimination in death penalty sentencing procedures. In the case of *Turner v. Murray* (1986), the U.S. Supreme Court ruled that it was allowable to ask venirepersons about racial attitudes and beliefs in murder cases involving a defendant and a victim of different races. This ruling seemed to implicitly acknowledge the specter of racial discrimination in capital punishment. However, a district court case two decades earlier had rejected statistical evidence of racial disparities in death sentencing, suggesting that a defendant would need to present evidence showing purposeful discrimination in the specific case (*Maxwell v. Bishop*, 1966). A year after *Turner*, the Supreme Court similarly rejected statistical evidence of racial disparities and reached a similar conclusion (*McCleskey v. Kemp*, 1987). In the majority's view, disparities are an inevitable part of sentencing.

A sixth theme that emerged is the death penalty eligibility of offenders. For much of American history, the list of capital crimes was long and included numerous non-homicide crimes, and virtually anyone who committed such crimes was potentially eligible for the death penalty. This was especially true for African Americans due to race-dependent capital crimes. In the period leading up to *Furman* and *Gregg*, murder and rape were the primary capital crimes. However, over the next several decades, rape alone was excluded as a death eligible offense (*Coker v. Virginia,* 1977; *Kennedy v. Louisiana*, 2008). The Court also delineated capital murder, in essence, by ruling that the death penalty was unconstitutional for offenders lacking murderous intent or prior awareness (*Enmund v. Florida*, 1982); the "insane" (*Ford v. Wainwright*, 1986); offenders with incompetency (*Madison v. Alabama*, 2019; *Panetti v. Quarterman*, 2007); offenders with (severe) intellectual disabilities (*Atkins v. Virginia*, 2002); and minors who were under the age of 18 when the crime was committed (*Roper v. Simmons*, 2005).

A seventh and final theme in the death penalty related to Supreme Court cases involves the method of execution. Firing squad (*Wilkerson v. Utah*, 1879), electrocution (*In re Kemmler*, 1890), and three-drug lethal injection led by sodium thiopental (*Baze v. Rees*, 2008) have all been ruled as constitutional. Recently, the Supreme Court ruled that the method of execution must not add substantial pain to the inmate for what is necessary for execution (*Bucklew v. Precythe*, 2019) and does not take the place of a substantially less harmful alternative (*Glossip v. Gross*, 2015).

In more recent cases, such as *Atkins* v. *Virginia* (2002), the U.S. Supreme Court has referenced international law and policy in its decisions, suggesting that the U.S. is beginning to look to other countries as evidence of legal trends (however, it does not use international law or policy as the basis for a standard of decency) at least in terms of the death penalty. The U.S. has been late to abolish the death penalty for people with (severe) intellectual disabilities and juveniles when compared to advanced Western cultures. This fits with the notion that U.S. death penalty laws are lagging the global abolition trend rather than leading it. Some critique the U.S., stating that the U.S. is late in abolishing the death penalty as global trends suggest an advanced Westernized culture should have done so by now, calling into question the (global) moral leadership of the U.S. (Kurtis, 2004).

Religion and the U.S. Death Penalty

It is quite difficult to untangle religion and the death penalty, especially Christianity and the American death penalty (see Naas, 2012). The Christian scriptures include numerous references to death penalty support and death penalty opposition (Bornstein & Miller, 2009; Latzer & McCord, 2011). Many contemporary writings wrestle with the complexity of this particular topic (see Owens et al., 2004). The specific directive from the Christian perspective is simply unclear, and scholars and authors still discuss the morality of the death penalty and the role of Christianity (Garvey, 2000).

The U.S. essentially adopted and applied the death penalty seamlessly from colonial America, including much of its religious interpretation, and America was founded in a religiously and politically pro-death penalty era (Banner, 2002; Douglas, 2000; Latzer & McCord, 2011; McBride, 1995). The Catholic Church and Protestant institutions, which were both dominant religions in the founding era, favored the death penalty (Douglas, 2000). One goal of executions was encouraging repentance, often accompanied by sermons at the time of execution, and sometimes executions were delayed so that the offender would have enough time to repent and pray (Banner, 2002; Latzer & McCord, 2011).

Over the course of the nineteenth and twentieth centuries, Christian religious institutions began changing stances from support to opposition, coinciding with a major overhaul of the modern death penalty in the 1970s. However, the religious population in the U.S. did not seem to follow the institutional stances (Douglas, 2000). It is possible that the people were unaware of the institutional stances or that the influence of religious institutions on people's social attitudes waned as religion became more individualized and personalized and institutions were less trusted (e.g., Banner, 2002; Versteeg & Roeland, 2011). Another explanation could be that the death penalty serves a ritualistic purpose, signifying a population's willingness to sacrifice one or more categories of people, which has changed over time, to symbolize a society's effort to root out evil (Kurtis, 2004; McBride, 1995). In this case, the death penalty is an outgrowth of the Christian idea that good conquers evil and moral violators are not tolerated but that vulnerable populations need protection, explicit in theme six of the death penalty case history. There are several Christian references to protecting children, the widowed, poor, needy, outcasts, and so on. It is possible that this explains why the death penalty for vulnerable populations has been systematically excluded over time despite strong death penalty support from religious groups, and why the death penalty for non-homicide child rape was allowed long after (approximately 30 years) the death penalty for rape of an adult was considered unconstitutional.

Religion and the Jury Trial

Religion emerges in numerous aspects of the trial process. Even the derivation of 12 jurors is suggested to be possibly based on the biblical reference to the 12 disciples, 12 stones, and 12 judges (Frank & Rashkow, 1966). The 12 jurors reflect a biblical theme of 12 as an important aspect of governmental structure, authority, and nation building (Buch, 1999; Forman, 2010). Increasing authority in the 12 jurors, post-*Gregg* (as explained in the first theme in the death penalty case history), also increases reliance on a symbolic representation of authority in the Bible. Even subtle cues (such as the presence of a Bible in oaths or deliberations) could prime religion, which could increase the salience of religion among trial attendees and affect the extent to which religion influences the case disposition (see Malavanti et al., 2012; Yelderman & Miller, 2017). However, these religious cues are passive symbols and not direct appeals to consult religion or religious moral authority to determine sentences.

Both the prosecution and the defense make some of the primary invocations of religion during death penalty trials. This occurs both as an argument for rendering a death penalty and against rendering a death penalty, primarily in closing arguments, sentencing remarks, or at some other time during the penalty phase (Brooks, 1999; Thomas, 1962). However, this practice is quite controversial. In *Carruthers v. State* (2000) and *Sandoval v. Calderon* (2001), the prosecuting attorneys invoked biblical scripture stating that God approved or even required the death penalty. However, in both of these cases, the ruling was that the attorney erred and it was not acceptable to appeal to a higher moral authority outside of the law. In other cases, attorneys successfully used religious appeals to denounce the death penalty (Brooks, 1999). These cases are notable for two reasons. First, they lend some credence to the notion that religious appeals affect sentencing decisions (e.g., see Miller & Bornstein, 2006). If the appellate courts did not think so, the attorneys' conduct would not have been considered inappropriate or consequential enough to be disallowed. Second, these cases show the precise crossroads between religious moral law and state law discussed in previous sections. Even with the separation of church and state, the cognitive contemplation between one's legal duties and religious moral duties substantiates the inability to truly separate religion from law (e.g., Garnett, 2003). Attorneys with strong religious beliefs might still use their beliefs as a foundation to seek the death penalty in the first place, submit certain aggravators, choose which mitigating evidence to submit, craft arguments, provide specific advice to clients, or take certain cases, which specifically pertains to the third theme identified in the case history of the death penalty (Buckingham, 1982; Stanford, 2003). It is unclear as to whether religious appeals impact sentencing decisions. Nevertheless, the debate about if and how religious appeals affect death sentences persists in the scholarly discourse and research literature.

Religious Jurors

Because jurors are the fact finders in capital cases, it is their religious beliefs (or lack thereof) that provide the cognitive, moral, and evaluative framework by which they interpret the trial evidence. One of the most notable ways that religion has been studied among jurors, and found influential, in death penalty attitudes and decisions is through religious affiliation (Morin, 2011). Catholics supported the death penalty up until the latter part of the twentieth century, but their support has decreased over the past few decades (Anderson et al., 2017; Uelmen, 2005). Protestants are typically supportive of the death penalty, especially evangelical and fundamentalist Protestant denominations (Anderson et al., 2017; Eisenberg et al., 2001; Grasmick, Cochran et al., 1993); however, Wozniak and Lewis (2010) suggest that there might be more of a difference between harsh denominations and unaffiliated individuals than there are interdenominational differences. While religious affiliations and denominations differ in their attitudes and beliefs about the death penalty, this means they fare differently in the death qualification process. Most notably, Catholics and Jews are likely to be removed from the jury pool through death qualification because of their oppositional views (relating to theme four in the case history of the death penalty), potentially increasing the jury population with more punitive religious beliefs (e.g., Ellsworth, 1984; Summers et al., 2010).

Because religious beliefs are becoming less institutionalized and more individualized, it might be imprecise to measures differences in religion at the denomination or affiliation level. Instead, it is likely more valid to assess individual religious beliefs and behaviors to capture the variation in death penalty support among religious believers. One of the primary behaviors studied is religious service attendance. In general, religious service attendance is negatively related to death penalty support (Bias et al., 2011; Messner et al., 2006; Price, 2006). Another form of religiousness is religiosity, which is typically the degree to which a person considers themselves religious. Religiosity is also negatively related to death penalty support (Unnever & Cullen, 2007). Accordingly, the more a person engages in religious activities and sees themselves as religious, the less punitive they are.

Another aspect of religion is religious salience, the extent to which a person contemplates their religious beliefs at any given time. Consistent with service attendance and religiosity, religious salience is negatively associated with death penalty support, and it is worth pointing out that Catholics tend to be higher in religious salience than non-Catholics (Britt, 1998; Robbers, 2004; Unnever & Cullen, 2006). It is possible that religious salience is part of the explanation for Catholics' oppositional attitudes. However, some studies find religious salience to be associated with death penalty support (Evans & Adams, 2003; Robbers, 2004). Religious salience describes religious cognitive presence in a person's mind, but it does not measure which specific religious beliefs or thoughts are present. Therefore, better ascertaining how specific religious beliefs relate to the death penalty might provide a better picture of how religious salience works.

Arguably, the most robust religious belief predictor of death penalty support is religious fundamentalism (see Bornstein & Miller, 2009). The proportion of fundamentalists is positively associated with the number of death sentences at both the county level and the state level (Amidon, 2018; Amidon & Eassey, 2021), and religious fundamentalism is associated with death penalty support and harsher verdicts in death penalty mock juror studies (Britt, 1998; Miller & Hayward, 2008; Stack, 2003; Yelderman et al., 2019; Young, 1992). What drives fundamentalism's relationship with death penalty support might be correlates such as conservatism, dispositional attributions, biblical literalism, and authoritarianism (Grasmick et al., 1993; Miller & Hayward, 2008; Young, 2000; Stack, 2000, 2003). Fundamentalist beliefs are also associated with a reluctance to endorse mitigating evidence (Yelderman et al., 2019). Thus, despite the moral nature of mitigating evidence and the increased legal emphasis and importance placed on mitigating evidence, described in the second theme of the case history of the death penalty, mitigating evidence is filtered through a person's religious beliefs. Because fundamentalism is associated with a greater belief in personal responsibility, these beliefs create a higher threshold, which mitigating evidence must meet before any reduction in punishment might be considered (Yelderman & Miller, 2016; Yelderman et al., 2019). Additionally, a punitive image of God, belief that God supports the death penalty, and beliefs in Hell all are related to increased support for the death penalty (Bones & Sabriseilabi, 2018; Grasmick et al., 1993; Miller & Hayward, 2008). It is possible that religious beliefs also evoke racialized views of the death penalty, increasing punitiveness toward African Americans primarily, and potentially other minorities, which might explain some of the disparities in death sentencing as examined in theme five of the case history of the death penalty (Barkan & Cohn, 1994).

Religious beliefs have been evoked in death penalty legislation in other countries as well. For example, Papua New Guinea recently abolished the death penalty citing the religious beliefs of the nation and, specifically, a reference to "thou shalt not kill," one of the ten biblical commandments (Togiba, 2022). However, this is a semantic reference to a policy adoption and not an association between measured citizens' religious beliefs and death penalty attitudes/decisions.

Conclusion

The link between the death penalty and religion might be unique to the U.S., due the historical significance of religion in the development of law, justifications for the death penalty, and moral foundations of the country. Comparing the role of religion in the U.S. with other Western countries might be a fruitful avenue of inquiry. For example, religion was unrelated to death penalty support in studies of Indian and Japanese college students (Jiang et al., 2010; Lambert et al., 2008). Religious doctrines often have multiple and mixed messages, including judgment and peace, which are reflected in the U.S. law as well. These messages manifest in different ways for different people. Religious-based explanations and justifications for death penalty support (or opposition) might be resilient to attacks and persuasion and difficult to change (Bohm, 1987). This could perhaps explain some of the reasons why religion has remained a consistent predictor of death penalty support over time, despite cultural changes (e.g., institutional shifts in death penalty support) and large-scale oppositional events (e.g., national moratorium on executions). The legal trend in the death penalty points toward abolition or increasing isolation in fewer and fewer states. It is quite possible that the state-level abolition of the death penalty will depend upon the religious population in that state, and the federal abolition of the death penalty might depend upon religious beliefs of the U.S. Supreme Court justices. However, short of abolition, religious determination to keep the death penalty paired with religious-based compassion might play a role in the continued dwindling of the applicability of the death penalty. For example, it is possible that the evolution in execution method, outlined in theme seven of the death penalty case history, serves to both retain the death penalty and ease concerns for religious people who have qualms with executions, justifying support and limiting resistance. Death penalty support might be increasingly concentrated in a group of staunch supporters who have individualized their beliefs, deviated from their religious institution's official stance, and justified their death penalty support through their religion. To help address potential predictions about the role of religion in the death penalty's legal future, we find it critical to examine possible explanations of the derivation order regarding religious beliefs and death penalty attitudes.

One explanation is that death penalty attitudes, and subsequent decisions, are derived from people's religious beliefs. Independent of when a person acquires religious beliefs, religion provides a moral framework on which to base one's attitudes and behaviors when facing a moral dilemma. When attorneys make religious appeals at trial, they are trying to remind the jury about their own religious beliefs and to consult those beliefs and interpret them consistent with the attorneys' arguments. These appeals seat religion as the foundation for why the death penalty is (un)justified. Most of the work in this chapter approaches the relationship between religion and the death penalty from this perspective.

A second explanation is that death penalty attitudes are intuitive, in that they are developed when people are able to engage in critical moral reasoning (e.g., Haidt, 2001). Prior to that, people are simply repeating or reflecting someone else's attitudes, such as parents or teachers, and so on. In this case, once a person can contemplate morality, they are intuitively for or against the death penalty. Once the person is cognitively aware of these moral attitudes, they search for justifications. At this point, religion becomes a frame of reference to justify their stance on the death penalty. Thus, religion is not the basis for their death penalty attitudes; instead, it is ad-hoc reasoning. This might explain why people of the same denomination and faith come to different conclusions about the death penalty using the same text and why people persist in their death penalty beliefs despite shifts in institutional stances. In this case, the scriptural basis acts as a confirmation bias rather than a true origin of their death penalty attitudes.

There might also be a bit of both of these explanations occurring and different people might experience different derivations of their death penalty attitudes, some in religion and some outside of religion. At this point, these theoretical explanations have not been tested in comparison. However, future research might begin to move beyond post-formative death penalty attitudes and religious beliefs to investigate theoretical explanations for the role of religion in one's death penalty attitude development.

Overall, it is difficult to state exactly how religion has shaped the U.S. death penalty and how the evolution of the U.S. death penalty has shaped how people think about their religious views. This is especially true given confounding events such as the Second World War, the Vietnam War, the civil rights movement, and the Jesus movement. One thing that we believe is clear, is that religion and the death penalty both involve some of the most foundational moral questions and undoubtedly are intertwined.

References

Amidon, E. (2018). Politics and the death penalty: 1930–2010. *American Journal of Criminal Justice, 43*, 831–860.

Amidon, E., & Eassey, J. M. (2021). Examining county-level political considerations associated with declining reliance on the death penalty from 1990 to 2010. *Criminology, 59*, 318–350.

Anderson, A., Lytle, R., & Schwadel, P. (2017). Age, period, and cohort effects on death penalty attitudes in the United States, 1974–2014. *Criminology, 55*(4), 833–868.

Atkins v. Virgina, 536 U.S. 304 (2002).

Banner, S. (2002). *The death penalty: An American history*. Harvard University Press.

Baze v. Rees, 553 U.S. 35 (2008).

Berman, H. (1980). The interaction of law and religion. *Mercer Law Review, 31*, 405–422.

Berman, H. (1983). Religious foundations of law in the West: An historical perspective. *Journal of Law and Religion, 1*(1), 3–43.

Bias, T., Goldberg, A., & Hannum, T. (2011). Catholics and the death penalty: Religion as a filter for political beliefs. *Interdisciplinary Journal of Research on Religion, 7*, 1–11.

Bohm, R. M. (1987). American death penalty attitudes: A critical examination of recent evidence. *Criminal Justice and Behavior, 14*(3), 380–396.

Bones, P. D. C., & Sabriseilabi, S. (2018). Sinners in the hands of an angry God: An exploration of religions forces on support for the death penalty. *Journal for the Scientific Study of Religion, 57*(4), 707–722.

Britt, C. L. (1998). Race, religion, and support for the death penalty: A research note. *Justice Quarterly, 15*(1), 175–191.
Brooks, E. A. (1999). Thou shalt not quote the Bible: Determining the propriety of attorney use of religious philosophy and themes in oral arguments. *Georgia Law Review, 33*(4), 1113–1180.
Buch, J. (1999). The biblical number 12 and the formation of the ancient nation of Israel. *Jewish Bible Quarterly, 27*, 49–57.
Bucklew v. Precythe, 587 U.S. ___ (2019).
Carruthers v. State, Supreme Court of Georgia, 528 S. E. 2 d 217 (2000).
Coker v. Georgia, 433 U.S. 584 (1977).
Douglas, D. M. (2000). God the executioner: The influence of Western religion on the death penalty. *William & Mary Bill of Rights Journal, 9*(1), 137–170.
Dunn v. Smith, 141 S. Ct. 725, 209 L. Ed. 2d 30 (2021).
Eisenberg, T., Garvey, S. P., & Wells, M. T. (2001). Forecasting life and death: Juror race, religion, and attitude toward the death penalty. *Journal of Legal Studies, 30*(2 – Part 1), 277–312.
Ellsworth, P. C. (1984). Due process vs. crime control: Death qualification and jury attitudes. *Law and Human Behavior, 8*(1–2), 31–51.
Enmund v. Florida, 458 U.S. 782 (1982).
Espy, M. W., & Smykla, J. O. (2016). *Executions in the United States, 1608–2002: The ESPY file*. Ann Arbor, MI: Inter-university Consortium for Political and Social Research.
Evans, T. D., & Adams, M. (2003). Salvation or damnation? Religion and correctional ideology. *American Journal of Criminal Justice, 28*(1), 15–35.
Ford v. Strickland, 696 F.2d 804 (1983).
Ford v. Wainwright, 477 U.S. 399 (1986).
Forman, J. (2010). Numerical symbolism in the dedication of the altar. *Jewish Bible Quarterly, 38*(1), 52–54.
Frank, H., & Rashkow, B. (1966). Right to trial by jury: Is it necessary? *DePaul Law Review, 15*(2), 398–402.
Furman v. Georgia, 408 U.S. 238 (1972).
Garnett, R. W. (2003). Christian witness, moral anthropology, and the death penalty. *Notre Dame Journal of Law, Ethics & Public Policy, 17*(2), 541–560.
Garvey, S. P. (2000). Introduction to the symposium: Religion's role in the administration of the death penalty. *William & Mary Bill of Rights Journal, 9*(1), 29–30.
Glossip v. Gross, 576 U.S. ___ (2015).
Godfrey v. Georgia, 446 U.S. 420 (1980).
Grasmick, H. G., Bursik, R. J., & Blackwell, B. S. (1993). Religious beliefs and public support for the death penalty for juveniles and adults. *Journal of Crime and Justice, 16*(2), 59–86.
Grasmick, H. G., Cochran, J. K., Bursik, R. J., & Kimpel, M. (1993). Religion, punitive justice, and support for the death penalty. *Justice Quarterly, 10*(2), 289–314.
Greenberg, D. F., & West, V. (2008). Siting the death penalty internationally. *Law & Social Inquiry, 33*(2), 295–343.
Gregg v. Georgia, 428 U.S. 153 (1976).
Hamburger, P. A. (1992). Natural rights, natural law, and American constitutions. *Yale Law Journal, 102*, 907–960.
Hurst v. Florida, 577 U.S. ___ (2016).
In re Kemmler, 136 U.S. 436 (1890).
Jiang, S., Pilot, R., & Saito, T. (2010). Why Japanese support the death penalty? *International Criminal Justice Review, 20*(3), 302–316.
Jurek v. Texas, 428 U.S. 262 (1976).

Kennedy v. Louisiana, 554 U.S. 407 (2008).

Kurtis, B. (2004). *The death penalty on trial: Crisis in American justice.* New York Public Affairs.

Lambert, E. G., Pasupuleti, S., & Jiang, S. (2008). Views on the death penalty among college students in India. *Punishment & Society, 10*(2), 207–218.

Latzer, B., & McCord, D. (2011). Death penalty cases: Leading U.S. Supreme Court cases on capital punishment (3rd ed.). Elsevier.

Lockett v. Ohio, 438 U.S. 586 (1978).

Madison v. Alabama, 586 U.S., ___ (2019).

Malavanti, K. F., Johnson, M. K., Rowatt, W. C., & Weaver, C. (2012). Subtle contextual influences on racial bias in the courtroom. *Jury Expert, 24*(3), 2–8.

Mathias, M. D. (2013). The sacralization of the individual: Human rights and the abolition of the death penalty. *American Journal of Sociology, 118*(5), 1246–1283.

Maxwell v. Bishop, 257 F. Supp. 710 (E.D. Ark. 1966).

Maynard v. Cartwright, 486 U.S. 356 (1988).

McBride, J. (1995). Capital punishment as the unconstitutional establishment of religion: A Girardian reading of the death penalty. *Journal of Church and State, 37*(2), 263–288.

McKoy v. North Carolina, 494 U.S. 433 (1990).

McCleskey v. Kemp, 481 U.S. 279 (1987).

McGautha v. California, 402 U.S. 183 (1971).

Messner, S. F., Baumer, E. P., & Rosenfeld, R. (2006). Distrust of government, the vigilante tradition, and support for capital punishment. *Law & Society Review, 40*(3), 559–590.

Miller, M. K., & Bornstein, B. H. (2006). The use of religion in death penalty sentencing trials. *Law and Human Behavior, 30*, 675–684.

Miller, M. K., & Hayward, R. D. (2008). Religious characteristics and the death penalty. *Law and Human Behavior, 32*, 113–123.

Morgan v. Illinois, 504 U.S. 719 (1992).

Morin, C. (2011). Do race, religion, or gender affect death penalty support in the United States? *Perspectives, 3*(1), 18–23.

Muryani, M. A., & Rosyidah, N. (2020). The concept of death penalty in a Pancasila State (perspective of official religion in Indonesia). *Walisongo Law Review, 2*(2), 131–158.

Naas, M. (2012). The philosophy and literature of the death penalty: Two sides of the same sovereign. *The Southern Journal of Philosophy, 50*, 39–55.

Owens, E. C., Carlson, J. D., & Elshtain, E. P. (Eds.). (2004). *Religion and the death penalty: A call for reckoning.* Wm. B. Eerdmans.

Panetti v. Quarterman, 551 U.S. 930 (2007).

Paternoster, R., Brame, R., & Bacon, S. (2008). *The death penalty: America's experience with capital punishment.* Oxford University Press.

Peterson, T. S. (2020). *Why criminalize?* Springer.

Price, M. (2006). *God's will or linked fate: Race and religion in African American views of the death penalty (a qualitative and quantitative approach).* Doctoral dissertation, University of Michigan. Available at SSRN 907318.

Proffitt v. Florida, 428 U.S. 242 (1976).

Purba, N., Tanjung, A. M., Sulistyawati, S., Pramono, R., & Purwanto, A. (2020). Death penalty and human rights in Indonesia. *International Journal of Criminology and Sociology, 9*, 1356–1362.

Ring v. Arizona, 536 U.S. 584 (2002).

Robbers, M. L. P. (2004). Extremists of believers? Religious salience, literalness, attribution styles and attitudes toward the death penalty among students: An empirical examination of main and moderating effects. *Journal of Crime and Justice, 27*(2), 119–149.

Roberts v. Louisiana, 428 U.S. 325 (1976).

Roper v. Simmons, 543 U.S. 551 (2005).

Sandoval v. Calderon, 241 F. 3d 765 – Court of Appeals, 9th Circuit (2001).

Spaziano v. Florida, 468 U.S. 447 (1984).

Stack, S. (2000). Support for the death penalty: A gender-specific model. *Sex Roles, 43*(3/4), 163–179.

Stack, S. (2003). Authoritarianism and support for the death penalty: A multivariate analysis. *Sociological Focus, 36*(4), 333–352.

Stanford, J. W. (2003). The Christian lawyer: Defending apparently guilty defendants and using deceptive courtroom strategies and tactics: An evangelical biblical view. *Regent University Law Review, 16*(2), 275–300.

Strickland v. Washington, 466 U.S. 668 (1984).

Summers, A., Hayward, R. D., & Miller, M. K. (2010). Death qualification as systematic exclusion of jurors with certain religious and other characteristics. *Journal of Applied Social Psychology, 40*(12), 3218–3234.

Thomas, G. L. (1962). John Brown's courtroom speech. *Quarterly Journal of Speech, 48*(3), 291–296.

Togiba, L. (2022, January 21). Papua New Guinea repeals death penalty 30 years after reintroduction. *The Guardian*. Retrieved from www.theguardian.com/world/2022/jan/21/papua-new-guinea-repeals-death-penalty-30-years-after-reintroduction.

Trop v. Dulles, 356 U.S. 86 (1958).

Turner v. Murray, 476 U.S. 28 (1986).

Uelmen, G. F. (2005). Catholic jurors and the death penalty. *Journal of Catholic Legal Studies, 44*(2), 355–378.

Unnever, J. D., & Cullen, F. T. (2006). Christian fundamentalism and support for capital punishment. *Journal of Research in Crime and Delinquency, 43*(2), 169–197.

Unnever, J. D., & Cullen, F. T. (2007). The racial divide in support for the death penalty: Does white racism matter. *Social Forces, 85*(3), 1281–1302.

Versteeg, P., & Roeland, J. (2011). Contemporary spirituality and the making of religious experience: Studying the social in an individualized religiosity. *Fieldwork in Religion, 6*(2), 120–133.

Wainwright v. Witt, 469 U.S. 412 (1985).

Walton v. Arizona, 497 U.S. 639 (1990).

Weems v. United States, 217 U.S. 349 (1910).

Wiggins v. Smith, 539 U.S. 510 (2003).

Wilkerson v. Utah, 99 U.S. 130 (1878).

Williams v. Taylor, 529 U.S. 362 (2000).

Witherspoon v. Illinois, 391 U.S. 510 (1968).

Woodson v. *North Carolina*, 428 US 280 (1976).

Wozniak, K. H., & Lewis, A. R. (2010). Reexamining the effect of Christian denominational affiliation on death penalty support. *Journal of Criminal Justice, 38*, 1082–1089.

Yelderman, L. A., & Miller, M. K. (2016). Religious fundamentalism and attitudes toward the insanity defense: The mediating roles of criminal attributions and attitudes toward the mentally ill. *Psychiatry, Psychology and Law, 23*(6), 872–884.

Yelderman, L. A., & Miller, M. K. (2017). Religious fundamentalism, religiosity, and priming: effects on attitudes, perceptions, and mock jurors' decisions in an insanity defense case. *Psychology, Crime & Law, 23*(2), 147–170.

Yelderman, L. A., West, M. P., & Miller, M. K. (2019). Death penalty decision-making: Fundamentalist beliefs and the evaluation of aggravating and mitigating circumstances. *Legal and Criminological Psychology, 24*, 103–122.

Young, R. L. (1992). Religious orientation, race, and support for the death penalty. *Journal for the Scientific Study of Religion, 31*(1), 76–87.

Young, R. L. (2000). Punishment at all costs: On religion, convicting the innocent, and supporting the death penalty. *William & Mary Bill of Rights Journal, 9*(1), 237–246.

Zant v. Stephens, 462 U.S. 862 (1983).

14

ISLAM AND RELIGIOUS HATE CRIME

Exploring the Role of Religion and Crime

Kim McGuire and Michael Salter

Introduction

Issues of legality and religion, which mediate religious hate crimes laws, are intertwined in numerous and analytically and politically challenging ways (Sandberg 2011; Iganski & Levin 2015). One of the initial challenges lies in identifying and differentiating 'religion' from 'non-religion' (*R (Hodkin) v Registrar General of Marriages* [2013] UKSC 77, [2014] 2 WLR 23 at [57] by Lord Toulson). Another issue lies in balancing freedom of religion and expression of religious doctrines with no less core liberal rights of freedom of expression concerning the critique of religious doctrines and practices. Does a further issue concern whether membership of a religious group or abuse from co-religionists that stems from, say, a Moslem announcing she has decided to change her religion, fall within the rationale of hate crimes laws?

In April 2021, Pakistan's prime minister, Imran Khan, stated his intention to launch a campaign seeking Muslim countries' support to raise the simmering issues of blasphemy and 'Islamophobia' at international forums, including the UN and the European Union (EU). 'When we begin a campaign by bringing together all Muslim countries [against Islamophobia and blasphemy], it will make a difference and change will come in the West,' Khan said at a televised ceremony in the capital Islamabad (Latif 2021). One possible realisation of his call would be for Britain to reinstate special protections for Islam over and above those currently contained in existing religious-related hate crimes laws, as noted in *The Guardian* (*The Guardian* 1 December 2018). Unfortunately, *The Guardian* article did conflate Islamophobia with racism, confusing the issue, as discussed below.

Several consultees to the Law Commission's review of hate crime laws called for specific references to particular religions. The commission itself stated: 'the evidence base for the inclusion of "religion" in hate crime laws derives primarily from

DOI: 10.4324/9781003276593-17

anti-Semitic and Islamophobic hatred; both of which remain very serious concerns' (Law Commission, 2021, 4.87).

> However, consistent with existing hate crime and anti-discrimination laws, we do not believe it is desirable to define specific forms of prejudice (such as antisemitism and islamophobia) in primary legislation, which focuses on the identification of protected characteristics such as 'race' and 'religion'
>
> *Law Commission, 2021, 4.108*

In the period since 9/11/2001, we have witnessed calls for extra and special protection for one religion, namely Islam. Indeed, there have been calls to make 'Islamophobia' a new offence, providing more protection than that offered for race and religion in current 'hate crime' legislation. Such calls are supported by claims of rising aggression towards followers of Islam, especially since 9/11. However, can such a move can be justified at the level of principle? Furthermore, would its enactment prove not only difficult but counterproductive and divisive?

In recent years, religious and political leaders have been accused of violating hate-speech laws by voicing their religious convictions in ways that others find insulting, offensive, and discriminatory. Hate-speech laws prohibit incitement to religious hatred. Many argue religious freedom includes a right to radically critique religions, even if the effect is to offend and insult religious believers. Any credible response to suggestions for special protections for Islam must consider a range of both in principle and in practice objections, including those we set out here (Rehman, 2010).

This chapter will revisit religious hate crime issues, but the foci are the legal definitions of 'religious hate crime' and incitement to religious hatred. Our particular concern is effectively reinstating 'blasphemy' for one specific religion, preventing critique and potentially sanctioning abuse. Islamic and Christian blasphemy law in the UK will be the main foci because any proposal to give special legal protection to Islam will face similar principled objections to those that the former faced, which led in part to its abolition. Rehman is particularly useful here, for example, discussing sharia law and the Quran. (Rehman, 2010)

Transnational Dimensions

There is no global or even pan-European-wide consensus within European states claiming liberal-democratic status on whether to enact religious hate speech laws or other hate crime measures. Indeed, there is a significant variation in the characteristics that are protected, the legal tests that are applied to identify the offence for the purposes of criminal law, and the mechanism by which such laws recognise the behaviour as a hate crime (Law Commission, 2021, Summary: 3). Although the details addressed in this short chapter are primarily related to the UK, the issues and dilemmas we address have far wider relevance to any modern liberal democratic state that strives to find a coherent relationship between competing imperatives (Bielefeld et al., 2016, 494–95; Temperman, 2017), for instance, those dilemmas related to European and international human rights protections of 'freedom of religion,' which includes freedom to hold and express religious views about more issues relating to sexuality and same-sex marriage that groups specifically protected by hate crimes laws might find offensive and insulting, as well strongly held critiques of other religions and 'deviant' co-religionists (Perrone, 2014). Yet even international human rights measures endorsing freedom of speech make provision for legal restrictions based on indeterminate grounds of 'public morals' and 'public order' (International Covenant on Civil and Political Rights, 1966, Art 19(3)b). This dilemma even features in the deliberations and policies of the UN (Cox, 2015; UN, 2013).

Not surprisingly, international as well as European human rights lawyers have weighed in on this topic from a diversity of incompatible perspectives (Dobras, 2009; Bennett, 2009; Holzaepfel, 2014). Most modern liberal democratic states struggle to strike a balance somewhere between no restrictions on speech and, at the other extreme, laws that permit only officially sanctioned opinions and beliefs related to religious issues (Law Commission, 2021). Every modern society with liberal democratic aspirations must strive to protect itself from the danger of overreach from both the sides of intolerant militant secularism and religious extremism, in which, at a minimum, laws against incitement to violence cannot avoid including contextually inappropriate expressions of religious criticism (Temperman, 2016). Yet this debate occurs within a pluralist context where the possibility of achieving a rational consensus on even the definition of the terms of the debate is extremely unlikely (Cox, 2020; O'Flaherty, 2012).

In this respect, our critical analysis of British provisions can be read as a case study of dilemmas intrinsic to the whole enterprise of deploying criminal laws, including blasphemy and hate crime measures, to regulate and criminalise religious and religious-related speech that has transnational implications. This question has transnational relevance in a context where nearly 50% of states have blasphemy-related laws (Hicks 2015, 51; Liu, 2020). Finally, there are also transnational dimensions to encoded forms of religious hate speech, especially anti-Semitism, arising from Holocaust denial (Cox, 2014; Salter, 2017). In short, while these transnational dimensions cannot be surveyed in this short chapter, our treatment of British legal regulation can be read as a case study of issues that transcend the border of any single legal regime.

The Current Religious Hate Crime Legislation in England and Wales.

Currently in the UK, for all 'hate crimes offences,' a *base* criminal offence must be committed, motivated by, or demonstrate hostility towards a protected 'religion,' or indeed, atheism. Religion itself is not specifically defined. These crimes are covered by the Crime and Disorder Act (CDA)1998 and section 66 of the Sentencing Act 2020, which allows prosecutors to apply for an uplift in sentence for those convicted of a hate crime. 'Religious group' is defined in section 28(5) of the CDA 1998 as a 'group of persons defined by reference to religious belief or lack of religious belief.'

The scope of 'lack of religious belief' means the simple absence of religious belief, such as 'atheists' or 'apostates (Addison, 2006, 126; The Equality Act, 2010, s10). Hostility towards a group defined by non-religious beliefs or philosophies that extend beyond mere lack of religious belief (for example, humanism) is therefore excluded. Whether a cult or a similar group is protected will depend on whether their beliefs are 'religious in nature.' The inclusion of groups defined by a lack of religious belief is especially interesting. It means that if, for example, an offender is motivated to assault a fellow Muslim because the latter is considering rejecting this or any other religious belief, thereby becoming 'apostate,' the offender would be guilty of a religiously aggravated offence. The same applies to sectarian hostility between Sunni and Shia Muslims, or Catholics and Protestants as such scenarios are also covered by the definition of 'religious group' (Law Commission, 2021, 2.34).

The prosecution must prove not only that the underlying or 'base' offence was committed, but also that the defendant demonstrated, or the offence was motivated by, racial or religious hostility. The hostility does not need to be the sole or even the main motivation for committing the base offence (Babbs, 2007, 8). There is no legal definition of either the meaning or the scope of 'hostility' (or hatred). Hatred, which must be directed at a group, not merely an individual as such, is not defined in the POA 1986 and

> it can be taken to bear its ordinary meaning. It is generally thought that 'hatred' is a stronger term than 'hostility.' As a term which appears very rarely in criminal statutes, there is limited further definition in case law, and it is ultimately a question for the trier of fact (jury or magistrates) whether this standard has been met.
>
> Law Commission, 2021, *2.132–34*

So, legal outcomes cannot but be determined by: 'everyday understanding of the word which includes ill-will, spite, contempt, prejudice, unfriendliness, antagonism, resentment and dislike' (CPS, 2022). Especially relevant to our points on sectarian inter-Moslem conflict, 'hostility' can be demonstrated by the defendant towards someone of the defendant's own racial or religious group (White, 2001, 20).

There are also relevant provisions of the Racial and Religious Hatred Act 2006 – Stirring Up Religious Hatred. This offence is committed if a person uses threatening words or behaviour, or displays any written material which is threatening, providing that person intends thereby to stir up religious hatred. Here, it is *threatening* that is the operative word, *not abusive or insulting*. Possession, publication, or distribution of inflammatory material is also an offence. The offence can be committed in a public or a private place but not within a dwelling, unless the offending words and behaviour were heard outside the dwelling and were intended to be heard. A vital point for the viability of prosecutions is that the defendant *must intend* to stir up religious hatred; recklessness is not enough. In terms of the realisation of the policy goals that include deterrence, the need for 'intend to stir up' is a relatively high threshold.

The Public Order Act 1986 (POA) contains wide protection for comment, criticism, and debate on religious beliefs and practices, including comic treatment amounting to ridicule. Unlike the parallel offences relating to other protected groups, such as race, there is a 'freedom of expression' defence contained in Section 29J, (Foreign & Commonwealth Office, 2014, March 24) which both asserts and affirms that:

> Nothing in this Part shall be read or given effect in a way which prohibits or restricts discussion, criticism or expressions of antipathy, dislike, ridicule, insult or abuse of particular religions or the beliefs or practices of their adherents, or of any other belief system or the beliefs or practices of its adherents or proselytising or urging adherents of a different religion or belief system to cease practising their religion or belief system.
>
> *POA, 1986, 29J*

There are no reported cases interpreting this provision. In the absence of appellate judicial interpretation, it is hard to assess the meaning and scope of this 'free speech provision' (Law Commission, 2021, 2.139). Traditional defences of Christianity-only blasphemy laws faced the objection that it was impossible to determine the content of the protected tenets with the type of precision needed for criminal law. Yet the same point applies to Islam. It has, for example, proven difficult to determine whether alleged 'hostility' accompanying a criminal offence against followers of Islam is due to either racial or religious bias, to which it demonstrates hostility. The aggravated offences under the CDA 1998 were extended to *religious* aggravation as part of a package of measures introduced by the Anti-terrorism, Crime and Security Act 2001 in the name of equal treatment: some religious groups, such as Jews and Sikhs, which were also ethnic groups, previously were afforded the protection of *racially* aggravated offences, but this was not available to multi-ethnic religions, such as Christianity and Islam. This received criticism within Parliament, and from Muslim groups, which, having lobbied for the extension, were troubled by its inclusion in a Bill concerning terrorism (Law Commission, 2021, 2.113). To prosecute, the protected characteristic must be clearly identified (Hansard (HL), 27 Nov 2001, vol 629, col 150).

As Sealy argues: 'Islamophobia has been a controversial concept ever since it first gained popular currency. One of the main sticking points over the term is whether or not it refers to religion' (Sealy 2021:1). Furthermore,

> Debates about the term itself, whether we should instead use anti-Muslim racism or anti-Muslimism for instance, as well as debates about whether it

> refers to religion, ethnicity, or culture, have been the focus of much academic as well as political commentary.
>
> *Sealy, 2021, 1; Halliday, 1999; Allen, 2010; Sayyid & Vakil 2011; Jackson 2018*

The updated report *Islamophobia: Still A Challenge for Us All* (Runnymede, 2017) and the All-Party Parliamentary Group on British Muslims (APPGBM) report *Islamophobia Defined* (APPGBM 2018), shared the definition of Islamophobia as anti-Muslim racism: 'Islamophobia is rooted in racism and is a type of racism that targets expressions of Muslimness or perceived Muslimness' (cited in Sealy, 2021, 1). However, this definition was rejected by the government (*The Guardian* 16 May 2019). Such rejection makes sense insofar as it conflates Islam with questions of racial exclusivity which, to its credit, Islam itself rejects. If Muslim extremists blow up Christian churches in Sri Lanka, for example, it is surely unjustifiable to accuse the perpetrators of 'Christianophia rooted in racism' (DeVotta, 2009).

Whilst 'Islamophobia' may coincide with racism in certain contexts, this is not always the case. According to Greer, '"Islamophobia" generally refers to irrational antagonism towards Islam and/or Muslims typically based on myth, caricature, and misleading stereotype. Strictly speaking, a "phobia" is a clinically observable anxiety disorder defined by recurrent and excessive fear of an object or situation' (Greer, 2019). However, we argue that many who express intense critiques do not have a phobia of Islam per se, nor an excessive irrational fear. Rather fear may arise from a concern over the extreme version of Islam proposed by organisations such as the Islamic State of Iraq and al-Sham (ISIS), or the Taliban, and the symbiotic linking of politics, law, and religion. The Taliban are a predominantly Pashtun, Islamic fundamentalist group. Since their return to power in Afghanistan in 2021 and the imposition of their interpretation of Islamic law, many have been fearful of even further expansions of this illiberal ideology. The especially negative consequences for established legal and constitutional rights of women have been noted (Ibrahim, 2021). The fact that interpretations can be defined as 'classical' and a strict interpretation has created difficulties for critique, even from within their communities of belief.

The Need to Offer Critique

However, the practice of critique cannot be restricted to the potentially negative consequences of repressive policies justified by reference to a particular interpretation of Islamic doctrine. Instead, as with any other form of rights repression, critique must also address the motivating power of the ideological basis that reinterprets such repression as a righteous – indeed obligatory – act of religious observance.

Different versions of Islam are noticeable even within extremist factions. As with other extreme approaches, including the political far-right and left, there is a tendency towards factionalism, as well as sectarianism: one that may be driven by the personal ambitions of would-be leaders of what is rhetorically represented as 'the one true version of Islam.' Once such fusion of non-religious motivations with religious movements takes place, those who dissent or oppose the leader of one faction, possibly on entirely reasonable grounds based upon credible interpretations of Islamic teaching, risk being subjected to hostility and discriminatory treatment justified by their alleged status as 'apostates.'

Members of faith groups can be as vulnerable to religiously related hostility and violent abuse from members of 'their own' religious communities, broadly defined, as from outsiders. To give one illustration of religious interpretation, the Islamic State, also known as ISIS, follows one distinctive variety of Islam, which differs from the Muslim Brotherhood in Egypt. It is claimed that the Islamic State views leaders of the Muslim Brotherhood as 'apostates' meriting murder (Wood, 2022). Hence, legal measures to address ill-defined instances of 'Islamophobia' risk generating more prosecutions of Muslims than anyone else. Furthermore, this could publicise a mass of details of sectarian prejudice that far-right racist groups would regard with malicious glee as a massive 'own goal' in the sense of representing a propaganda boost and source of further recruitment.

Legal measures having a chilling effect upon religious debates and disagreements within Muslim or any other communities of religious faith, must be avoided (Marshall & Shea, 2011). The health of any religion lies in its constant reinterpretation through a process of informed debate regarding its basic principles, and appropriateness to prevailing social contexts. A version of Islam rooted in rural Afghanistan and Pakistan is one thing, the preconditions for the acceptability of Islam among ultra-Westernised teenagers from a South Asian cultural heritage in Manchester quite another.

Laws relating to religion must surely respect, indeed encourage, open and free debate between incompatible narratives. As Sandberg and Colvin note: 'Powerful narratives that invoke religious concepts – *jihad*, *Sharia*, *shahid*, *Caliphate*, *kuffar*, and *al-Qiyāmah* – have accompanied jihadi violence but also inspired robust counter-narratives from Muslims' (Sandberg & Colvin 2020, 1585). It was also noted that:

> Authorities on Islam have offered high-profile rejections of the jihadi readings, for example when several hundred Islamic scholars signed a letter denouncing IS and its theological views.
>
> *Open Letter to Al-Baghdadi, in Sandberg & Colvin, 2020, 1586*

Hence, the arguably unresolvable practical difficulty facing proposals to give Islam special legal protection superior to that afforded to Judaism and so on, can be summed up in the slogan 'Islam, which Islam?' In practice, academic evidence from theologians could render prosecution for critiques of Islam ambiguous or even ill-founded, since different views on the core tenets are common, evoking tensions between more traditional and liberalising views.

A possible counterargument could be that only expressions of Islamophobia from non-Muslims would fall under revised legislation to bypass the issue of sectarian hostilities within Islamic faith communities. Yet, the parallel here would be, for example, that black people can subject brown and white-skinned persons to racist hostility with legal impunities that would not apply in the reverse. That no such proposals for law reform have arisen even from the most fervent anti-racist pressure groups is surely telling. It suggests that anti-discrimination laws are based on the practical enforcement of liberal doctrines of equal rights for all citizens irrespective of their religion, race, and ethnicity.

A related point is that membership of religious faith communities does not preclude belonging to ideologies of extreme intolerance targeting those they identify as gay, bisexual, and transgendered persons, and/or who exhibit hostile forms of xenophobia and religious sectarianism. Although in legal principle the categories of perpetrator and victims of religious hate crime are utterly distinct, in real-world cases such as drunken teenagers clashing outside a nightclub both groups can be legally classified as 'perpetrators' (who are merely incidentally 'victims') or as 'victims' (who are merely incidentally 'perpetrators.')

The Problems with Resurrecting Blasphemy Laws

We argue that British political and everyday culture, as well as other Western nation states, have enhanced their orientation towards all manner of expressions that had for many centuries been subjected to censure, even criminalisation, as supposedly 'deviant.' The form of ideological bigotry that conflates one's own specific beliefs to a divine moral order, which provides the religious rationale for punishing those who disagree with one as 'heretics' and 'apostates,' now appears to belong to a distant and thankfully long-departed historical era: one with no claims to be respected or missed. The last British citizen to be sent to prison for blasphemy was John William Gott. In 1922 he was sentenced to nine months' hard labour for comparing Jesus with a circus clown. In Scotland, there has not been a public prosecution since 1843 (BBC, 1984).

The long-standing rationale for opposition to British blasphemy laws is of special interest because the criticisms remain relevant for the idea of prioritising Islam within a revised hate crime legislation. The British Humanist Association developed a critique arguing that any form of blasphemy law is a threat to rights to free speech. The latter argument was echoed in 2008 by a House of Lords select committee which stated that any future blasphemy prosecution would fail because it would clash with the right to free speech in the European Convention on Human Rights, itself part of British domestic law (House of Commons, Hansard Debates for 09 Jan 2008 (pt 0026) (parliament.UK), 9 Jan 2008, Column 442).

Although the offence of blasphemous libel has been legally challenged as contrary to the freedom of speech provisions in the Convention, particularly Article 10, the results have been mixed and controversial. In *Wingrove v UK* (1996), the European Court of Human Rights (ECtHR) decided that it was within the state's margin of appreciation to restrict free speech in a case where the content is deemed 'blasphemous.' *Wingrove* involved a film board's refusal to issue a classification certificate to a film accused of blasphemy. The court found no violation of the right to freedom of expression because the interference was properly prescribed by law and pursued a 'legitimate aim' of protecting the Christian faith from blasphemous expressions. However, Judge Lohmus wrote a dissenting opinion, arguing that because the aim of the criminal law of blasphemy was only to protect the Christian religious belief, there remains a question of whether the interference could indeed be interpreted as 'necessary' in a multi-faith democratic society (*Wingrove v UK* 1996).

Further, shifting societal and cultural attitudes can be seen in the following examples. In 1977, a trial judge in the prosecution of *Gay News* for blasphemous libel, *Whitehouse v Lemon*, argued that this crime was committed: 'if a publication about God, Christ, the Christian religion or the Bible used words which were scurrilous, abusive or offensive, which vilified Christianity and might lead to a breach of the peace' (BBC 1984). This case arose from a private prosecution by Mary Whitehouse against *Gay News* for publishing an erotic poem depicting a centurion's sexual love for Christ. Arguably, her position is analogous with some British Muslims unsuccessfully calling for the author Salman Rushdie to be tried under the law after the publication of his controversial novel, *The Satanic Verses* (Rushdie, 2012).

Our main issue is further advanced if we reconstruct how the offence of blasphemy was first introduced and then abolished in the UK. Their original rationale and abolition have been marked by social and historical contingencies. Within the UK, common law criminal laws prohibiting blasphemy and blasphemous libel hark back to the mediaeval fourteenth century supplemented, in some special cases, by legislation (Temperman, 2017). The common law offences of blasphemy and blasphemous libel were formally abolished in England and Wales in 2008 (Criminal Justice and Immigration Act, 2008, s.79), but abolition in Scotland – where issues of religious sectarianism persist – only occurred in 2021 (Sandberg & Doe, 2008). In May 2017, Stephen Fry and the Irish broadcaster RTE were under investigation for the crime of blasphemy in Ireland (*The Telegraph*, 9 May, 2017). Ripples from the affair prompted New Zealand and Denmark to repeal their still existing blasphemy laws, with many in shock that they were still in place (Nash, 2017). Ireland was the first country in the world to hold a referendum on ending blasphemy law, which resulted in a constitutional amendment in 2018 and in repealing the offence of blasphemy with effect in 2020. Given these divergences, it can hardly be argued that laws regulating religious and anti-religious expression can be reduced to the realisation of any type of immutable universal principles and ahistorical 'natural rights.' Indeed, their promotion and abolition owe more to policy arguments, and perceptions of promoting 'peace.'

Policy Issues

In a 1949 speech later quoted in Parliament, Lord Denning, despite placing the blasphemy laws in the past, suggested a social policy goal he believed they contained:

> The reason for this law was because it was thought that a denial of Christianity was liable to shake the fabric of society, which was itself founded upon the Christian religion. There is no such danger to society now and the offence of blasphemy is a dead letter.
>
> *Denning, 1949, 46*

However, in 1977, when giving judgement on the *Gay News* case, Lord Scarman said that 'I do not subscribe to the view that the common-law offence of blasphemous libel serves no useful purpose in modern law. The offence belongs to a group of criminal offences designed to safeguard the internal tranquillity of the kingdom' (*Whitehouse v Lemon* [1979], AC, 617). Furthermore, Lord Scarman thought that blasphemy laws should cover *all* religions and not just Christianity and sought strict liability for those who 'cause grave offence to the religious feelings of some of their fellow citizens or are such as to tend to deprave and corrupt persons who are likely to read them.' On the first hearing, the prosecuting counsel, John Smythe, stressed that the whole of 1970s morality was on trial with his assertion that it was a test case of 'whether anything is to remain sacred.' The conclusion of this case differs from the incitement to religious hatred currently enacted, which requires intent (Racial and Religious Hatred Act, 2006; Public Order Act, 1986, ss 29B to 29G) .

It is, however, vital to emphasise that the criminalisation of religious hate crime and speech is not a purely conceptual-linguistic issue of legal semantics. Being convicted of a religious or any other type of hate crime or hate speech may have devastating consequences for a person's reputation and even career. Only in those rarer cases where an offender belongs to a brutal subculture of violent religious (or racial etc.) intolerance and ideologically driven sectarian hatred will a conviction function as a desirable symbolic rite of passage and a badge of honour. Yet in this area, there remains the permanent danger that the chronic ambiguities within the doctrinal and procedural laws are not always consistently interpreted in favour of the accused according to general liberal criminal law doctrine, with extensions of criminalisation through creeping judicial reasoning by analogy.

Conclusion

Presently, the goal of advocates of religious hate crime laws typically includes bolstering the voices of supposedly especially 'vulnerable' and less-resilient religious groups deemed from discriminatory abuse. Whether this is the case, such special legislative protections inevitably require the *partial silencing* of the speech of other religious groups or even members of the protected group. Affording legal and constitutional protection of freedom of religious expression by, for example, religious hate speech legislation, must factor in protection from abusively intolerant co-religionists (*Wingrove v UK*, 1996).

It must also be recognised that actions that are readily classified as 'Islamophobia' are also carried out by Moslems. No legal measure designed to protect the peaceful expression of Islamic views can be framed in ways that exclude prosecutions of a co-religionist. Expressions of hateful intolerance can arise from sectarian disagreements within religious groups.

We argue that within modern multifaith liberal democratic societies, the right to offer critique, even insult, is important. Such critique may challenge and offend an individual's intimately held religious beliefs and convictions, but should not be prevented. We understand reactions to cartoons satirising the prophet Muhammad, to burnings of the Koran, and offensive anti-Islam videos, but Islam is not the only religion affected (WION Web Team, 2020). As a Foreign and Commonwealth Office report states, 'many of the cases taken to the European Court of Human Rights (ECtHR) and communicated to the UN Human Rights Committee concern other beliefs, including Christianity and Judaism' (Foreign Office Report, 2016). We do not dispute that in recent years an increase in high-profile cases related to Islam is evidenced (Home Office, 2019–2020).

In both practice and principle, it is doubtful whether religious hate speech laws ever protect all those who speak out on religious or religious-related controversial matters. Yet, this is surely the only credible justification for any claimed right to legal protection deemed to be universal. We should strive to equalise all protected headings, not prioritise any of them. Only in this way can we avoid the paradox of striving to formulate a legislative definition of the defining characteristics of religious hate speech related to Islam, whilst contravening the dignity and rights of all others. If we reinstate blasphemy for Islam or any other religion, how can this avoid effectively preventing critique of 'religiously supported' views: potentially opening the floodgates for expressions that detrimentally affect others? Unless and until these challenges are credibly and convincingly answered, the case for enhanced legal protection for Islam is not made.

References

Addison, N. (2006). *Religious Discrimination and Hatred Law.* Taylor & Francis.

Allen, C. (2010). *Islamophobia* (1st edition). Routledge.

Allen, C. (2016). *Still a Challenge for Us All? The Runnymede Trust, Islamophobia and Policy.* Routledge.

All-Party Parliamentary Group (APPG). (2018). *Islamophobia Defined: Report on the Inquiry into a Working Definition of Islamophobia/anti-Muslim Hatred.* Retrieved from: www.camden.gov.uk/documents/20142/4794543/APPG+Definition+of+Islamophobia.pdf/f747d5e0-b4e2-5ba6-b4c7-499bd102d5aa

Babbs [2007]. EWCA Crim 2737, [2007] All ER (D) 383 (Oct).

BBC (1984). Q & A: Blasphemy laws. Retrieved from: http://news.bbc.co.uk/2/hi/uk_news/3753408.stm

Bennett, G.L. (2009). Defamation of Religions: The End of Pluralism, *Emory International Law Review* 23(1) (2009), 69–84.

Bielefeld, B. et al. (2016) *Freedom of Religion or Belief: An International Commentary.* Oxford University Press, pp. 494–95.

Crown Prosecution Service (CPS). (2020). *Racist and Religious Hate Crime – Prosecution Guidance*: (2020, February 16). Retrieved from: www.cps.gov.uk/legal-guidance/racist-and-religious-hate-crime-prosecution-guidance

Crown Prosecution Service (CPS). (2022). Hate Crime. https://www.cps.gov.uk/crime-info/hate-crime

Cox, N. (2015). Pourquoi Suis-Je Charlie? Blasphemy, Defamation of Religion, and the Nature of Offensive Cartoons, *Oxford Journal of Law and Religion* 4(3), 343–67.

Cox, N. (2014) Blasphemy, Holocaust Denial and the Control of Profoundly Unacceptable Speech, *American Journal of Comparative Law* 62, no. 3: 739–74

Cox, N. (2020). Justifying blasphemy laws: Freedom of expression, public morals, and international human rights law. Journal of Law and Religion, 35(1), 33–60.

Crime and Disorder Act 1998. HMSO.

Criminal Justice and Immigration Act 2008. HMSO.

Denning, Lord. (1949). Freedom under the Law. Hamlyn Lectures. 1st Series. London: 46. Quoted by Nick Herbert Hansard 9 Jan 2008: Column 452.

DeVotta, N. (2009, 25 April). Sri Lanka's Christians and Muslims Weren't Enemies, *Foreign Policy*. Retrieved from: https://foreignpolicy.com/2019/04/25/sri-lankas-christians-and-muslims-werent-enemies/

Dobra, D. (2012). The antinomy tradition-modernity at another level. Online Journal Modelling the New Europe, (06), 71-74.

Dobras, R.J. (2019). Is the United Nations Endorsing Human Rights Violations? An Analysis of the United Nations' Combating Defamation of Religions Resolutions and Pakistan's Blasphemy Laws, *Georgia Journal of International and Comparative Law* 37(2), 341–80.

Durrant, R., & Poppelwell, Z. (2017). Religion, Punishment, and the Law. In: *Religion, Crime and Punishment* (pp. 127–60). Palgrave Macmillan.

Ecclesiastical Courts Jurisdiction Act 1860.

Elgot, J. (2019, 15 May). Government Criticised for Rejecting Definition of Islamophobia, *The Guardian*. Retrieved from: www.theguardian.com/news/2019/may/15/uk-ministers-criticised-rejecting-new-definition-islamophobia.

Foreign & Commonwealth Office. (2014, 24 March). *Hate Speech, Freedom of Expression and Freedom of Religion: A Dialogue*. GOV.UK. Retrieved from: www.gov.uk/government/publications/hate-speech-freedom-of-expression-and-freedom-of-religion-a-dialogue

The Guardian (2015, 1 December). Muslims Demand Full Legal Protection from Islamophobia. Retrieved from: www.theguardian.com/uk-news/2018/dec/01/muslims-demand-full-legal-protection-from-islamophobia

Halliday, F. (1999). 'Islamophobia' Reconsidered, *Al Jazeera*. Retrieved from: www.aljazeera.com/news/2021/8/23/hold-the-taliban-and-sharia-law-in-afghanistan.

Home Office. (2020). *Hate Crime England and Wales (2019–2020)*. Retrieved from: https://assets.publishing.service.gov.uk/government/uploads/system/uploads/attachment_data/file/925968/hate-crime-1920-hosb2920.pdf.

Holzaepfel, C. (2014). 'Can I Say That?' How an International Blasphemy Law Pits the Freedom of Religion against the Freedom of Speech, *Emory International Law Review* 28(1), 597–648.

House of Commons, Hansard Debates for 9 Jan 2008 (pt 0026) (parliament. UK) 9 Jan 2008: Column 442).

HRCR.org. (1996). Freedom of Religion and Other Beliefs. Retrieved from: http://www.hrcr.org/safrica/religion/Otto.html.

Iganski, P., & Levin, J. (2015). *Hate Crime: A Global Perspective*. Routledge.

Jackson, L. B. (2018). *Islamophobia in Britain: The Making of a Muslim Enemy*. Palgrave Macmillan.

Latif, A. (2021, 19 April). Pakistan to Launch Global Appeal against Blasphemy. AA, Andalou Agency. Retrieved from: www.aa.com.tr/en/asia-pacific/pakistan-to-launch-global-campaign-against-blasphemy/2213493.

Law Commission. (2021). *Hate Crime Laws: Final Report*. HMSO.
Greer, S.(2019, 22 August). Know Your Enemy: Racism and Islamophobia. University of Bristol Law School Blog. Retrieved from: https://legalresearch.blogs.bris.ac.uk/2019/08/know-your-enemy-racism-and-islamophobia/
Liu, J. (2020, 30 May). Laws Penalizing Blasphemy, Apostasy and Defamation of Religion are Widespread. Pew Research Center's Religion & Public Life Project. Retrieved from: www.pewforum.org/2012/11/21/laws-penalizing-blasphemy-apostasy-and-defamation-of-religion-are-widespread/.
Mcguire, K. (2021). Extending the Concept, or Extending the Characteristics? Misogyny or Gender? In I. Zempi and J. Smith, eds, *Misogyny as Hate Crime*, Routledge. Retrieved from: www.routledge.com/Misogyny-as-Hate-Crime/Zempi-Smith/p/book/9780367903176.
Mcguire, K. (2022). Gender Empowerment through Legislation: Extend the Concept, or Extend the Characteristics of Hate Crime? In M. Kitchener, ed., *Handbook for Creating a Gender-Sensitive Curriculum: Teaching and Learning Strategies* Oxford Brookes University, page 16–17. Retrieved from: www.brookes.ac.uk/ocsld/publications/.
McGuire, K., & Salter, M. (2014). Legal Responses to Religious Hate Crime: Identifying Critical Issues, *King's Law Journal* 25(2), 159–84.
Mcguire, K., & Salter, M. (2019). *From the Experience of Hate Crime: Towards a Phenomenological Approach*. Springer.
Marshall, P., & Shea, N. (2011). *Silenced: How Apostasy and Blasphemy Codes Are Choking Freedom Worldwide*. Oxford University Press.
Nash, D. (2017, 15 November). Blasphemy on Trial, *History Today*. Retrieved from: www.historytoday.com/miscellanies/blasphemy-trial.
O'Flaherty, M. (2012). Freedom of Expression: The International Covenant on Civil and Political Rights and the Human Rights Committee's General Comment No. 34, *Human Rights Law Review* 14(4), 627–54.
Otto-Preminger-Institut v. Austria, Series A no. 295-A (1994).
Participation, IN. (2020). Sentencing Act 2020. GOV.UK. Retrieved from: www.legislation.gohttp://www.hrcr.org/safrica/religion/Wingrove.htmlv.uk/ukpga/2020/17/contents.
Perrone, R. (2014). Public Morals and the European Convention on Human Rights, *Israel Law Review* 47(3), 361–78.
Public Order Act 1986. HMSO.
R (Hodkin) v Registrar General of Marriages [2013] UKSC 77, [2014] 2 WLR 23 at [57] by Lord Toulson.
Racial and Religious Hatred Act 2006. HMSO.
Rehman, J. (2010). Freedom of Expression, Apostasy, and Blasphemy within Islam: Sharia, Criminal Justice Systems, and Modern Islamic State Practices: Javaid Rehman Investigates the Uses and Abuses of Certain Interpretations of Sharia Law and the Quran, *Criminal Justice Matters* 79(1), 4–5.
Rushdie, S. (2012). *Joseph Anton*. Literatura Random House.
Salter, M. (2017). Genocide Denial in Relation to the Nuremberg Trials'. In Brehens, P., Nicholas, T. and Jensen, O. *Holocaust and Genocide Denial: A Contextual Perspective*. Routledge, pp. 33–50.
Salter, M., & McGuire, K. (2015). Issues and Challenges in the Application of Husserlian Phenomenology to the Lived Experience of Hate Crime and Its Legal Aftermath: An Enlightenment Prejudice against Prejudice? *Journal of Interpersonal Violence* 30(10), 1782–802.
Sandberg, R. (2011). *Law and Religion*. Cambridge University Press.

Sandberg, S., & Colvin, S. (2020). 'ISIS Is Not Islam': Epistemic Injustice, Everyday Religion, and Young Muslims' Narrative Resistance. *The British Journal of Criminology* 60(6), 1585–605.

Sandberg, R., & Doe, N. (2008). The Strange Death of Blasphemy, *The Modern Law Review* 71(6), 971–986.

Sayyid, S., & Vakil, A. (2010). *Thinking through Islamophobia: Global Perspectives*. Hurst.

Sealy, T. (2021). Islamophobia: With or without Islam? *Religions* 12, 369–383.

The Telegraph (2017, 9 May). Stephen Fry Blasphemy Prosecution in Ireland Reportedly Dropped. Retrieved from: www.telegraph.co.uk/news/2017/05/09/stephen-fry-blasphemy-prosecution-ireland-reportedly-dropped/

Temperman, J. (2016). *Religious hatred and international law: the prohibition of incitement to violence or discrimination* (No. 118). Cambridge University Press.

Temperman, J. et al. (Eds.) (2017). *Blasphemy and Freedom of Expression: Comparative, Theoretical and Historical Reflections after the Charlie Hebdo Massacre*. Cambridge University Press.

Villa, V. (2022). Four-in-Ten Countries and Territories Worldwide Had Blasphemy Laws in 2019. Pew Research Center. Retrieved from: www.pewresearch.org/fact-tank/2022/01/25/four-in-ten-countries-and-territories-worldwide-had-blasphemy-laws-in-2019-2/.

White [2001] *EWCA Crim 216,* [2001] 1 WLR 1352.

Wingrove v. UK, (Application no. 17419/90) Judgment of 25.11.96, RJD 1996-V; 24 EHRR.

WION web team, (2020, 19 November). Swedish Prosecution Says Quran Burning Not 'Illegal', Decides Not to Press Charges. *WION*. Retrieved from: www.wionews.com/world/swedish-prosecution-says-quran-burning-not-illegal-decides-not-to-press-charges-344065.

Wood, G. (2015, March). What ISIS Really Wants, *The Atlantic*. Retrieved from: www.theatlantic.com/magazine/archive/2015/03/what-isis-really-wants/384980/

United Nations. (2013). *Report of the United Nations High Commission for Human Rights on the Expert Workshops on the Prohibition of Incitement to National, Racial or Religious Hatred A/HRC/22/17/Add. 4 (January 11, 2013)*. Retrieved from: www.ohchr.org/Documents/Issues/Opinion/SeminarRabat/Rabat_draft_outcome.pdf.

United Nations Human Rights Committee (UNHRC). (2011). General Comment No. 34, Freedom of Opinion and Expression, CCPR C/GC/34, 48 (September 12). Retrieved from: www2.ohchr.org/english/bodies/hrc/docs/gc34.pdf.

Acknowledgements: The authors would like to thank research assistant Luyao Xu for editorial support.

15

RELIGION AND TERRORISM

Is Far-Right Terrorism Another Form of Religious Terrorism?

Shamila Ahmed and Garth den Heyer

Introduction

This chapter explores how the constructions of far-right extremism and extreme nationalism[1] have contributed to non-religious inspired terrorism and extreme nationalism. The chapter explores how within the Covid-19 pandemic, far-right extremists, Islamists and populists have exploited the impact of national policies and geopolitical transnational policies on structural inequality, resources and services to promote anti-state, anti-immigrant and anti-European Union (EU) sentiments. It demonstrates the equally pervasive ability of religious and non-religious terrorism to gain support for ideologies premised on replacing existing social and political structures.

Global crises such as Covid-19 demonstrate the problematic nature of such constructions through revealing how such crises can be used to gain support and promote far-right ideologies. As the chapter demonstrates, the failures of national and transnational institutions within the Covid-19 pandemic have led to the production of extremist narratives through which to view, interpret and understand Covid-19 and question the legitimacy and effectiveness of existing social and political structures. . In exploring the Covid-19 pandemic in relation to different forms of terrorism, the chapter further validates how the construction of 'religious' terrorism and 'secular' terrorism as distinct entities obscures the threat of secular terrorism.

The Intersectionality of Ideology

Although global crises, including the financial crisis of 2007–2008 and the refugee crisis of 2015–2016, have been used by extremists and populists to further their own aims and ideology, Covid-19 is barely comparable to any of the world's previous

DOI: 10.4324/9781003276593-18

major crises (Mallin & Margolin, 2020). The Covid-19 pandemic emerged after a decade marked by an increase in populist and nationalist parties, and targeted political violence. Islamist radicalisation, far-right extremism and the growth of extreme nationalism, most notably in Hungary (Viktor Orbán), Switzerland (the Swiss People's Party), Denmark (the Danish People's Party), Finland (the Finns Party), Sweden (the Sweden Democrats), Holland (Geert Wilders et al.), Germany (the AfD), Greece (the Golden Dawn neo-Nazis and the New Democracy Party), Italy (Lega Nord), and the UK (British National Party, Britain First), demonstrate the increasing existence of various polarising groups and ideologies across Europe (Stavrakakis, 2017). Through advocating hostility to European integration and existing national political structures (Mallin & Margolin, 2020), these groups threaten the existence of the EU and social cohesion across and within EU nation states. Similarly, the US has also seen an increase in nationalism and far-right extremism, culminating in the 'storming' of the Capitol building in Washington, DC. In this Covid-19 environment, national policies and geopolitical transnational policies have become increasingly important. According to the United Nations (2020), it is these political responses to the pandemic which risk further exacerbating conditions conducive to extremism and violence.

Gunning and Jackson (2011) argue that the construction of religious terrorism and secular terrorism as distinct entities dismisses the similarities between these forms of terrorism. This distinction also serves to create religious terrorism as ideologically unique and more powerful, thus serving to legitimise more draconian and contentious counterterrorist policies and actions. Extremist narratives incorporate distinctive ideologies which advocate changing existing political and social structures and removing the state and or ruling structure (Hall, 2016; Neumann, 2011). During the Covid-19, pandemic real or perceived failures in states have been exploited to promote anti-state sentiments and accelerationist narratives (UN, 2020). Therefore, extremist groups have appealed to the fears, expectations and aspirations of vulnerable groups (Malik, 2020) to validate and legitimise their central ideology of replacing existing social and political structures. Within far-right extremism, accelerationists have also used Covid-19 to advocate racial genocidal wars that will lead to the establishment of ethno-states (Bloom, 2020; Kiesel, 2020). Through this process of self-legitimisation, where global disasters such as Covid-19, the financial crisis and the refugee crisis are exploited and manipulated, is seems worthy and important to ask, will extremist groups continue to exploit global disasters to delegitimise and facilitate distrust against national and global political structures? And if global disasters continue to be exploited to exacerbate distrust against national and global political structures, then what are the implications for the growth, existence and threat of extremism and populism?

The capacity to arouse anti-state sentiments is of vital importance in Islamic radicalisation, which has been defined as people embracing opinions, views and ideas which could lead to acts of terrorism and seeking to make changes to the existing political and social structure (Neumann, 2011). Similarly, far-right extremism and extreme nationalism have been defined as seeking to replace the existing social order, with far-right extremism advocating the use of violence to remove the state or ruling structure, and thus being the more 'ultra-right' version of extreme nationalism (Eatwell, 2000). Therefore, one can note how the rejection of existing social and political structures is a core component of both radicalisation and extremism, leading to radicalisation becoming synonymous with the adopting of extremist beliefs (Allen, 2007). In relation to the far-right, frustration with existing governments often facilitates support and acceptance of an extremist group offering an alternative and possible change in government (Mercy Corps, 2016).

Walker (2005) distinguishes between what he calls the 'thin' global-level obligations and the 'thicker' local obligations. It could be argued that far-right extremism and nationalism are a reaction to the thin-level obligations of so-called elites in national capitals and/or Brussels (EU) who are regarded as pursuing policies for their own self-interest (Eatwell and Goodwin, 2018; Shipman, 2017). These grievances lead to the rejection of existing political structures, with far-right groups and nationalist groups advocating their groups as truly representing nationalist interests via thicker local obligations which incorporate resources and services (Bötticher & Mares, 2012; USAID, 2011). Perceptions, evaluations and judgements of injustice do not simply come to exist but are informed through various factors such as opportunities, resources and equality. 'Doing justice' therefore 'means giving what is due' (Hudson, 2009: 703). The importance of perceived equality is that equal treatment by the state translates into 'equal moral worth' which informs citizens of their value (Brock & Brighouse, 2005). Within this conceptualisation it is possible to understand how extremists exploit state deviations from their ethical duties, and perceptions of injustice to legitimise the need for alternative political structures that are able to meet their ethical duties, because after all, if existing structures were able to provide justice and ethics via resources and services, then this would significantly decrease the need for alternative structures. As is discussed later, Covid-19 has significantly impacted government policies, and through exacerbating anti-state sentiments it has increased the power, legitimacy and pull of extremist groups.

Expectations, Trust and Covid-19

Unmet economic needs can lead marginalised groups to feel that the state has abandoned them (USAID, 2011), with evidence demonstrating that violent extremists have exploited economic marginalisation, high levels of poverty and a lack of access to basic services to attract followers (Avis, 2020). Thus, dissatisfaction via perceptions of state failures is crucial in informing beliefs that a change in governance is required and in communities turning to extremist groups for services (Allan et al., 2015).

Covid-19 has had a profound effect on governance, social polarisation and unrest, the economy, the information landscape and political discourse (Comerford & Davey, 2020). Most of the world's governments, European leaders and EU institutions have been widely criticised for acting slowly, selfishly and without sufficient planning (Mallin & Margolin, 2020), through governments whose legitimacy is already weak, facing a crisis of trust and aggravation of domestic struggles in the Covid-19 pandemic (Clarke, 2020). Such a view has been heightened since the pandemic with allegations of the West controlling the patents and distribution of the Covid-19 vaccines. The pandemic has therefore been pivotal in stimulating and increasing anti-establishment sentiments, thus providing the perfect sociopolitical and economic opportunities for the far-right, Islamists and populists to further their own ideological aims (CCE, 2020; Clarke, 2020). Low levels of employment have been noted as a contributory factor to radicalisation, with extremist groups radicalising individuals through narratives of restored agency and purpose, which are of vital importance for individuals who are experiencing the loss of dignity that usually accompanies losing employment (Avis, 2020). However, as Ackerman (2020) identifies, unemployment can also lead to a new demographic to recruit.

Coupled with increases in unemployment has been the impact of Covid-19 on resources and services. Empirical research has demonstrated that extremist groups have been able to gain support in local communities via providing a service delivery role and filling the vacuum created by poor public services and weak state capacity (ICG, 2013). Existing research has also highlighted the importance of community approaches, relationships and belonging to divert individuals away from extremism (Borum, 2004; Ranstorp, 2016; Sageman, 2004). This local 'community' space is vital in facilitating extremism, with the Radicalisation Awareness Network (RAN, 2017) defining radicalisation as a local issue that requires local solutions and active communities. During the Covid-19 pandemic, extremists have employed 'community politics' via the provision of essential services, including those relating to health, social care and the providing of scarce everyday items such as flour, toilet paper and groceries to portray themselves as guarantors of order and stability (UN, 2020: Zeller, 2020). Thus, the extremist exploitation of local space has not only capitalised upon state failures to meet citizens' expectations (Clarke, 2020), but through doing so it has responded to citizens' needs and anxieties which have been exacerbated within the pandemic.

According to the Centre for Mental Health, understanding inequalities in mental health during Covid-19 has intensified pre-existing structural inequalities in society (Allwood and Bell, 2020). It has also exacerbated structural inequalities within Black, Asian and Minority Ethnic (BAME) communities with the Public Health England Covid-19 disparity report concluding that BAME communities are more likely to catch and die from the disease because of racism, discrimination and social inequalities (Tapper, 2020). The failure to deliver services – coupled with lack of trust in government – leads communities to feel neglected by their governments and support extremists, believing that such support will lead to the stability that has not been provided by government (Allan et al., 2015; Botha & Abdile, 2014). Research also indicates that a lack of trust in the system is generally higher amongst those who are most prone to believing conspiracy theories (Hermansson. 2020). Where distrust is prevalent, extremists are able to reach out to 'sentiment pools' who share a set of common grievances and then 'reframe' these issues as grievous injustices which give sanction and moral legitimacy to violence against the perceived wrongdoer (Wiktorowicz, 2005). Where extreme nationalism is concerned, it was the ability of Brexit strategists in 2016 to link immigration to loss of jobs and benefit cuts that swung so many Labour voters to Brexit (Shipman, 2017). State failures that lead to unemployment, reductions in resources and services and exacerbate structural inequality directly impact belonging via disrupting and reducing individuals' trust in states and their political and social institutions. Covid-19 thrust forward issues of resources, services, expectations and duty.

A set of nation polls conducted in June 2020 revealed that the British government had the lowest domestic approval rating in the world (alongside Mexico) for its handling of the pandemic (Woodcock, 2020). Just 41 percent of Britons questioned by YouGov said that Boris Johnson's administration was dealing with the outbreak well, against 56 per cent who said it was not – giving an overall rating of −15 (YouGov, 2020). The decline in trust in the UK government has occurred across the political spectrum, including among those on the right (down 10 percentage points), as well as among people in the centre (down 19 percentage points) and on the left (down 24 percentage points) (Fletcher et al., 2020). However, not only was trust down, but there was also a substantial increase in the percentage of people who said they are concerned about false or misleading information about the coronavirus from the UK government (up 11 percentage points since April) and from politicians (up 9 percentage points) (Fletcher et al., 2020). In the US, President Donald Trump's ratings plummeted following his response to the pandemic (Walker, 2020).

Extremist groups have also highlighted transnational political failures within the Covid-19 pandemic. Covid-19 represented the biggest crisis since the Great Depression and needed a coherent response from the 19 member states of the EU (Boffey, 2020). However, EU failures led to those within political structures and those outside political structures questioning the need for and purpose of transnational political structures. Rather worryingly, in a survey conducted in nine countries by the European Council on Foreign Relations think tank, 63 percent of Italians said the EU failed its citizens, with only 4 percent citing the EU as a useful ally, and large majorities in all the nations surveyed felt that either their country was left to cope alone or they simply did not know who their most helpful ally was and the majority cited the EU bloc as being 'irrelevant' (Butler, 2020a).

Although as previously stated, extremist ideologies incorporate the rejection of universal human rights and transnational institutions that exist beyond the national level (Bötticher & Mares, 2012), Covid-19 led to some national leaders also questioning the necessity and viability of such systems and institutions. Criticism of the anti-cosmopolitan individualism displayed by EU member states was also highlighted by European Commission President Ursula von der Leyen, when she stated, 'when Europe really needed to be there for each other, too many initially looked out for themselves […] when Europe really needed an "all for one" spirit, too many initially gave an "only for me" response' (cited Chadwick, 2020). The necessity for and viability of the World Health Organisation (WHO) has also been questioned, with US president Trump withdrawing American funding to the WHO, contending that the WHO was 'very China-centric' in its approach (Al-jazeera, 2020). This withdrawal has had major consequences due to the US contributing $400 million in the past, almost double the second-largest member-state contribution (Al-jazeera, 2020). During the Covid-19 pandemic, the anti-cosmopolitan individualism that Trump espoused in his 'America First' agenda has been echoed by many politicians, and not just those who could be conceptualised as constituting extreme nationalists and/or the far-right.

It could therefore be argued that, in the absence of citizens having their immediate local and daily concerns, anxieties and hardships addressed via transnational policies, global crises – as demonstrated by the Covid-19 pandemic – will continue to erode the foundations of transnational political and social structures. In such a climate, where organisations that exist to serve humanity and transcend differences are reduced, difference will become the primary definer of social and political relationships. Therefore, whereas Covid-19 could promote commonality via a shared humanity through transnational policies, the lack of a unified and coordinated response has been capitalised upon to exacerbate national interests via advocacy of anti-cosmopolitan individualism.

Covid-19 represents the interconnectedness between the global and the local and how this can be exploited by extremists to advocate anti-cosmopolitan individualism. The extremist exploitation of Covid-19, as Ahmed (2020) suggests in relation to Islamic radicalisation whereby Islamists highlight state practices, state failures and state crimes to achieve legitimacy, follows the same utilisation of state practices, state failures and state crimes to maintain validity. Within this selective use of reality, extremists have been able to highlight national and geopolitical transnational policies to create new and to exacerbate existing anti-state and anti-EU sentiments. As the next section details, such sentiments when combined with anti-cosmopolitan individualism and the rejection of cosmopolitan humanity, lead to anti-immigration sentiments, thus fracturing the very notion of humanitarian responsibility and civilisation.

Covid-19: Anti-immigration, Anti-state and Anti-EU Sentiments

As this chapter has demonstrated, Covid-19 has facilitated extremism through exacerbating unemployment, structural inequality, lack of resources and services, distrust of states, and anti-immigration, anti-state and anti-EU sentiments. Extremists across the ideological spectrum have integrated Covid-19 into their narratives (Aymenn, 2020), with Covid-19 being used to feed into xenophobia and anti-immigration, anti-state and anti-EU feelings.

Far-right extremism and Islamic radicalisation are both transnational movements. The far-right movement includes Americans and white supremacist training camps in Poland, Bulgaria and even the UK (Weiner, 2020). Similarly, Islamic radicalisation is a global phenomenon. As transnational movements, both forms of extremism are well placed to use the Covid-19 pandemic to mobilise transnational support. According to leading ISIS propaganda analyst Laith al-Khouri, jihadists' main objective is to sow the seeds of mistrust of government, while simultaneously using unfolding events to substantiate their view of the world and validate their predictions (cited Bloom, 2020). Laith al-Khouri also highlights how jihadists are undermining the credibility of governments which are knowingly suppressing information about the virus and lying about the virus (such as Iran, Egypt, and Turkey) to recruit new followers who perceive the terrorist groups as more capable or more honest than their own governments (cited Bloom, 2020). Therefore, aspects of Covid-19 directly feed into extremist narratives and provide aspects of these narratives with grains of legitimacy and truth. Jihadist groups, including the Islamic State (ISIS) and al-Qaeda (AQ), have released several official statements expressing that the pandemic is 'the wrath of Allah' and the damage it afflicts on governments and economies should be celebrated (Clarke, 2020). In highlighting religion as the cause of the pandemic, the pandemic becomes another evident example of 'God's will' and how governments that do not follow Islam are deserving and legitimate enemies (International Crisis Group, 2020). ISIS has also encouraged its followers to launch attacks on vulnerable populations in Europe and the United States (Kiesel, 2020). Moreover, the spread of the pandemic has not only fed into ISIS' apocalyptic and end-of-time narratives, but it has further weakened the anti-ISIS coalition as Canada, the UK, France and Spain have withdrawn their troops from Iraq (Nicholls, 2020).

Far-right groups on social media have encouraged anyone who becomes infected with Covid-19 to spread the virus at synagogues, law enforcement offices and other government buildings and neighbourhoods with high minority populations (Weimann & Masri, 2020). For far-right extremists, the pandemic has presented an opportunity to promote their narratives and conspiracy theories online – for example, a post on a Telegram channel called Eco-Fascist Central circulated in March 2020 advocating for members to target Jewish communities by simply coughing on the door handles of local synagogues (*The Jerusalem Post*, 2020). The call to spread Covid-19 is of great concern given the ease with which individuals can 'weaponise the COVID-19 virus' (Ong & Azman, 2020: 20).

The linking of anti-immigrant sentiments with Covid-19 has further fuelled extremist narratives of such groups posing threats and being problematic. In Germany, far-right extremists including Weg oder Die Rechts, AfD and Young Nationalists, have advertised themselves as 'Germany's largest patriotic citizen network' (TAZ, 2020). These groups, as demonstrated by the Nationaldemokratische Partei Deutschlands (NPD), patrol cities, claiming that the state is unable to protect its citizens and they are able to provide protection (TAZ, 2020). Members of the NPD have offered to go shopping for the elderly and vulnerable and help homeless individuals, with members of the neo-Nazi party The Third Way (Der Dritte Weg) providing neighbourhood aid and dispersing conspiracies regarding the 'true' cause of Covid-19 (Zeller, 2020). These groups are also divisive in practice through only providing assistance to 'Germans', and thus demonstrating the importance they place on nationalist anti-immigrant xenophobic ideologies (TAZ, 2020). Anti-state and anti-EU sentiments have also been prevalent in Germany.

When expressing Germany's role within a unified EU response to Covid-19, German chancellor Angela Merkel said a recovery fund was in Germany's interest, and that her country would have to make greater contributions to the EU budget (Rankin, 2020). However, this spirit of solidarity has been exploited by extremist groups, which claim that elites are diverting essential resources and services to other countries, thereby serving to facilitate the ideology that national interests will be better supported by far-right and nationalist groups (TAZ, 2020).

Covid-19 has also had an enormous impact on extremism in America. Over recent years there has been an increase in both international transnational white supremacism and white supremacism within the US (Hewitson, 2020). In February 2020, the FBI and Department of Homeland Security (DHS) warned members of Congress about the increasing international threat of white supremacist terror and how extremist groups such as Atomwaffen, The Base and Sonnenkrieg are becoming sophisticated in their online communications and messaging (Hewitson, 2020). The increase can be noted from the following statistics which demonstrate that in 2016, far-right extremism accounted for only 20 percent of terrorism-related deaths in the US, and by 2018, that figure had increased to 98 percent, with 2019 marking the deadliest year of white supremacist violence since the Oklahoma City bombing in 1995 (Weiner, 2020). According to the US DHS, there have been two attempted attacks by homegrown violent extremists against medical facilities since the Covid-19 outbreak (DHS, 2020). As Hewitson (2020) states, these incidents indicate an elevated security risk from homegrown violent extremists who are exploiting the ongoing pandemic. Since September 2019, 36-year-old Timothy Wilson had been the subject of an FBI domestic terrorism investigation which revealed him to be a homegrown violent extremist motivated by racial and anti-government sentiments associated with white supremacy (Tribune, 2020). Wilson changed his initial target of an Islamic Center or a synagogue or a Walmart headquarters, believing that the coronavirus would increase the impact and attention of his attack on a hospital healthcare facility in Missouri (Counter extremism project, 2020). Wilson was part of the larger accelerationist and neo-Nazi communities, often communicating with members of the neo-Nazi group Atomwaffen Division and expressing sympathy for a similar group, The Base (Kiesel, 2020). According to DHS, white supremacists have advocated violence against critical infrastructure and faith-based and minority communities – including Asian Americans – in response to the Covie-19 outbreak (Mallin and Margolin, 2020). Covid-19 has also been exploited by Islamic radicals with DHS discovering a clipping from an ISIS newsletter urging supporters to conduct attacks against overburdened healthcare systems in various Western countries (Counter extremism project, 2020). The pandemic is therefore being used by extremist groups to further their ideologies via exacerbating anti-state, anti-EU and anti-immigrant sentiments.

Italy was one of the first EU countries to experience a Covid-19 outbreak. Immigration policy is an ongoing debate in Italian politics, especially given the recent ascent of far-right populist parties that employ explicit anti-immigrant rhetoric. Since the start of the pandemic, extremist social media reports have blamed the outbreak on migrants and ethnic minorities (Kiesel, 2020), using the coronavirus pandemic to feed existing anti-immigrant sentiment across the country (DFRLAB, 2020). The DFRLAB conducted a search of recent articles across Italian media and identified the following narratives on the pandemic: the Italian government is encouraging new arrivals of immigrants, despite the fact that Italians are suffering from Covid-19, and recent Italian governments have cut public healthcare funding while increasing financial support to help immigrants, and that if they had done the reverse, the crisis could have been averted (DFRLAB, 2020). These themes clearly demonstrate how the Covid-19 pandemic has been linked to anti-state and anti-immigrant sentiments.

In conjunction with anti-immigration and anti-state feeling, there has also been an increase in anti-EU feeling. As stated previously, Ahmed (2020) argues that some extremist anti-state narratives contain elements of truth. During the Covid-19 pandemic, some Italians would claim that anti-EU sentiments also contain segments of truth based on the EU failing to support and respond to the Italian government's calls for assistance. In late January 2020, the Italian government banned all flights to and from China and sought a meeting of EU health ministers to push for stricter entry screening measures across Europe (Boffey et al., 2020). However, the meeting took three weeks to organise as cases continued to rapidly increase. By late February 2020, the numbers of Italians known to be infected with the coronavirus was tripling every 48 hours, leading the Italian prime minister, Giuseppe Conte, to appeal to fellow EU member states for help (Boffey et al., 2020). The specifications of Italy's needs were uploaded onto the EU's Common Emergency Communication and Information System (CECIS), with no member state responding to Italy's request, according to Janez Lenarčič, the European commissioner responsible for crisis management (Boffey et al., 2020). European countries acted individually to impose restrictions on the export of key medical supplies to neighbours, with a total of 15 member states placing restrictions on the movement of equipment, leading countries to accuse each other of undermining EU solidarity and the single market (Boffey et al., 2020). As Mallin and Margolin (2020) contend, the EU is seen as a last-resort mechanism when national governments are overwhelmed, and the post-1950 strenuous efforts to build peace, security and rule of law through multiple treaties and common policies have raised expectations with regard to a higher level of protection. The tensions between expectations of the EU and the reality of help received, manifested with the populist Matteo Salvini using the Covid-19 pandemic to question Italy's EU membership (Charles Grant cited Butler, 2020b). Covid-19 was used to produce similar anti-immigration and anti-EU sentiment in France. In France, activists called for sending non-white populations back to their 'home' countries (Kiesel, 2020), and the leader of France's far-right, Marine Le Pen, declared the EU as the 'first death' of the pandemic when speaking out about the bloc's 'incapacity' to act (Chadwick, 2020).

There has been an increase in the threat of the far-right in the UK, with official figures released earlier this year revealing that around a quarter of individuals referred to deradicalisation services had ties to right-wing ideology – 10 percent higher than those with Islamist leanings (DW, 2020). Similarly, like other countries, evidence has also demonstrated that far-right politicians and news agencies have capitalised on the virus to push forward their anti-immigrant and populist message. The recent Commission for Countering Extremism report on how Covid-19 has impacted extremism in the UK noted that there will be an increase in anti-government conspiracy theories across the ideological spectrum (CCE, 2020). As with other countries, the national coordinator for Prevent has warned that the impact of Covid-19 and social isolation may exacerbate grievances that make people more vulnerable to radicalisation and extremists (Counter Terrorism Police, 2020).

Extremism in a Post-Covid-19 World

Covid-19 will continue to have a significant impact on geopolitical transnational policies and national policies in the 'post-Covid-19 world' (UN, 2020: 5) and demonstrate the potential and ability of extremist groups to exploit global crises. Global crises can have severe impacts on resources and services, structural inequality and governance via transnational and national policies. During these times, as has been the case with Covid-19, citizens expect governments to act, and where there is a failure, extremist groups are able to appeal to citizens' fears, expectations and aspirations (Malik, 2020) via meeting their needs and employing 'community politics' (Zeller, 2020). Thus, the grave danger is that extremist groups can use such events to reach out to 'sentiment pools' (Wiktorowicz, 2005). As has been the case with Covid-19, through highlighting failures in national and geopolitical transnational responses and policies, this process feeds directly into the legitimacy of extremist narratives, thus serving to validate the anti-state and anti-EU sentiments that exist within extremist narratives.

An analysis of Covid-19 demonstrates the potential and ability for global crises to facilitate extremists and extremist narratives, such as acceleration theory. According to Avis (2020: 14), 'disasters and emergencies play into the central tenant of "acceleration" theory, which posits that the liberal-democratic order is a failure'. Extremist narratives such as acceleration theory highlight how individuals can change the social and political policies which impact their lives. They therefore empower individuals to believe that change is possible. During the Covid-19 pandemic, in countries such as the UK, this empowerment has become a stark contrast to state approaches which have failed to acknowledge the negative impact of policies on individuals. This chapter, via its analysis of Covid-19, therefore demonstrates that as Ahmed (2020) has argued, state practices, including state crimes, facilitate the legitimacy, validity and authenticity of extremist narratives, and therefore state practices should be acknowledged and included as variables that facilitate radicalisation and more generally extremism. As Covid-19 demonstrates, the academic and policy failure to include state practices and state crimes in explanations of radicalisation and extremism has led to the neglect of the anti-state and anti-EU sentiments that are such a pivotal part of extremist narratives and directly legitimise the extremist aim of changing and removing existing political structures.

Conclusion

The extremist aim of changing political structures is inherently based on negative evaluations of existing structures. At times of global crises, as evidenced by the Covid-19 pandemic, expectations become increasingly important, and thus to neglect state practices and responses as facilitators of radicalisation and extremism is to dismiss the vast duty and role they have in meeting citizens' expectations and responding to global crises. Further, it should be noted that during times of global crisis, citizens are often desperate for services, and this vulnerability and desperation, coupled with perceptions of political structural betrayal, provides the perfect socio-political and economic context for national and transnational structures to validate extremist narratives.

Note

1 Elsewhere 'extremist ideologies' and 'extremism' are used to denote these ideologies.

References

Ackerman, S. (2020, 20 March). US military pauses training missions in Iraq for coronavirus. *Daily Beast.*

Ahmed, S. (2020). *The 'war on terror,' state crime & radicalization: A constitutive theory of radicalization.* Palgrave.

Al-jazeera. (2020). *Under fire for COVID-19 response, Trump says 'WHO really blew it'; World Health Organization rejects US president's critique saying 'now not the time to cut back on funding'.* Retrieved from: www.aljazeera.com/news/2020/04/trump-threatens-deny-funding-world-health-organization-200408012719572.html.

Allan, H., Glazzard, A., Jesperson, S., Reddy-Tumu, S. & Winterbotham, E. (2015). *Drivers of violent extremism: hypotheses and literature review.* Royal United Services Institute.

Allen, C. (2007). *Threat of Islamic radicalization to the homeland. Testimony before the U.S. Senate Committee on Homeland Security and Government Affairs.* Retrieved from: www.investigativeproject.org/documents/testimony/270.pdf.

Allwood, L. & Bell, A. (2020). *Covid 19: Understanding inequalities in mental health during the pandemic.* Centre for Mental Health. Retrieved from: www.centreformentalhealth.org.uk/covid-19-inequalities-mental-health.

Aly, A. & Strieghher, J-L. (2012). Examining the role of religion in radicalization to violent Islamist extremism. *Studies in Conflict & Terrorism*, 35(12), 849–862.

Avis, W. (2020). The COVID-19 pandemic and response on violent extremist recruitment and radicalisation. Retrieved from: http://reliefweb.int/sites/reliefweb.int/files/resources/808_COVID19%20_and_Violent_Extremism.pdf.

Aymenn, A-T. (2020). Coronavirus and official Islamic State output: An analysis, global network on extremism & technology. Retrieved from: https://gnet-research.org/2020/04/15/coronavirus-and-official-islamic-state-output-an-analysis/.

Beck, U. (2006). *The cosmopolitan vision*. Polity Press.

Bloom, M. (2020). *How terrorist groups will try to capitalize on the coronavirus crisis*. Just Security. Retrieved from: www.justsecurity.org/69508/how-terroristgroups.

Boffey, D. (2020, 6 May). *Coronavirus threatens future of eurozone, Brussels warns*. *The Guardian*. Retrieved from: www.theguardian.com/business/2020/may/06/coronavirus-threatens-future-eurozone-brussels-economic-social-divisions-pandemic.

Boffey, D., Schoen, C., Stockton, B. & Margottini, L. (2020, 15 July). Revealed: Italy's call for urgent help was ignored as coronavirus swept through Europe. *The Guardian*. Retrieved from: www.theguardian.com/world/2020/jul/15/revealed-the-inside-story-of-europes-divided-coronavirus-response" www.theguardian.com/world/2020/jul/15/revealed-the-inside-story-of-europes-divided-coronavirus-response.

Borum, R. (2004). *Psychology of terrorism*. University of South Florida.

Botha, A. & Abdile, M. (2014). *Radicalisation and al-Shabaab recruitment in Somalia*. Institute for Security Studies.

Bötticher, A. & Mares, M. (2012). *Extremism: Theories, concepts, forms*. Oldenbourg Verlag.

Brock, G. & Brighouse, H. (2005). Introduction. In G. Brock & H. Brighouse (Eds.), *The political philosophy of cosmopolitanism* (pp. 1–9). Cambridge University Press.

Butler, K. (2020a, 23 June). Coronavirus: Europeans say EU was 'irrelevant' during pandemic. *The Guardian*. Retrieved from: www.theguardian.com/world/2020/jun/23/europeans-believe-in-more-cohesion-despite-eus-covid-19-failings.

Butler, K. (2020b, 12 April). After coronavirus: How will Europe rebuild? *The Guardian*. Retrieved from: www.theguardian.com/world/2020/apr/12/after-coronavirus-how-will-europe-rebuild.

Chadwick, L. (2020, 27 March). The future of the European project is at stake': EU in crosshairs of coronavirus pandemic. *Euronews*. Retrieved from: www.euronews.com/2020/03/27/the-future-of-the-european-project-is-at-stake-eu-in-crosshairs-of-coronavirus-pandemic.

Clarke, C. (2020). Yesterday's terrorists are today's public health providers. *Foreign Policy*. Retrieved from: https://foreignpolicy.com/2020/04/08/terrorists-nonstate-ungoverned-health-providers-coronavirus-pandemic/.

Comerford, M. & Davey, J. (2020). Comparing Jihadist and far-right extremist narratives on COVID-19. Global Network on Extremism & Technology. Retrieved from: https://gnet-research.org/2020/04/27/comparing-jihadist-and-far-right-extremist-narratives-on-covid-19/.

Commission for Countering Extremism (CCE). (2020). *COVID-19: How hateful extremists are exploiting the pandemic*. Retrieved from: www.gov.uk/government/publications/covid-19-how-hateful-extremists-are-exploiting-the-pandemic.

Counter Extremism Project. (2020). *COVID-19*. Retrieved from: www.counterextremism.com/news-free-tags/covid-19.

Counter Terrorism Police. (2020). *CTP warn about greater risk of radicalisation during COVID-19 lockdown*. Retrieved from: www.counterterrorism.police.uk/ctp-look-to-bolster-prevent-referrals-during-lockdown.

Couture, J. & Nielsen, K. (2005) Cosmopolitanism and the compatriot priority principle. In G. Brock & H. Brighouse (Eds.), *The political philosophy of cosmopolitanism* (pp. 180–193). Cambridge University Press.

DFRLAB. (2020). Pro-right Italian media target African immigrants over coronavirus. *Medium*. Retrieved from: https://medium.com/dfrlab/pro-right-italian-media-target-african-immigrants-over-coronavirus-5d0e741cdb8c.

Dower, N. (2008). Questioning the questioning of cosmopolitanism. In W. Van de kerckhove & H. Stan Van (Eds.), *Cosmopolitan corporate responsibilities, 3-20*. Springer.

DW. (2020). UK: Fears of resurgent terrorism as COVID-19 lockdown ends. Retrieved from: www.dw.com/en/uk-fears-of-resurgent-terrorism-as-covid-19-lockdown-ends/a-54124486.

Eatwell, R. (2000). The rebirth of the 'extreme right' in Western Europe? *Parliamentary Affairs*, 53(3), 407–425.

Eatwell, R. & Goodwin. M. (2018). *National populism and the revolt against liberal democracy*. Pelican.

EU Expert Group. (2008). *Radicalisation processes leading to acts of terrorism: A concise report prepared by the European Commission's Expert Group on violent radicalisation*. The European Commission.

European Union. (2020). *The common EU response to COVID-19*. Retrieved from: https://europa.eu/european-union/coronavirus-response_en.

Fletcher, R., Kalogeropoulos, A. & Nielsen, R. (2020). Trust in UK government and news media COVID-19 information down, concerns over misinformation from government and politicians up. Reuters Institute. Retrieved from: https://reutersinstitute.politics.ox.ac.uk/trust-uk-government-and-news-media-covid-19-information-down-concerns-over-misinformation.

Hall, M. (2016, 12 July) Radicalisation, extremism and terrorism: Words matter. European Parliamentary Research Service. Retrieved from: https://epthinktank.eu/2016/07/12/radicalisation-extremism-and-terrorism-words-matter/.

Hermansson, P. (2020). Trust no one: Understanding the drivers of conspiracy theory belief. HOPE not hate. Retrieved from: www.hopenothate.org.uk/wp-content/uploads/2020/04/conspiracy-report-2020-04-v1-copy.pdf.

Hewitson, W. (2020). Homegrown violent extremism in the United States: Exploiting COVID-19. Intelligence Fusion. Retrieved from: www.intelligencefusion.co.uk/blog/homegrown-violent-extremism-in-the-united-states-exploiting-covid-19.

Hudson, B. (2009). Justice in a time of terror. *The British Journal of Criminology*, 49(5), 702–717.

International Crisis Group (ICG). (2013). Tunisia: Violence and the Salafi challenge. www.crisisgroup.org/~/media/Files/Middle%20East%20North%20Africa/North%20Africa/Tunisia/137-tunisia-violence-and-the-salafi-challenge.pdf.

International Crisis Group (ICG). (2020). Contending with ISIS in the time of coronavirus. Retrieved from: www.crisisgroup.org/global/contending-isistime-coronavirus" www.crisisgroup.org/global/contending-isistime-coronavirus.

The Jerusalem Post. (2020). Far-right obsession with bioterror could lead to work with al-Qaeda, Iran. Retrieved from: www.jpost.com/international/far-right-obsession-with-bioterror-could-lead-to-work-with-al-qaeda-iran-632662.

Kiesel, S. (2020). The Pandora Report, viruses and violence: How COVID-19 has impacted extremism. Retrieved from: https://pandorareport.org/" https://pandorareport.org/.

Lee's Summit Tribune. (2020, 25 March). FBI statement regarding March 24, 2020 incident in Belton, MO. Retrieved from: https://lstribune.net/index.php/2020/03/25/fbi-statement-regarding-march-24-2020-incident-in-belton-mo/.

Malik, N. (2020, 26 March). Self-isolation might stop coronavirus, but it will speed the spread of extremism. *Foreign Policy*.

Mallin, A. & Margolin, J. (2020). Homeland Security warns terrorists may exploit COVID-19 pandemic: The bulletin notes there is 'no information' yet on specific plots. ABC News. Retrieved from: https://abcnews.go.com/Politics/homeland-security-warns-terrorists-exploit-covid-19-pandemic/story?id=69770582.

Mercy Corps. (2016). *Motivations and empty promises: Voices of former Boko Haram combatants and Nigerian youth*. Mercy Corps. Retrieved from: www.mercycorps.org/sites/default/files/Motivations%20and%20Empty%20Promises_Mercy%20Corps_Full%20Report_0.pdf.

Neumann, P. (2011). *Preventing violent radicalization in America*. Bipartisan Policy Center's National Security Preparedness Group.

Nicholls, D. (2020, 19 March). *Army redeploys troops home from Iraq as coronavirus forces end to training mission. The Telegraph*. Retrieved from: www.telegraph.co.uk/news/2020/03/19/armyredeploys-troops-home-iraq-coronavirus-forces-endtraining/.

Ong, K. & Azman, N. (2020). Distinguishing between the extreme far right and Islamic State's (IS) calls to exploit COVID-19. *Counter Terrorist Trends and Analyses*, 12(3), 18–21.

RAN. (2017). Preventing radicalisation to terrorism and violent extremism: Approaches and practices. Retrieved from: https://home-affairs.ec.europa.eu/system/files/2021-05/ran_collection-approaches_and_practices_en.pdf

Rankin, J. (2020, 23 April). EU leaders clash over trillion-euro Covid-19 aid in online meeting. The Guardian. Retrieved from: www.theguardian.com/world/2020/apr/23/clashes-predicted-over-trillion-euro-covid-19-aid-as-eu-meets-online.

Ruggiero, V. (2007). War, crime, empire and cosmopolitanism. *Critical Criminology: An International Journal*, 15(3), 211–221.

Sageman, M. (2004). *Understanding terror networks*. University of Pennsylvania Press.

Schomerus, M. & El Taraboulsi-McCarthy, S. (2017). *Countering violent extremism*. University of Birmingham Press.

Shipman, T. (2017). *All-out war*. Collins.

State of New Jersey. Office of Homeland Security and Preparedness. (2020). Online extremists exploit COVID 19 to inspire supporters. Retrieved from: www.njhomelandsecurity.gov/analysis/online-extremists-exploit-covid-19-to-inspire-supporters#:~:text=Supporters%20of%20domestic%20and%20international,the%20deaths%20of%20their%20enemies.

Stavrakakis, Y., Katsambekis, G., Nikisianis, N., Kioupkiolis, A. & Siomos, T. (2017). Extreme right-wing populism in Europe: Revisiting a reified association. *Critical Discourse Studies*, 14(4), 420–439.

Tapper, J. (2020, 13 June). Minorities more at risk from Covid-19 because of racism, says report. *The Guardian*. Retrieved from: www.theguardian.com/inequality/2020/jun/13/leaked-report-says-racism-and-inequality-increase-covid-19-risk-for-minorities.

Taylor, M. & Horgan, J. (2006). A conceptual framework for addressing psychological process in the development of the terrorist. *Terrorism & Political Violence*, 18(4), 585–601.

TAZ. (2020). Solidarity with borders. Retrieved from: https://taz.de/Nazis-nutzen-Coronakrise/!5678947/.

United Nations. (2020). The impact of the COVID-19 pandemic on terrorism, counter-terrorism and countering violent extremism. Retrieved from: www.un.org/sc/ctc/wp-content/uploads/2020/06/CTED-Paper%E2%80%93-The-impact-of-the-COVID-19-pandemic-on-counter-terrorism-and-countering-violent-extremism.pdf.

USAID. (2011). The development response to violent extremism and insurgency policy. Retrieved from: www.usaid.gov/sites/default/files/documents/1870/VEI_Policy_Final.pdf.

Walker, B. (2020). Polls show the UK has lost faith in the government's ability to handle the Covid-19 crisis. *New Statesman*. Retrieved from: www.newstatesman.com/politics/health/2020/06/uk-government-coronavirus-response-boris-johnson-approval-poll.

Walker, N. (2005). Making a world of difference? Habermas, cosmopolitanism and the constitutionalization of international law. EUI Working Papers Law No. 2005/17. 10 December 2010. Retrieved from: http://papers.ssrn.com/sol3/papers.cfm?abstract_id=891036.

Weimann, G. & Masri, N. (2020). *The virus of hate: Far-right terrorism in cyberspace*. International Centre for Counter-terrorism. Retrieved from: www.ict.org.il/Article/2528/The_Virus_of_Hate#gsc.tab=0.

Weiner, R. (2020, 23 June). The growing white supremacist menace: COVID-19 has been a boon for far-right extremists. *Foreign Affairs*. Retrieved from: www.foreignaffairs.com/articles/united-states/2020-06-23/growing-white-supremacist-menace.

Wiktorowicz, Q. (2005). *Radical Islam rising: Muslim extremists in the West*. Rowman & Littlefield.

Woodcock, A. (2020). Coronavirus: Confidence in UK government's handling of pandemic plummets to lowest in world after Dominic Cummings scandal. *The Independent*. Retrieved from: www.independent.co.uk/news/uk/politics/coronavirus-uk-government-confidence-dominic-cummings-boris-johnson-a9554946.html.

YouGov. (2020, 17 March). YouGov COVID-19 tracker: government handling. Retrieved from: https://yougov.co.uk/topics/international/articles-reports/2020/03/17/perception-government-handling-covid-19.

Zeller, M. (2020). Extremists thrive in times of crisis: The COVID-19 pandemic is no exception. openDemocracy. Retrieved from: www.opendemocracy.net/en/global-extremes/extremists-strive-times-crisis-covid-19-pandemic-no-exception/.

16

RELIGION AND TERRORISM

What Can We Learn from the State Policy Responses to the Christchurch Mosque Shootings?

William Hoverd, Garth den Heyer and Ian de Terte

Introduction

On the 8 December 2020, a Royal Commission of Inquiry (RCOI) report into the terrorist attack on the Christchurch Masjidain was submitted to the New Zealand Parliament (RCOI 2020). The RCOI had investigated how much the New Zealand State had known about the Christchurch Mosque shooter who had, on 15 March 2019, attacked the Al Noor and Linwood Ave Mosques in Christchurch during afternoon prayer. Using first a semi-automatic shotgun and then an AR-15 semi-automatic assault rifle, the attacker killed 51 worshippers and seriously injured another 40. Specifically, the RCOI's mandate was to produce "an independent and authoritative report on these matters to reassure the New Zealand public, including its Muslim communities, that all appropriate measures were being taken by relevant state sector agencies to ensure their safety and protection" (New Zealand Legislation 2019). The RCOI's report critiqued historic state surveillance of the Muslim community. It pointed to the question of how to efficaciously deliver effective domestic counterterrorism and policing efforts to credibly engage with religious communities whilst remaining attentive to the threat of faith-based extremism, a question which this chapter is devoted to exploring.

The state surveillance of Muslim communities throughout the Western world has been subject to sustained academic and public criticism (Blackwood et al., 2016; Qurashi, 2018; Wilson, 2019). While there is little empirical evidence of this occurring in New Zealand, research from Australia has suggested that a "militant democratic approach" to counterterrorism had unintended negative consequences for its Muslim population (Tittensor et al., 2020). Moreover, it was found that surveillance-based approaches had decreased the Muslim community's willingness to engage in counterterrorism initiatives (Murphy et al., 2020) and fuelled a general distrust of police legitimacy (Ali et al., 2021). It is the question of how to enact

DOI: 10.4324/9781003276593-19

counterterrorism policy ethically and unbiasedly after the Christchurch Mosque attack on which this chapter is focused. The discussion is structured over three parts. The first part outlines the historical tensions inherent in New Zealand policy engagements around religious communities and counterterrorism, and how they evolved in response to the recommendations contained within the RCOI; the second explores how in the New Zealand context, government engagement with religious communities might best occur after the Christchurch Mosque shootings, particularly when it comes to concerns around terrorism. The third part theorises what New Zealand's now reconceived relationship between religion and terrorism means in the international context?

Counterterrorism Policy and Religious Communities

In this section, we detail how both the New Zealand Muslim community and the state viewed counterterrorism policy in years leading up to the Christchurch Mosque attack before turning to demonstrate how it was reconceived after the release of the RCOI report. Before Christchurch, it outlines an environment where the Muslim community felt alienated from the state and subject to Islamophobia from the general population. This section details these differences and the problems as they existed before the Christchurch attack. It then briefly reviews the findings of the RCOI report before turning to review the subsequent reconceived state counterterrorism policy that has emerged since the release of the RCOI report.

The RCOI's focus and terms of reference were intended to produce a coordinated response to the New Zealand Muslim community's evidence that their systematic efforts at airing their security concerns in the years before the attack had made little progress with the government (in particular with its counter-terrorism apparatus) and a general population in which an embedded Islamophobia was commonplace (Rahman, 2019). In 2011, a New Zealand academic wrote that Islamophobia was a "projection of the West's darkside" (Buehler, 2011). The extant subsequent academic literature now empirically supports the argument that wide-spread Islamophobia is prevalent across New Zealand whether it be in universities (Boamah & Salashour, 2021), sport (Thorpe et al., 2020), the preferencing of religious communities (Oxholm et al 2021), media (Shaver et al., 2017), discrimination against women (Ash et al., 2019, Ash et al., 2020), and that it is simply embedded in the colonial structure of this Western settler nation (Ali, 2021; Elers & Jayan 2020).

Writing and speaking on Radio New Zealand, in response to the attack on 17 March 2019, Ms Anjum Rahman, spokesperson for the Islamic Women's Council of New Zealand, argued that this widespread Islamophobia had led to "increasing pressure on our communities from rising levels of discrimination in this country, and the social issues that came with that. The issues we were seeing were too much for our community to resolve on a volunteer basis" (Rahman 2019). Rahman noted that the Islamic Women's Council had sought and held meetings with politicians, the Department of Prime Minister and Cabinet (DPMC) (responsible for national security coordination), the New Zealand Security Intelligence Service (NZSIS) (responsible for human intelligence and domestic terrorism threat assessments), the State Services Commission (SSC), the Department of Internal Affairs (DIA), and the Human Rights Commissioner. The implication was that the New Zealand State had ignored the requests for assistance from the community and had been too focused on the jihadi terrorist threats posed by both the Islamic State and Al Qaeda to consider the ramifications of Islamophobia when it came to fuelling the general discrimination (and subsequent terrorist massacre) faced by the domestic New Zealand Muslim population. In 2019, Rahman ended her speech with a broad call for government accountability in response to the Christchurch Mosque attack:

> I want, I need accountability. My community wants and needs accountability. I need those public servants to sit in front of all of us who presented to them in March 2017 and tell us what they have done since. Tell us what resources and programmes you put in place. I want the politicians from both parties that we personally spoke to, to sit in front of us and tell us what they did as a result of our meetings with them. We need answers.
>
> *Rahman, 2019*

Rahman's words on national radio evidenced a demand for accountability which in concert with the fact that the attacker had been undetected, was a powerful motivator for the RCOI. The question was where exactly had the New Zealand security sector and its counterterrorism focus been prior to the attack? To answer that question, we need to look at how the New Zealand government had responded to the rise of the Islamic State. In 2014, then-Prime Minister John Key in his only national security speech had explicitly signalled that New Zealand was responding for the rise of the Islamic State in Syria and the Levant (ISIL) (Key, 2014). Key argued that "ISIL's ability to motivate Islamist radicals, as well as its growth, ambition, resources and methods, make it a brutal threat, not only to stability in the Middle East, but regionally and locally too" (Key, 2014). Key was clear that ISIL represented an immediate terrorist threat to New Zealand. He went on to detail the New Zealand terrorism threat environment at that time:

> As in other Western countries, ISIL has been successful in recruiting New Zealanders to its cause. Government agencies have a watch list of between 30 and 40 people of concern in the foreign fighter context. These are people in or from New Zealand who are, in various ways, participating in extremist behaviour. Some of those on the watch list have travelled to Syria to engage in fighting and remain there. [...] it is important to note that there are individuals here who are attracted to carrying out domestic attacks of the type we have seen prevented in Australia and recently take place in Canada. Our agencies do everything in their powers to prevent that happening here and to keep New Zealanders safe.
>
> *Key, 2014*

Key (2014) pointed out that the immediate threat was not indicative of the New Zealand Muslim community as a whole rather certain "individuals." But for Key, those individuals and their links to ISIL represented such a threat that they required significant national security agency attention.

> I want to assure New Zealanders that our agencies are doing everything they can to monitor the potential threat posed by radicalised individuals [...] My Government will ensure the agencies have the resources and tools they need to do this work.
>
> *Key, 2014*

He went on to detail what additional funding would be supplied and the additional surveillance that this would provide.

> The New Zealand Security Intelligence Service will be given a funding injection of almost $7 million across the current and next financial year to increase the number of staff it has available to work on monitoring and investigating foreign terrorist fighters. As I noted earlier, while we know of between 30 and 40 individuals who are on the watch list, there is also another group of people who require further investigation. The funding injection for the SIS will allow it to continue to focus on the highest risk individuals but also strengthen its understanding of the potential threat posed by others.
>
> *Key, 2014*

Key's speech represents ISIL both as a domestic and international terrorist threat that transcended global barriers and the only way to mitigate the threat was investment in broadening surveillance of members of the New Zealand Muslim population. A Muslim population that was in 2019 subject to a massacre conducted by a white extremist. A type of extremist who escaped the counterterrorism apparatus of the New Zealand State that had been expanded to combat the Islamic State. Consequently, through the words of both Ms Anjum Rahman and Sir John Key, we see a Gordian knot laid bare in which the New Zealand government conducted surveillance on its Muslim population because of intelligence about the Islamic State inspired jihadi threats whilst simultaneously potentially facilitating an environment which fuelled an Islamophobia alienating that population from civil society. It is also possible that the focus on the ISIL terrorist threat created a form of institutional bias and/or that Islamophobia was present in the priorities of certain national security agencies.

In 2017, New Zealand's current prime minister, Jacinda Ardern, appointed the Honourable Andrew Little as minister for the government communications and signals bureau and the NZSIS. Speaking in 2018, Andrew Little stated that terrorism and cyberthreats were the greatest national security threats to New Zealand (Little, 2018). Similar to John Key, when it came to terrorism, he framed the threat in relation to ISIL and their ability to fuel domestic terrorism.

> The continued instability in Syria and other parts of the Middle East is still a cause of threats worldwide, especially as radical extremist messages are easy to propagate through social media. Those messages now easily reach into otherwise benign communities like New Zealand. We are not immune to the possibility of extremist action here.
>
> *Little, 2018*

Little (2018) also repeated that the New Zealand security agencies were focused on a list of some 30–40 people. Battersby (2018) asked the question why a jihadi attack had not occurred in New Zealand? He noted historical examples of what might now be defined as terrorism (e.g. the 1985 *Rainbow Warrior* bombing). In terms of contemporary threats, Battersby focused on the intelligence community watch list and a number of minor jihadi convictions, but concluded that New Zealand lacked the mass and history of migration and the external drivers for a developed jihadi terrorist threat. After the Christchurch attack, drawing on interviews with security sector staff, Battersby and Ball (2019) argued that:

> While Islamist inspired terrorism has been the predominant identified threat in recent years, the primacy of any particular threat historically did not blind New Zealand's security sector to others, and various Right-Wing extremist (RWE) risks had been identified, investigated and mitigated periodically since at least 1990.
>
> *Battersby & Ball, 2019, 296*

Overall, a brief historical review of the high-level New Zealand policy statements and the few articles on counterterrorism suggested that the primary focus of the national security apparatus had been expanded to focus on jihadi terrorist threats since 2014. Importantly, the argument here is not to discount the potential threat of jihadi violent extremism, but to emphasize that this discourse was dominant and that as a corollary intended to alienate the Muslim population and make them a terrorist target. Consequently, after Christchurch the development of new ways to enact counterterrorism policy ethically, efficaciously and unbiasedly is essential.

Royal Commission of Inquiry Findings

In the immediate aftermath of the attack, Prime Minister Jacinda Ardern put considerable public effort into reframing it as an attack on all New Zealanders and went out of her way to explicitly integrate the Muslim community into the New Zealand community (Besley & Peters, 2020) through strong messages of inclusion (Jalalian & Rahim, 2020) and her wearing of the hijab (Rahman, 2020). In general, these efforts were well received domestically and internationally (Hashemi & Na, 2021). Other measures were introduced such as the ban on semi-automatic firearms (Hoverd, 2019) and the Christchurch Call, which asked social media companies to start banning terrorist and violent extremist content online (Hoverd et al., 2021).

However, deeper structural reconciliation and accountability between the community and government was to be initiated through the RCOI report (RCOI, 2020). The first four sections of the RCOI (2020) report focused on the question of whether government agencies were at fault in respects relevant to the attack. It concluded that:

> there was an inappropriate concentration of counter-terrorism resources on the threat of Islamist extremist terrorism, but the reasons for this require some teasing out. Our concern with the focus of counter-terrorism resources on Islamist extremist terrorism is one of process. There are two aspects to this. First, there had been no substantial assessments of other potential threats of terrorism. So, the concentration of counter-terrorism resources was not based on a comparative risk analysis. Second, there had been no informed system-wide decision to proceed on this basis. By this we mean a decision made by all relevant Public sector agencies with the knowledge that there were other potential threats of terrorism that were not well understood. This also requires brief explanation. The New Zealand Security Intelligence Service had decided to concentrate its scarce counter-terrorism resources on the presenting threat of Islamist extremist terrorism. This was in part because it had a lack of capacity until mid-2018 both to deal with that threat and, at the same time, to baseline other threats. *RCOI, 2020*

The RCOI report found that the state had devoted its scarce security counter-terrorism resources to the threat it perceived to be the greatest, that of Islamic violent extremism. After the attack, other issues around the state's approach to counterterrorism had been noted by various academic commentators, that the state had no consistent language to describe terrorism or to differentiate between extremism and violent extremism (Vanderberg & Hoverd, 2020), and that the counterterrorism strategy promoted by DPMC was problematic (Ball et al., 2020). Both critiques suggested that there was a lack of internal alignment in the national security sector when it came to thinking about terrorism and extremism. The findings of the RCOI in terms of the national security sector's concentration on jihadi terrorism were then considered in terms of the everyday Islamophobia and violence faced by the Muslim population. Section 8 of the executive summary explicitly noted:

> From whānau [family] of the 51 shuhada [martyrs], and the survivors and witnesses of the terrorist attack and their whānau we heard about the ongoing impacts of the terrorist attack, including challenges in obtaining government support. Through broader engagement with Muslim communities we learned about frustrations with the Public sector that go back many years. Muslim communities talked candidly about racism, discrimination and experiences of being suspected of being, or treated as, terrorists as well as their fear of being the targets of hate speech, hate crime and terrorism.
>
> *RCOI, 2020*

The report recommended that both the Muslim community and the Commission itself felt that the adoption of a concerted social cohesion approach to government policy would offer benefits for improving diversity, inclusion and for countering violent extremism (Peace et al., 2005). The RCOI recommended across government that a concerted effort was required to ensure that New Zealand Muslims were treated in an inclusive manner in all policy, which leads to the question of pragmatic implementation. How does the state operationalise an inclusive counterterrorism policy when it has explicitly stated the primary violent extremist threat is jihadi?

The Post-RCOI Counterterrorism Environment

Post-RCOI, evidence is emerging of counterterrorism policy language that is intentionally inclusive or focused on carefully defined threat categories. The government accepted all the recommendations of the RCOI unconditionally. The first implementation step to develop a new cohesive relationship between the Muslim community and the state took place on 15 June 2021 at the He Whenua Taurikura: New Zealand's first Hui (meeting) on Countering Terrorism and Violent Extremism. The conference included Ms Anjum Rahman and the director of the NZSIS, Ms Rebecca Kitteridge, as speakers. Speaking at the conference, the Honourable Andrew Little noted, "This hui builds on the progress we have made since the 15 March attack and will be an important annual event to help counter terrorism and violent extremism" (Little, 2021a). The Honourable Andrew Little, speaking on the need for including social cohesion into national security policy, stated:

> This new focus on social cohesion in our national security is a somewhat novel approach internationally. It is, perhaps, a uniquely New Zealand response to a tragedy on our soil. It recognises that our increasing diversity in recent decades can be a source of strength when our collective goals and aspirations are aligned.
>
> *Little, 2021b*

Post-RCOI, social cohesion and inclusion are being integrated into national security policy. For example, a revised counterterrorism strategy has been released by the DPMC (NZ Government 2021). In the foreword to this strategy, Prime Minister Jacinda Arden stated: "While the aim of terrorism is to shake our beliefs and divide us, New Zealand instead responded with compassion, empathy and solidarity" (Ardern, 2021, 3). Evident is the inclusive approach to reconciling a community after terrorism. Elsewhere, there has been careful standardised language employed to describe the terrorism threat environment. The standardised violent extremist ideological framework has been developed and released by the Combined Threat Assessment Group (New Zealand Security Intelligence Service, 2022). In particular, it now differentiates between "faith motivated violent extremism" (jihadis) and "Identity motivated violent extremism" (Tarrant), with two additional categories "Politically motivated violent extremism" and "Single issue-motivated violent extremism." Importantly, terrorism remains a threat and there is a need for careful policy. In June 2021, New Zealand's Countering Terrorism and Violent Extremism Strategy (2021, 7) noted that "Terrorism continues to threaten the cohesion of communities globally and in New Zealand." The strategy notes that the Christchurch terrorist attack is still impacting a small number of "White Identity Extremists." It also states: "Support for ISIL in New Zealand has very likely declined [...] [however] There are a small number of New Zealand based extremists who continue to support ISIL" (NZ Govt, 2021, 7). The language is careful. The language is balanced. It covers a variety of violent extremist threats. Individuals are the concern rather than communities.

Critically, this new cohesive approach to counterterrorism has already been tested. On 2 September 2021, New Zealand experienced its first Islamic State–inspired violent extremist attack (BBC, 2021). A man known to the state, who had been followed by New Zealand Police, entered an Auckland Countdown supermarket, took a knife from the shelves and stabbed six people. He was shot dead within 60 seconds and no lives were lost. Noting that the attacker had previously been in jail and had been under surveillance since 2016, Prime Minister Ardern stated, "It was hateful, it was wrong. It was carried out by an individual, not a faith [...] He alone carries the responsibility for these acts" (Al Jazeera, 2021). Arden carefully delineated that the attack was an Islamic State–inspired terrorist act, but that it originated from an individual rather than a community.

Under the new parlance, New Zealand has now experienced two terrorist attacks: one white identity violent extremist attack and one faith-motivated violent extremist attack. In November 2021, the Honourable Andrew Little, in a discussion of national security, compared the 3 September attack to the 15 March attack, stating:

> If March 15 didn't make it clear then September 3 should make it undeniable that New Zealand is not immune from the terrorist atrocities that happen in our world. There remains a small number of individuals that the security intelligence agencies know about, and who give cause for concern because of their potential to mobilise to violent extremism. But there are likely other unknown unknowns that the agencies don't yet know about. The international experience shows us terrorist threats will continue to evolve, including online radicalisation and increasingly sophisticated lone actor threats.
>
> *Little 2021b*

Minister Little makes it clear that New Zealand exists in a threat environment where it remains at risk of violent extremist attacks from a variety of motivated actors; consequently, it must sustain a counterterrorism apparatus. However, after Christchurch, that apparatus must be attentive to implications of its surveillance and operations for broader communities. Some violent extremists are lone actors and are clearly quite isolated; others are part of communities the state must be careful about not alienating.

We now turn to consider the operational question how might, in the New Zealand context, government engagement with religious communities best occur after the Christchurch Mosque shootings, particularly when it comes to counter-terrorism concerns?

Engagement with Religious Communities around Concerns of Terrorism

This section is focused on how terrorist attacks can be prevented. This is an extremely difficult question and one that is not answered easily. However, one of the key drivers to preventing any such terrorist attack is information. It should be noted that in most crimes, or in this case terrorism, the event does not "just happen." There is always an escalation by the criminal or extremist to such an event. One of the initial acts will be that the religious community will become aware of the extremist either by a veiled threat or information from a third party. Such information needs to be provided to the appropriate government agency. However, leaders or people in religious communities do not know what is the appropriate avenue that information needs to be given to government agencies. In addition, people in such communities may think that such information may be innocuous. This innocuous information may be a piece in the puzzle that government agencies require to prevent such a terrorist attack. This suggests that the first thing that government agencies can undertake is an engagement with the religious community, in this case the Muslim community.

This engagement is so that trust is developed between the government agency and the Muslim community. The reason that trust needs to be developed between the two parties is so that information can be shared, no matter how innocuous the information may be. Bedrov et al. (2021) argued that trust needs to be established so that any "secret" that a person is maintaining, is shared. Therefore, an ongoing relationship between the government agency and the Muslim community is vital so that any information is shared with the appropriate people in law enforcement agencies.

This engagement needs to develop in an open and transparent way between the government agency and the religious community. The main purpose of this engagement is to develop trust or a bond between the two groups, so information can be shared. We appreciate that there is certain information that the government agency cannot share with the religious community, so it is important to develop "rules" about the relationship at the very beginning of this engagement. The government agency that would be involved in such a relationship would be police personnel. Due to the transient nature of particular police roles, it would be important that at least two members of the police engage in this role. This is to ensure some continuity in the personnel who maintain this relationship with the religious community. The people from the government agencies that engage with these community groups need to be from the appropriate sections within the government agencies. The other important aspect to this relationship is the regular occurrence of these meetings. These engagement meetings must proceed whether or not the parties believe there is anything to discuss. The regular occurrence of these meetings will increase the trust between the parties. The final element of these engagement meetings that needs to be addressed is the location of such meetings. These meetings should occur at the premises of the religious community. The reasons for the location of the engagement meetings mean the police are aware of potential security issues at the premises and any terrorist may see that the police regularly go to the premises of any such communities. It should be noted that the timings of these meetings would be irregular, so any such terrorist cannot identify a pattern for when the police personnel visit the premises.

Once trust between the two parties has been developed and information starts to be shared, it is envisaged that some of this information would be about potential groups of people or individuals who are potential extremists. It is extremely important for any information regarding extremists to be thoroughly investigated by the government agencies involved. This investigation would be completed via usual investigative techniques that are open to the government agencies involved. The difficult part is the feedback to the religious community regarding the information that has been supplied and what the government agency has done about that information. We appreciate the need for secrecy, but it is vitally important that there is a feedback loop about the information that has been given to the government agencies for two reasons. First, if there is not any feedback to the religious community, then there may be a reluctance to give further information in the future and this information may be critical. Second, there may be further information that the religious community is cognisant of that needs to be supplied to the government agency.

Overall, it is imperative that the government agency engages with the religious community to develop trust between the two parties. There are several ways to develop trust, which are beyond the scope of this chapter, but it is imperative that there is some continuity of the people involved in such relationships; that the meetings regularly occur but are random; that the location of such meetings needs to be at the religious community's premises; that any information supplied to government agencies needs to be thoroughly investigated; and that the outcome of the information supplied needs to be reported back to the religious community.

Conclusion

Prior to the attack by the Norwegian right-wing extremist Anders Behring Breivik, other than in the United States of the America, the world had only experienced a few isolated incidents of right-wing extreme violence or attacks. Since the Breivik attacks, however, the world has experienced an increase in the occurrence of right-wing extremist violence.

The incidences of religion-based, and white extremist/supremacy terrorism have been on the rise around the world since the 1970s. The Global Terrorism Index reveals the proportion of unaffiliated attacks, or attacks committed by individuals with no link to a terrorist group, has risen from under 5% in the mid-1970s to above 70% for the period between 2014 and 2018 (Institute for Economics & Peace, 2020).

New Zealand has a unique, social and tolerant demographic make-up and a liberal and progressive acceptance of other faiths and ethnicities (Lipson, 2011). It also has different organisational structures of law enforcement and intelligence agencies than other Western democracies. However, the Christchurch Mosque shootings are no different to the international trends, as is the incidence of terrorism within New Zealand. This is in contrast to some commentators (e.g., Hunt, 2019) who have claimed that there is no terrorism in New Zealand. The country has a chequered terrorism history that has included both domestic and international (even state-sponsored) terrorists. The domestic terrorists were primarily attackers motivated by political or religious causes, involving lone actors or small groups (Battersby & Ball, 2019). Possibly the most infamous terrorist act was the bombing and sinking of the Greenpeace ship the *Rainbow Warrior*, in Auckland Harbour on 10 July 1985, which was undertaken by the French foreign intelligence services.

Similarly, the perpetrator of the Christchurch Mosque attacks was typical of a lone wolf terrorist, as has been experienced elsewhere. The perpetrator acted alone, was radicalized by the internet, was difficult to detect and was able to undertake the attack without warning or coming to the notice of the police or intelligence services (Battersby & Ball, 2019). He was also in contact with the approximately 60 right-wing groups within the country (Spoonley, 2020).

What is different in the New Zealand context in comparison to what has been experienced in other countries is that, although there were claims that the government had been focusing too much on Islamic extremism and ignoring the rise of the far right, the security sector was not blind to the threat and that a number of right-wing risks had been identified and investigated since the 1990s (Battersby & Ball, 2019). The problem, however, was that at the political level, there was little concern and as a result, resources were not allocated to manage the risk.

The threat from lone wolf racial or religion-based terrorism is nothing new. Such terror attacks are most likely be low capability and conducted by a lone actor or a small group using a firearm. The problem is that such terrorists are now well supported through networks and social media platforms. They are also more sophisticated than those of the past, which means that police and intelligence agencies need to be provided with the appropriate government support and legal frameworks to be able to identify, investigate and apprehend such actors.

References

Al Jazeera. (3 Sept 2021) 'It was hateful, it was wrong': Six injured in NZ stabbing attack. Retrieved from: www.aljazeera.com/news/2021/9/3/new-zealand-pm-says-mall-stabbing-a-terrorist-attack 3rd September 2021.

Ali, K. (2021) "Unsettling" the Christchurch Massacre foregrounding settler colonialism in studies of Islamophobia. *Journal of the Contemporary Study of Islam, 2*(2), 87–111. Retrieved from: http://contemporarystudyofislam.org/index.php/jcsi/article/view/74

Ali, M. M., Murphy, K., & Cherney, A. (2021) Counter-terrorism measures and perceptions of police legitimacy: The importance Muslims place on procedural justice, representative bureaucracy, and bounded-authority concerns. *Journal of Criminology, 55*(1), 3–22. July 2021. http://doi.org/10.1177/26338076211030955

Ardern, J. (2021) Foreword. *New Zealand's Countering Terrorism and Violent Extremism Strategy*. New Zealand Government, July 2021.

Ash, E., Kahu, E., & Tuffin, K., (2020) Interrogating antipodean angst: New Zealand's non-Muslim majority talk about Muslims. *Journal of Muslim Minority Affairs*, 40(4), 559–575, http://doi.org/10.1080/13602004.2020.1847781

Ash, E., Tuffin, K., & Kahu, E. (2019) Representing Islam: Experiences of women wearing hijab in New Zealand. *New Zealand Journal of Psychology*, 48(1), 114–121.

Ball, R., Battersby, J., & Nelson, N. (2020). New Zealand's Counter Terrorism Strategy: A Critical Assessment. *National Security Journal*, 2(1), 1–19.

Battersby, J. (2018) Terrorism Where Terror Is Not: Australian and New Zealand Terrorism Compared. *Studies in Conflict & Terrorism*, 41(1), 59 76, http://doi.org/10.1080/1057610X.2017.1287501

Battersby, J., & Ball, R., (2019) Christchurch in the Context of New Zealand Terrorism and Right-Wing Extremism. *Journal of Policing, Intelligence and Counter Terrorism*, 14(3), 191–207, http://doi.org/10.1080/18335330.2019.1662077

BBC (Sept 3rd, 2021) New Zealand PM Ardern says supermarket stabbing was 'terrorist attack'. Retrieved from: https://www.bbc.com/news/world-asia-58405213.

Bedrov, A., Gable, S., & Liberman, Z. (2021) It Takes Two (or More): The Social Nature of Secrets. *Wires Cognitive Science*, 12, e1576, https://doi.org/10.1002/wcs.1576

Besley, T., & Peters, M., (2020) Terrorism, Trauma, Tolerance: Bearing Witness to White Supremacist Attack on Muslims in Christchurch, New Zealand. *Educational Philosophy and Theory*, 52(2), 109–119, http://doi.org/10.1080/00131857.2019.1602891

Boamah, E., & Salahshour, N. (2021) Information Culture: Exploring Muslims' Values and Attitudes to Information When Facing Discrimination at New Zealand Universities. *Kōtuitui: New Zealand Journal of Social Sciences Online*, http://doi.org/10.1080/1177083X.2021.1940218

Buehler, A. (2011). Islamophobia: A Projection of the West's 'Dark Side'. *ICR Journal*, 2(4), 639–653, https://doi.org/10.52282/icr.v2i4.603

Elers, C., & Jayan, P. (2020) 'This is us': Free Speech Embedded in Whiteness, Racism and Coloniality in Aotearoa, New Zealand. *First Amendment Studies*, 54(2), 236–249, http://doi.org/ 10.1080/21689725.2020.1837654

Hashemi, A., & Na, K. S. (2021). A Critical Discourse Analysis of a News Report on Two Mosques Shooting in Christchurch-New Zealand. *International Journal of Social Sciences and Education Research*, 7(1), 24–32, http://doi.org/ 10.24289/ijsser.838397

Hoverd, W. (2019) The Changing New Zealand National Security Environment: New Threats, New Structures, and New Research. *National Security Journal*. Issue 1, 17–34.

Hoverd, W. J., Salter, L., & Veale, K. (2021) The Christchurch Call: Insecurity, Democracy and Digital Media – Can It Really Counter Online Hate and Extremism? *Social Sciences* 1(2), https://doi.org/10.1007/s43545-020-00008-2.

Hunt, E. (2019, 15 March) New Zealand Felt Removed from the Global Voices of Hatred. No Longer. *The Guardian*. Retrieved from: www.theguardian.com/commentisfree/2019/mar/15/newzealand-voices-hatred-christchurch-mosque-attacks" www.theguardian.com/commentisfree/2019/mar/15/newzealand-voices-hatred-christchurch-mosque-attacks.

Institute for Economics & Peace. (2020) *Global Terrorism Index 2020: Measuring the Impact of Terrorism*. National Consortium for the Study of Terrorism and Responses to Terrorism (START), University of Maryland.

Jalalian Daghigh, A., & Abdul Rahim, H. (2020) Representation of Muslim Minorities in Politicians' Discourse: Jacinda Ardern vs. Donald Trump. *Journal of Muslim Minority Affairs*, 40(2), 179–195, http://doi.org/ 10.1080/13602004.2020.1773099

Key, J. (2014) Speech to NZ Institute of International Affairs. 6 November. Retrieved from: www.beehive.govt.nz/speech/speech-nz-institute-international-affairs-0" www.beehive.govt.nz/speech/speech-nz-institute-international-affairs-0.

Lipson, L. (2011) *The Politics of Equality: New Zealand's Adventures in Democracy*. Victoria University Press.

Little, A. (2018) Andrew Little addresses Massey University National Security Conference. Retrieved from: https://defsec.net.nz/2018/07/20/andrew-little-addresses-massey-university-national-security-conference/.

Little, A. (2021a) He Whenua Taurikura: New Zealand's First Hui on Countering Terrorism and Violent Extremism. Retrieved from: www.beehive.govt.nz/release/he-whenua-taurikura-new-zealand%E2%80%99s-first-hui-countering-terrorism-and-violent-extremism"www.beehive.govt.nz/release/he-whenua-taurikura-new-zealand%E2%80%99s-first-hui-countering-terrorism-and-violent-extremism.

Little, A. (2021b) Intelligence and Security in our Changing World – Speech to the Victoria University of Wellington Centre for Strategic Studies. Retrieved from: www.beehive.govt.nz/speech/intelligence-and-security-our-changing-world-speech-victoria-university-wellington-centre.

Murphy, K., Madon, N., & Cherney, A. (2020) Reporting Threats of Terrorism: Stigmatisation, Procedural Justice and Policing Muslims in Australia. *Policing and Society*, 30(4), 361–377, http://doi.org/ 10.1080/10439463.2018.1551393

New Zealand Government. (2021) *New Zealand's Countering Terrorism and Violent Extremism Strategy*.

New Zealand Security Intelligence Service. (2022) Combined Threat Assessment Group (CTAG). Retrieved from: www.nzsis.govt.nz/our-work/counter-terrorism/combined-threat-assessment-group-ctag/. Last retrieved 18 March 2022.

Oxholm, T., Rivera, C., Schirrman, K., & Hoverd, W. (2022) Representing New Zealand Religious Diversity? The Removal of the Words 'True Religion' and 'Jesus Christ' from the Parliamentary Prayer. *Journal of Church and State*, 64(1), (Winter), 87–109, https://doi.org/10.1093/jcs/csab004

Peace, R., Spoonley, P., Butcher, A., & O'Neill, D. (2005) Immigration and Social Cohesion: Developing an Indicator Framework for Measuring the Impact of Settlement Policies in New Zealand. Working Paper 5 (1) Prepared for the Centre for Social Research and Evalation Te Pokapu Rangahau Arotaki Hapori, Wellington.

Qurashi, F. (2018) The Prevent Strategy and the UK 'War on Terror': Embedding Infrastructures of Surveillance in Muslim Communities. *Palgrave Communications*, 4(17), 1–13, https://doi.org/10.1057/s41599-017-0061-9Alimahomed" https://doi.org/10.1057/s41599-017-0061-9Alimahomed

Rahman, A. (2019) Islamic Women's Council Repeatedly Lobbied to Stem Discrimination. RNZ. Retrieved from: www.rnz.co.nz/news/on-the-inside/384911/islamic-women-s-council-repeatedly-lobbied-to-stem-discrimination.

Rahman, K. (2020) News Media and the Muslim Identity after the Christchurch Mosque Massacres. *Kōtuitui: New Zealand Journal of Social Sciences Online*, 15(2), 360–384, http://doi.org/10.1080/1177083X.2020.1747503

Royal Commission of Inquiry into the Terrorist Attack on Christchurch Masjidain on 15 March 2019 (December 2020). Retrieved from: https://christchurchattack.royalcommission.nz/.

Royal Commission of Inquiry into the Terrorist Attack on Christchurch Mosques on 15 March 2019 Order 2019. Retrieved from: www.legislation.govt.nz/regulation/public/2019/0072/latest/LMS183988.html.

Shaver, J., Sibley, C., Osborne, D., & Bulbulia, J. (2017) News Exposure Predicts Anti-Muslim Prejudice. *PLoS ONE*, 12(3), e0174606, https://doi.org/10.1371/journal.pone.0174606

Spoonley, P. (2020) Far-Right Extremists Still Threaten New Zealand, a Year on from the Christchurch Attacks. The Conversation. Retrieved from: https://theconversation.com/far-right-extremists-still-threaten-new-zealand-a-year-on-from-the-christchurch-attacks-133050.

Thorpe, H., Ahmad, N., Marfell, A., & Richards, J. (2020) Muslim Women's Sporting Spatialities: Navigating Culture, Religion and Moving Bodies in Aotearoa New Zealand. *Gender, Place & Culture*, 8(4–5), 668–691, http://doi.org/10.1080/0966369X.2020.1855123

Tittensor, D., Hoffstaedter, G., & Possamai, A. (2020) Hyper-Securitisation and Belonging: Understanding the Plight of Young Muslims in Melbourne, Australia. *Journal of Muslim Minority Affairs*, 40(3), 480–496, http://doi.org/10.1080/13602004.2020.1819127

Vanderberg, H., & Hoverd, W. J. (2020) The Inconsistent Usage of the Terms 'Extremism' and 'Terrorism' around the Christchurch Mosque Attacks. *National Security Journal*, 2(1), 1–13.

Wilson, S. (2019) When the FBI Knocks: Racialized State Surveillance of Muslims. *Critical Sociology*, 45(6), 871–887, http://doi.org/10.1177/0896920517750742

17

THE CHALLENGES BELIEF IN WITCHCRAFT AND SORCERY POSE FOR NATIONAL AND INTERNATIONAL JUSTICE SYSTEMS

Miranda Forsyth

Introduction

This chapter addresses a fundamental question: How do you legislate around belief? In some parts of the world today, legislating in regard to belief in witchcraft and sorcery forces legislators to confront a situation where one part of the population – perhaps the vast majority – has a fundamentally different view of what causes both fortune and misfortune to those responsible for developing the laws. It also gives rise to situations where a crime that the majority considers to be morally abhorrent and terrifying – witchcraft– is officially considered to be an imaginary concern. In working through these issues, it is important to be aware that for people who live in a world where witches exist, fear of them is very real.

Although questions of witchcraft and magic may appear esoteric and of marginal contemporary relevance to national governments and international institutions, this assumption is incorrect on three bases. First, belief in the supernatural is linked to a range of harms perpetuated across the globe today. Research into its scope found over 20,000 victims of harmful practices related to accusations of witchcraft and ritual attacks from media reports across 60 countries during 2019–2020. This includes over 5,250 unlawful or wrongful killings, 60 disappearances in suspicious circumstances, 14,700 attempted killings and physical attacks, 420 trafficking incidents, and 90 grave robberies. A significant number of victims are persons with albinism, older persons, persons with mental illnesses, women, and children (WHRIN, 2020).

Second, there is every reason to believe that harms arising from these beliefs are likely to increase in number, level of severity, and geographic coverage in the short to medium term. Historical and anthropological scholarship show that accusations of witchcraft, scapegoating, and out-casting are correlated with periods

DOI: 10.4324/9781003276593-20

of uncertainty, doubt, anxiety, and fear – all characteristics of our current global trajectory. Factors like unusual weather events, plague, and war, all phenomena currently trending upwards, have historically led to an inward focus, in which old fears and desire to blame others surface more easily. Given climate change, it is salient to remember that the European witch-hunting craze occurred during the Little Ice Age, when reduced growing seasons placed pressures on agricultural production (Behringer, 1999).

Third, core philosophical and juridical questions raised by the criminalisation and condemnation of acts surrounding beliefs in sorcery and witchcraft have broad relevance to a wide range of concerns advanced democracies are facing, such as rising threats posed by extremist vigilante groups and misinformation entrepreneurs. As discussed below, questions about how the state should deal with a Papua New Guinean diviner (known as *glasman*) who uses a bamboo stick to identify a suspected witch, raise surprisingly similar questions to more apparently modern threats. All raise questions such as: Where is the balance between freedom of religion and other rights? How does the law accommodate different understandings of reality amongst citizens?

The relationship between law and magic has a long history. Europe provides the example of jurisdictions where an official belief in witchcraft was transformed into an equally vehement disbelief, and law was central in both reflecting and creating that transformation. As recently as March 2022, Scotland's first minister issued an official apology in Parliament to "all those accused, convicted, vilified or executed under the Witchcraft Act of 1563" (Cramer, 2022). This law made "witchcraft or consulting with witches" a capital offence, enabling the execution of an estimated 2,500 people. In colonialism's later period, colonial governments across the global South were confronted with beliefs they categorised as witchcraft (discussed below) and went to torturous lengths to grapple with the state's positionality. As illustration, the Preamble to Papua New Guinea's Sorcery Act 1971 (passed in the colonial administration's twilight days, repealed in 2013) states:

> There is a widespread belief throughout the country that there is such a thing as sorcery and that sorcerers have extraordinary powers [...] used sometimes for good purposes but more often for bad ones, and because of this belief many evil things can be done and many people are frightened or do things that otherwise they might not do [...]
>
> There is no reason why a person who uses or pretends or tries to use sorcery to do, or to try to do, evil things should not be punished just as if sorcery and the powers of sorcerers were real, since it is just as evil to do or to try to do evil things by sorcery as it would be to do them, or to try to do them [...]
>
> There is a danger that any law that deals fully with sorcery may encourage some evil-intentioned people to make baseless or merely spiteful or malicious accusations that their enemies are sorcerers solely to get them into trouble with other people, and this is a thing that the law should prevent.

Today, many countries have repealed their colonial-era sorcery laws, with many only doing so in the past decade (SMH, 2005). Yet, they are left with the questions of how and whether to use law to address harms perpetrated due to belief systems incorporating magic, sorcery, witchcraft, or other engagements with the supernatural. These harms are many and varied, taking on particular forms in different geographical locations, like public torture of women in Papua New Guinea's (PNG's) highlands, out-casting of child "sorcerers" in Nigeria, ritual killing of people with albinism for their body parts as magical charms in Malawi, and exorcism and killing of children accused of witchcraft in the UK (WHRIN, 2020).

There are many questions about the role of law in responding to these harms. This chapter addresses one of the seemingly most simple, but actually deceptively complex and far-reaching – that of terminology.

This chapter is largely based on my own experiences as a Western academic working on sorcery accusation-related violence (SARV) and law in navigating terminological minefields over the past decade. I have worked at two different scales – a national scale in Papua New Guinea where I have been involved in research and advocacy since 2013, and an international scale, where I was involved in the passage of the historic Human Rights Council resolution on harmful practices related to accusations of witchcraft and ritual attacks (UNGA, 2021), formally adopted in July 2021.

This chapter shares some of the issues that arose and insights into debates that occurred at both scales to inform, and ideally better frame, an approach for those confronting similar challenges, that is, legislating around competing worldviews. Part one introduces the theoretical framework I and colleagues working at several research institutions in PNG have developed. This frame, which we call "worldview pluralism," is helpful in situating questions of terminology and approach. Part two identifies various terminological debates that arose during PNG national policy development, international conferences, and development of the resolution, together with the navigation routes developed in response. Part three discusses the vexed question of culture and its accommodation in legislation, and part four argues that worldview pluralism requires finding ways to address anxieties caused by worldviews that are incommensurate with that privileged through a legal response.

Before proceeding, I acknowledge I have not as yet defined what I mean by witchcraft and sorcery – and that I have juxtaposed and perhaps conflated other terms, such as supernatural, ritual attacks, and magic. Discussion about these choices awaits in part two.

Part 1 – Worldview Pluralism

> Viewed from the outside, from a post-Enlightenment perspective, witchcraft is delusion, even if it has its uses, as anthropologists show it to have. Viewed from the inside, by its believers, witchcraft has a reality whose denial puts them at peril.

The statement above from Seigel (2006, p. 15) highlights vast differences in perspective between a worldview in which magic is real, and one in which magic is superstitious nonsense. Kirsten Renwick Moore (2012, Appendix B) defines a worldview as "the basic cognitive orientation of an individual or society, [...] the framework of ideas and beliefs through which the actor perceives, interprets, and interacts with the world." She perceives worldviews as singular, but here I advocate for the concept of "worldview pluralism."

A landscape characterised by worldview pluralism displays not only multiple worldviews within a given population, but many individuals who contain within themselves multiple worldviews. Our PNG research identified that the vast majority of the population have what we termed a magical worldview – accepting the possibility of direct communication between natural and supernatural dimensions of reality unmediated by God or Satan (Forsyth & Gibbs, 2021). However, many *also* held worldviews partly or entirely cognitively inconsistent with this magical worldview, like a belief in scientific causes of death or a Christian faith commitment. The ability to maintain such cognitive dissonance was high amongst our study cohort. The avalanche of worldwide anecdotal accounts from the past two years about the prevalence of individuals possessing both scientific understandings of the world and non-scientific views about Covid-19 vaccines suggests the PNG population is not atypical in this regard (for example, Rozbroj, 2020).

A pluralistic perspective recognises both that people may possess multiple worldviews and that they may favour one over another in certain circumstances. Adopting a framing of worldview pluralism means that rather than thinking in binary terms about replacing one worldview with another, or deciding that one is right, or one is fixed, it is more helpful to accept there will be fluidity and movement between worldviews within both individuals and populations. Moreover, this movement is likely to be dynamic and responsive to circumstances, such as changing emotional environments (fear, anxiety, doubt) or sets of external pressures (misfortune, peer pressure, uncertainty). Understanding what factors drive people to adopt different worldviews in particular contexts is a critical empirical question.

A framework of worldview pluralism is helpful for contextualising the role of law in responding to beliefs in sorcery and witchcraft. In particular, it suggests three fundamental starting points. First, legal sanctions should focus on harm caused by individuals and groups resulting from ideas about sorcery, witchcraft, or the supernatural, rather than on the beliefs themselves (see part two). Second, beliefs of individuals should not be treated as necessarily fixed or as being singular, but as dependent upon circumstances and hence open to change. This relates to the issue of cultural essentialism or sensitivity (see part three). Third, intervening legislatively will eventually privilege one worldview over others in ways that may leave people feeling vulnerable and possibly distressed. This vulnerability needs addressing through other means, in parallel processes with legal provisions (see part four).

Part 2 – Debating Terminology, Navigating Through

Broad versus Specific Terminology

Terminology rears its head early in any initiative concerning sorcery, witchcraft, the supernatural, magic, occult powers, and so forth – the list of terms is extensive. The belief systems coalescing around these terms and their non-English synonyms vary intensely across time and place. Moreover, these are intimate beliefs, often having particular resonances – and gendered implications – within families, and amongst clans or ethnic communities, or within nation states. In PNG, there are 850 different language groups and many different terms used to relate overlapping ideas (Forsyth & Eves, 2015).

Thinking of these terms as referring to shared family characteristics, rather than as synonymous with each other, can help. Generally, shared characteristics of these belief systems revolve around a set of ideas wherein an individual in the physical world can manipulate the supernatural world to influence the former. This is why sorcery or witchcraft frequently appears in questions of causation, particularly about misfortune: Why did crops fail? Why did Joe have a heart attack? Why did my son fail school and her daughter pass? All these questions are often answered by reference to sorcery or its belief family. In some belief systems, manipulation of the supernatural is intentional, and associated with deliberate actions (like making potions, chanting spells, sacrificing animals, etc.). In others, it is unintentional (like when people are possessed by spirits/demons that cause them to behave in certain ways). Sometimes, the divide between intentional and unconscious manipulation is undefined. Intentional and learned manipulation of the supernatural is often associated with male sorcery and unconscious manipulation with female sorcery, but these are also generalisations (see Hutton, 2017).

Manipulation of the supernatural world can occur with both positive and malevolent intentions. Many societies around the world utilise weather magic, healing magic, and magic over agriculture as part of everyday life. Wiccans and modern pagans are adamant their practice is entirely beneficial and justifiably resent framings implying witchcraft causes harm. Traditional healers in countries such as South Africa have been concerned by legislative interventions that curtail them in practising their craft (Ashforth, 2005).

Use of a singular term, like witchcraft, to cover the entire family of diverse beliefs is clearly problematic. It inappropriately homogenises the immense diversity, including the underpinning systems of logic of these belief systems. It casts the shadow of one particular culturally, geographically, and temporally specific understanding about the phenomenon – the European witch figure – over a broad range of practices in ways likely to be highly misleading. For example, the gendered nature of the term "witchcraft" imported into PNG has meant, in my experience, that it is intensely difficult to move donor and international organisations past assuming that all victims of sorcery are female, although even newspapers report an almost fifty-fifty split of victims (Forsyth et al., 2017).

These issues were extensively debated in all the forums I was involved in at both national and international levels. The concept of "path dependency" points to the significant influence initial decisions about terminology can have, and the difficulty of moving away from them. For example, internationally, the term "witchcraft" had already become known and utilised in existing instruments; therefore, switching terminology was difficult. Generalising broadly, both forums I was involved with reached the conclusion that there are intense problems with all possible terminology, and no good solution. Only a "least worst" solution exists, which appears to be using the generic English words "witchcraft" or "sorcery," or both, alongside definitions making it clear which family characteristics are being referred to.

Targeting Beliefs or Behaviour?

The second major issue confronting the forums was how to protect an individual's right to their beliefs, whilst simultaneously condemning and sanctioning harmful behaviour linked to those beliefs. This presents key issues of framing and terminological concern. The first concerns human rights law and protection of the right to practice a religion or manifest a belief. Individuals who identify witchcraft as a religion, such as Wiccans or modern-day pagans, raise concerns about any legislation potentially threatening that right (Hume, 1995, p. 141). In other contexts, such legislation may be seen as threatening religious practices, even by those not identifying themselves as practising witchcraft but rather a more mainstream religion. For example, in the Indian state of Maharashtra that passed the *Maharashtra Prevention and Eradication of Human Sacrifice and other Inhuman, Evil and Aghori Practices and Black Magic Bill 2013*, campaigns against the legislation ensued, claiming it was anti-religious (BBC News, 2013).

The next concern stems from understanding that, from the perspective of people possessing those worldviews, the practice of witchcraft or sorcery has both beneficial and harmful sides. Sorcery or witchcraft is highly correlated with traditional healers, who perform the role of primary healthcare workers across much of the developing world. For many, it has beneficial uses, often combined with other forms of knowledge, like herbal lore, psychological care, and therapeutic massage.

Concerns about overreach of legislative sanction that impugn an individual's freedom of belief or put at risk valued traditional practices, particularly with healing or cultural value, have been significant sticking points in many of the forums I participated in.

Broadly, the same navigational approach has been developed to respond to both sets of concerns. This involves making a clear distinction in policy and legislation/treaty between belief systems around sorcery and witchcraft – which all are free to participate in – and the harm caused by behaviour associated with these beliefs – which is condemned and sanctioned. In the PNG context, the agreed terminology in policy documents is "Sorcery Accusation Related Violence," which emphasises the fact that the violence targeted comes from the accusation of sorcery, and not from sorcery itself. Legislation is directed against a wide variety of harms, two broad categories of which aim at prohibiting, first, making accusations of witchcraft against an individual (either self-practice or practice leading to harmful acts like murder); or, second, pretending/tricking people into believing a person has supernatural powers and taking advantage of that belief (Forsyth, 2016).

While this approach privileges a worldview in which sorcery or witchcraft is not accepted as a legitimate explanation of causation, it limits privileging that worldview to the boundary of causing harm to a person or property. As one author of the Maharashtra legislation has argued, the legislation does not prohibit a person from performing a miracle; it only prohibits someone cheating another through claiming to perform a miracle (DNA, n.d.).

In international law, grounds for distinguishing between the right to hold a belief and the right to act upon it are expressed as the need to balance competing rights. In other words, where the result of exercising a belief infringes upon enjoyment of other rights, such as the right to be free from torture, then that right to manifest a religion or belief can be limited by law. In the UN resolution, this balance is evidenced by the statement,

> [t]aking note also of general comment No. 22 (1993) of the Human Rights Committee, in which the Committee affirmed the unconditional right to freedom of thought, conscience and religion, including the freedom to hold beliefs, and noted that restrictions on that freedom were permitted only if limitations were prescribed by law and were necessary to protect public safety, order, health or morals, or the fundamental rights and freedoms of others.
>
> *UNGA, 2021, p. 2*

In the UN resolution, the "harmful practices" concept was adopted as part of terminology identifying what the resolution is designed to oppose. The full term is "Elimination of harmful practices related to accusations of witchcraft and ritual attack." The term "harmful practices" had a developed usage in the UN system, for example, in joint general recommendation No. 31 of the Committee on the Elimination of Discrimination against Women and general comment No. 18 of the Committee on the Rights of the Child, which each allowed emphasis on the harm rather than on the beliefs themselves. A specific notation further required that members adopting the resolution recognise "traditional or complementary or integrative medicine, as defined by the World Health Organization, as a field distinct from harmful practices related to witchcraft accusations and others rituals attacks violating or abusing human rights." This ensures that "good" magic connected with healing is not covered by the resolution.

It remains open how easy this distinction is to maintain in practice. One possible area of difficulty, for example, involves what some call "magical vaccines" – praying over people or other non-violent interventions that seek to alleviate anxieties about sorcery within the belief structure. For example, religious leaders may claim to rid people of evil spirits or cure them through prayer or rituals. While arguably this may enable a peaceful but meaningful way to address concerns, it risks reinforcing beliefs and stigmatising individuals, making them more vulnerable to future accusations. The act of submitting to cleansing rituals or prayer healing may reinforce suspicions in the minds of community members that the person "really" used magic, and when misfortune reoccurs, this suspicion may lead to harm. Additionally, some rituals associated with exorcisms, such as fasting, beating, application of water, and so forth, may themselves cause significant harm, and even sometimes prove fatal (Dodd, 2005).

Part 3 – Navigating the Relationship between Law and Cultural Change

Cultural respect and the relationship between law and culture is a significant issue when considering legislative intervention. There is a fine line between due acknowledgement of the need to accommodate cultural values, and the dangers of allowing cultural relativism to justify non-intervention. Other domains where this issue has arisen, such as treatment of women in multicultural or Islamic contexts, can provide helpful guidance. Feminist theories engaging with multiculturalism and Islam advocate rejecting an either/or approach to culture and human rights (Shachar, 2001; Abu-Lughod, 2013). This scholarship argues that paying greater attention to the "internal dialogue of the cultural community" provides supportive approaches to projects that champion women's cultural rights and gender equality (Williams, 2011, p. 66). Suggesting a constructivist model of culture, this recognises the internally contested and negotiated character of cultural practices, opening up the possibility for change (Young, 2002; Song, 2007). In the Melanesian context, scholars examining how gender identities are reshaped through interaction with global ideas show the impact of human rights discourses, new economic models, and new forms of Christianity (Macintyre & Spark, 2017). These scholars identify both the flux of contemporary Melanesian society and the attraction and power of static conceptions of "custom" and "tradition" in assertions of authority and justification of violence (Macintyre & Spark, 2017). This scholarship suggests a need for scepticism about claims of cultural continuity, focusing attention towards the power dynamics involved in such claims instead.

In the context of harmful practices relating to accusations of witchcraft and sorcery, several factors complicate the terrain. One is the colonial legacy of generally incompetent legislative attempts to intervene in the first place, resulting in problematic colonial legacies of witchcraft acts across the globe (see Keenan, 2015). The historical context of lawmaking around harmful practices concerning beliefs in witchcraft, at both national and international scales, is imbued with colonial assumptions about the power and legitimacy of law to assert imported, and often profoundly violent, interpretations of morality contrary to local understandings. This historical, and in many cases continued, experience of reliance on the coercive power of law makes it is critically important to be careful about using law to impose standards of morality fundamentally at disjuncture with those of the general population. On the other hand, attentiveness to history also clarifies real dangers in allowing for cultural sensitivities to block legislative interventions intended to prevent harmful practices justified by reference to belief in witchcraft. In some cases, over-cautiousness about intervening in cultural practices will enable exploitation of the weak by those with sufficient power to legitimise their behaviour through reference to cultural authority.

The nature of the harm under consideration also matters. Accusations of witchcraft and ritual attacks frequently involve extreme violence (Forsyth 2016). Even where no physical harm is inflicted, being publicly accused of using witchcraft can cause profound psychological damage, and lead to intense feelings of insecurity (Forsyth et al., 2021). Whereas the principle of progressive realisation of human rights may be appropriate in the context of socio-economic entitlements like work, when the rights are fundamental – such as the right to life – the law must prefer a protective function.

Debates over the extent to which culture should be accommodated in legal frameworks concerning sorcery are also complicated by the mix of disciplines and backgrounds in the debate. Ranging across anthropologists, human rights lawyers, gender equality advocates, religious studies experts, religious leaders, historians, public health scholars, and others, the diversity of backgrounds results in many different framings to position the issue. Culture is often seen to play a significant, but different, role according to which of these framings one refers. For example, many anthropologists today view harms related to beliefs in witchcraft as arising from fear, confusion, desperation, and poverty, where witchcraft is a reality of daily life manifesting in response to contemporary pressures (Ashforth, 2002; Ashforth, 2015; Comaroff & Comaroff, 1993). Older anthropological understandings of witchcraft saw it through a largely static and functionalist lens, explaining its various roles in ordering societies (Evans-Pritchard, 1937). A gender equality lens, on the other hand, tends to view witchcraft practices as stemming from underlying misogyny and discrimination against women, attitudes often deeply entrenched in existing culture.

Against this background, I propose that the question of cultural accommodation may be assisted by reference to worldview pluralism. The premise of worldview pluralism is that many different worldviews coexist in society, and are generally more fluid and accommodating than often presented. Conceptually, rather than assuming any fixed or static cultural underpinning of practices and beliefs associated with sorcery or witchcraft, we should treat the stability of the beliefs over time as a question to be subjected to empirical enquiry. Therefore, the historical environment from which witchcraft-related knowledge and practices have emerged in particular locations, and the extent to which they continue to evolve, must be investigated.

A rich literature documents the ways in which many practices and belief systems associated with sorcery and witchcraft around the world today that claim or are assumed to be cultural or deeply rooted in tradition, have actually been profoundly shaped by forces like colonialism, Christianity/other world religions, and capitalism (e.g. Comaroff & Comaroff, 1999; Geschiere, 1997). Overall, the literature shows that beliefs and practices associated with witchcraft can and do change dramatically over time. Often, contemporary practices are not a continuation of old traditions, but a dynamic phenomenon responsive to time, place, and power dynamics. In PNG, for instance, torture for confessions and ritualised trials are new practices, likely developed in response to imported colonial conceptions of demanding proof and evidence of wrongdoing.

Clear evidence from around the globe shows that many individuals, often in positions of power, exploit these beliefs to harm or profit from others (e.g. PLD, 2014). In parts of the world, this happens through various religious institutions or individuals claiming religious authority of some form or another. In others, it occurs through exercising cultural authority (see OKH, 2020). Or, it happens through seeking to control women, for example, through using belief in juju curses over women involved in sex trafficking (van der Watt & Kruger, 2019). In our PNG fieldwork, we noted it was common for a woman to be accused of having killed her husband through sorcery, to clear her out of the way and enable an uncle or brother to expropriate the deceased husband's land or property.

The inherent fluidity of worldviews can usefully be threaded into consideration about the role of law concerning harms arising from beliefs in sorcery and witchcraft. Essentially, the argument is that law should not be viewed as a tool to force people to replace one worldview with another, but rather as a mechanism to make courses of action associated with one worldview more attractive. As noted above, in conditions of worldview pluralism, individuals have different worldviews coexisting at any one time. Often there is no need to make a choice between these worldviews, so they coexist without friction and with tolerance of cognitive dissonance. However, occasionally, particular choices about how to behave in a given situation do need to be made. When this happens, different worldviews will dictate different courses of behaviour, some of which may orient towards violence, some towards non-violence. For example, if someone is desperately ill, do you first send for a doctor to provide medicine? Or do you call a diviner to find out who used sorcery to cause the illness and then torture that person until they reverse the sorcery? Or do you see a priest to pray for recovery? At both individual and community levels, conflict and contestation about such choices will often exist, as different worldviews jostle for domination (Subbotsky, 2000). While this may manifest in people trying out one option and then another, our research has also found that factors like charismatic leaders, and even the environment, can play significant roles in activating dominance of one worldview over another (Forsyth & Gibbs, 2021).

Law can play an important role in such a context through promoting behaviour associated with a worldview that does not encourage violence. The assumption is there will be voices within individuals and within communities opposed to inflicting violence and harm, and law can usefully provide both leverage and support for voices arguing for those non-violent approaches. In our PNG SARV research, we sought to understand which arguments were most successful in persuading people making accusations of sorcery against someone to instead resolve their anxieties in a peaceful manner. Somewhat unexpectedly, given the limited reach of state law in PNG, one of the most convincing arguments was that using violence against those accused of sorcery is against the law. This research suggests that even in contexts where the vast majority of cases of SARV are neither reported to police nor prosecuted, law can still be effectively enrolled as a source of moral support and authority by those seeking to avoid violence.

For law to play a useful role in navigating worldview pluralism, however, clarity and consistency of terminology and intent is crucial. Witchcraft and sorcery are slippery and elusive concepts, constantly giving rise to misunderstandings. It is therefore essential to ensure clarity over what is intended in any legislative change, and for this to be consistent with rules of evidence and procedure, including providing judicial training for when judicial proceedings arise. A current example of inconsistency in the Pacific Islands region involves many existing acts or sections within general criminal codes adopting an ambiguous positionality concerning the reality of witchcraft. For instance, the Vanuatu Penal Code provides, "[n]o person shall practise witchcraft or sorcery," and the Solomon Islands Penal Code Act provides any person who "performs any magical ritual" is guilty of an offence (Forsyth, 2006). Yet, both provisions are required to be proven within the existing framework of a secular court and rules of evidence that do not permit evidence of magic or the supernatural (see Forsyth, 2006). Further, the nomenclature of legislation and any awareness-raising done based upon it must be carefully considered. Legislation titled with terms such as Witchcraft or Sorcery, even if used to address harmful practices, may be misunderstood by local populations as official recognition of the reality of such beliefs. In my own research into understandings about the law concerning sorcery in PNG, I was frequently confronted with the total confusion that the repeal of the Sorcery Act had caused. I have interviewed many individuals, sometimes even in the justice system, who were convinced the "Sorcery Repeal Act" was actually new legislation seeking to address the problem of sorcery through "repealing" it. The potential for confusion cannot be overstated.

Satisfying the Needs of Other Worldviews Other Than through State Law

While it is appropriate for law, international treaties, and policies to privilege a worldview in which sorcery and witchcraft are not real, it cannot be expected this will itself lessen the degree to which people continue to possess a worldview in which magic is real. As noted already, beliefs in sorcery exert considerable influence over, and structure the lives of, many populations around the world. Ignoring concerns and anxieties produced by a belief that sorcery is real makes it likely that associated harmful practices will either continue or will be forced even further underground.

Therefore, to be effective, any legislation or new policy directive in this area must develop a comprehensive package to address these anxieties. This must be done in ways that do not reinforce the beliefs in sorcery that lead to harmful practices, but rather lessen concerns around them. It may be appropriate, for example, to create or support informal mediation processes that assist community members concerned about use of magic or witchcraft, or to develop partnerships with religious institutions in a proven position to provide assistance in non-stigmatising ways. Above all, it is necessary to have good answers for those operationalising laws/policies, to enable them to effectively respond to the most common questions, like "what do I do if someone is using sorcery against me?" and "why is the state protecting the witch who killed my child?" Our research into the impact of repealing the *Sorcery Act 1971* in PNG, shows that a failure to institute a clear programme responsive to these genuine anxieties has led not only to great community level concern, but also to confusion and misinformation on behalf of law enforcement and judicial officers.

Conclusion

This chapter has introduced the concept of worldview pluralism as a way to navigate through the complexities of legislative intervention directed towards eliminating harmful practices related to beliefs in sorcery and witchcraft. Worldview pluralism identifies the multiplicity and dynamism of worldviews often present in individuals and communities, particularly in the postcolonial world. It recognises that understandings about causation of events may be guided by one of a number of worldviews, including one based on understandings about the reality of magic. I emphasised that, while the law should adopt a worldview that denies the existence of sorcery, the state should actively seek to provide support mechanisms to aid those for whom these beliefs generate significant anxieties, a factor that a purely rationalist approach to law tends to overlook.

I have argued that the choice of terminology used in legislation and policy is fraught, but it is also key to properly addressing the issue. This was explained through discussing the background behind various terminological choices made recently in both international and national forums. In examining law's role in addressing behaviours connected with culture, I have argued that approaching cultural traditions as dynamic and subject to ongoing change and contestation provides an important space within which law can operate.

To conclude, this topic demonstrates the complexities of the relationship between law and society, meaning that legislative interventions are susceptible to creating problematic and unintended consequences. There are therefore two key requirements in any consideration of laws role in such a context: (1) a starting position of humility and acknowledgement of the limits of law, and (2) the development of active feedback loops capable of monitoring and evaluating legislative and policy impacts, to allow for ongoing course correction (Martin, 2020).

References

Abu-Lughod, L. (2013). *Do Muslim women need saving?* Harvard University Press.
Ashforth, A. (2002). An epidemic of witchcraft? The implications of AIDS for the post-apartheid state. *African Studies, 61*, 121–43.

Ashforth, A. (2005). Muthi, medicine and witchcraft: Regulating 'African science' in Post-apartheid South Africa? *Social Dynamics, 31*(2), 211–242

Ashforth, A. (2015). Witchcraft, justice and human rights in Africa: Cases from Malawi. *African Studies Review, 58*(1), 5–38.

BBC News. (2013). Nerendra Dabholkar: India's Maharashtra state bans black magic after killing. Retrieved from: www.bbc.com/news/world-asia-india-23776406.

Behringer, W. (1999). Climatic change and witch-hunting: the impact of the Little Ice Age on mentalities. *Climatic Change, 43*, 335–351.

Comaroff, J., & Comaroff, J. L. (1993). *Modernity and its malcontents. Ritual and power in post-colonial Africa*. University of Chicago Press.

Comaroff, J., & Comaroff, J. L. (1999). Occult economies and the violence of abstraction: Notes from the South African postcolony. *American Ethnologist, 26*, 279–303.

Cramer, M. (2022, 9 March). Scotland apologizes for history of witchcraft persecution. *New York Times*. Retrieved from: www.nytimes.com/2022/03/09/world/europe/scotland-nicola-sturgeon-apologizes-witches.html?smid=em-share.

DNA. (no date). Anti-superstition law drafted in such a way that Warkaris will not oppose it: Shyam Manav. Retrieved from: www.dnaindia.com/pune/report-anti-superstition-law-drafted-in-such-a-way-that-warkaris-will-not-oppose-it-shyam-manav-1894433.

Dodd, V. (2005, 4 June). More children 'victim of cruel exorcisms'. *The Guardian*. Retrieved from: www.theguardian.com/society/2005/jun/04/childrensservices.childprotection.

Evans-Pritchard, E. E. (1937). *Witchcraft, oracles, and magic among the Azande*. Clarendon Press.

Forsyth, M. (2006). Sorcery and the criminal law in Vanuatu. *LawAsia, 2*, 1–27.

Forsyth, M. (2016). The regulation of witchcraft and sorcery practices and beliefs. *Annual Review of Law and Social Science, 12*, 331–351.

Forsyth, M., & Eves, R. (Eds.) (2015). *Talking it through: Responses to sorcery and witchcraft beliefs and practices in Melanesia*. ANU Press.

Forsyth, M., & Gibbs, P. (2021). Causal stories and the role of worldviews in analysing responses to sorcery accusations and related violence. *International Journal for Crime, Justice and Social Democracy, 9*(2), 37–59.

Forsyth, M., Losoncz, I., Gibbs, P., Hukula, F., & Kipongi, W. (2021). Sorcery accusation-related violence in PNG, Part 7: The harm of SARV. Department of Pacific Affairs. In Brief 2021/07. Retrieved from: https://dpa.bellschool.anu.edu.au/experts-publications/publications/7989/ib-202107-sorcery-accusation-related-violence-png-part-7-harm.

Forsyth, M., Putt, J., Bouhours, B., & Bouhours, T. (2017). Sorcery accusation related violence in Papua New Guinea part 2: Key characteristics of incidents, victims and perpetrators. Department of Pacific Affairs. In Brief 2017/29. Retrieved from: https://dpa.bellschool.anu.edu.au/sites/default/files/publications/attachments/2017-11/ib-2017-29_forsyth-et-al.pdf.

Geschiere, P. (1997). *The modernity of witchcraft: Politics and the occult in postcolonial Africa*. University Press Virginia.

Hume, L. (1995). Witchcraft and the law in Australia. *Journal of Church and State, 37*(1), 135–150.

Keenan, M. (2015). The Western legal response to sorcery in colonial Papua New Guinea. In M. Forsyth & R. Eves (Eds.), *Talking it through: Responses to sorcery and witchcraft beliefs and practices in Melanesia*. ANU Press, pp. 197–212.

Macintyre, M., & Spark, C. (2017). *Transformations of gender in Melanesia*. ANU Press.

Martin, R. L. (2020). *When more is not better: Overcoming America's obsession with economic efficiency*. Harvard Business Review Press.

On Knowing Humanity Journal (OKH). (2020). Special Issue: Child witchcraft accusations and the church. *On Knowing Humanity Journal, 4*(1).

Partners for Law in Development (PLD). (2014). *Contemporary practices of witch hunting: A report on social trends and the interface with law.* Retrieved from: https://papers.ssrn.com/sol3/papers.cfm?abstract_id=2660070.

Renwick Moore, K. (2012). *Ethics in an age of terror and genocide: Identity and moral choice.* Princeton University Press.

Rosbroj, T. (2020). Vaccine refusers are health literate and believe they're pro-science. But this just reinforces their view. *The Conversation.* Retrieved from: https://theconversation.com/vaccine-refusers-are-health-literate-and-believe-theyre-pro-science-but-this-just-reinforces-their-view-144068.

Shachar, A. (2001). *Multicultural jurisdictions: Cultural differences and women's rights.* Cambridge University Press.

Siegel, J. T. (2006). *Naming the witch.* Stanford University Press.

Song, S. (2007). *Justice, gender, and the politics of multiculturalism.* Cambridge University Press.

Subbotsky, E. (2000). Phenomenalistic perception and rational understanding in the mind of an individual: The fight for dominance. In K. S. Rosengren, C. N. Johnson, & P. L. Harris (Eds.), *Imagining the impossible: Magical, scientific, and religious thinking in children.* Cambridge University Press, pp. 35–74.

Sydney Morning Herald (SMH). (2005, 21 July). Victoria clears witches for take-off. Retrieved from: www.smh.com.au/national/victoria-clears-witches-for-take-off-20050721-gdlq66.html.

United Nations General Assembly (UNGA). (2021). General Assembly resolution 47/L.9, Elimination of harmful practices related to accusations of witchcraft and ritual attacks, A/HRC/47/L.9 (5 July). Retrieved from: https://undocs.org/Home/Mobile?FinalSymbol=A%2FHRC%2F47%2FL.9.

Van der Watt, M., & Kruger, B. (2019). Breaking bondages: Control methods, 'juju', and human trafficking. In J. Winterdyk & J. Jones (Eds.), *The Palgrave International Handbook of Human Trafficking,* 935-951. Palgrave Macmillan.

Williams, S. H. (2011). Democracy, gender equality, and customary law: Constitutionalizing internal cultural disruption. *Indiana Journal of Global Legal Studies, 18*(1), 65–85.

Witchcraft & Human Rights Information Network (WHRIN). (2020, 18 November). UN Concept note: In support of advocacy for the elimination of harmful practices: Accusations of witchcraft and ritual attacks. Retrieved from: www.whrin.org/un-concept-note-in-support-of-advocacy-for-the-elimination-of-harmful-practices-accusations-of-witchcraft-and-ritual-attacks/.

Young, I. M. (2002). *Inclusion and democracy.* Oxford University Press.

18

UNDERSTANDING CLERGY-PERPETRATED CHILD SEXUAL ABUSE AS ORGANISED OFFENDING

Networks versus Individuals

Jodi Death, Kelly Richards and Kathleen McPhillips

Introduction

Through ongoing research and public inquires, the systemic nature of clerical child sexual abuse (CSA) and its management has been established (McPhillips, McEwan, Death, & Richards, 2022; McPhillips, Death, Richards, & Fitzgerald, 2022). Whilst systemic issues have been acknowledged, the body of work that examines clergy CSA as organised remains in development. Understanding institutional violence as systemic includes focusing on organisational factors that enable abuse (such as culture and policy). Understanding abuse as organised considers actors as agents involved in networks of ties that facilitate abuse (Burcher, 2018). This chapter first outlines why the movement of perpetrators to developing nations is important for understanding clerical CSA as organised crime. Factors that may have allowed organised clerical offending in developed nations to occur in undisrupted ways are then discussed, including a reliance on faith-based organisations (FBOs) to provide services to vulnerable populations, limitations to criminal and civil justice systems, and a weakened media. These factors have been important in disrupting clerical CSA in developing nations.

It is important to state from the outset that we are not arguing that the entire Roman Catholic Church (RCC) is a criminal network. Our argument is that there is evidence that the systemic nature of clerical CSA points to elements of organised offending that drew on the licit functions of the Church to facilitate and cover offending behaviour. Insofar as this is our objective, Dark Networks Theory (DNT) and Social Network Analysis (SNA) provide mechanisms to critically explore and understand organised clerical CSA.

DOI: 10.4324/9781003276593-21

Background

In the 1980s Finklehor developed the widely espoused 'Four Preconditions Model' to explain the conditions that were necessary for child sexual abuse to occur (Finkelhor, 1984). The model argues that in order for an adult to sexually abuse a child, they must: 1) possess the motivation to sexually abuse a child; 2) overcome internal inhibitors; 3) overcome external inhibitors; and 4) overcome any resistance on the part of the child. Finkelhor's model, and later explanatory models of CSA (e.g. Seto (2019) – Motivation-Facilitation Model) are widely considered to explain individual drivers of offending; however. they are not sufficient to explain offending more broadly, or as a network of actors. In the context of clergy overcoming both internal and external barriers to offending, particularly offending multiple times, aid was provided by Church policy and culture through secrecy around sexuality of clergy, diminished offender responsibility for offending when behaviours were detected, the prioritising of the reputation of the Church to protect offenders, repeated affirmation of the authority and purity of clergy, and continued facilitation of access to vulnerable children (Gardner, 2021). There is also evidence that perpetrators within Church networks facilitated access to victims, assisted individuals with narratives to overcome internal barriers to abuse, and drew individuals into offending as both victims and perpetrators (Muytjens, 2019; Royal Commission into Institutional Responses to Child Sexual Abuse [RCIRCSA], 2017). The nature of this was systemic and, as we have argued elsewhere (McPhillips, Death, Richards, & Fitzgerald, 2022), indicates a level of organisation that goes beyond management of individuals and points to organised facilitation of abuse.

Despite this increased awareness of sexual offending and improved mechanisms to address it, Salter and Woodlock (2021; Salter, 2013) point to an unwillingness, and backlash against, understanding sexual offending as organised. We understand organised crime to be Gottschalk (2009: 5), 'crime committed by criminal organisations whose existence has continuity over time and across crimes, and that may use systematic violence and corruption to facilitate their criminal activities'.
This leads to ongoing vulnerability of children and adult survivors. We argue that many of the conditions in which clerical CSA has thrived historically in developed nations continue to exist in developing nations, leaving children at increased vulnerability to networks of perpetrators. These networks include offending clergy being sent to developing nations to escape prosecution for offences, complaints of communities, and as a means of disrupting scrutiny on the Church (O'Neill, 2020). Developing nations often have a colonial background that has resulted in the increased vulnerability of Indigenous peoples through the disruption to traditional legal systems, changing and conflicting social norms and values (including sexual and relationship norms), dispossession of people from their traditional lands, diminishing mental and physical health, increased substance abuse, and the imposition of 'western values' (Paton, 2017; Strakosch & Macoun, 2020). Christian

churches, including the Catholic Church, have been, and continue to be, a mechanism of colonialism in developing nations including in delivering foreign aid and in 'development' agendas (Anderson, 2015; Clarke, 2015; Jewkes, Jama-Shai, & Sikweyiya, 2017). This is also so where nation states have experienced, or are experiencing, civil conflict and FBOs provide services and aid (O'Neill, 2020). This is relevant to understanding organised clerical sexual abuse insofar as the result has been the creation of systems in which Catholicisms have been empowered by the state to provide welfare, health, education, and other services to vulnerable people. This often occurs when nation states have few resources to implement mechanisms for accountability and/or there are cultural inhibitors to recognising, reporting, and addressing sexual violence (O'Neill, 2020).

Barriers to reporting, and the implicitly secretive nature of child sexual offences, have meant that the 'dark figure of crime' is an ongoing challenge for researchers, policymakers, and communities in developed and developing nations (Cashmore & Shackel, 2014; Falshaw, Friendship, & Bates, 2003). Similarly, identifying numbers of perpetrators in communities and organisations is difficult. The John Jay study (John Jay College of Criminal Justice, 2004) established the rate of offenders amongst Catholic clergy in the United States to be 4%. In Australia, the Royal Commission into Institutional Responses to Child Sexual Abuse (RCIRCSA) examined religious orders in detail and reported rates of perpetrators in the top five religious orders, between 1950 and 2010, as follows: St John of God 40.4%, Christian Brothers 22%, Del La Salle Brothers 13.8%, Marist Brothers 20.4%, and Salesians of Don Bosco 20.8% (RCIRCSA, 2017: 16). Diocesan priests were 30% of all known alleged perpetrators in claims of sexual abuse considered by the Royal Commission (RCIRCSA, 2017: 15). These figures bear recalling here as they emphasise that clerical CSA was more pervasive in some contexts than others. Unsurprisingly, religious orders with higher levels of perpetrators often had a focus on provision of services to children; however, understanding potential ties between perpetrators is important to a detailed picture of how clerical CSA persisted in orders and amongst diocesan clergy. The use of SNA will assist in this aim.

What Is Social Network Analysis?

SNA has become an important tool in addressing organised crime (Bakker, Raab, & Milward, 2012; Burcher & Whelan, 2018; Everton & Cunningham, 2013). Whilst used in other disciples such as sociology, business, and hard sciences, criminology has embraced SNA as a means of understanding and disrupting a range of organised offending, including terrorist networks (Demiroz & Kapucu, 2012), corrupt police networks (Lauchs, Keast, & Chamberlain, 2012), drug trafficking (Boivin, 2014), and outlaw motorcycle gangs (Lauchs, 2019). DNT, which underpins SNA's application in understanding organised offending, identifies three levels of organised offending networks: the *light network* of a licit organisation, which is knowingly or unknowingly, used as a cover and mechanism of organising and distributing network resources; the *grey network* of actors who, either knowingly or unknowingly, facilitate the activities of the *dark network*, and the dark network of illicit offenders. Network analysis can include location; resources such as money, arms, illegal substances or victims; individual offences; individual actors in each level of the network; and links between actors, locations, and offences (Brinton Milward & Raab, 2006; Cunningham, 2016). The benefit of the theoretical-methodological pairing of SNA and DNT is that it facilitates an understanding of how criminal behaviour is organised. This can be achieved through recognising patterns of offending, roles of individuals in the network, the structure of a network, and ways in which a network adapts to adverse situations as well as opportunities. For criminal networks this can assist in forming strategies of disrupting offending either in the short term locally or in ways that decrease resilience of the network and its ability to rebuild (Bakker, Raab, & Milward, 2012; Burcher & Whelan, 2018; Everton & Cunningham, 2013).

In applying DNT to clergy offending in the RCC, the light network consists of the licit activities of the church, the grey network consists of actors who have facilitated the cover-up of abuse, whether deliberate or not, and the dark network is clergy offenders. If offenders and their management are only considered on an individual basis, critical information and an accurate historical picture may be missed (McPhillips, Death, Richards, & Fitzgerald, in press). Our thesis is that clergy abuse in the RCC is not characterised by individual actors in poorly managed systems, but that patterns of offending, the movement of perpetrators, and ties between actors indicate organised offending. The movement of perpetrators to developing nations is an element of organised offending.

A central aim of DNT is to utilise SNA to better understand how networks function so as to better understand how to disrupt them. Research has shown that disruption of a network varies depending on the shape of the network and its resilience (Cunningham, 2016; Everton & Cunningham, 2015). Whilst some networks that are highly centralised may be disrupted by removing a pivotal individual, even this is reliant on the ability of the network to replace that individual. Other networks may be dispersed, with actors relatively isolated from each other until such a time as it is necessary to draw together – such as in a terrorist attack. The benefit of a dispersed network with isolated actors is that the chance of detection is much lower and even were one actor detected, it would be unlikely to affect the rest of the network adversely (Everton & Dan, 2015). This means that strategies for disrupting networks may need to be diverse and have different objectives. A second objective may be to create environments that make the activities and function of the network more difficult (Obokata & Payne, 2017)

What Indicators Are There of Organised Clerical CSA?

Understanding clergy abuse as organised challenges the dominant understanding that clerical CSA is a problem of individual offenders in poor systems. Whilst establishing that factors such as canon law, institutional secrecy, and clericalism contributed to the ongoing perpetration of clergy abuse has been a significant achievement of research and public inquiry, this does not adequately explain the extent of clergy abuse, its ongoing nature across decades, the cover-up of abuse, or the significance of ties between actors (Doyle, 2006; Keenan, 2012). Additionally, where groups of offenders are known to have been co-located, these have been described as paedophile networks in media and public inquiry and these claims should be tested. SNA offers the opportunity to examine ties between actors in ways that are important to the ongoing prevention of clerical CSA. It is not only historic disruptions to networks that are important but being able to understand how networks adapt, develop resilience to, and recover from disruptions so as to prevent the formation of potential future networks of abusers (Bakker et al., 2012; Cavallaro et al., 2020).

Muytjens' (2019) work was the first to complete a large-scale mapping project that included perpetrators of abuse, survivors of abuse, and those engaged in managing perpetrators in four dioceses of Victoria, Australia (Melbourne, Ballarat, Sandhurst, and Sale). The project found that the movement of perpetrators was not random, that clusters of perpetrators existed between 1950 and 2010, and that perpetrators shared victims, strategies, and techniques of abuse. Muytjen's (2019) work further evidences a grey network that facilitated the cover-up of abuse and, either knowingly or unknowingly, further access to victims. Death (2018) examined the Christian Brothers in Western Australia (WA), noting that five out of eight Brother Superiors at the boys' home Bindoon have been accused of sexual offences by former residents, that cultures of violence aided in concealing abuse, and that the Brother Superiors each supervised multiple perpetrators. Lynch's (2019) work examined opportunities for perpetrator collaborations in the Christian Brothers of Western Australia and reported that Brothers accused of CSA were more likely to be transferred between the four WA institutions, that there was evidence of Brothers knowing of perpetration by other Brothers, and there was evidence of abuse by multiple perpetrators.

There are other indicators that are consistent with the function and strategies of organised offending. While organisations may legitimately seek to protect their own interests, Robertson (2010: 3) observed that in the management of clerical CSA, the Catholic Church had become 'a law unto itself, providing a concurrent system of secret proceedings under which abusive priests found forgiveness, victims were silenced, and national law enforcement was frustrated'. Organised crime often has methods for protecting and disciplining members to avoid detection by external authorities and promote loyalty (Meier, Pierce, Vaccaro, & La Cara, 2016). Having internal policies to address organisational problems is not uncommon and can be beneficial to organisations in legitimate ways. However, the history of the Catholic Church using internal policies and canon law to actively resist intervention from external authorities, to disavow accountability to civil and criminal law, and to protect its members from detection and prosecution has been extraordinary. This is consistent with what Duxbury and Haynie (2019: 314) state is the organised criminal group's challenge, 'the need to conceal activity under constant threat of detection and resulting risk of legal consequences'. A part of Church efforts to manage clerical CSA has been the movement of priests away from wealthy developed nations to less wealthy or developing nations. O'Neill (2020) has termed this transnational clerical sexual abuse. Utilisation of borders to avoid detection, the use of internal 'justice' and discipline mechanisms, the silencing of victims and those who would draw attention to illegal activity, and the utilising of licit networks for illicit means are recognised elements of organised crime groups (Obokata & Payne, 2017).

Why Developing Nations Are Important to Understanding Organised Clerical CSA?

Including developing nations in understanding clerical abuse as a network is important for several reasons. First, perpetrators who were detected by Church authorities in developed nations were often sent to developing nations. Second, developing nations often continue to rely on FBOs for the provision of children's services and have done so historically. Third, systems that would ordinarily lead to accountability for offending, including criminal justice, child services, education, health, and media, are frequently less advanced and equipped in developing nations. This poses an ongoing problem to justice responses for survivors of clergy abuse and accountability for the Church's management of offending.

Perpetrators Often Sent to Vulnerable Populations

The RCC has been widely criticised for utilising a strategy of moving perpetrators between parishes once offending was detected (RCIRCSA, 2017). Motivations for these movements tend to be attributed to a range of concerns including a desire to protect the reputation of institutions, overstated belief in clergy, difficulty in recognising that clergy could abuse children sexually, the treatment of sexual violence as a moral failure, and a consequential belief in the moral redemption of clergy (RCIRCSA, 2017). Despite an apparent lack of national and international organisational policy the RCIRCSA found that responses across jurisdictions in Australia were remarkably similar. These responses are also evident in international inquiries that have sought to understand church responses to clerical offending, including the movement of perpetrators (Death, 2018; Rashid & Barron, 2018). The movement of offending clergy was not geographically isolated to a region, state, or country; rather, international transfers were used to avoid prosecution for offences, to provide treatment for offenders, to return them to ministry with a fresh start, and to avoid increased scrutiny and potential reputational damage for individuals and the RCC (O'Neill, 2020). The effect of these movements was a widening of opportunities to offend without a reduced chance of detection and/or consequence for offenders (Rashid & Barron, 2018).

Whilst perpetrators were moved globally, many were transferred to developing nations. As an example, Case Study 13 of the RCIRCSA considered the case of Father Denis McAlinden, who had multiple victims in the Maitland/Newcastle diocese across 50 years. After concerns as to McAlinden's behaviour towards children were raised, he was moved between a number of locations including those in

Australia, Papua New Guinea (PNG), the Philippines, Ireland, and New Zealand (Cunneen, 2014). We do not currently know the extent of McAlinden's offending, or that of other perpetrators sent to developing nations; however, the NSW Special Commission of Inquiry (Cunneen, 2014: 4) found that:

> Given McAlinden's modus operandi, the five decades his abuse spanned, and the time he spent in Western Australia and overseas in Papua New Guinea, Ireland, New Zealand and the Philippines, undoubtedly there are other victims of his abuse who have not come forward and might never do so.

For potential victims of McAlinden in PNG, opportunities to disclose abuse would be diminished due to civil conflict, lack of faith in systems, shame, cultural prohibitors, an increased tolerance for violence against women and children, a reliance on the Church for the provision of goods and services, and the impact of clericalism in positioning clergy as holy, powerful, and beyond rebuke (Biersack, Jolly, & MacIntyre, 2016; Forster, 2009; Jewkes et al., 2017; Paton, 2017). Consequently, only one victim of McAlinden has come forward from his time serving in PNG, who has allegedly received compensation from the Church (Collins, 2017; PNG Attitude, 2012). McAlinden is just one example of a clergy perpetrator who benefited from international transfers that extended potential networks for offending.

Although we know they occurred with varying frequency, the extent of perpetrator movements internationally is unknown, as are potential patterns of movements. SNA provides an opportunity to point to likely locations where parts of an international network of offenders may have existed, and given the right conditions, may still exist. SNA also provides the opportunity to understand how geographical sites and jurisdictions were used in the management of offenders. As an example, specific locations were used similarly to sites in Victoria where offenders were often sent to communities that had already hosted a perpetrator and been groomed or there were other motivations for location choice (Muytjens, 2019).

Reliance on RBO's for the Provision of Children's Services

One mechanism that has facilitated the movement of perpetrators is the role that the Catholic Church has played in the development of nations across the globe (Artaud de La Ferrière, 2020; Gooren, 2015). In developing nations, failure of market economies, governments, and disruptions to civil societies have often led to entrenched poverty at individual and community levels. It is often FBOs that have stepped into a gap. This comes on a long missionary history in many nations states where FBOs have historically cared for vulnerable individuals and communities (Barrera, 2018). The benevolence of FBOs appears to remain an assumption in partnerships between states and FBOs where emerging or poorer states are reliant on FBOs for the provision of services.

This is of interest to those utilising SNA and DNT as there is potential for asymmetrical relationships to be perpetuated in vulnerable communities and it is these relationships structures that increase vulnerability to sexual violence (Gardner, 2021). Further, where institutions such as the RCC have established a long-standing presence, Catholic spirituality is held in high regard, and is the basis of common identity and community. Moreover, in these contexts, clericalism perpetuates the idealisation of clergy. As a consequence, the capacity for clergy to offend, avoid detection, and if detected to avoid potential consequences, is magnified. We know these factors are significant because they have become central in understanding historical clerical CSA in developed nations. These are the conditions that surrounded clergy offending from the 1950s to the early 2000s (Davis, 2015; Keenan, 2012) in the developed world. The question as to whether these conditions that facilitated organised offending in developed nations, such as Australia, also enabled organised offending in developing nations is important to public accountability for religious institutions and the ongoing protection of vulnerable children.

In developed nations, changes to social policy have led to some preventative mechanisms to protect against clerical CSA. One policy includes a move away from large-scale children's institutions to foster or kinship care (Swain, 2014). Institutions have historically been vulnerable to clusters of offenders and cultures of violence, secrecy, and the continued disempowerment of residents that prevented reporting of abuse. Often the presence of geographical or social isolation further inhibited disclosures of abuse and multiple perpetrators were able to find haven and access to victims in institutions (Death, 2018). Geographical isolation placed residents in a position of being unable to physically remove themselves from perpetrators. Running away often led to detection, punishment, and further abuse. Social isolation meant a lack of external visitors willing to speak with children, recognise and respond to signs of violence, and facilitate accountability for perpetrators. Social isolation was enhanced by the low social standing of residents who were often state wards through poverty or family violence, orphans, 'delinquents', and children with disabilities who lacked the social capital necessary to be valued and heard. These were children whose only source of support was often those who would abuse them (RCIRCSA, 2014).

Developed nations have also seen changes to civil and criminal processes that better enable investigation and prosecution of offences, criminalise failure to report CSA, and remove statutes of limitation and other mechanisms institutions have relied onto avoid accountability (Mathews, 2019; Mizzi, 2019). Alongside this increased social and political awareness of the realities of CSA in institutions, greater efforts in ensuring institutions have child safeguarding policies and practices, and continued willingness to recognise the voices of survivors helps create environments that make offending and its concealment more difficult and responses more effective (Firmin, 2020). This is not to idealise developed nations and their responses as it is clear there is much work still to do.

Many organisations and governments, in developing nations, are also making efforts towards enhanced child protection and criminal justice systems in efforts to prevent the abuse of children and respond meaningfully when abuse occurs (Afiaz, Masud, & Mansur, 2021; Mathews & Dallaston, 2020). These efforts have often been made in contexts of civil conflict, little or no funding, systemic corruption, and impediments to democracy that enable accountability for governments and institutions (Afiaz et al., 2021; Mathews, 2016). Historically, the Catholic Church has used gaps in service provision in developing nations to move clergy offenders to places where they are less likely to be detected and have opportunities to offend further (RCIRCSA, 2017).

Media Accountability and Advocating Awareness of CSA

An independent media is an important arm of democracy. The ideal of a free and independent media is compromised even in developed nations where media services are often privatised and profit driven (Budarick, 2019). Budarick (2019: 2) argues that journalism increasingly has a contentious relationship with democracy as defined by 'a lack of interest in experts, the rise of fake news, and a deteriorating relationship between political leaders and journalists'. Even in developing nations the role of media to hold governments to account can be impacted by restrictions on reporting significant issues such as human rights violations (Brevini, 2017; Rae, Holman, & Nethery, 2018). Nonetheless, most democratic nations offer a range of media sources that have been diversified by the increasing presence of social media as a source of information (Rae et al., 2018). For understanding and advocating awareness of clerical CSA, media representation has been essential (Death, 2018).

Beginning in the USA in the 1980s, media representation of the problem of clerical CSA was sporadic until the groundbreaking work of the *Boston Globe* in the early 2000s. It was this work that first pointed to the systemic nature of clerical CSA and its cover-up in the RCC (Marcel, 2013; The Investigative Staff of the *Boston Globe*, 2002). Pressure from media has led to governments initiating public inquiries, including the RCIRCSA, legislative reforms in criminal and civil spheres, and consciousness-raising that prioritises the well-being and protection of children over institutions and individuals in positions of power (Death, 2018).

As little research, and few public inquiries, have been conducted into clerical CSA in developing nations, media remains central to building awareness and understanding. Media is important as it has the capacity to apply pressure to internal governments as well as illicit intervention from external governments and oversight bodies where there may be human rights violations associated with clerical abuse, including the United Nations (Rashid & Barron, 2018). The threat of exposure is central to understanding network function and disruption (Everton & Cunningham, 2015). Where this exposure has not been brought through official government channels, such as criminal justice, it may be brought through media representation (Death, 2018). Where media has been used to bring accountability to the Catholic Church in developed nations, so it can be used in developing nations. Whist media is increasingly transnational and global, a strong and independent media that is able to challenge large institutions is still essential to these objectives and not always present or uncompromised in developing nations.

Where there is an absence of research, civil and criminal litigation, and public inquiry, media can also provide a source of data for networking projects (Muytjens, 2019). Media analysis is a recognised tool in qualitative research, and, despite limitations, mapping media reports may provide a foundation for further work (Berger, 2019). This could give insight into the need for further examination of where a network may extend, where perpetrators were moved, and whether clergy perpetrators are primarily local or are imported priests in developing nations. As media has been recognised for contributions to combating corruption more widely, so it may also prompt accountability for a global church that has facilitated transnational clergy offending (Dutta & Roy, 2016; Prabowo, Hamdani, & Sanusi, 2018).

Conclusion

In this chapter we have argued that clergy-perpetrated CSA should be understood as a form of organised criminal activity. This explanation has begun to gain traction and amass empirical support in developed nations (McPhillips, McEwan, Death, & Richards, 2022; McPhillips, Death, Richards, & Fitzgerald, 2022). However, we argue here that the lessons learned from framing clergy-perpetrated CSA in this way remain highly relevant for understanding – and critically, disrupting – clergy-perpetrated CSA in developing nations. The extent of clergy CSA in developing nations is largely unknown; however, it has been recognised as occurring, and developing nations continue to be vulnerable to offenders going undetected due to cultural, political, and social conditions. As has been demonstrated in developing nations, disruption of clergy CSA has relied on a range of social, political, and legislative measures. SNA and DNT provide tools for critically exploring the extension of organised clergy offending into developing nations. There is, however, much work to be completed in this space.

References

Afiaz, A., Masud, M. S., & Mansur, M. (2021). Impact of child's cognitive and social-emotional difficulties on child abuse: Does mother's justification of intimate partner violence also play a role? *Child Abuse & Neglect, 117*, 105028. https://doi.org/10.1016/j.chiabu.2021.105028

Anderson, J. (2015). Struggling with 'this gender relations thing' in the Papua New Guinea Church Partnership Program. *Gender, Place and Culture: A Journal of Feminist Geography, 22*(10), 1357–1373. https://doi.org/10.1080/0966369X.2014.970133

Artaud de La Ferrière, A. (2020). The Catholic Church in Tunisia: a transliminal institution between religion and nation. *The Journal of North African Studies, 25*(3), 415–446. https://doi.org/10.1080/13629387.2019.1611428

Bakker, R. M., Raab, J., & Milward, H. B. (2012). A preliminary theory of dark network resilience. *Journal of Policy Analysis and Management, 31*(1), 33–62. https://doi.org/10.1002/pam.20619

Barrera, A. (2018). *Catholic missionaries and their work with the poor: Mitigating market-government failure in emerging nations*. Routledge.

Berger, A. A. (2019). *Media analysis techniques* (6th ed.). SAGE.

Biersack, A., Jolly, M., & MacIntyre, M. (2016). *Gender violence & human rights: Seeking justice in Fiji, Papua New Guinea and Vanuatu*. ANU Press.

Boivin, R. (2014). Risks, prices, and positions: A social network analysis of illegal drug trafficking in the world-economy. *International Journal of Drug Policy, 25*(2), 235–243. https://doi.org/10.1016/j.drugpo.2013.12.004

Brevini, B. (2017). Metadata laws, journalism and resistance in Australia. *Media and Communication (Lisboa), 5*(1), 76–83. https://doi.org/10.17645/mac.v5i1.810

Brinton Milward, H., & Raab, J. (2006). Dark networks as organizational problems: Elements of a theory 1. *International Public Management Journal, 9*(3), 333–360. https://doi.org/10.1080/10967490600899747

Budarick, J. (2019). *Ethnic media and democracy from liberalism to agonism*. Springer International.

Burcher, M., & Whelan, C. (2018). Social network analysis as a tool for criminal intelligence: Understanding its potential from the perspectives of intelligence analysts. *Trends in Organized Crime, 21*(3), 278–294. https://doi.org/10.1007/s12117-017-9313-8

Cashmore, J., & Shackel, R. (2014). Responding to historical child sexual abuse and the needs of survivors. *Current Issues in Criminal Justice, 26*(1), 1–4.

Cavallaro, L., Ficara, A., De Meo, P., Fiumara, G., Catanese, S., Bagdasar, O., ... Liotta, A. (2020). Disrupting resilient criminal networks through data analysis: The case of Sicilian Mafia. *PLoS One, 15*(8), e0236476–e0236476. https://doi.org/10.1371/journal.pone.0236476

Clarke, M. (2015). Innovative delivery mechanisms: Australian aid partnership with churches in Papua New Guinea. *Journal of International Development, 27*(8), 1462–1478. https://doi.org/10.1002/jid.3185

Collins, S. (2017, 30 January). Lawyers seek victims of Catholic paedophile priest Fr Denis McAlinden. *New Zealand Herald*. Retrieved from: www.nzherald.co.nz/nz/lawyers-seek-victims-of-catholic-paedophile-priest-fr-denis-mcalinden/3OCLZAQRQMPGSKYJMYKANEQNYQ/

Cunneen, M. (2014). *Special Commission of Inquiry into matters relating to the investigation of certain child sexual abuse allegations in the Catholic Dioceses of Maitland-Newcastle Report Volume 2*. Retrieved from: www.dpc.nsw.gov.au/__data/assets/pdf_file/0005/163922/Report_-_Volume_2_-_Hunter_Special_Commission_of_Inquiry.pdf

Cunningham, D. (2016). *Understanding dark networks: A strategic framework for the use of social network analysis*. Lanham, MD: Rowman & Littlefield.

Davis, F. (2015). The Royal Commission into institutional responses to child sexual abuse: Learning from the past. *Australian Feminist Law Journal, 41*(2), 213–218. https://doi.org/10.1080/13200968.2015.1079353

Death, J. (2018). *Governing child abuse, voices and victimisation: The use of public inquiry into child sexual abuse in Christian institutions*. Oxon Routledge.

Demiroz, F., & Kapucu, N. (2012). Anatomy of a dark network: The case of the Turkish Ergenekon terrorist organization. *Trends in Organized Crime, 15*(4), 271–295. https://doi.org/10.1007/s12117-012-9151-7

Doyle, T. P. (2006). Clericalism: Enabler of clergy sexual abuse. *Pastoral Psychology, 54*(3), 189–213. https://doi.org/10.1007/s11089-006-6323-x

Dutta, N., & Roy, S. (2016). The interactive impact of press freedom and media reach on corruption. *Economic Modelling, 58*, 227–236. https://doi.org/10.1016/j.econmod.2016.05.008

Duxbury, S.W., & Haynie, D. L. (2019). Criminal network security: An agent-based approach to evaluating network resilience. *Criminology (Beverly Hills), 57*(2), 314–342. https://doi.org/10.1111/1745-9125.12203

Everton, S. F., & Cunningham, D. (2013). Detecting significant changes in dark networks. *Behavioral Sciences of Terrorism and Political Aggression: Applying Social Network Analysis to Terrorism, 5*(2), 94–114. https://doi.org/10.1080/19434472.2012.725225

Everton, S. F., & Cunningham, D. (2015). Dark network resilience in a hostile environment: Optimizing centralization and density. *Criminology, Criminal Justice, Law & Society, 16*(1), 1–20.

Everton, S. F., & Dan, C. (2015). Dark network resilience in a hostile environment: Optimizing centralization and density. *Criminology, Criminal Justice, Law & Society, 16*(1), 1–20.

Falshaw, L., Friendship, C., & Bates, A. (2003). *Sexual offenders – measuring reconviction, reoffending and recidivism*. Home Office.

Finkelhor, D. (1984) *Child sexual abuse: New theory & research*. The Free Press.

Firmin, C. (2020). *Contextual safeguarding and child protection: Rewriting the rules*. Routledge.

Forster, C. (2009). Sexual offences law reform in Pacific Island countries: Replacing colonial norms with international good practice standards. *Melbourne University Law Review, 33*(3), 833–864.

Gardner, F. (2021). *Sex, power, control: Responding to abuse in the institutional church*. The Lutterwoth Press.

Gooren, H. (2015). The growth and development of non-Catholic churches in Chile. *Review of Religious Research, 57*(2), 191–218. https://doi.org/10.1007/s13644-014-0180-3

Gottschalk, P. (2009). *Entrepreneurship and organised crime: Entrepreneurs in illegal business*. Edward Elgar.

The Investigative Staff of the Boston Globe. (2002). *Betrayal: The crisis in the Catholic Church*. Little Brown and Company.

Jewkes, R., Jama-Shai, N., & Sikweyiya, Y. (2017). Enduring impact of conflict on mental health and gender-based violence perpetration in Bougainville, Papua New Guinea: A cross-sectional study. *PLoS One, 12*(10), e0186062-e0186062. https://doi.org/10.1371/journal.pone.0186062

John Jay College of Criminal Justice. (2004). *The nature and scope of the problem of sexual abuse of minors by Catholic priests and deacons in the United States* Retrieved from: www.jjay.cuny.edu/Churchstudy/main.asp

Keenan, M. (2012). *Child sexual abuse & the Catholic Church: Gender, power, and organizational culture*. Oxford University Press.

Kevin Lewis, O. N. (2020). The unmaking of a pedophilic priest: Transnational clerical sexual abuse in Guatemala. *Comparative Studies in Society and History, 62*(4), 745–769. https://doi.org/10.1017/S0010417520000274

Lauchs, M. (2019). Are outlaw motorcycle gangs organized crime groups? An analysis of the Finks MC. *Deviant Behavior, 40*(3), 287–300. https://doi.org/10.1080/01639625.2017.1421128

Lauchs, M., Keast, R., & Chamberlain, D. (2012). Resilience of a corrupt police network: The first and second jokes in Queensland. *Crime, Law, and Social Change, 57*(2), 195–207. https://doi.org/10.1007/s10611-011-9337-y

Lynch, G. (2019). *Possible collusion between individuals alleged to have sexually abused boys at four Christian Brother's institutions in Western Australia, 1947–1965: A secondary analysis of material collated by historical abuse inquiries*. Retrieved from: file:///C:/Users/jodid/iCloudDrive/Documents/Dark%20Networks%20Project/Christian%20Brothers/Alleged%20abusers%20at%20CBs%20institutions%20in%20WA%20(version%20for%20KAR%20upload,%2025.01.21).pdf

Marcel, M. (2013). Victim gender in news coverage of the priest sex crisis by the *Boston Globe. Women's Studies in Communication, 36*(3), 288. https://doi.org/10.1080/07491409.2013.832088

Mathews, B. (2016). Developing countries and the potential of mandatory reporting laws to identify severe child abuse and neglect. In S. Deb (Ed.), *Child safety, welfare and well-being: Issues and challenges*. Springer, India, pp. 335–350.

Mathews, B. (2019). *New international frontiers in child sexual abuse: Theory, problems and progress*. Springer.

Mathews, B., & Dallaston ,E. (2020). Reform of civil statutes of limitation for child sexual abuse claims: Seismic change and ongoing challenges. *UNSW Law Journal, 43*(2): 386–416.

McPhillips, K., Death, J., Richards, K., & Fitzgerald, J. (2022). Innovative methodological approaches to understanding institutional gender-based violence through mapping organized clerical child sexual abuse networks. In D. Llewellyn, S. Hawthorne, & S. Sharma (Eds.) (in press), *Bloomsbury handbook of religion, gender and sexuality*. Bloomsbury Press.

McPhillips, K., McEwan, T., Death, J., and Richards, K. (forthcoming). Exploring narratives of gender in sexual violence against children in religious organisations. *Religion and Gender* 11(2).

McPhillips, K., Death, J., Richards, K., & Fitzgerald, J. (in press). Innovative methodological approaches to understanding institutional gender-based violence through mapping organized clerical child sexual abuse networks. In D. Llewellyn, S. Nawthornde, & S. Sharma (Eds.), *Bloomsbury Studies in religion, gender, and sexuality*. Bloomsbury Publishing.

Meier, S., Pierce, L., Vaccaro, A., & La Cara, B. (2016). Trust and in-group favoritism in a culture of crime. *Journal of Economic Behavior & Organization, 132*, 78–92. https://doi.org/10.1016/j.jebo.2016.09.005

Mizzi, P. (2019). Balancing prosecution with the right to a fair trial: The child sexual abuse reforms in NSW. *Judicial Officers Bulletin, 31*(2), 11–18.

Muytjens, S. (2019). *An exploration of the existence of clergy child sexual abuse dark networks within the Victorian Catholic Church*. Queensland University of Technology,

Obokata, T., & Payne, B. (2017). *Transnational organised crime: A comparative analysis*. Routledge.

O'Neill, K. L. (2020). The unmaking of a pedophilic priest: Transnational clerical sexual abuse in Guatemala. *Comparative Studies in Society and History, 62*(4), 745–769. https://doi.org/10.1017/S0010417520000274

Paton, M. (2017). De-colonising human rights: Customary justice and child protection in Papua New Guinea. *The International Journal of Children's Rights, 25*(3–4), 622–657. https://doi.org/10.1163/15718182-02503003

PNG Attitude. (2012, 18 November). Abusive priest Fr Denis McAlinden: the PNG link. Retrieved from: www.pngattitude.com/2012/11/abusive-priest-fr-denis-mcalinden-the-png-link.html

Prabowo, H., Hamdani, R., & Sanusi, Z. (2018). The new face of people power: An exploratory study on the potential of social media for combating corruption in Indonesia. *Australasian Accounting, Business & Finance Journal, 12*(3), 19–40. https://doi.org/10.14453/aabfj.v12i3.3

Rae, M., Holman, R., & Nethery, A. (2018). Self-represented witnessing: The use of social media by asylum seekers in Australia's offshore immigration detention centres. *Media, Culture & Society, 40*(4), 479–495. https://doi.org/10.1177/0163443717746229

Rashid, F., & Barron, I. (2018). Critique of the Vatican's role in recent child protection practice: A brief report. *Journal of Child Sexual Abuse, 27*(2), 141–153. https://doi.org/10.1080/10538712.2018.1425948

Robertson, G. (2010). *The case of the Pope: Vatican accountability for human rights violations*. Penguin Books.

Royal Commission into Institutional Responses to Child Sexual Abuse. (2014). *Report of Case Study No. 11: Congregation of Christian Brothers in Western Australia response to child sexual abuse at Castledare Junior Orphanage, St Vincent's Orphanage Clontarf, St Mary's Agricultural School Tardun and Bindoon Farm School.* Retrieved from: http://childabuseroyalcommission.gov.au/public-hearings/findings

Royal Commission into Institutional Responses to Child Sexual Abuse. (2017). *Analysis of claims of child sexual abuse made with respect to the Catholic church institutions.* Sydney: Royal Commission into Institutional Responses to Child Sexual Abuse.

Salter, M. (2013). *Organised sexual abuse.* Routledge.

Salter, M., & Woodlock, D. (forthcoming). The antiepistemology of organised abuse: Ignorance, exploitation, inaction. *British Journal of Criminology, 20,* 1–17. https://doi.org/10.1093/bjc/azac007

Seto, M. C. (2019). The motivation-facilitation model of sexual offending. *Sexual Abuse, 31*(1), 3–24. https://doi.org/10.1177/1079063217720919

Strakosch, E., & Macoun, A. (2020). The violence of analogy: Abstraction, neoliberalism and settler colonial possession. *Postcolonial studies, 23*(4), 505–526. https://doi.org/10.1080/13688790.2020.1834930

Swain, S. (2014). *History of child protection legislation.* The Royal Commission into Institutional Responses to Child Sexual Abuse. Retrieved from: http://www.childabuseroyalcommission.gov.au/policy-and-research/our-research/published-research/history-of-child-protection-legislation

19

RELIGION AND RESTORATIVE JUSTICE

A Mutual Critical Dialogue

Myra N. Blyth

Introduction

The conviction of practical theologians writing on criminal justice, is that public debate on issues of justice is enriched and deepened when lawyers and theologians engage with one another (Forrester, 2012, 256–7; Sagovsky, 2008, xviii; Gorringe, 1996, 17). Viewing theology and law as dialogue partners can be mutually enriching. Each brings something different and distinctive to the discussion. More than 40 years ago, Bishop David Jenkins (1980) made this case, arguing that theology can best serve the quest for an answer to how society responds to crime by keeping alive in criminology those awkward questions that are frequently neglected about the struggle to be human (Jenkins, 1980, 178).

In this chapter, I seek to pursue that quest. I will contend that Christian atonement theology has shifted its focus during the twentieth/twenty-first centuries from punishment to restoration and reconciliation, and that this shift mirrors in part the modern criminal justice debate and particularly the emergence of restorative justice. I shall use the definition of restorative justice offered by Tony Marshall and adopted by the UN as my starting point, and from there propose three principles – radical participation, moral seriousness, and reintegration – to frame a critical dialogue between restorative justice and atonement theology. In the final section, drawing on the example of the Prison Fellowship Sycamore Tree Project, I will consider how faith-inspired restorative practice measured against restorative principles can enrich restorative justice policy and practice development in the criminal justice system. While I write as a Christian theologian, I am convinced that the main principles explored here and the hermeneutic proposed for evaluating faith-based programmes will have strong resonances and practical relevance across diverse faith communities.

DOI: 10.4324/9781003276593-22

Marshall's definition of restorative justice emphasises the importance of the role of crime victims and community members: 'Restorative justice is a process whereby parties with a stake in a specific offence collectively resolve how to deal with the aftermath of the offence and its implications for the future' (Marshall, 1999, 5).

This holds offenders directly accountable to the people and communities they have violated. It seeks to restore the emotional and material losses of victims, and to provide for a range of opportunities for dialogue, negotiation, and problem-solving, which can lead to a greater sense of community safety, social harmony, and peace for all involved. It redefines crime, interpreting it not so much as breaking the law or offending against the state but as a wrong done to another person or persons. The resonances between restorative justice, defined this way, and contemporary atonement theories are very striking. Both regard justice as relational and, consequently. a participatory process; both understand the purpose of punishment as being restorative rather than retributive; and both understand the goal of justice to be reconciliation. These common concerns create a unique potential for mutual critical dialogue.

Atonement Theology Reappropriated

Rather than pursue an old line of argument which polarises debate between two classic models of atonement, penal (sometimes called 'substitutionary') and 'moral influence', I shall draw upon theologians who have constructively engaged with both these models in support of a restorative interpretation, first, Christopher Marshall's reappropriation of penal atonement theory, and second, Paul Fiddes' rehabilitation of the moral influence theory of medieval theologian Peter Abelard.

In his exploration of New Testament visions for crime and punishment, Marshall makes the case for a restorative emphasis in penal atonement thinking associated with the Pauline epistles. The understanding of atonement in question is, he argues, best understood not as penal substitution but as penal suffering:

> What Christ did was unique, yet Paul insists, we share in it, through our union with Christ in baptism. Humanity participating in Christ's death is such a strong idea in Paul's letters it makes representative over substitute the preferred translation for contemporary commentators.
>
> *Marshall, 2001, 61*

A main weakness in penal atonement theory is the place given to punishment and, specifically, the way terms such as wrath have been interpreted in the process of translation. Punishment or wrath clearly has a place in the picture, but it is not in Paul's theology vengeful or retributive. In Romans 1:24–28, Paul equates the wrath of God with the outworking of sin in the world. Sin or wrongdoing reaps its own punishment and produces considerable suffering to all concerned (Fiddes, 1989).

The wrath of God is 'the penalty of inherent consequences something intrinsic to the nature of the offense itself' (Fiddes 2000, 91). If the main weakness in penal atonement is a wrong emphasis on punishment, the flip side of this, according to Marshall, is a lack of focus on what is central in Paul's message, namely, forgiveness: 'God justifying sinful humanity is an act of forgiveness'. Paul's emphasis on forgiveness is what distances him from the negative associations of penal atonement theory with violent retribution (Mills, 2021, 57–74).

Marshall shows how legal models of atonement were reinterpreted by Paul from a restorative perspective; emphasis on forgiveness tempered the dominant place of punishment. The representative nature of Christ's sacrifice also moves the emphasis from spectating to participating in the work of the cross through sacrificial discipleship. This shift is important because at the heart of the criminal justice debate is long-standing and heated discussion about the place and meaning of punishment. In penal atonement theory, wrongdoing is taken seriously and there can be no room for cheap grace or pain-free reconciliation. At the same time, punishment serves the purposes of restoration and reconciliation, and is not an end in itself (Mills, 2021). This understanding of penal atonement points to forgiveness and reconciliation as the source and summit of atonement theology.

My second approach to atonement, known as 'moral influence', theory, is where the concern within the modern debate to see active participation on the part of humanity in the redemption and moral restoration of creation is most keenly addressed. The controlling idea is that the redeeming power of divine love, demonstrated through the death of Jesus, has the power to change the human condition:

> everyone is made more righteous, that is more loving towards God after the passion of Christ than he had been before because a realised gift incites greater love than that which is only hoped for. Therefore, our redemption through Christ's suffering is that supreme love in us which not only frees us from slavery to sin, but also acquires for us the true liberty of sons of God.
>
> *Fiddes, 1989, 143–4*

The necessity of the cross was not to satisfy God but to restore humanity. It is through our response of love to Christ that we are joined with him and benefit from his passion. Abelard's theory stemmed from his conviction that God's act of sacrificial love, the Crucifixion, was not to satisfy any prior conditions of honour or justice, but simply to satisfy his own nature of love: 'It is the essence of love to be ecstatic [...] creation and redemption are fitting for God as a logical outworking or "intrinsic necessity" of his nature' (Fiddes, 1989, 143). In turn, God's initiative of love kindles within hearts and minds an answering love (Fiddes, 1989, 143–4).

Abelard's model built upon on the Eastern concepts of deification and theosis, which may be captured in the words of Athanasius: 'The word became flesh that he might make man capable of Godhead' (Athanasius (ca. 360), II.59). The humanness of Christ in Abelard's writings underscores the reality of the incarnation and resonates with the restoration of humanity as described in Eastern theology through the notion of recapitulation. Christ becomes incarnate to retrace Adam's steps:

> but when He became incarnate, and was made man, He commenced afresh the long line of human beings, and furnished us, in a brief, comprehensive manner, with salvation; so that what we had lost in Adam-namely, to be according to the image and likeness of God – that we might recover in Christ Jesus.
>
> *Irenaeus, ca. 180, III. 18. I*

The Eastern fathers sought to emphasise that salvation is progressive. Humanity is not created perfect, but with the potential for perfection. Sin is about human frailty, and the work of atonement is about reorientation and transformation.

This model, even more than the penal model, offers a positive approach to human identity as beings-in-relationship. Christ's death invites participation and inspires a committed, forward-looking response. The emphasis is on healing and restoring the divine human relationship through costly sacrifice. The model has, according to Fiddes, a redemptive effect: 'love which is bestowed is at the same time the love which recreates' (Fiddes, 1989, 145). Drawing upon Abelard's letters, Fiddes identifies a deep psychological appreciation of the effect of the cross on the human mind. It does not simply evoke tears and inspire acts of love; it heals the diseased ego (Fiddes, 1989, 147).

Critical Dialogue: Atonement Theology and Restorative Principles

i. *First principle: 'radical participation'*

A common criticism of both atonement theology and restorative justice is that they each have a tendency, in different ways, to narrow down participation. In atonement theology, where objectivity has been emphasised over subjectivity, there has been a tendency to dehumanise and impersonalise the work of redemption. This is sometimes evident in presentations of the penal atonement model, which reduce redemption to a transaction in which humanity was a rather distant spectator. This impression runs counter to a key biblical theme in which humanity partners with God in recreating and redeeming the world, as in, for example, the Magnificat (Lk 1:46–65). Reappropriations of traditional atonement models, as discussed above, seek to redress the balance between the subject–object (divine–human) divide. They give new emphasis to a human response to and costly participation in the events of salvation. Atonement in contemporary theologies is not a distant event or a forensic transaction done for us, but a costly journey or an act of sacrificial love undertaken by God in Christ, into which humans are actively drawn.

At its best, atonement theology is participatory. Restorative justice, and particularly its principle of radical participation, acts as a timely reminder to the church that the journey of atonement is not and should not be treated as an individual, private matter. Atonement, understood as reconciliation between humans or with God, is costly. Genuine participatory encounters designed to redress wrong cannot be reduced to or replaced by quasi-magical or legal transactions. The challenge for restorative justice is that, whilst radical participation is recognised and understood as a demanding, costly, risk-taking exercise on the part of all those involved, this is not so clearly the mindset of traditional legal thinking and practice. The criminal justice system does not normally advocate a process in which the offender and victim hear the other and risk seeing their point of view; nor does it insist on the community being ready to hear all sides and to exercise moral persuasion.

Where restorative justice processes have been introduced into the criminal justice system, or function alongside it, there is always a risk that the principle of participation will be narrowed down or minimised. Regarding the principle of participation, the criminal judicial system is vulnerable on several points. First, the law is vulnerable because its precepts and processes risk leaving people on the sidelines as mere bystanders and spectators. Many victims affected by court proceedings are not engaged in the process in a way whereby they feel heard or believe that the damage done to them has been addressed. Second, the law is vulnerable when it comes to the principle of participation because community is an ambiguous and illusive notion in contemporary Western society. Whilst community in previous generations implied strong bonds between people based on kinship and shared faith values, this is not the case today.

The expectation that friends, family, and concerned citizens will participate in the process, and that they will accompany the offender for the long haul, is a huge assumption. If restorative justice is to realise its own goal of radical participation, it needs to turn to partners, including faith communities, where this expectation of committed participation can be nurtured and respected. The capacity of partners in civil society cannot, however, simply be assumed. The participation of faith organisations, like churches, in restorative justice processes is a realistic option, but as will be shown later, negotiating terms, and building the capacity for partnership need careful attention.

ii. Second principle: 'moral seriousness'

Where wrongdoing is not taken seriously, the accusation is rightly made that the criminal justice system or churches are not morally serious. In different ways, atonement models and restorative justice theory have found each other wanting in this regard. Concerning atonement theology, two criticisms need to be considered. First, it has been judged to be lacking in interpersonal moral seriousness because, in Christian practice, forgiveness and reconciliation frequently focus exclusively on the relationship between the individual and God. Scant attention has been given to the implications of harm and injury for relations between individuals and within communities. Restorative justice, under the plea of moral seriousness, challenges atonement thinking to give more regard to the human dimension of forgiveness and to recognise that righting wrong is not about covering up but uncovering the truth about a situation.

The human encounter between victim and offender in the company of the community is not secondary or peripheral to forgiveness and cannot risk being circumvented by means of a heavy dose of cheap grace. Sensitive to this charge, current atonement thinking, especially new readings of penal and moral influence theories, emphasises that reconciliation is two-dimensional. It involves a movement towards both God and neighbour, and it is a costly journey of forgiveness (Fiddes, 2016, 54–65). Atonement, both human and divine, requires vulnerability and risk-taking. Only by revisiting situations of harm and wrongdoing through encounters and meetings, and by listening to the other's story, can fresh awareness and understanding grow. The power of the Crucifixion is to transform relationships so that reconciliation becomes possible.

A second criticism of some atonement thinking is the very opposite of the view-point just discussed, namely, that it is excessively punitive. It is certainly true that there has been at times a strong punitive strand in atonement theology. However, a shift has taken place in the twentieth century towards a restorative stance. As the work of Hans Boersma and Christopher Marshall show, for example, there is growing recognition that, whilst the reality of crime and wrongdoing must be taken seriously, the judgement of God, properly understood, is not retributive but restorative in character. Punishment has a place in the righting of wrong, but the end goal of justice is not to inflict pain but to restore lives. Addressing harm done is a painful option for all concerned, but contemporary atonement theory suggests that the act of remembering rightly, that is, reliving the events which led to the injury, is worth the pain when this route of remembering opens the door to repentance, restitution, forgiveness, and reconciliation.

Concerns about how or whether atonement theology is weak or strong on punishment simply underline just how central to any discussion of criminal justice is the place and purpose of punishment within the sentencing system. This, more than anything, evokes the impression of moral seriousness. Having described how atonement theology can fall short of the principle of righting wrong in a morally serious way and needs the help of restorative justice to be held accountable, we may now turn to those areas where restorative justice practice falls short when measured against the principle of moral seriousness and needs the corrective insights of atonement thinking and practice.

First, to be morally serious, the process of righting wrong cannot be reduced or compressed into the minimum time available. Exploring and understanding a harmful situation takes time and effort. Restorative justice practitioners and policy makers are sometimes accused of minimising procedures by cutting out essential steps or lessening requirements to save on budgets or reach results quickly. Second, many people are the victims of structural injustice, and the damage done to them – physical, psychological, and economic – often lies outside of the scope of criminal law. Atonement theory confronts a world in which systems and powers generate feelings of hopelessness and powerlessness in people. The interest and scope of some of the oldest atonement language looks to overcome violence, which is systemic and cosmic, as well as to reconcile relations on the interpersonal level, whilst contemporary approaches have emphasised structural transformation. Mark Heim's Girardian focus on the cross as 'saved from sacrifice' (Heim, 2006, 329), and the presentation of the cross by liberation theologians as Christ's identification with the dispossessed and marginalised, both directly target structural and systemic wrongdoing.

By contrast, restorative justice within the UK criminal justice system is almost exclusively applied to reconciliation on an interpersonal level. It focuses on righting wrongs in the community at an individual level, between victim and offender. Its capacity, meanwhile, to address systemic violence and injustice in the community is largely untested. There are high-profile examples on the international level, where systemic violence and human rights abuse have been addressed through the courts using restorative justice measures, but this has not been replicated in local situations where structural crime and wrongdoing is evident. If, as Michael Taylor has argued, restorative justice cannot transform society at large, then it risks returning victims and offenders into situations of harm and failing to reduce recidivism or accomplish long-term results (Taylor, 2021a, 91–108).

iii. Third principle: 'reintegration'

Reintegration of victims and offenders back into the community is central to the restorative process. The context in which reintegration occurs is the community, and both restorative justice and atonement theology recognise the importance of community for restoring and maintaining just relationships (Blyth, 2021). However, their understandings and use of the term diverge, with significant implications for the treatment of members seeking reintegration.

Within restorative justice theory and practice there is, according to Paul McCold, a lack of agreement about what makes for community. He offers a twofold definition. First, micro-community includes individual communities of care, comprising victims, offenders, and their respective friends and families. Typically, the process followed would be mediation and family conferencing practices, and the participants themselves decide collectively what needs to be done. The primary goal is to repair the harm caused to individuals by the offending behaviour. Second is macro-communities, in which the primary objective is more widely defined as repairing the effect of crime in the victimised community, and limiting the potential threat posed to society by the offender's future behaviour (McCold, 2004, 155–60). The process removes magistrates and legal professionals, favouring citizens and representatives of the wider community dealing with the offender. It does not necessarily include victims or communities of care. The focus of the macro-community is typically more on outcomes than process. Unfortunately, the conflicting assumptions over the roles of these two types of communities mean that restorative justice advocates are divided in their conception of community. What is lacking is a holistic or unifying narrative.

The church, whilst complex and flawed, nevertheless understands itself to be a community whose gift and calling, patterned on the journey of forgiveness, is to embody the principles, values, and practices of restorative justice. Christians may advocate different models of community (as in different confessions or denominations), but the narrative they share is their unifying impetus. The ecclesial community is an organic body of people drawn together by shared values; it is universal and local; dispersed and gathered; shaped by a story which is past, present, and future. Such a claim for the church needs to be set in context. Modesty is needed in a Western secular culture where the church is a declining player. Nevertheless, local Christian communities, shaped by the unifying narrative of the atonement, have the potential to participate in restorative processes. Building their capacity and competence is a challenge which they need to embrace.

The church also understands that in the context of community, conflict is natural. The challenge is to manage conflict and turn it to good effect. By seeking to nurture kingdom values such as mercy, truth, justice, and peace amongst all people, the ecclesial community takes the vision of reconciliation and reintegration seriously. It is committed to safeguarding these values from one generation to the next. John Paul Lederach has written about and facilitated conflict transformation over the last 30 years and in *The Journey towards Reconciliation* he offers practical guidelines for local Christian communities using the biblical model of Matthew 18 (Lederach, 1999).

The church understands community in countercultural terms, so whilst restorative justice may not always enjoy political support, it can count on the support of the church, whose mission is to be an instrument of healing, restoration, and reconciliation. Whilst no longer politically powerful, it can make its voice heard by continuing to bear witness to restorative values in atonement thinking and provide a community context for reintegration. There is a strong case for an alliance between churches and restorative justice partners, based upon their common recognition of the need for restorative values to be nurtured and practiced in the context of community. The restorative justice movement arguably needs the church not only to help nurture and promote its values in wider society but in addition, needs and benefits from the church as a critical ally, helping to keep policymakers and practitioners alert to the dangers of trying to work too quickly and thus superficially. Values are not nurtured overnight; offenders are not transformed in an instant and victims cannot just produce forgiveness on demand. A community that journeys consistently and persistently with damaged people is vital to the success of restorative processes.

The alliance between restorative justice and the church is more than a social construct, however. That they have need of each other is certain, but that they essentially belong together, is a deeper and more substantive claim. Restorative justice is more than an effective democratic process and laudable system of values. It is, according to Marshall,

> a manifestation of something deeper than that – something that explains its power and cross-cultural applicability. It is a practice that reveals the inherent nature of the universe. It is a phenomenon that makes visible the way reality is, the way God has made human beings and under the wider moral order to function.
>
> *Marshall, 2002, 85*

Drawing on the New Testament claims that in Jesus we see God and that through the crucified and risen Christ the ultimate meaning and the destiny of all created reality is found, Marshall concludes that 'the central principle of creation is not naked power or control or order – but love: valuable, passionate, forgiving, reconciling, self-giving, triumphant love' (Marshall, 2002, 86). To claim that restorative justice reflects a transcendent order, is not new. Classical retributive justice also claimed a metaphysical basis whereby the moral universe operates on the principle of 'just deserts'. What is different is that Marshall's claim is not based on the perfect balance of deed and desert, but on redeeming, restoring interpersonal love. Restorative justice reflects the nature of the God we meet on the cross and is charged with the healing, restoring power of love.

Faith-Inspired Restorative Justice

Whilst reflecting upon and drawing lessons from faith-based restorative work, I do not want to overclaim for faith communities. I need first to acknowledge that, while faith can and does provide inspiration and motivation for some professionals and volunteers, many people who engage in restorative justice do not hold religious beliefs. Some contend that terms like 'restoration', 'reconciliation', and more controversially 'forgiveness', may have strong resonances in religious belief systems, but no faith has a monopoly on these concepts. Lode Walgrave makes this point forcefully:

> It is said that western ethical beliefs are rooted into Judeo-Christian traditions. Several texts on restorative justice indeed refer to Christianism as an inspiration for this option (Allard & Northey, 2001; Noakes-Duncan, 2017). Several restorative justice advocates explicitly refer to their Christian beliefs as a ground for their endeavour (Van Ness & Heetderks Strong, 2006, XI). While religion may be an inspiration for those who believe, claiming restorative justice as a kind of 'justice of God' seems to be out of proportion. As if disbelievers could not genuinely understand the essentials of restorative justice (Oudshoorn, 2013). Western civilisation may be deeply rooted into Christian culture and tradition, but it is not evident that this tradition really is fundamental for restorative justice. Also, other religions and great spiritual traditions, such as Buddhism, Confucianism, Hinduism, Islam, Judaism, or indigenous spiritualism, have produced texts and recommendations promoting virtues and values which are congruent with restorative justice values

> and virtues (Claessen, 2016), such as respect, compassion with the weaker, mercy, apology and forgiveness, social peace, and harmony.
>
> *Walgrave, 2021*

There is merit in Walgrave's argument, for certainly restorative justice thrives without religious belief. Yet, faith is not irrelevant when it inspires and motivates reform activists across the world. In a study of forgiveness as a restorative value, Michael Taylor offers a related observation:

> When it comes to the meaning of forgiveness, Christians appear to have nothing particularly new or different to say [...] What is distinctive is not the concept of forgiveness, or even the sources from which it is derived, but the motivation for practising it and advocating its practice by others, rooted as it is in faith in a forgiving God and one's own discipleship. (Taylor, 2021b, 54)

In this vein, evidence-based studies to which I will refer highlight that faith organisations can be a positive force in restorative justice.

In 1995, Prison Fellowship International gathered from around the world staff and volunteers with restorative justice expertise to develop a victim awareness programme that Prison Fellowship ministries could use. Daniel Van Ness coordinated the development of the programme. In 1996, a manual was published and distributed, including the six teaching sessions for the delivery of the Sycamore Tree Programme. In spring 1998, Prison Fellowship USA expanded the programme and piloted it. Shortly after this, Prison Fellowship New Zealand piloted the programme and then, in December 1998, Prison Fellowship England and Wales adapted, shortened, and piloted the programme at Her Majesty's Prison 'The Mount'. The Sycamore Tree Programme is described as a victim awareness programme which teaches the principles and application of restorative justice. The programme is offered to all regardless of faith, gender, or age, and is delivered by trained Prison Fellowship staff and volunteers. The programme consists of approximately 15 hours of structured discussion and activities and seeks to enable participants to: (1) understand the wider impact of their criminal behaviour and accept a greater level of personal responsibility; (2) identify with a victim's experience of crime and the need for victim/offender forgiveness and reconciliation; (3) learn about the process of restorative justice and how offenders, victims, and the wider community can take part; (4) plan steps to reduce offending behaviour whilst still in prison. Sycamore Tree courses are run in over 50 prisons within the UK. These prisons range from high-security to open detention centres. The participants in the courses have committed a wide range of crimes which are not known to the volunteers leading the courses. The course consists of six weekly sessions designed to improve desistance by changing attitudes that are known to be conducive to offending (Feasey & Williams, 2009).

A story-telling technique is used to raise awareness in offenders about their victims and to help them be honest with themselves about their crime. It is based around the biblical story of Zacchaeus ('Zach'), which keeps the conversation focused and rooted in restorative values and principles. As the story unfolds, words and images of confession, repentance, forgiveness, restitution, reparation, and reconciliation open in conversation amongst the offenders. They are encouraged to adapt and use these words and images freely to apply them to their own story. At the midpoint in the course, a surrogate victim comes into the prison to tell their story, and this opens a further space for the offenders to reflect on the impact of their own crime. At the end of the programme, prisoners are given the opportunity to make a symbolic act of restitution, taking the first step towards making amends for their past behaviour. Impact evaluation studies in 2004 and 2009 show many positive outcomes which this programme has achieved:

> The evidence indicates that the Sycamore Tree programme appears to have contributed towards a shift in how learners view their offence and wider impact of their actions, including greater empathy for their victims. At the same time, the findings reveal a number of other outcomes for learners engaged with the Programme. These include improvements in well-being and self-forgiveness, attitudinal and behavioural changes, improved relationships, and improved engagement with prison activities. Although not discussed explicitly by learners, these outcomes may be viewed as making a positive contribution towards an individual's pathway to desistance.
>
> *Feasey & Williams, 2009*

In 2010, a research study I undertook on 'the response of local Christian communities to crime and wrongdoing' included five case studies: three local congregations and two parachurch projects (street pastors and the Prison Fellowship Sycamore Tree Project). My objective was to evaluate in each case study the restorative impact of programmes being initiated. To do this, data gathered through interviews and programme observation was analysed using a hermeneutical lens comprising the three principles of restorative justice outlined in this chapter: radical participation, moral seriousness, and reintegration. In each case study the restorative impact of the responses to crime and wrongdoing was measured along two axes: personal–social, and indirect–direct. The conclusion was that, while many of the programmes adhered to one or more of the restorative principles, none fully expressed all three.

In the case study with the Prison Fellowship Sycamore Tree Project facilitators, the interviews were emotionally charged. The passion and commitment of the volunteers was evident and from their descriptions, the power of the programme to influence prisoners in a prosocial way was palpable. The positive impact of the programme has also been well documented in independent research studies (Feasey & Williams, 2009). My own study broadly agrees with the positive evaluation undertaken by other studies, but using the restorative hermeneutic as my interpretative tool, some concerns and critical questions emerged about capacity and competence. Where and how might the Sycamore Tree Programme become more restorative for the people involved and be a channel for advocating restorative approaches more widely in the prison system? The main concerns can be summarised as follows:

First, the Sycamore tree project does not fully conform to the first principle (radical participation) because it does not bring offenders face to face with their victim, and the community representation is quite limited, since it does not include family or significant others in the offender's life. Second, adherence to the second principle is partial. Moral seriousness depends greatly on the unique dynamic that emerges when offender and victim enter each other's stories. It is through mutual exchange that empathy forgiveness and reconciliation emerge, and this can only happen in a limited way when the actual victim is absent. The obvious next step is for offenders to be helped to reach out to their victims and to wider circles of family and community affected by their crime. Where offenders request this, it deserves priority attention and the appropriate investment of time and energy from prison and probation staff to make this happen. There is, to date, little evidence of this happening. Finally, with respect to reintegration, the programme nurtures a positive forward-looking perspective for offenders. The story of Zach entertains the possibility of new beginnings. However, there was a keen awareness amongst volunteers of the need for more to be done and poor provision for the reintegration of offenders was a major source of their criticism (Blyth, 2012, 185 and 233). They regarded this lack as potentially undermining the good done in this and other courses that seek to prepare the offender for life in mainstream society (Blyth, 2012, 191 and 233).

Conclusion

I have argued that the shift in theological discourse from retribution and punishment to restoration and reconciliation provides a clear rationale and support for congregations and faith-based organisations investing their time and energy in restorative justice work. The positive potential of faith communities to advocate for and practice restorative programmes with victims and offenders is well evidenced, but they face two interrelated challenges if their potential is to be realised. First, they must more critically reflect on the quality and impact of their restorative programmes. This is true even for flagship programmes like the Sycamore Tree Project. The restorative hermeneutic based on the core principles of restorative justice outlined in this chapter is one means by which they can do this.

Second, and perhaps more contentiously, faith-based organisations and actors need to reflect more critically on the root causes of crime and wrongdoing and on the reasons for the systemic failure of justice systems. Their best restorative efforts will only ever have partial impact if systemic problems that cause or exacerbate criminal behaviour remain unchallenged or unchanged. Faith-based organisations urgently need to 'up their game' and show more political nerve. Hesitating to speak out for fear of losing funding or favour is not an option. Creative partnership with other actors in the restorative justice movement is the way they can meaningfully advocate for radical and long-lasting change in the criminal justice system.

The tough challenge facing the whole restorative justice movement is to make the case for mainstreaming restorative justice. Embedding its values and practices right across the criminal justice system requires sustained and mutual critical dialogue between restorative justice actors and the architects of justice systems. To this end, all stakeholders – governments, lawyers, prison authorities, probation services, and the full range of restorative actors and agencies, including faith communities – need to work together as critical allies.

References

Athanasius (ca. 360). *Four Discourses against the Arians, II. 59.* Retrieved from: www.newadvent.org/fathers/28162.htm

Blyth, M. N. (2012). *Towards a Restorative Hermeneutic: Local Christian Communities responding to Crime and Wrongdoing* [Unpublished doctoral dissertation]. Birmingham University, UK.

Blyth, M. N., Mills, M. J., & Taylor, M. H. (Eds.) (2021). *Forgiveness and Restorative Justice: Perspectives from Christian Theology.* Palgrave Macmillan.

Feasey, S., & Williams, P. (2009). *Crime Pics II: An Evaluation of the Sycamore Tree Programme TP.* Sheffield Hallam University in partnership with Manchester Metropolitan University.

Fiddes, P. S. (1989). *Past Event and Present Salvation: The Christian Idea of Atonement.* Darton, Longman & Todd.

Fiddes, P.S. (2016). Restorative Justice and the Theological Dynamic of Forgiveness. *Oxford Journal of Law and Religion, 5*(1), 54–65.

Forrester, D. (2012). *Christian Justice and Public Policy.* Cambridge University Press.

Gorringe, T. J. (1996). *God's Just Vengeance.* Cambridge University Press.

Heim, S. M. (2006). *Saved from Sacrifice: A Theology of the Cross.* Wm B. Eerdmans.

Irenaeus (ca. 180). *Against Heresies.* Retrieved from: www.earlychristianwritings.com/text/irenaeus-book3.html

Jenkins, D. (1980). Possible theological responses to apparent criminological confusion. In Bottoms, A.E., & Preston, R.H. (Eds.), *The Coming Penal Crisis, 173-189.* Scottish Academic Press.

Lederach, J. P. (1999). *The Journey towards Reconciliation.* Herald Press.

Marshall, C. D. (2001). *Beyond Retribution: A New Testament Vision for Justice, Crime and Punishment.* Wm B. Eerdmans.

Marshall, C. D. (2002). Grounding Justice in Reality: Theological Reflections on overcoming Violence in the Criminal Justice System. In Roberts J. (Ed.), *Overcoming Violence in New Zealand, 66-73.* Phillip Garside Publishers.

Marshall, T. F. (1999). *Restorative Justice: An Overview.* UK Home Office.

McCold, P. (2004). What Is the Role of the Community in restorative Justice Theory and Practice? In Zehr, H., & Toews, B. (Eds.), *Critical Issues in Restorative Justice, 155-172.* Lynne Rienner Publishers.

Mills, M. J. (2021). Just Enough to Be Satisfied. In Blyth, M. N., Mills, M. J., & Taylor, M. H. (Eds.), *Forgiveness and Restorative Justice: Perspectives from Christian Theology, 57-74.* Palgrave Macmillan.

Sagovsky, N. (2008). *Christian Tradition and the Practice of Justice.* (SPCK).

Taylor, M. H. (2021a). Restorative Justice and Social Justice. In Blyth, M. N., Mills, M. J., & Taylor, M. H. (Eds.), *Forgiveness and Restorative Justice: Perspectives from Christian Theology, 91-108.* Palgrave Macmillan.

Taylor, M. H. (2021b). The Role and Meaning of Forgiveness. In Blyth, M. N., Mills, M. J., & Taylor, M. H. (Eds.), *Forgiveness and Restorative Justice: Perspectives from Christian Theology, 39-55.* Palgrave Macmillan.

Walgrave, L. (2021). *In Search of the Social-Ethical Foundation of Restorative Justice and its Social Relevance.* Unpublished paper presented at a UK-China symposium on Restorative Justice Philosophy and Practice, Oxford UK.

20

CHRISTIANITY AND DESISTANCE

Exploring Ex-prisoners' Journeys in New Faith

Alex Beaumont

Introduction

Desistance theory has long had clear theological links with religious sensibilities such as new beginnings, forgiveness, repentance and redemption (Skotnicki, 2019). The whole notion of identity change or even transformation has similar connotations to being 'born again' – as with Christianity – but when it comes to theorizing and researching the topic in relation to desistance and the conversion process *itself*, there has been a distinct lack of engagement. For the few who have ventured into this topic of faith, conversion and desistance, most have been prison-based projects (for example, Giordano et al., 2008; Hallett and Johnson, 2015; Johnson, Larson, and Pitts, 1997).

One of the most significant studies on conversions and prisoners comes from Maruna, Wilson, and Curran (2006), which argued that 'jailhouse' conversion narratives acted as a means of integrating 'disparate and shameful life events into a coherent, empowering whole, renew[ing] prisoners' sense of their own personal biography, and provid[ing] them with hope and a vision for the future' (p.180) – in sum, conversions acted as means of 'shame management' and coping strategies within the prison walls. This current research takes issue with such perspectives on narrative methods, and especially the notion of narrative rescripting (Maruna, 2001; Maruna et al., 2006), firstly, by taking such constructed narratives at face value (Hollway and Jefferson, 2000), and secondly, in presenting self-narratives purely as *objects* of data, as any transcendental elements of human subjectivity and experience are stripped away from the analysis, or left as a footnote, with the word 'emotion' left to seemingly encapsulate what is being unacknowledged.

Laws (2020) provides an insightful challenge to such overt focus upon the 'reflexive self'. For Laws, studying *the self* in such isolation is reductive to the point that understanding is configured by the self as the 'ego' (who we think we are),

DOI: 10.4324/9781003276593-23

which is to the detriment of acknowledging the *immediacy* of direct experience as typically preceding narrative expression. Laws (2020) asks us to look beyond the dualism set within reflexive performativity of action and self-narrative, but overall, falls short of being able to provide the tools through which to proceed down that pathway. At one point, Laws acknowledges Jacques Lacan's concept of *the Real*, in relation to the unknowable of the unconscious that drives us – as that which is 'beyond the domain of speech' – but this is more of a nod towards Lacan rather than something he chooses to enter into; something that this research and its theoretical framework will seek to supplement.

Method

This research used the free association narrative interview method (FANIM) (Hollway and Jefferson, 2000) due to its basis in psychoanalytic principles and its focus on the *defended subject*. The method requires some degree of 'invisibility' in the process of data collection, whereby participants are encouraged to speak freely in response to such questions as 'can you tell me about...?', and the interviewer must refrain from asking immediate follow-up questions. In this sense, the respondents were asked to openly discuss their lives starting with their childhood. It was not until the second interview where the respondents were asked to expand in more detail on specific areas. This is especially important given how commonplace it is for new converts to give their Testimony as an important rite of passage into the Christian community. Between two and three interviews were conducted per participant, accruing over 35 hours of transcripts in total across the entire sample, wherein a deductive/concept-driven approach was then used to code and then thematically analyse the data.

The sample consisted of 11 participants (10 male, 1 female) from nearly all corners of the United Kingdom, all of whom claimed to have not reoffended since their last sentence (not including occasional illicit drug consumption). Ages ranged between 35 and 60 years old, and length of desistance ranged between 20 years and 18 months at the time of interviewing (2020–21). Of the 11, three (3) were repeatedly imprisoned for shoplifting and robbery offences, associated with their chronic heroin addiction; four (4) were organised criminals; one (1) was convicted for drug smuggling; one (1) was convicted for arson; and two (2) were both convicted for manslaughter and attempted murder.

Findings

The following findings are presented under three major themes: *1. Trauma and Lack, 2. Event, and 3. Nurturing the Event* – all of which are underpinned with Lacanian psychoanalytic subthemes – the *big Other, Fantasy* and *Jouissance*. The findings centre on how (in the case of this research) the Christian conversion Event offers a 'circuit-breaker' through which to circumvent subjectivity, and the anxiety-inducing symbolic structures of meaning built throughout the life course; however such new identities are vulnerable without both organisational and faith community nurture and support.

1 Trauma and Lack

Winlow and Hall (2009, p.294) identify the damning impact trauma can have on the individual, and future behaviour, whereby 'emotionally charged images feed back into the very nature of identity and can become a crucial context for future social behaviour'. In order to move beyond the sense of lack (referred to as the 'lost object') experienced following traumatic events in the life course, defence mechanisms are unconsciously adopted, confining the subject within a state of melancholia; however, the melancholic subject can never truly achieve such resolution. Slavoj Žižek's (2000) clarification of the dichotomy between the melancholic and the mourning subject affirms that while the melancholic subject remains faithful to the lost object, refusing to renounce his or her attachment to it, 'mourning is a kind of betrayal, the second killing of the (lost) object' (p.658). The melancholic subject is unable to accept the loss experienced as a result of the trauma and remains attached to the lost object, whether conscious or unconscious, and will be unable to move beyond such trauma until he/she confronts it fully.

Marcus (aged 41), had suffered numerous traumatic events in his childhood, with an alcoholic father (ex-military) who struggled with schizophrenia, and with an absent mother, who had left very early in his life. Marcus had to grow up quickly, and he took control of the house to look after his younger siblings due to his father's general inability. However, at the age of 11, he was sexually abused by his uncle, at a family event, and from thereon, his life seemed to spiral, spending the remainder of his childhood and adolescence in and out of the care system, and eventually the criminal justice system. Whilst already regularly experimenting in other drugs, at the age of 18 he took heroin for the first time:

> Marcus: 'It [heroin] just worked […] It just worked for that … For so long it worked, it worked for a long time actually, quite a period, a couple of years where it was … I don't like saying, but it was "manageable", you know I hadn't realised that what, what it would eventually lead to, I didn't see that at all, it was just, it worked, I got rid of all the [uncle/abuse] stuff, all of my dad stuff, all of my mums stuff, you know … [her] abandoning my brother and sister was a big thing for me as well you know, erm … But you know … heroin worked as I tried everything pretty much by 18'.

The abuse by his uncle really sets the backbone to Marcus's self-narrative, which he was fully aware of, throughout his 20 years of addiction to drugs, concerning the reason he was in his situation. At no time during the three interviews with him did he provide 'condemnation scripts' (Maruna, 2001), and he was fully aware of the damage he was doing to himself.

Having a self-awareness of one's issues and the problems and damage they are causing to oneself, and others, is like a form of self-harm, or in Lacanian terms, *jouissance*, an innate drive to self-sabotage and annihilation through enjoyment. Here, we use the psychoanalytic term *fundamental fantasy* to explain this further, which is the image/fantasy of the world built upon our own subjective constructions; it is rigid and cannot be easily altered, and is (to some extent) something knowable to the subject. For example, as argued by Laurita (2010), a drug addict can be clearly aware of the relationship that exists between their drug use (one specific example of *jouissance* – pleasure and self-annihilation) and an event/person, which may have caused it; therefore, the drug addict is thus aware of their fundamental fantasy (p.130). This is one tangible example among many that we can use, relating to criminogenic behaviours and *jouissance* (see Winlow and Hall (2009) for similar discussions on male violence).

Where psychotherapy seeks to facilitate the resolution of such melancholia through symbolic death and rebirth of the ego, we can quite easily frame this psychodynamic process in the context of Christianity and conversion within the desisting offender, even more so when considering the influence trauma has to play in its role. As was the case with many of the other participants, Marcus had received numerous forms of treatment, and prior to his conversion, he had inadvertently agreed to go on an Alpha[1] Course at his local community church, six months after his final prison sentence:

> Marcus: 'So getting into treatment, like I said, I had done the "head knowledge", I'd done the CARAT course in prison [counselling, Assessment, Referral, Advice and Throughcare], whatever they call it these days. So I knew, I knew about recovery and that, and what's involved and what to do, and what not to do. When I got into treatment this time and then Alpha, Alpha did it for me, the one session I remember vividly was about Jesus dying on the cross for us all, when we're all sinners. So yeah [...] That resonated with me that one'.

Similarly, Simon (aged 48), who had spent ten years in prison on drug smuggling charges, had gone through numerous treatment and therapy programmes during his sentence, which had helped him so much to the extent that he later became an addiction counsellor. He described the therapy he had, especially the AA 12-Step programme, which left him very 'raw' inside:

> Simon: 'Somebody in the prison asked me to go on an Alpha course [...] if I would I do the Alpha course in the prison, and I refused at the time because I was like "no no no no [...] I got into the whole recovery 12-step programme" and of course, that was, that was the God I had, the God of my understanding, and I was going through the 12-steps [...] It really helped me to unravel all that was that had been going on over the years, you know? All the confusion, all the pain, all the hurt [...]'.

Whilst both Marcus's and Simon's life stories and their conversion experiences differ considerably, both discussed how important therapy was in helping them to understand their take on the world and themselves. As discussed earlier, our view of the world is unique to each one of us, which is why we refer to it as *fantasy*, and it is something therapy aims to unravel. But when we are talking fantasy, we are not using it in the sense of 'make believe', as Žižek explains:

> fantasy does not mean that, when I desire a strawberry cake and cannot get it in reality, I fantasize about eating it; the problem is rather, how do I know that I desire a strawberry cake in the first place? This is what fantasy tells me.
>
> *2014, p.26*

Understanding their fantasy construction was clearly beneficial for Marcus and Simon, but it did nothing to resolve the lack and emptiness they felt inside – *something* else was needed; and that something had to come externally.

Lacan and the Big Other

In a marked shift in direction from the Freudian psychosexual interpretation of human subjectivity and psychic development, for Lacan, the reality of human beings is constituted by three intertangled levels: the *Symbolic*, the *Imaginary* and the *Real*. Contrary to Freud's idea that the unconscious is the home of irrational drives (the id), in opposition to the rational conscious self (the ego), and one that must be tamed by the superego, for Lacan, the unconscious is where a traumatic truth speaks out (Žižek, 2000). At its core is a void, an emptiness, devoid of any signification: this is the Lacanian *Real*. Where Freud's *Oedipus complex* marks the cornerstone of the subjectivization process, following its successful resolution, for Lacan, it is our alienation into language itself that marks this event at the moment we are able to assign a name, or recognise symbols as signifying something – a stage he called *Name-of-the-Father* (Lacan, 1988). Our new knowledge of this symbolic system is transformative in that we begin developing our sense of coherence and meaning of the world around us. Before our subjectivity arises from this state, we are still bound within a realm of the *Imaginary* – a stage of primary narcissism that remains. Thereafter, we become 'divided' and 'intersubjective', where we are only able to see ourselves through others – by what we think the *other* wants from us – a process Lacan named the *Mirror Stage*.

Once the laws provided by the symbolic take hold (for Lacan, this is swift and transformative), the world opens up and begins providing meaning, allowing us to start developing a coherent sense of ourselves – it therefore becomes the job of the symbolic, thereafter, to safeguard the imaginary from returning to the *real*, and risk losing signification. In order for the symbolic order to remain coherent, and everyday reality comprehensible, there must be high levels of symbolic efficiency and agreement upon what the signifiers of the symbolic order actually signify (Homer and Nelson, 2005). The *big Other* frames our collectively shared knowledge of the world as a *fundamental logic*, intersecting between our psyche, culture and our socio-economic systems, but also as something deeply personal and felt individually; it is not only language and law, but it can be also reified into a single agent: God, or a Cause (i.e. freedom, communism, nationalism, climate change (Žižek, 2006, p.9)). Essentially, it is the guiding force within the Symbolic that acts like a yardstick that can be used to measure oneself (similar to the superego), and such is the implication here that the external–internal symbolic order speaks and thinks for us through the big Other.

2 Event

One of the aims of this chapter now is to demonstrate how we might reframe our current notions of identity change, cognitive transformation and even 'turning points', as used in desistance theory and research via the philosophical concept of 'Event'. For both Alain Badiou (2007) and Žižek (2014), an Event refers to specific moments in the lives of individuals that have the potential to change everything. However, both their conceptions differ quite significantly – for Badiou, an event is determined by the consequences of its aftermath (framing); whereas, for Žižek, the event compels us to revaluate our constructions of reality itself! (reframing). These are subjective experiences in the sense that one event is not necessarily relative to another person's view of the same event, but nevertheless it creates a 'cut' or rupture in the way we view the world. The majority of the conversion experiences found within the sample certainly mirrored this sentiment, with the more overtly transformative experiences adhering to the Žižekian event (or what he refers to as 'act'), and the less emotive, yet still transformative, being more aligned to Badiou's – rather mechanical and structured account – something more akin to standard narrative rescripting and redemption sequences (Maruna, 2001).

Of the 11 participants, eight had a primary conversion 'event' while inside prison – five became Christians as a result, lasting for the remainder of their sentence; one drifted away from her faith after a few months, and two were released from prison very soon afterwards. Secondly, two of the 11 participants had their primary conversion outside of prison, at some point following their final sentence. And finally, there was one (outlier) participant who had been a devout evangelical Christian since his primary conversion event, at age 18, but drifted away later in life, only to end up in prison for the first time, where he fully reconnected with his faith again – a self-reported 'prodigal son'.

The Badiouian Event can be illustrated in one of the prison converts, Michael (aged 54), who described himself as always having had 'some sense of wonder about the world and the universe' and that there must be some higher power, but he had no pre-emptive desire to convert – for him it was sudden and unexpected.

> Michael: 'So, I was in my cell at night time and a Nigerian came into my cell, he just got locked up and he just came in, and he was supposedly a Christian, so he came in and he look and he see a bible on my bed, you know, I'm on the

> top bunk by myself, and he comes in and he presume and he goes "I'm glad to be in a cell with another Christian", so that's what he said because in his head he thought I was a Christian [...] and that was my Damascus Road, like the apostle Paul in the Bible [...] I jumped off the top of my bunk bed and stood on the floor and said "now I believe in Jesus Christ!!" and I know when I come out of prison I know I'm going to be going to church – that was my moment of salvation [...]'.

Michael's event, as with every one of the respondents, marked a sudden change from spiritual 'belief' to 'knowledge'. Here, he swiftly sees his direct external–internal connection to the symbolic made clear through the big Other. Across all three of his interviews, he consistently refers to his life and his work (in Christian youth outreach) as not through his own strengths, but through God and Jesus Christ:

> Michael: 'but for me God isn't a crutch – he is real, I know because he's taken me from somewhere [...] I know the truth of what God's Word says [...] It's not of my own strength – He has given me gifts and he's given me skills and abilities that I can use as best I can in order to benefit myself and benefit other people and benefit you know, society at large, and ultimately as I'm a person of faith, to glorify God [...] because I want it all to point back to him and say all of this that I have comes from him"

There is a distinct difference for the Žižekian event, as, unlike Badiou, there is a pre-emptive evental promise which necessitates an evental subjectivization. Here, one's fantasy cannot suddenly be halted, set aside and left, but rather one must shatter its foundations by submitting to it, accepting it and thereby *traversing* it – Žižek (2014: 28).

To demonstrate this, there is the case of Liam (aged 38), who had successfully desisted for 14 years. He had been a prolifically violent man, who had built his reputation on fear for the purposes of being respected, something he said he was always aware of. His narrative starts at a point in his childhood where he was being bullied for his appearance during school, humiliated by his teachers, and having a very dysfunctional early start to life in his family. He later waged war on authorities and police, especially in the prison system, rising to 'top boy' in the many prisons he was transferred around the country. He had built up such an excess of masks that there was no longer any 'diamond in the rough' to be found, that is, until he happened upon an Alpha course whilst in prison, which later led on to his conversion event.

> Liam: 'I just remember him [chaplain] saying, "right, I'm gonna pray and then you pray". And he started to pray in the tongues, they say praying in tongues, don't they [...] I just remember feeling proper uncomfortable, and thinking "what's he doing, man?" and "what's that?" [...] And what happened was, he said "pray", and I said "what do I do? How do you pray, what do I do?" He said

"just, from your heart, just pray", and I found myself saying "God [...] I hate who I am, I hate who I've become, come into my life [...]"'.

As Liam approached his 'moment of truth', he did what he had never done in front of anyone before – what scared him the most – and faced his traumatic encounter with the *real*, facing up to what he had avoided his whole life:

Liam: 'So I'm trying to hold the feeling of crying in, telling myself "do NOT cry in a max security prison", and I'm trying to hold it in, and so I'm holding it and holding it, and the more I'm trying not to cry, the more it was feeling like I was gonna cry. Then it started rising up a bit more, rising up a bit more, rising up, this feeling, this energy feeling, then it just shot [!] [...] felt like it shot out my body, and I just uncontrollably sobbed and sobbed and sobbed, and just cried my eyes out"'.

His conversion is certainly at the far end of the continuum, clearly illustrating the shattering experience in no uncertain terms, how someone is able to traverse the fundamental fantasy of their own subjectivity. As is the case in both Badiouian and Žižekian notions of event, to *be* one, it must be named. For Michael, it was a new prison cellmate giving it a name, 'Christian', that became swiftly inscribed into his symbolic world, framing it as an event that would reshape the rest of his life. In the Christian sense of becoming 'born again', and in a Lacanian sense – a resubjectivization event that reinstates the *Name-of-the-Father*. The same goes for Liam's reframing event:

Liam: 'And then he [chaplain] said to me, he said "that's the Holy Spirit" [...] which I'd [....] I just cried and cried. Do you know what, it was weird, cos I knew [...] it was like I knew, it was like [...] I dunno if you've heard this sort of thing before, but I've been alive all my life, but it was if I hadn't, and I was new. And I just knew God was real, I just *knew* [!] and I was just like "God is real, God is actually real"'.

Whilst Liam's outpouring of emotion followed a 'defiant act' of going against his number one rule to never show weakness, especially to a system he had waged war against – such was his enjoyment and satisfaction (*jouissance*) of suffering at the hands of prison guards and spending extended periods of time in segregation; alongside maintaining his well-established reputation of fear, both inside and outside the prison walls – it was the chaplain's naming and confirmation of the Event that made it so. For Žižek (2010), such an *event* is political in itself, as it presents its own revolutionary capacity through which to counter late capitalism's neoliberalist entrapment and subjugation of the ego. One must commit to this, defying the logic of the fantasy, and sublimating enjoyment (*jouissance*) elsewhere, in that it may defy the predetermined a priori coordinates that can themselves be absorbed into everyday living and view of reality. Through the support and love provided through the new Christian community (Holy Spirit), Liam entered into at that moment, the law of the new symbolic/big Other. Whilst Badiou explicitly centres the Event on it being named as so, fidelity to its rupture and significance must be upheld at all time (McGowan, 2010); however, as this chapter will now move on to, many of the participants described falling away from their new faith, whilst never denying the symbolic death and rebirth of the original (primary) conversion Event.

3 Nurturing the Event

Overall, the research findings revealed the extent and impact that individuals working in church prison ministry, community chaplaincies and the larger faith-based organisations all have on supporting prison leavers. Of the 11 participants, five fell away from practising their faith and fell back (briefly) into their former habits; however, such was the impact of the primary conversion that for many, reconnecting to their faith and practicing their faith followed a secondary (framing) event, with renewed fidelity.

Daniel (aged 40) had been a heroin and crack cocaine addict from the age of 14 years old. As a prolific shoplifter and burglar, with occasional drug dealing, he served four separate prison sentences, and spent the best part of 25 years in active addiction; it was during his final sentence where he had his conversion experience, amid a psychotic breakdown in his cell, whilst taking the drug spice.

> Daniel: 'my cell door is locked I'm on my own on in my cell in the afternoon, and I've had a spliff [spice]. And about half an hour later I get oppressed by an evil spirit, the worst things you could think of and going over and over in my head [...] It's like erm, what I can describe as a glimpse of hell [...] I thought I was going to be in that state of mind forever, stuck like that forever. And then I said "father" [...] And all the evil force stopped. The atmosphere in that cell changed. And I heard the audible voice of God saying "Daniel, you are a chosen one". I wept I fell to my knees, cried my eyes out like a baby. And, from that day I've never done heroin or crack again, and 25 years of drug addiction was broke in that afternoon, in that prison cell. I woke up the next day and I was like "whoa! What happened" [...] I felt different. Something had changed in my heart."'

Daniel spent the remaining six months of his prison sentence studying the Bible, both in his cell and in Bible study classes in the chaplaincy. His mother had noticed such a positive difference in him as a consequence of his conversion, when visiting him in prison, and shared his real concern about being released back into a 'drug or bail hostel', knowing he would fall back into his old life of drugs as a result. She found him a placement at a 'discipleship home' that was part of a larger faith-based organisation that works with prison leavers, which he ended up spending 18 months at:

> Daniel: 'So, I got released from prison straight into the discipleship home, and I got "discipled", where every day I would wake up read the Bible every day [...] We were able to do courses on trust, courses on leadership, spiritual warfare [...] We would serve at places, we would work one day a week and we would go and volunteer at a lot of places [...] So yeah [...] I now realise that there is no other way, for so many years I was trying to fill that void in my heart. And I'm content now I know that God got a plan for my life and I don't need all those drugs, I'm confident in who I am, but if I take my eyes off of Jesus – I just know I'll go back to that life, so I just need to keep growing in my faith and I feel purpose is a big thing for me. I wanna be serving God I want to be helping people [...]"'.

As with Maruna's (2001) notion of the *redemption script*, whereby desistance occurs via the 'help of some outside force, someone who "believed in" the ex-offender' (p.87) – the majority of the participants in this research all spoke of specific mentors who were integral to their through-the-gate journeys. Armstrong's (2014) research on how trustworthiness is played out between newly released prisoners and faith-based volunteers, and how this impacts upon community reintegration efforts, found that 'trust' is insurmountable within the mentoring process. When trust is proactively placed in the volunteer–prisoner relationship, it is not based upon the expectation that it is unbreakable; rather, that it is something that would be able to withstand disappointments. From here, her findings suggest that the love/care being offered by the volunteers was seen as authentic by the prisoner, and not something that arose from superiority, piety or pity (p.307). In the past, trust given by criminal justice professionals towards supporting faith-based organisations and their volunteers has been unforthcoming, due to there being an assumed naivety and potential conflicting levels of professionalism (Lorimer, 2010); but the 'spiritual capital' that churches offer with the ability to *bond* identities with a community, *bridge* relationships (socio-economic and cultural), and *link* individuals with these groups to wider networks (Jones, 2010, p.191), such attitudes of mistrust are now being discouraged (MoJ, 2021).

The sheer vulnerability of those prison leavers, including being released on temporary license (ROTL), often found barriers in the community that did not exist within the prison environment, as John (the 'outlier' participant now working in community chaplaincy) explains with one particular story about his church welcoming a prison leaver. His concern came following the significant mistakes made previously by the church's 'welcomers':

> John: 'So they gave him the ROTL, and we planned the day because you've got to do risk assessment and all that kind of thing. So, I said to the folk who lead the prison ministry in my church – *"we need to keep this as understated as possible, this is the first time this guy has ever stepped foot inside anything that looks like church, or church community"*. He'd come from a completely atheist background,

> got saved in prison, had a, you know, faith experience and so had never been to church or experienced other Christians outside of prison before. So I said, "we could get this really wrong if we're not careful.''

The psychological vulnerabilities and other various pains and barriers of desistance that prison leavers face are well established. Firstly, in what McNeill (2015) refers to as tertiary desistance, those attempting to desist will struggle significantly without having a sense that they belong in the community they have (re-)entered into. Considering how someone leaving prison, away from the predictability of structured day-to-day living, who is for the first time entering into a community with a new faith and symbolic identity, either with expectations (rejection or being welcomed) or with none – having a community that is unaware or unprepared for any potential unpredictability and lack of social/cultural capital, and knowledge of specific church practices (as numerous participants in this research divulged) can be highly detrimental.

Conclusion

This chapter has sought to present a case for extending academic focus within criminology and criminal justice on the conversion process itself, through re-evaluating and refining our current ontological and epistemological methods of analyses. First, by specifically focusing on the Christian (Incarnational) Event, it has attempted to refine current approaches to theorising 'jailhouse conversions', going beyond the prison wall. Second, it has aimed to dispel the belief that religion and psychology are in conflict with each other, where in fact, following Barbour (1997), we should seek to identify their parallels, their shared dialogue and how they may integrate with one another. For example, in the 1960s, Lacan argued that religion will one day triumph over psychoanalysis, because religion offers more 'certainties' than science can – science is constantly evolving, it is often at odds with itself in the pursuit of truth amidst continuous existential threats, creating acute anxiety due to fast-paced changes to science and technology, and modern warfare, all of which serve to create an ingrained deep level of anxiety and lack (Lacan, 2013).

With an increased drive focusing on faith as a human right, the *Ministry of Justice Diversity & Inclusion Strategy 2017–2020* (MoJ, 2017) expected outcomes has aimed to establish partnerships with faith communities, integrating services, improving release planning and a continuation of care; supporting community chaplaincy projects through increasing current funding for through-the-gate provisions; and establishing a more quality assured governance. These proposals have carried through in the HMPPS *Framework for Anglican Chaplaincy 2021–24 report* (MoJ, 2021), which sets out a strategy framework to effectively resource and support (including funding) Anglican prison chaplaincies. This is a step in the right direction for nurturing the Event, as essential for supporting ex-prisoners' journeys in their new faith. Hopefully, they will make good on their promise.

Note

1 The Alpha Course is an 11-week course aimed at providing an introduction to the Christian faith. As a global phenomenon, over 23 million people have participated worldwide. What is pertinent to this project is its prevalence within prisons worldwide, 'running in more than 900 prisons and secure facilities, in 46 countries. In 2018, over 53,000 people experienced Alpha in prison' (https://alpha.org/prisons/).

References

Armstrong, R. (2014). Trusting the untrustworthy: The theology, practice and implications of faith-based volunteers' work with exprisoners. *Studies in Christian Ethics, 27*(3) 299–317.

Badiou, A. ([1988]2007). *Being and event.* A&C Black.

Barbour, I. (1997). *Religion and science: Historical and contemporary issues.* Harper.

Chamberlain, J. M. (2012). *Understanding criminological research: A guide to data analysis.* SAGE.

Giordano, P. C., Longmore, M. A., Schroeder, R. D., & Seffrin, P. M. (2008). A life-course perspective on spirituality and desistance from crime. *Criminology, 46*(1), 99–132.

Hallett, M., and McCoy, J. S. (2015). Religiously motivated desistance: An exploratory study. *International Journal of Offender Therapy and Comparative Criminology, 59*, 855–872.

Hollway, W., and Jefferson, T. (2000). *Doing qualitative research differently: Free association, narrative and the interview method.* SAGE.

Homer, B. D., & Nelson, K. (2005). Seeing objects as symbols and symbols as objects: Language and the development of dual representation. In B. D. Homer & C. S. Tamis-LeMonda (Eds.), *The development of social cognition and communication.* Lawrence Erlbaum Associates, pp. 29–52.

Johnson, B. R., Larson, D. B., & Pitts, T. C. (1997). Religious programs, institutional adjustment, and recidivism among former inmates in prison fellowship programs. *Justice Quarterly, 14*(1), 145–166.

Jones, C. (2010). Crime, well-being and society: reflections on social, 'anti-social' and 'restorative' capital. In I. Steedman, J. R. Atherton, and E. Graham (Eds.), *The practices of happiness: Political economy, religion and wellbeing.* Routledge, pp. 184–194.

Lacan, J. (1988). *The Seminar. Book II. The ego in Freud's theory and in the technique of psychoanalysis, 1954–55.* Trans. Sylvana Tomaselli. Cambridge University Press.

Lacan, J. (2013). *The triumph of religion.* Polity.

Laurita, C. (2010). *Working with the drive: A Lacanian psychoanalytic approach to the treatment of addictions* (Doctoral dissertation). Duquesne University. Retrieved from: https://open.metu.edu.tr/bitstream/handle/11511/69305/12625735.pdf.

Laws, B. (2020). Reimaging 'the Self' in criminology: Transcendence, unconscious states and the limits of narrative criminology. *Theoretical Criminology, 26*(3), 475–493. First published online 12 May 2020. https://doi.org/10.1177/1362480620919102

Lorimer, C. (2010). Supporting offenders: A faith-based initiative. In I. Steedman, J. R. Atherton, and E. Graham (Eds). *The practices of happiness: Political economy, religion and wellbeing.* Routledge, pp. 215–224.

Maruna, S. (2001). *Making Good: How ex-convicts reform and rebuild their lives.* American Psychological Association Books.

Maruna, S., Wilson, L., & Curran, K. (2006). Why God is often found behind bars: Prison conversions and the crisis of self-narrative. *Research in Human Development, 3*(2–3), 161–184.

McGowan, T. (2010). Subject of the event, subject of the act: The difference between Badiou's and Žižek's systems of philosophy. *Subjectivity, 3*(1), 7–30.

McNeill, F. (2015). Desistance and criminal justice in Scotland. In H. Croall, G. Mooney, and M. Munro (Eds.), *Crime, justice and society in Scotland.* Routledge, pp. 212–228.

Ministry of Justice (2017). *MoJ Diversity & Inclusion Strategy 2017–2020: Executive Summary* [online] Retrieved from: https://assets.publishing.service.gov.uk/government/uploads/system/uploads/attachment_data/file/712842/moj-equality-objectives-2017-2020.pdf

Ministry of Justice (2021). *Framework for Anglican Prison Chaplaincy 2021–24* [online]. Retrieved from: https://assets.publishing.service.gov.uk/government/uploads/system/uploads/attachment_data/file/1008040/Framework_for_Anglican_Prison_Chaplaincy_2021-24.pdf.

Skotnicki, A. (2019). *Conversion and the rehabilitation of the penal system: A theological rereading of criminal justice.* Oxford University Press.

Winlow, S., & Hall, S. (2009). Retaliate first: Memory, humiliation and male violence. *Crime, Media, Culture, 5*(3), 285–304.

Žižek, S. (2000). Melancholy and the Act. *Critical Inquiry, 26*(4), 657–681.

Žižek, S. (2006). *How to read Lacan.* Granta.

Žižek, S. (2010). Paul and the Truth Event. In J. Milbank, S. Žižek and C. Davis (Eds.), *Paul's new moment: Continental philosophy and the future of Christian theology.* Brazos Press, pp.74–99.

Žižek, S. (2014). *Event: Philosophy in transit.* Penguin.

INDEX

For Product Safety Concerns and Information please contact our EU representative GPSR@taylorandfrancis.com Taylor & Francis Verlag GmbH, Kaufingerstraße 24, 80331 München, Germany